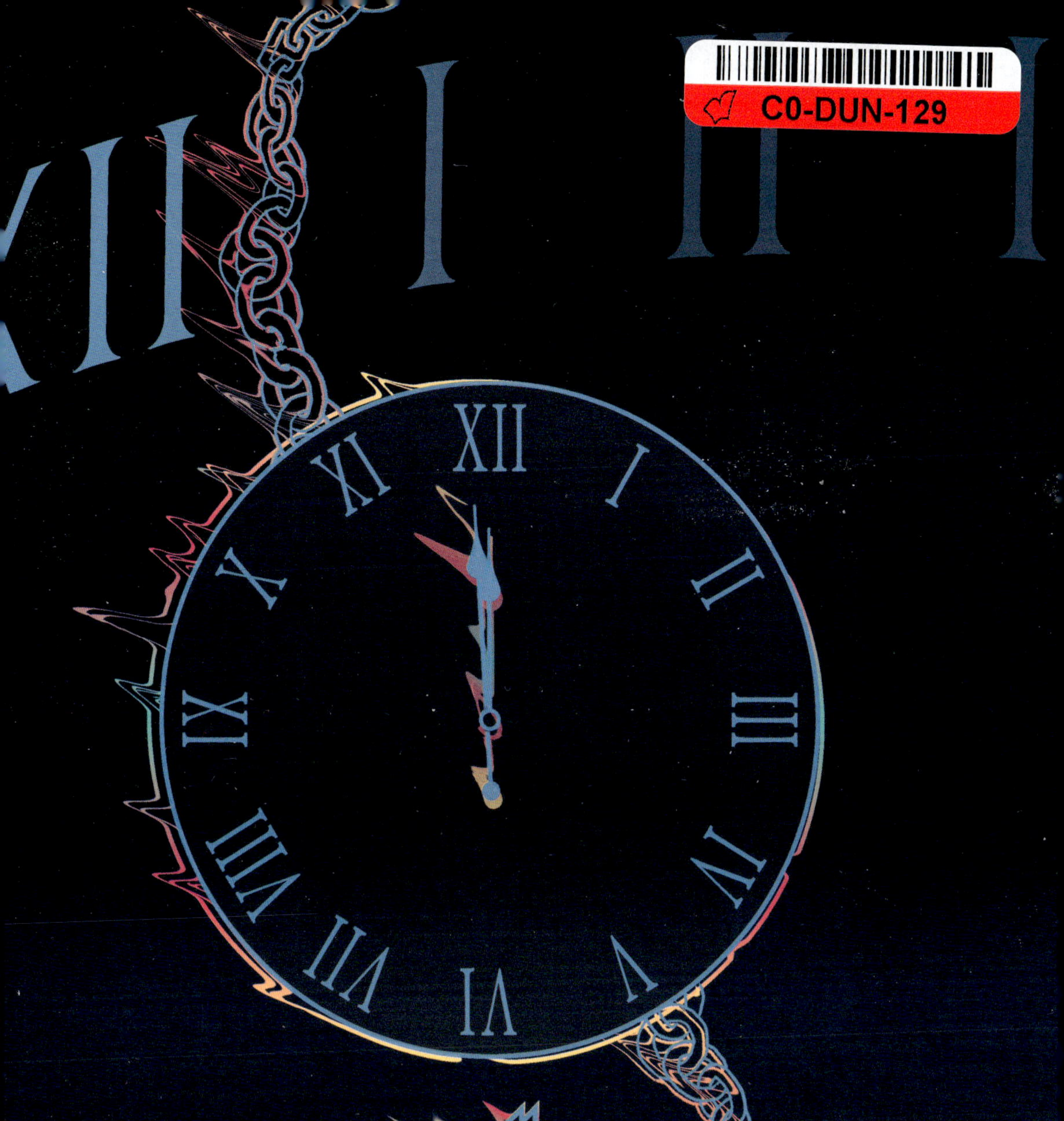

EDITORIAL
ADRIAN WASSEL – CCO & EDITOR-IN-CHIEF
DER-SHING HELMER – MANAGING EDITOR
DESIGN & PRODUCTION
TIM DANIEL – EVP, DESIGN & PRODUCTION
NATHAN GOODEN – CO-FOUNDER & SENIOR ARTIST
ADAM CAHOON – SENIOR DESIGNER & PRODUCTION ASSOCIATE
SALES & MARKETING
DAVID DISSANAYAKE – VP, SALES & MARKETING
SYNDEE BARWICK – DIRECTOR, BOOK MARKET SALES
BRITTA BUESCHER – DIRECTOR, SOCIAL MEDIA
OPERATIONS & STRATEGY
DAMIAN WASSEL – CEO & PUBLISHER
CHRIS KANALEY – CSO
F.J. DESANTO – HEAD OF FILM & TV

II III IV

STEVE
ORLANDO   GIOPOTA   ANDWORLD
writer   artist   letterer

SIMON BOWLAND
letterer, Issue #1

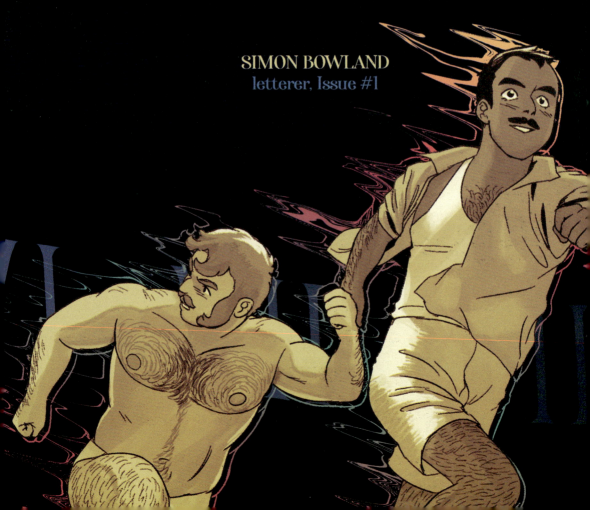

V VI VII

VAULT COMICS
PRESENTS

SAINTED LOVE

IX X XI

new york

chapter I

1907

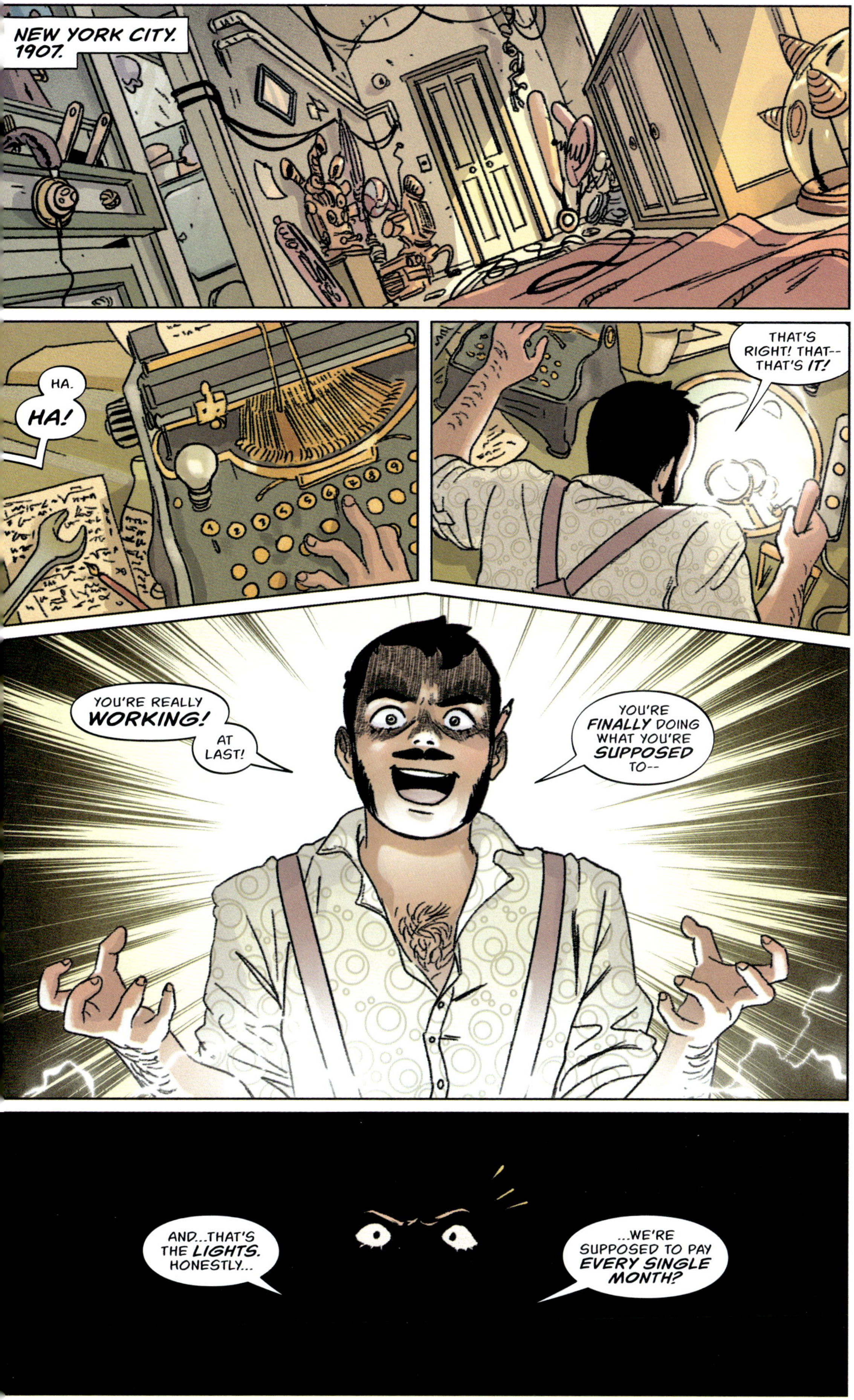
NEW YORK CITY. 1907.
HA.
HA!
THAT'S RIGHT! THAT-- THAT'S IT!
YOU'RE REALLY WORKING!
AT LAST!
YOU'RE FINALLY DOING WHAT YOU'RE SUPPOSED TO--
AND...THAT'S THE LIGHTS. HONESTLY...
...WE'RE SUPPOSED TO PAY EVERY SINGLE MONTH?

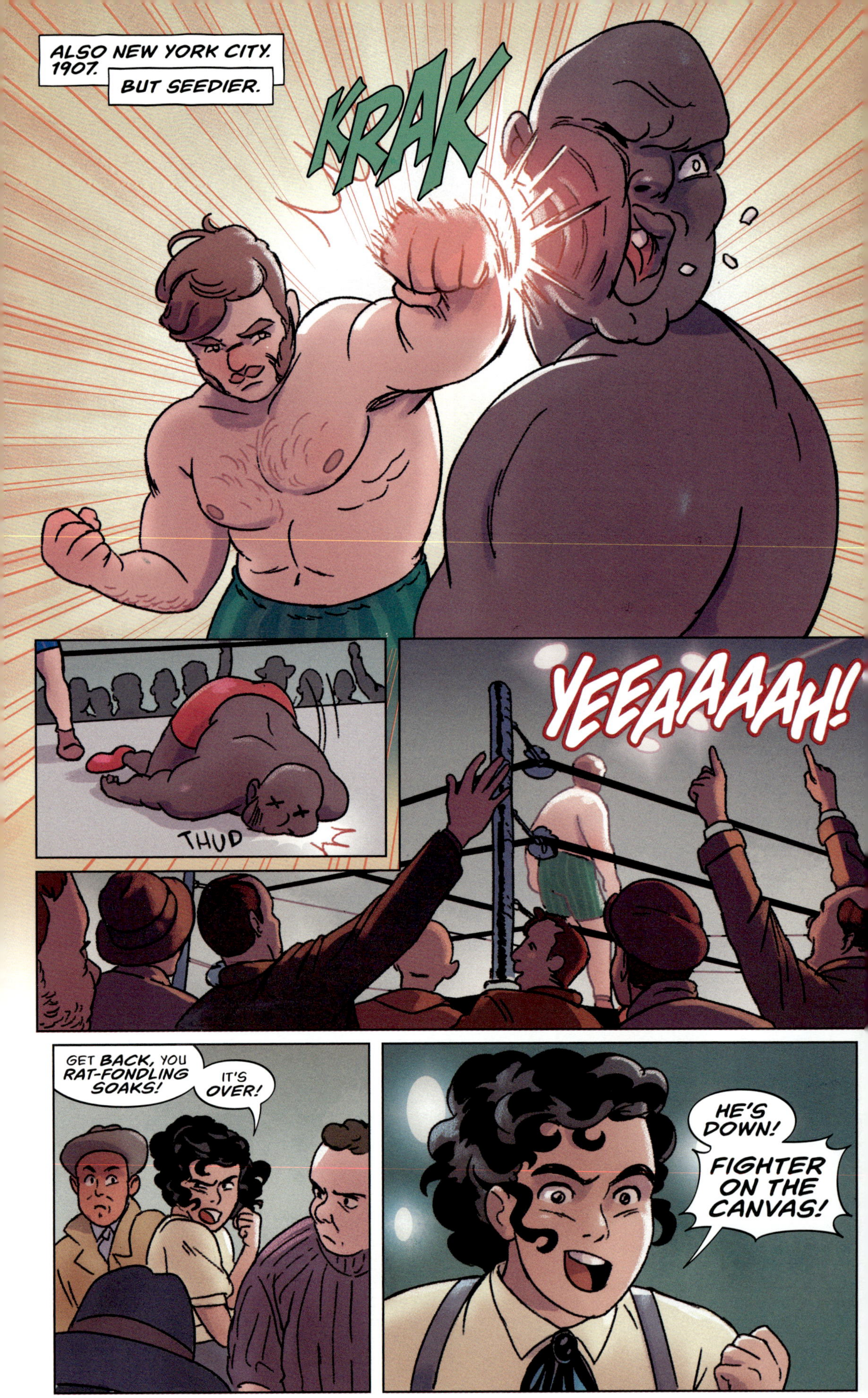
ALSO NEW YORK CITY. 1907.
BUT SEEDIER.
KRAK
THUD
YEEAAAAH!
GET BACK, YOU RAT-FONDLING SOAKS!
IT'S OVER!
HE'S DOWN!
FIGHTER ON THE CANVAS!

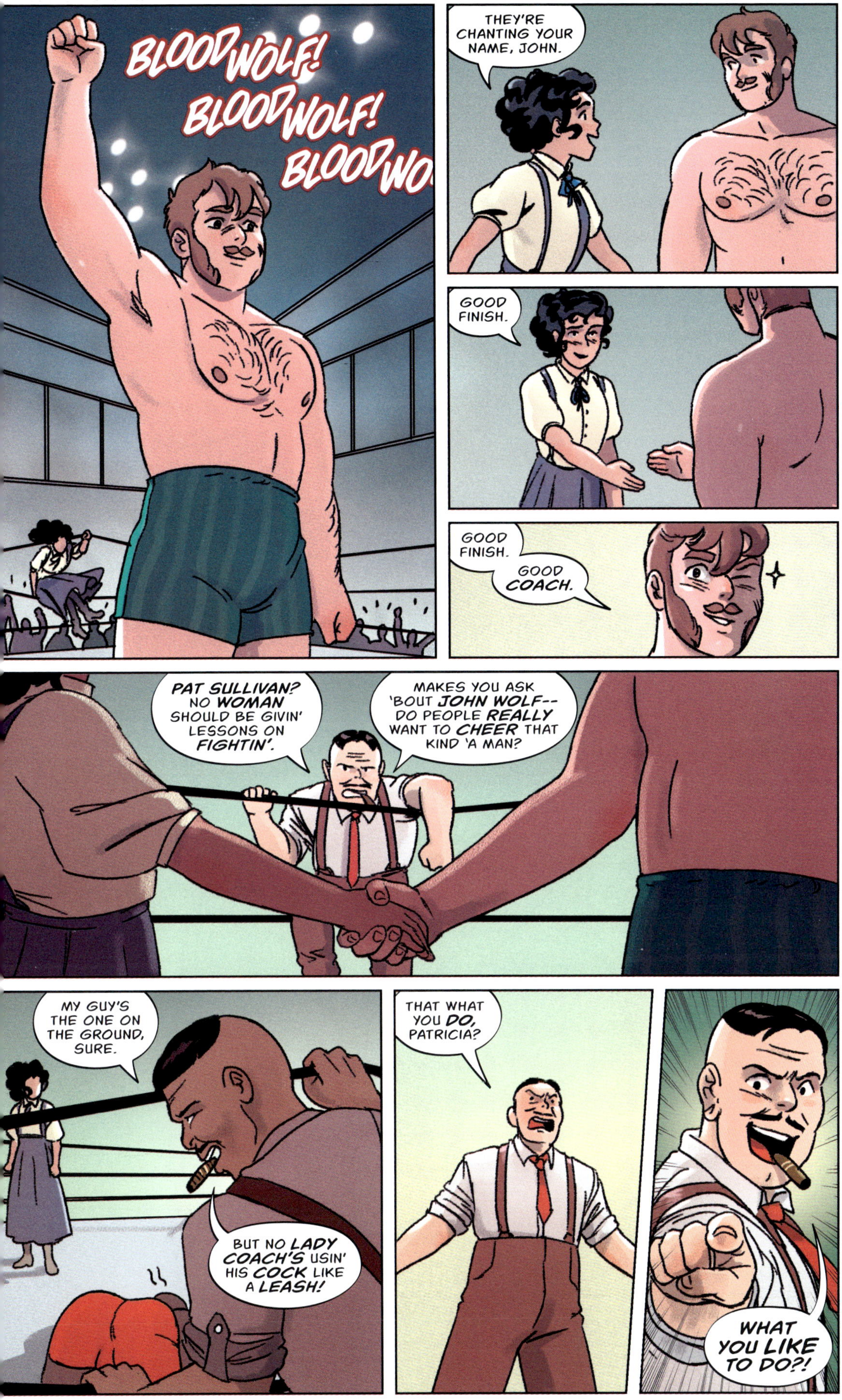
BLOODWOLF!
BLOODWOLF!
BLOODWO
THEY'RE CHANTING YOUR NAME, JOHN.
GOOD FINISH.
GOOD FINISH.
GOOD COACH.
PAT SULLIVAN? NO WOMAN SHOULD BE GIVIN' LESSONS ON FIGHTIN'.
MAKES YOU ASK 'BOUT JOHN WOLF-- DO PEOPLE REALLY WANT TO CHEER THAT KIND 'A MAN?
MY GUY'S THE ONE ON THE GROUND, SURE.
BUT NO LADY COACH'S USIN' HIS COCK LIKE A LEASH!
THAT WHAT YOU DO, PATRICIA?
WHAT YOU LIKE TO DO?!

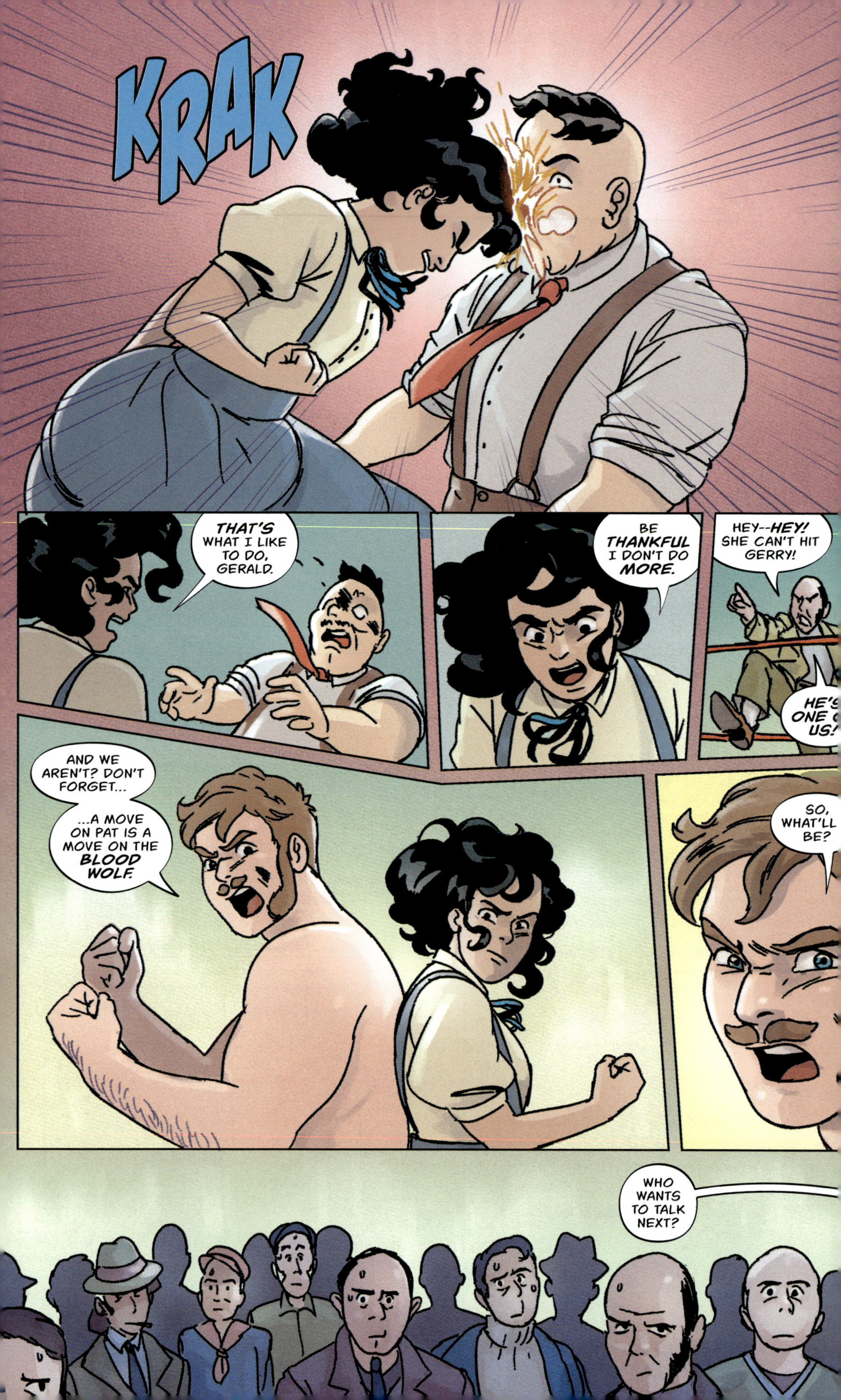
KRAK
THAT'S WHAT I LIKE TO DO, GERALD.
BE THANKFUL I DON'T DO MORE.
HEY--HEY! SHE CAN'T HIT GERRY!
AND WE AREN'T? DON'T FORGET...
...A MOVE ON PAT IS A MOVE ON THE BLOOD WOLF.
SO, WHAT'LL BE?
WHO WANTS TO TALK NEXT?

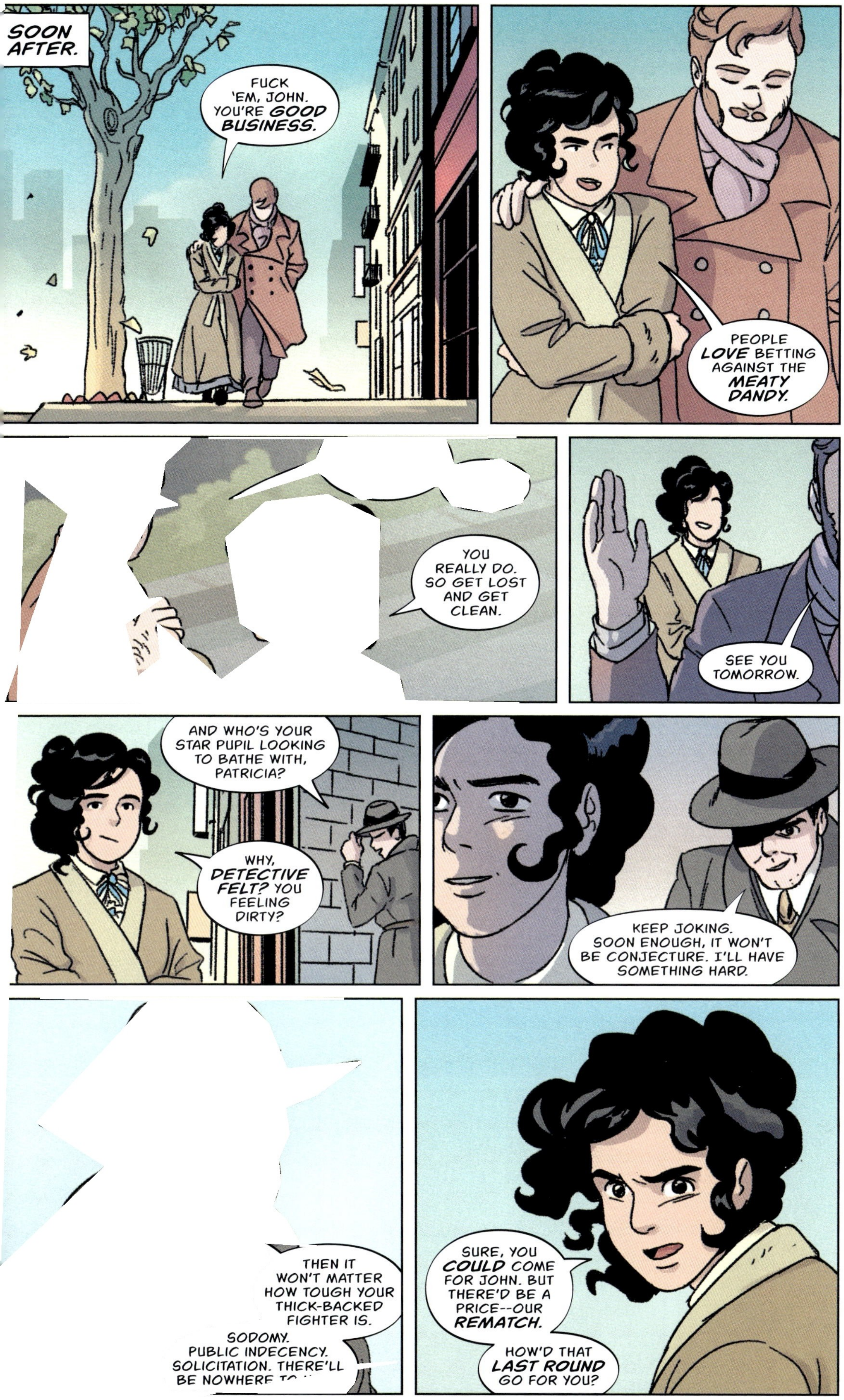
SOON AFTER.
FUCK 'EM, JOHN. YOU'RE GOOD BUSINESS.
PEOPLE LOVE BETTING AGAINST THE MEATY DANDY.
YOU REALLY DO. SO GET LOST AND GET CLEAN.
SEE YOU TOMORROW.
AND WHO'S YOUR STAR PUPIL LOOKING TO BATHE WITH, PATRICIA?
WHY, DETECTIVE FELT? YOU FEELING DIRTY?
KEEP JOKING. SOON ENOUGH, IT WON'T BE CONJECTURE. I'LL HAVE SOMETHING HARD.
THEN IT WON'T MATTER HOW TOUGH YOUR THICK-BACKED FIGHTER IS.
SODOMY. PUBLIC INDECENCY. SOLICITATION. THERE'LL BE NOWHERE
SURE, YOU COULD COME FOR JOHN. BUT THERE'D BE A PRICE--OUR REMATCH.
HOW'D THAT LAST ROUND GO FOR YOU?

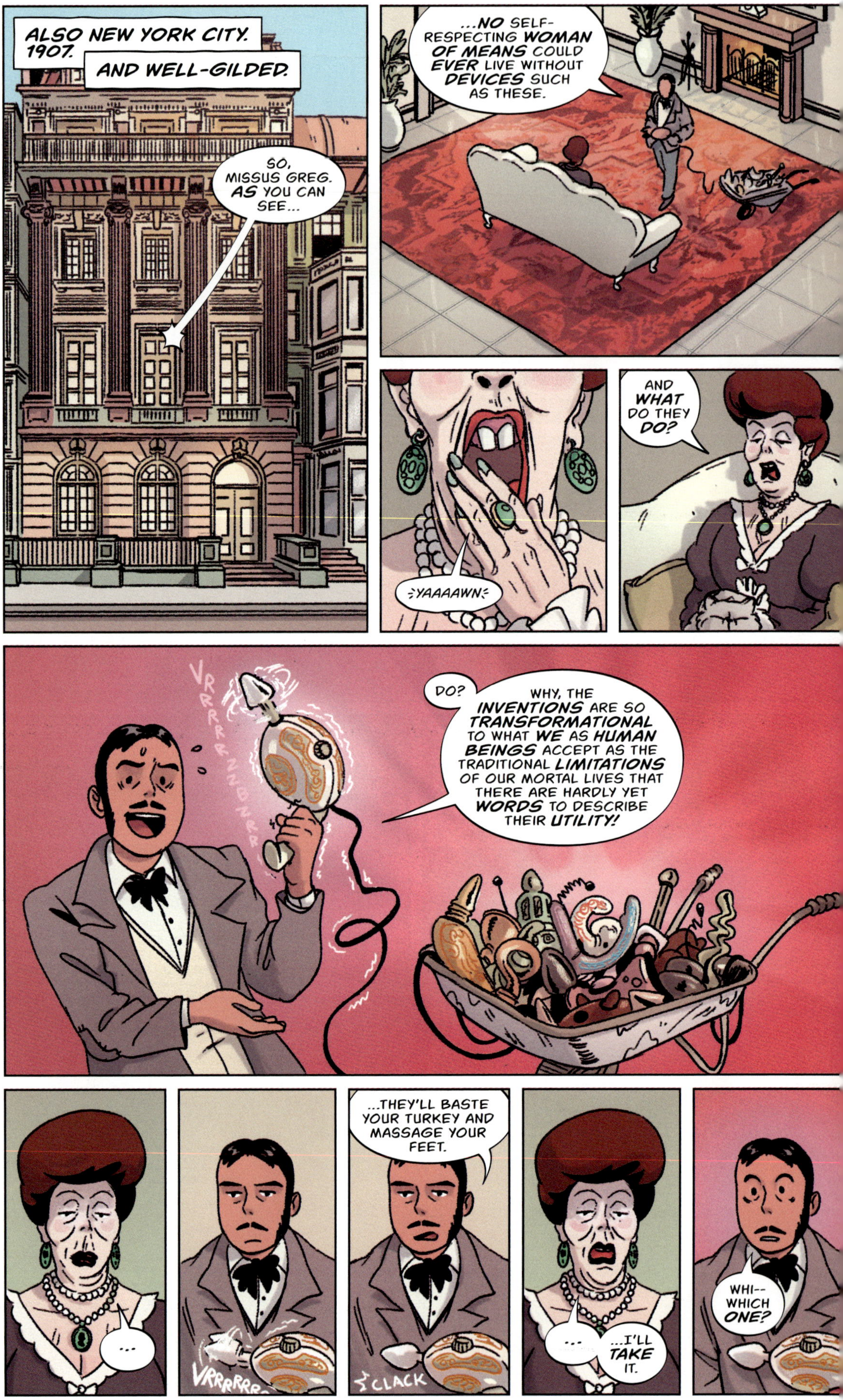
ALSO NEW YORK CITY. 1907.
AND WELL-GILDED.
SO, MISSUS GREG. AS YOU CAN SEE...
...NO SELF-RESPECTING WOMAN OF MEANS COULD EVER LIVE WITHOUT DEVICES SUCH AS THESE.
YAAAAWN
AND WHAT DO THEY DO?
VRRRRRZZZRRR
DO?
WHY, THE INVENTIONS ARE SO TRANSFORMATIONAL TO WHAT WE AS HUMAN BEINGS ACCEPT AS THE TRADITIONAL LIMITATIONS OF OUR MORTAL LIVES THAT THERE ARE HARDLY YET WORDS TO DESCRIBE THEIR UTILITY!
...
VRRRRRR
...THEY'LL BASTE YOUR TURKEY AND MASSAGE YOUR FEET.
CLACK
...
...I'LL TAKE IT.
WHI-- WHICH ONE?

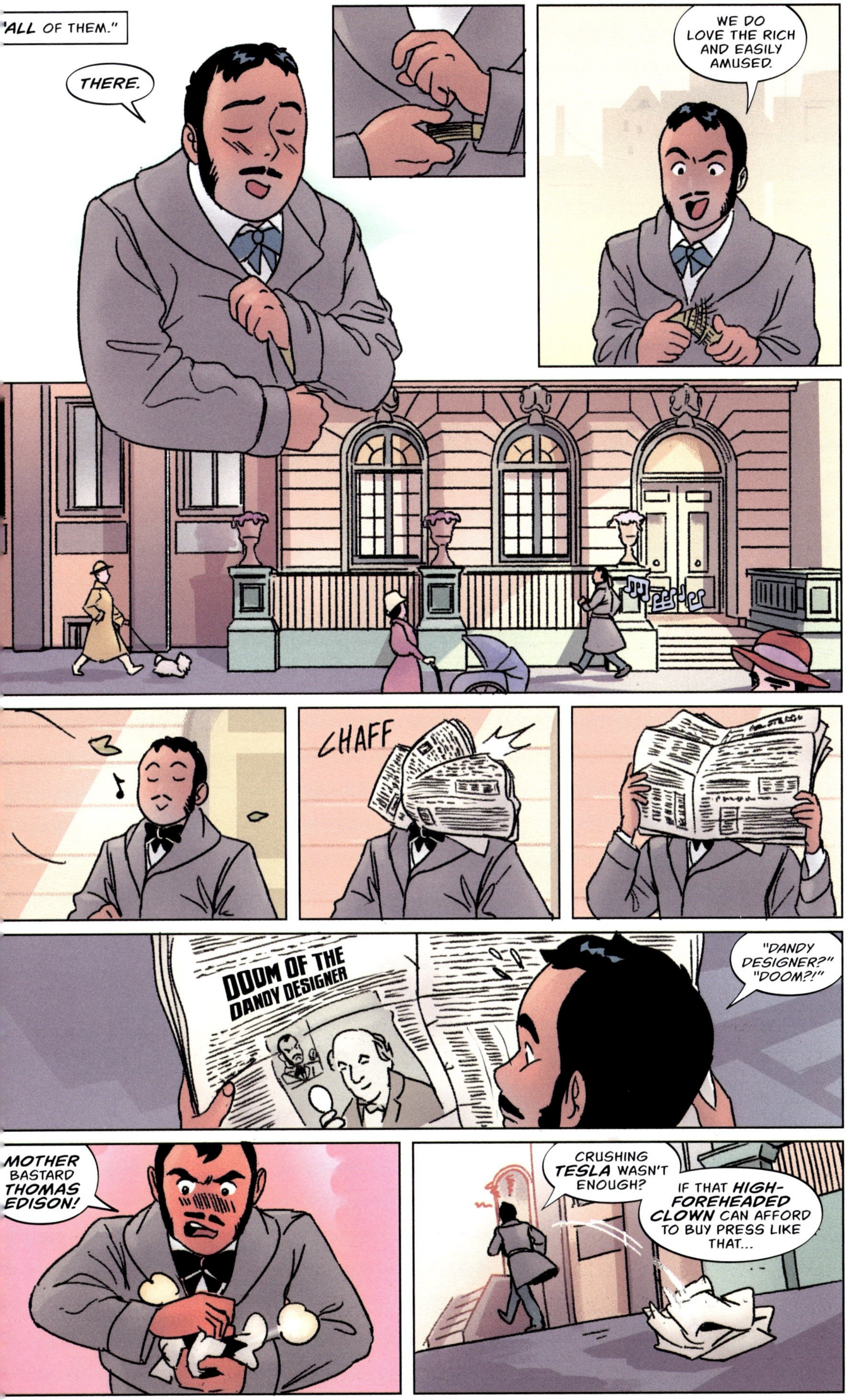
"ALL OF THEM."
THERE.
WE DO LOVE THE RICH AND EASILY AMUSED.
CHAFF
DOOM OF THE DANDY DESIGNER
"DANDY DESIGNER?" "DOOM?!"
MOTHER BASTARD THOMAS EDISON!
CRUSHING TESLA WASN'T ENOUGH?
IF THAT HIGH-FOREHEADED CLOWN CAN AFFORD TO BUY PRESS LIKE THAT...

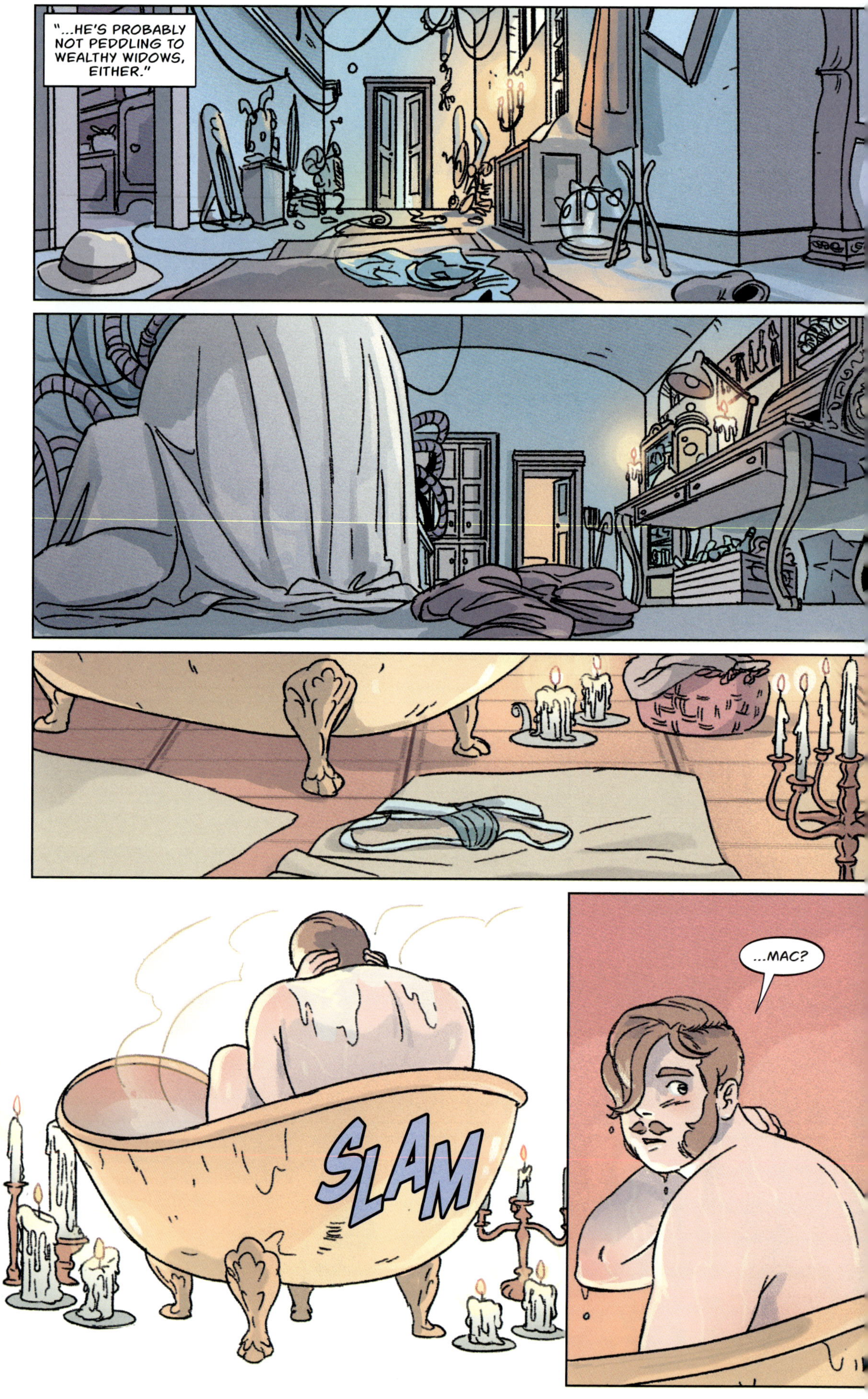
"...HE'S PROBABLY NOT PEDDLING TO WEALTHY WIDOWS, EITHER."
SLAM
...MAC?

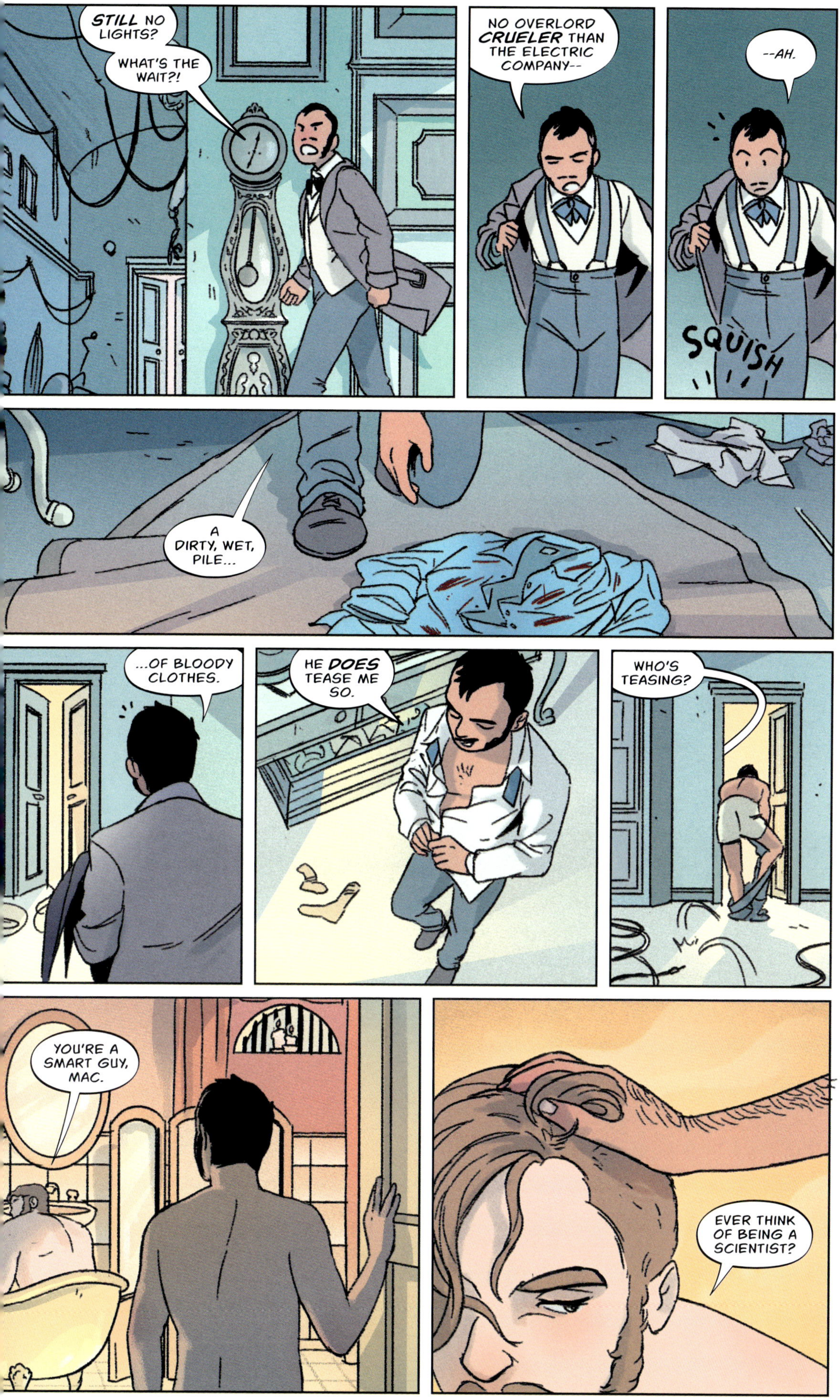
STILL NO LIGHTS?
WHAT'S THE WAIT?!
NO OVERLORD CRUELER THAN THE ELECTRIC COMPANY--
--AH.
SQUISH
A DIRTY, WET, PILE...
...OF BLOODY CLOTHES.
HE DOES TEASE ME SO.
WHO'S TEASING?
YOU'RE A SMART GUY, MAC.
EVER THINK OF BEING A SCIENTIST?

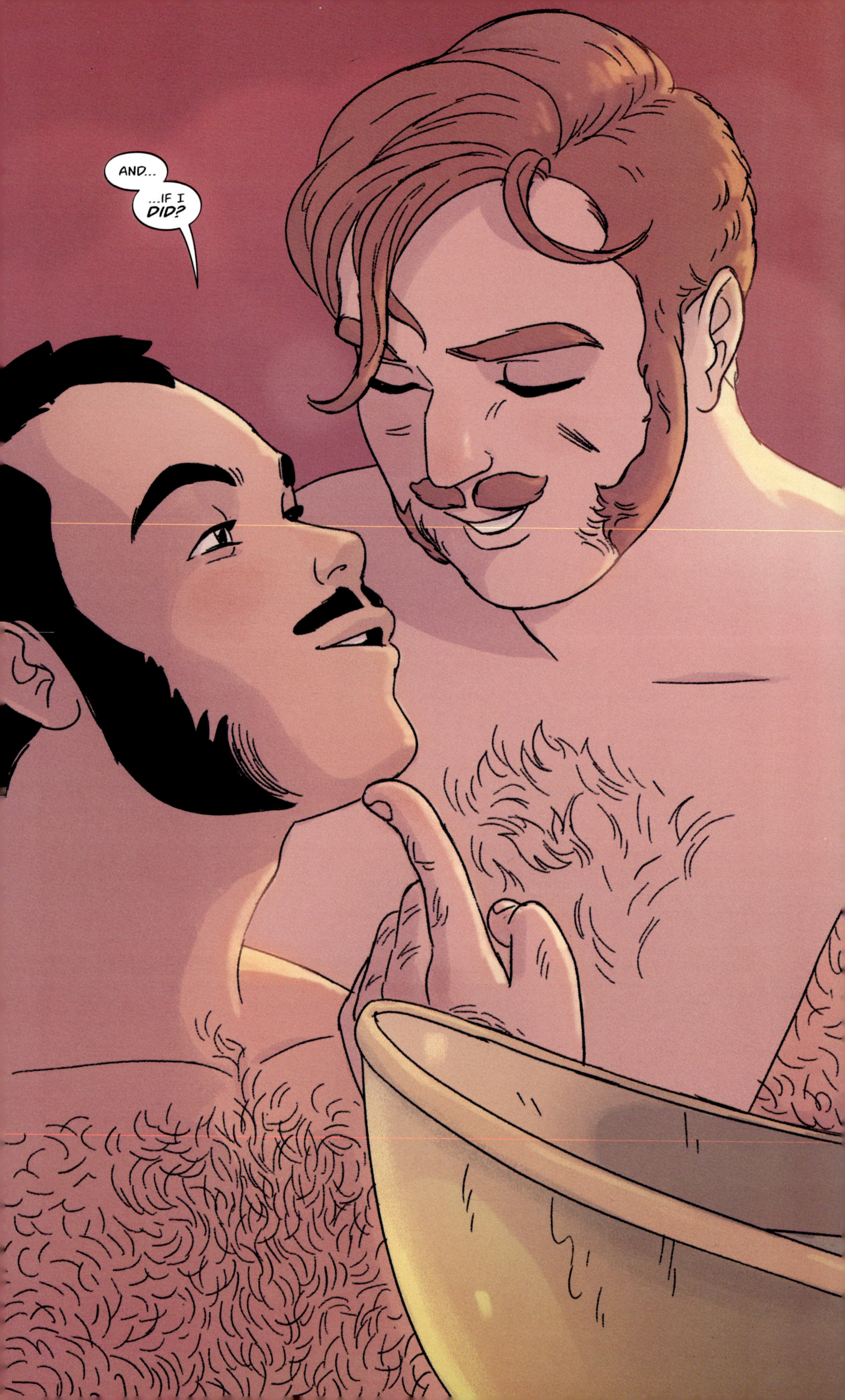
AND...
...IF I DID?

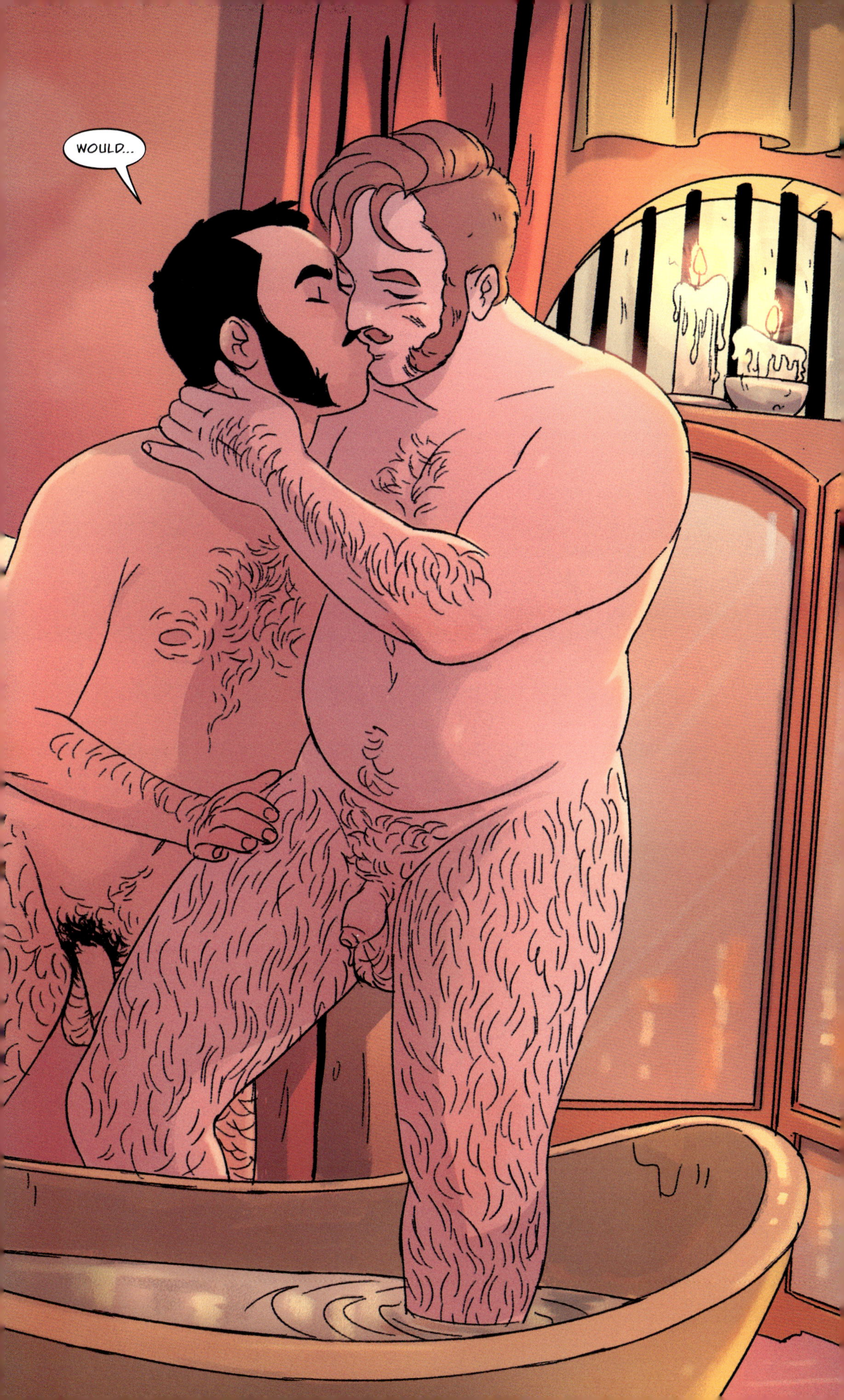
WOULD...

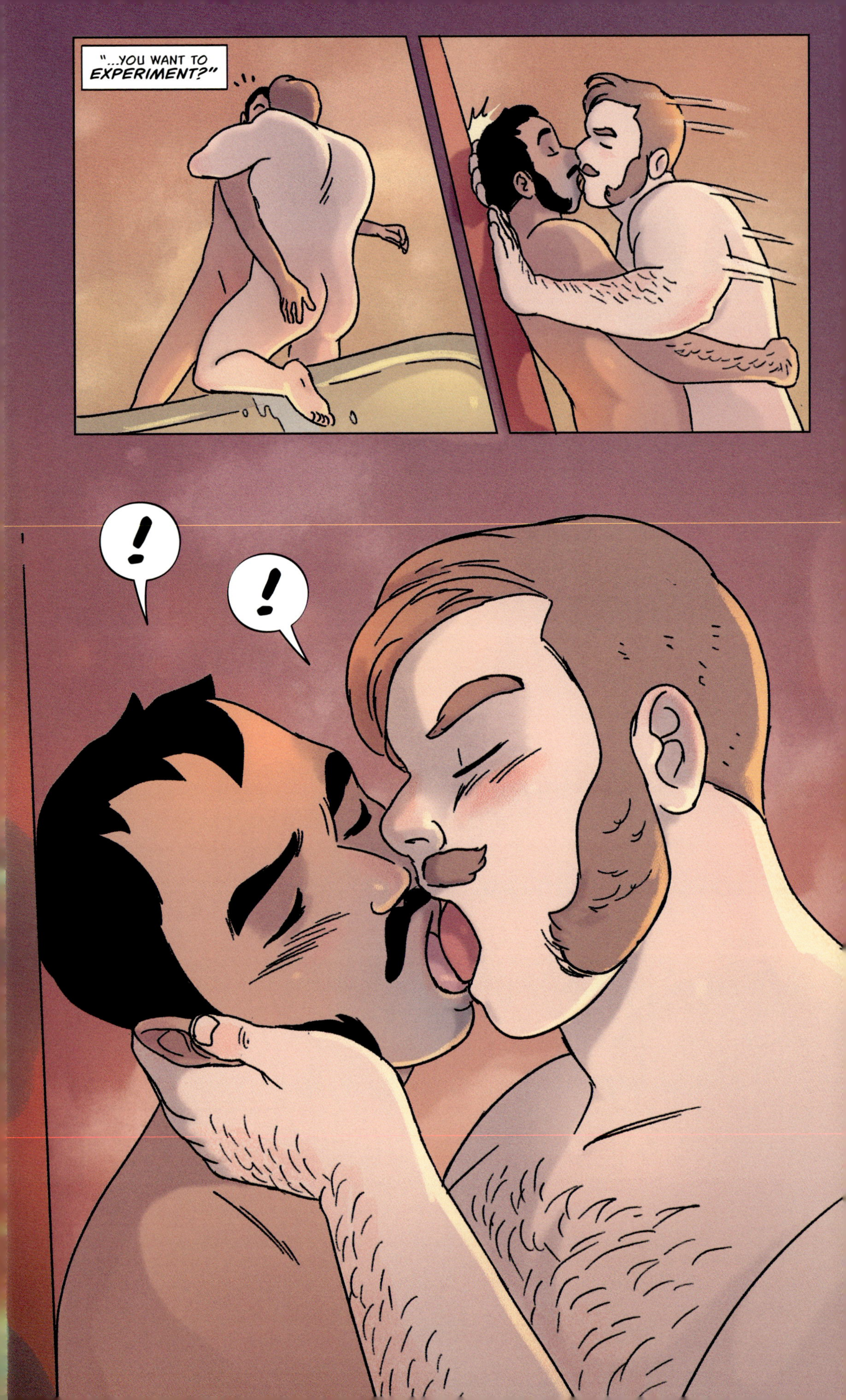
"...YOU WANT TO *EXPERIMENT?*"
!
!

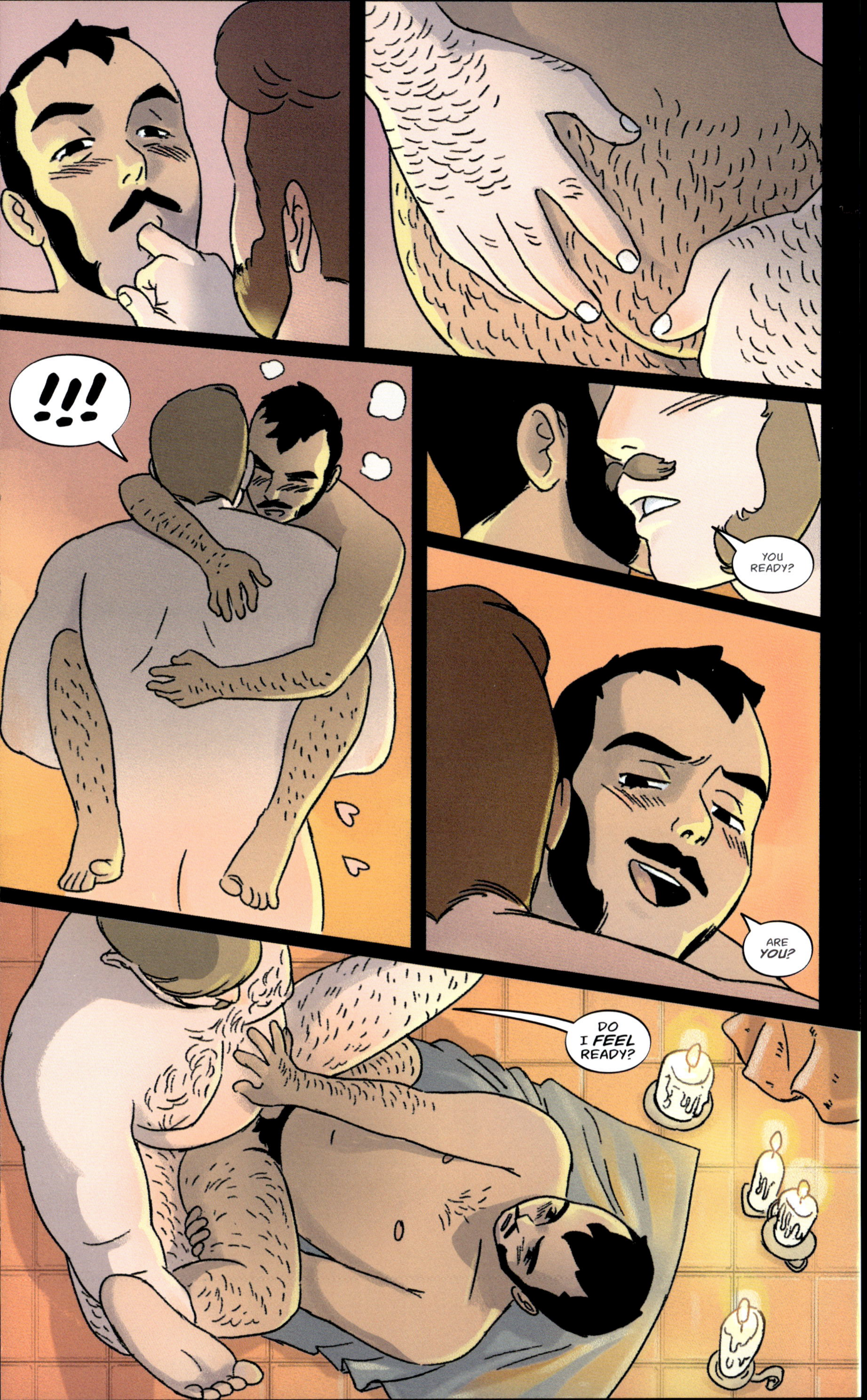

!!!
YOU READY?
ARE YOU?
DO I FEEL READY?

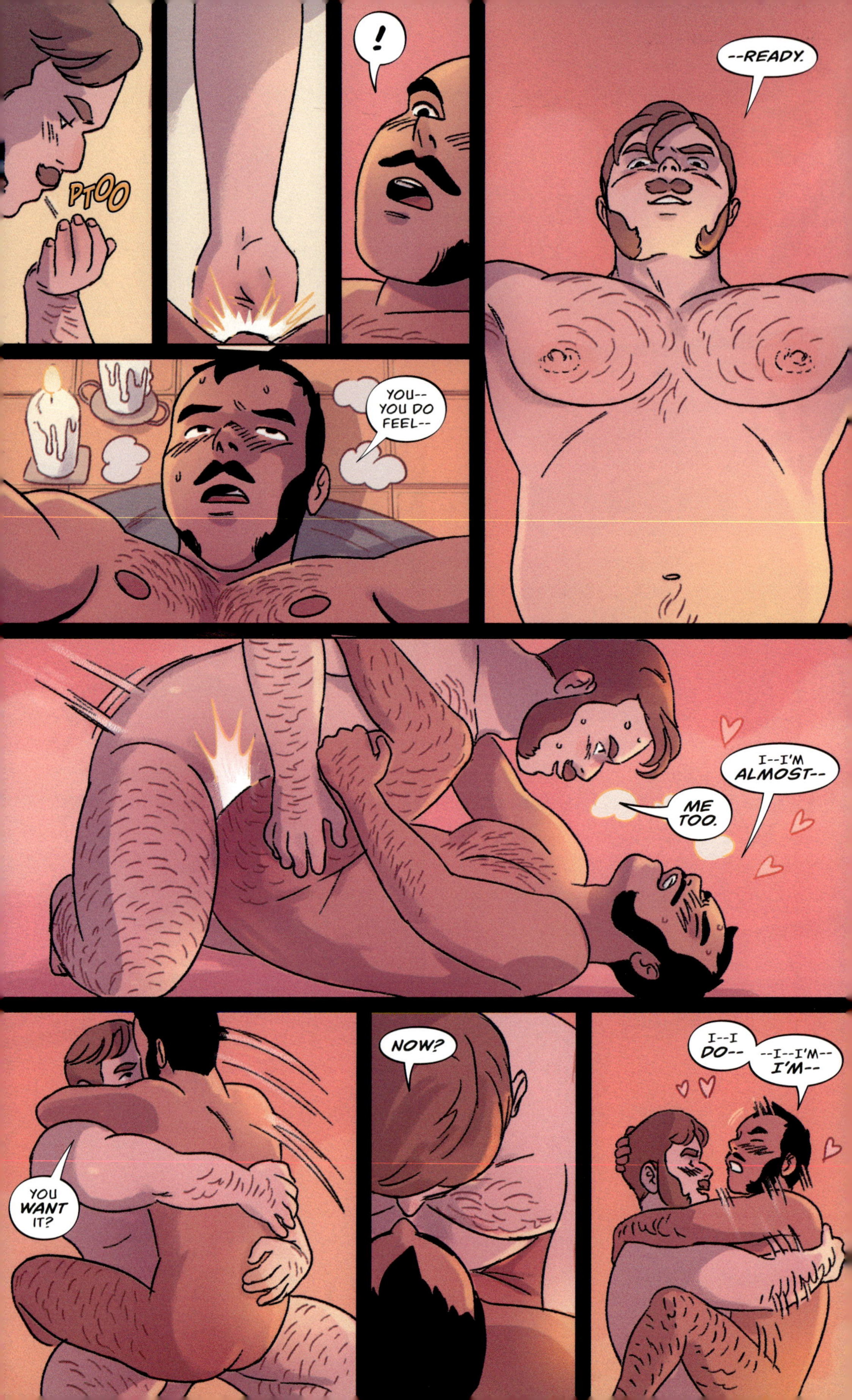
PTOO
!
--READY.
YOU--
YOU DO
FEEL--
I--I'M
ALMOST--
ME
TOO.
YOU
WANT
IT?
NOW?
I--I
DO--
--I--I'M--
I'M--

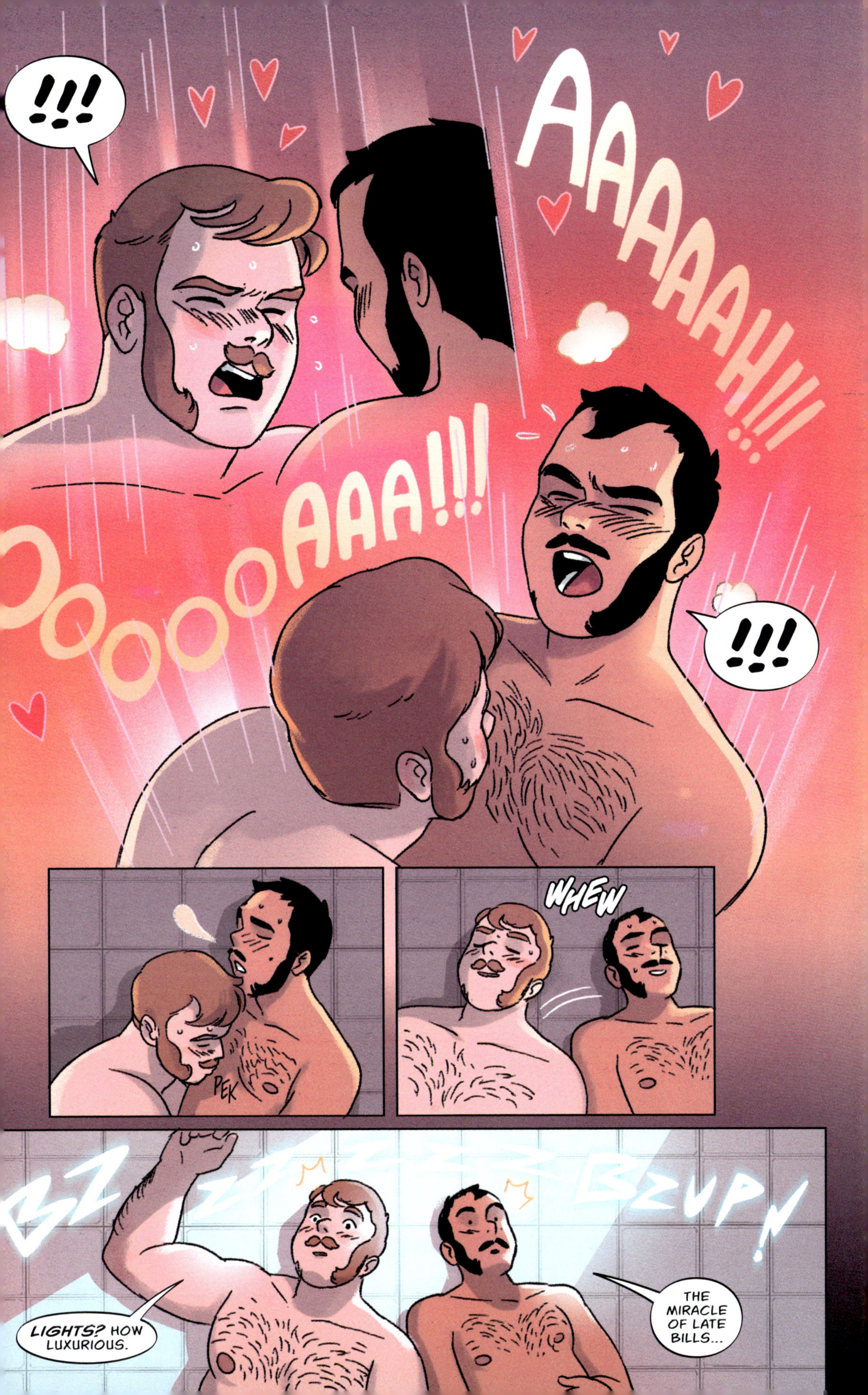
!!!
AAAAAAH!!!
OOOOOAAA!!!
!!!
PEK
WHEW
BZZZZZZT BZUPN!
LIGHTS? HOW LUXURIOUS.
THE MIRACLE OF LATE BILLS...

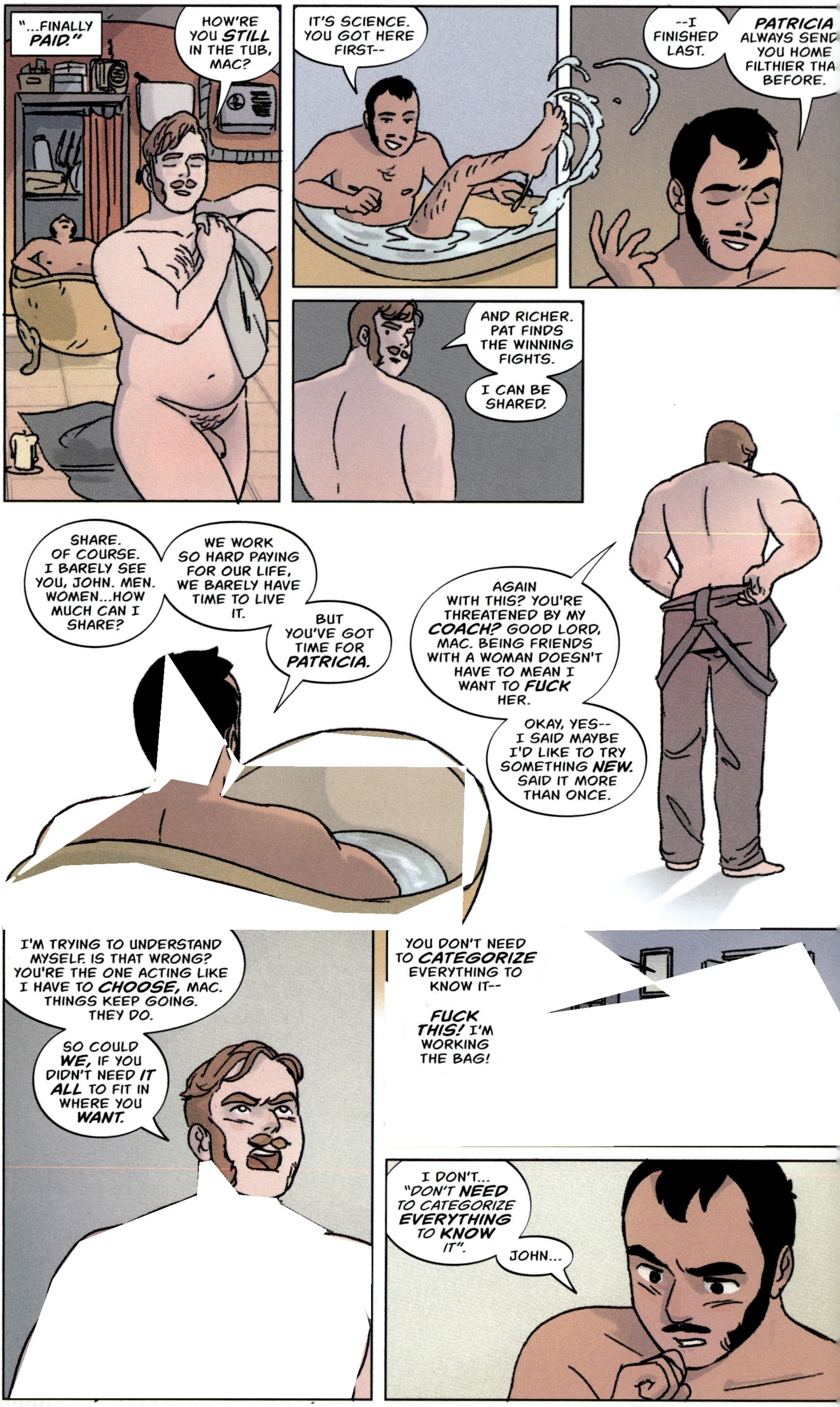

"...FINALLY PAID."
HOW'RE YOU STILL IN THE TUB, MAC?
IT'S SCIENCE. YOU GOT HERE FIRST--
--I FINISHED LAST.
PATRICIA ALWAYS SEND YOU HOME FILTHIER THA BEFORE.
AND RICHER. PAT FINDS THE WINNING FIGHTS.
I CAN BE SHARED.
SHARE. OF COURSE. I BARELY SEE YOU, JOHN. MEN. WOMEN...HOW MUCH CAN I SHARE?
WE WORK SO HARD PAYING FOR OUR LIFE, WE BARELY HAVE TIME TO LIVE IT.
BUT YOU'VE GOT TIME FOR PATRICIA.
AGAIN WITH THIS? YOU'RE THREATENED BY MY COACH? GOOD LORD, MAC. BEING FRIENDS WITH A WOMAN DOESN'T HAVE TO MEAN I WANT TO FUCK HER.
OKAY, YES-- I SAID MAYBE I'D LIKE TO TRY SOMETHING NEW. SAID IT MORE THAN ONCE.
I'M TRYING TO UNDERSTAND MYSELF. IS THAT WRONG? YOU'RE THE ONE ACTING LIKE I HAVE TO CHOOSE, MAC. THINGS KEEP GOING. THEY DO.
SO COULD WE, IF YOU DIDN'T NEED IT ALL TO FIT IN WHERE YOU WANT.
YOU DON'T NEED TO CATEGORIZE EVERYTHING TO KNOW IT--
FUCK THIS! I'M WORKING THE BAG!
I DON'T... "DON'T NEED TO CATEGORIZE EVERYTHING TO KNOW IT".
JOHN...

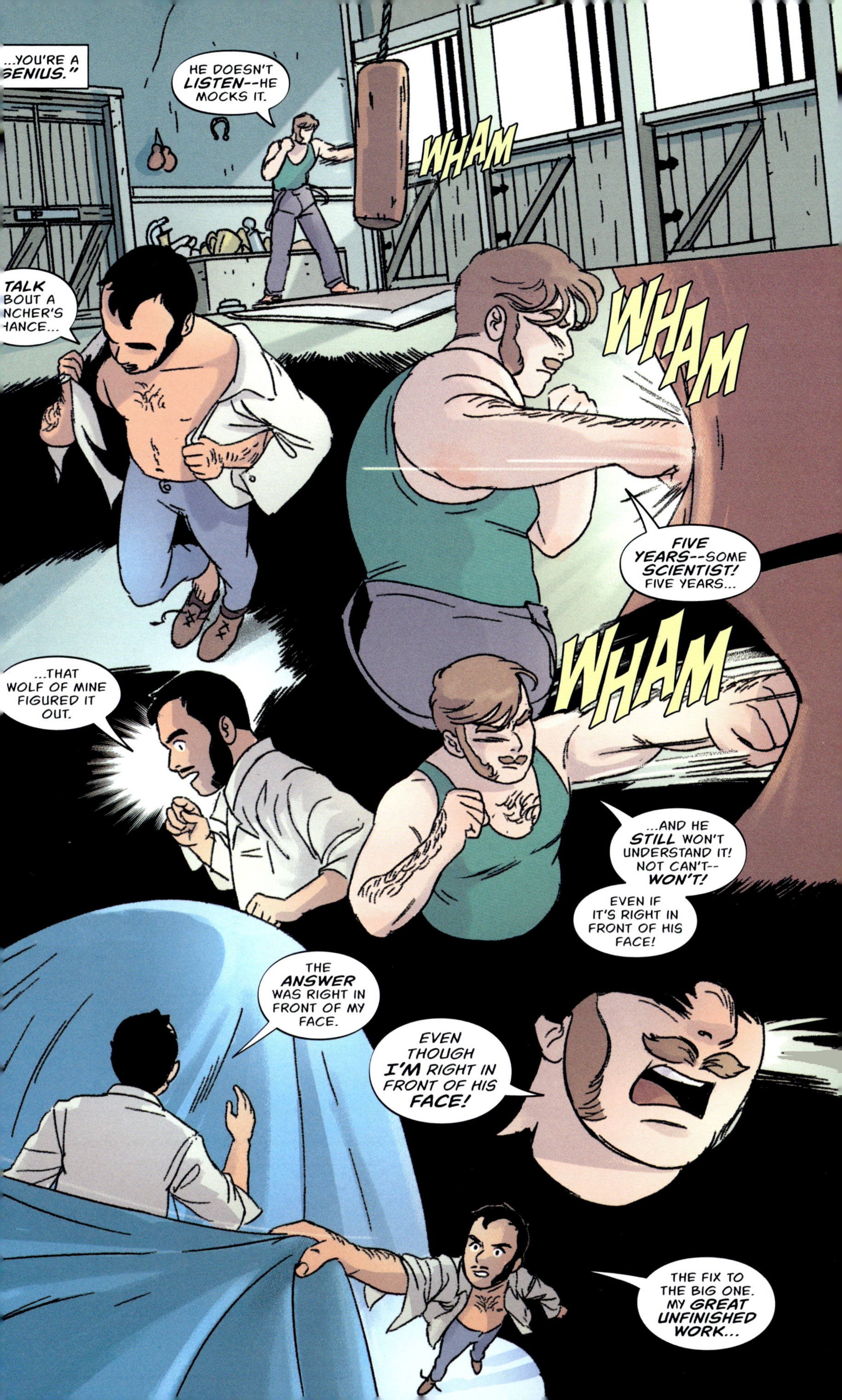
...YOU'RE A
GENIUS."
HE DOESN'T LISTEN--HE MOCKS IT.
WHAM
TALK
BOUT A
NCHER'S
HANCE...
WHAM
FIVE YEARS--SOME SCIENTIST! FIVE YEARS...
...THAT WOLF OF MINE FIGURED IT OUT.
WHAM
...AND HE STILL WON'T UNDERSTAND IT! NOT CAN'T-- WON'T!
EVEN IF IT'S RIGHT IN FRONT OF HIS FACE!
THE ANSWER WAS RIGHT IN FRONT OF MY FACE.
EVEN THOUGH I'M RIGHT IN FRONT OF HIS FACE!
THE FIX TO THE BIG ONE. MY GREAT UNFINISHED WORK...

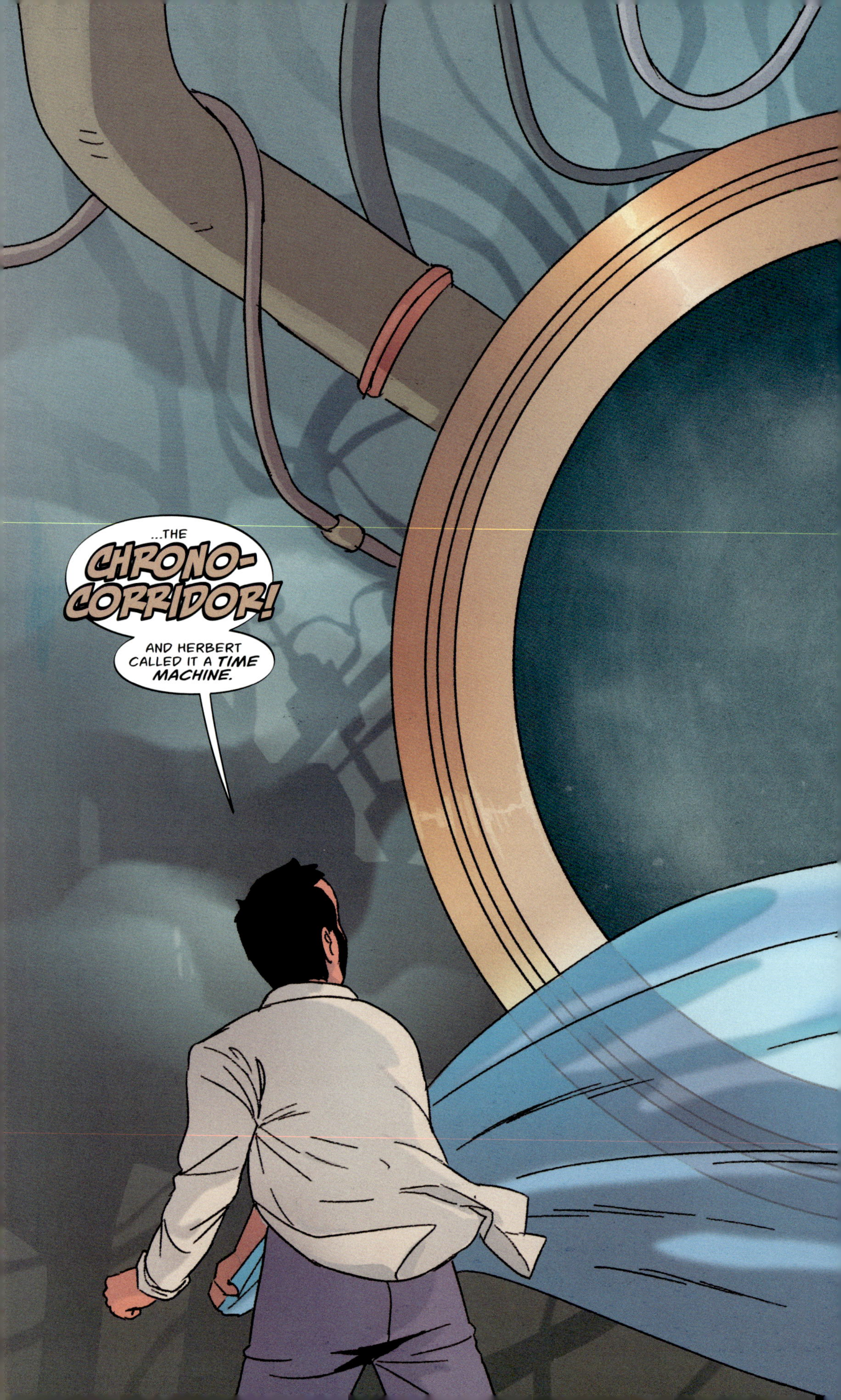
...THE
CHRONO-CORRIDOR!
AND HERBERT CALLED IT A *TIME MACHINE*.

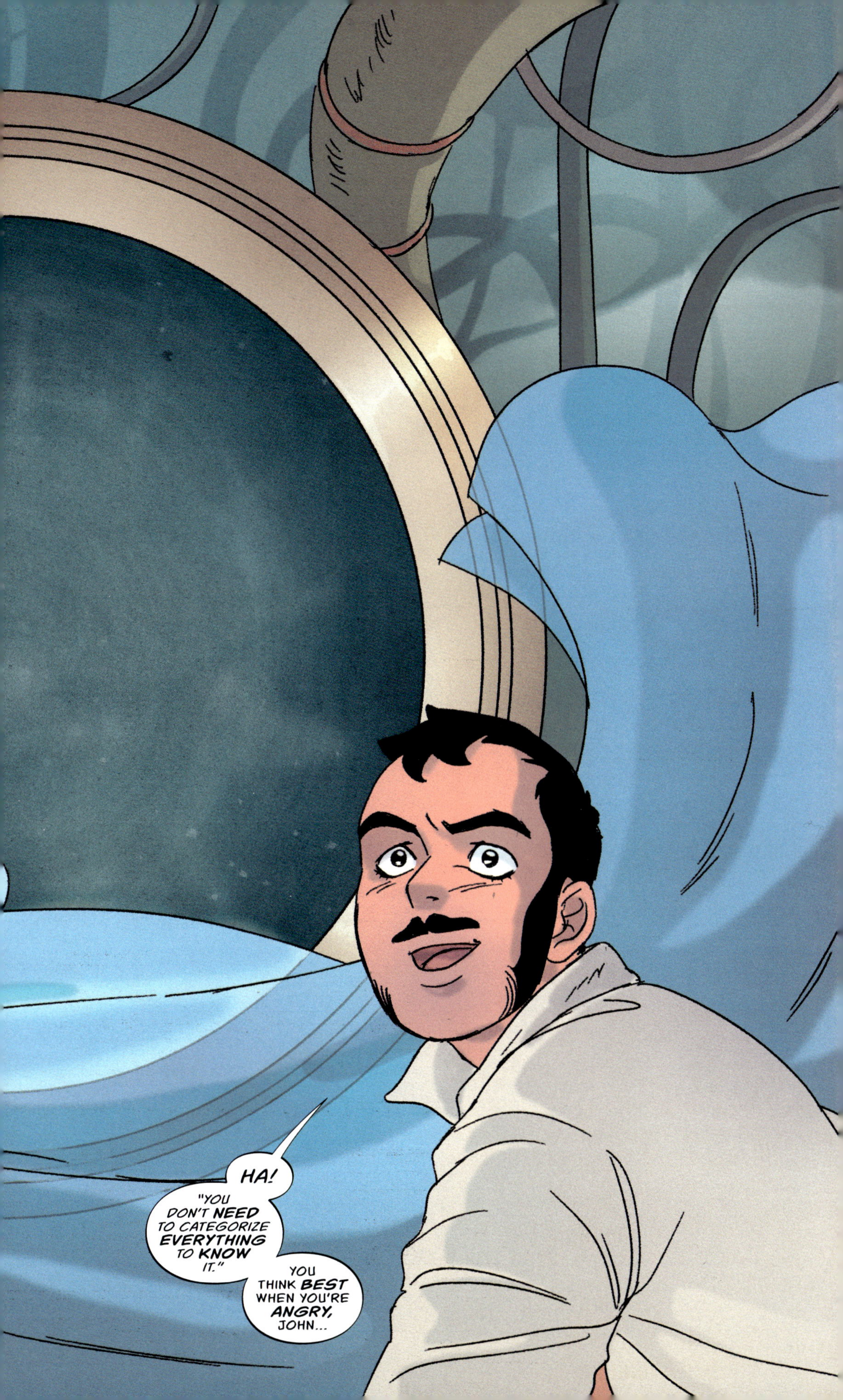
HA!
"YOU DON'T NEED TO CATEGORIZE EVERYTHING TO KNOW IT."
YOU THINK BEST WHEN YOU'RE ANGRY, JOHN...

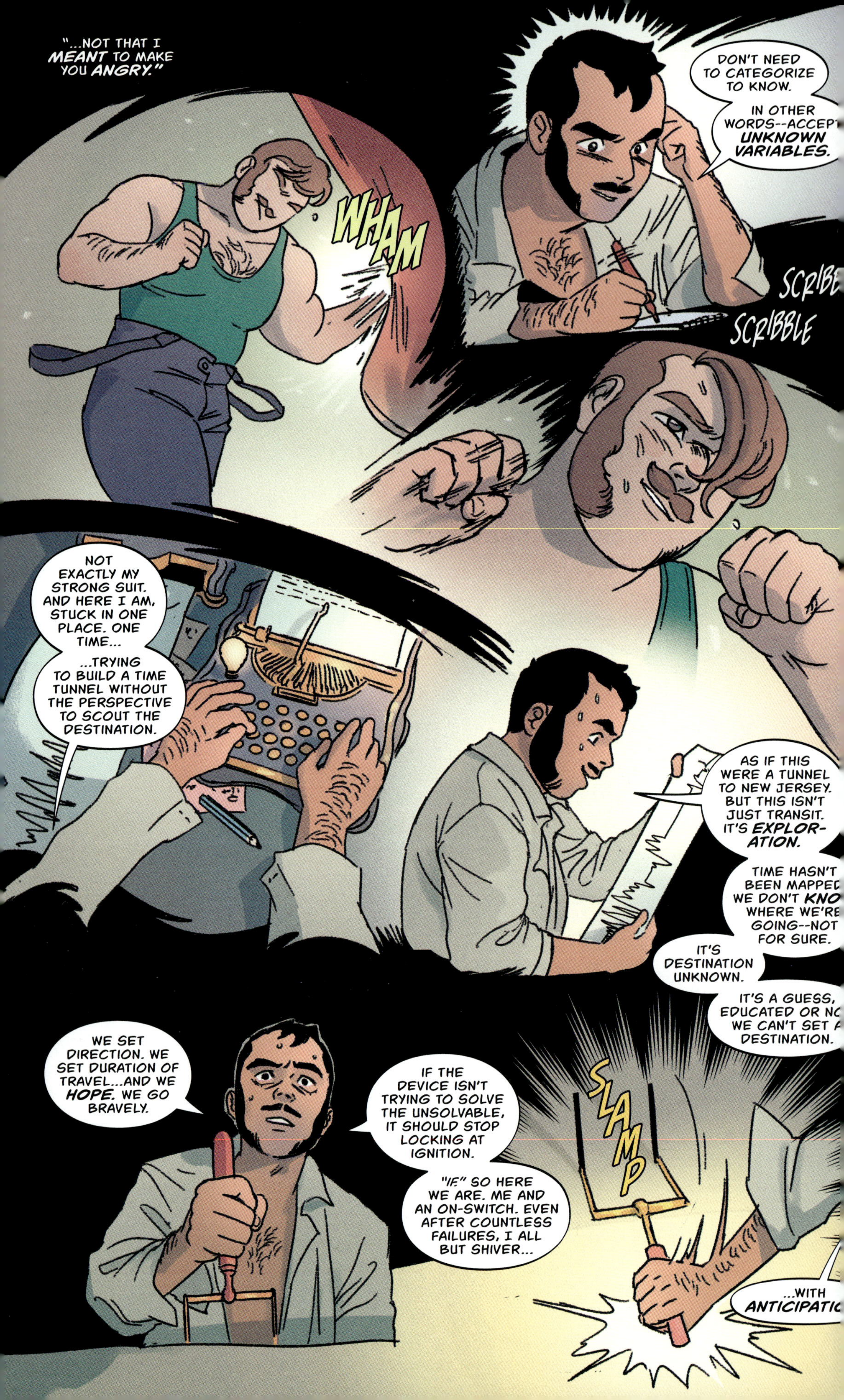
"...NOT THAT I MEANT TO MAKE YOU ANGRY."
DON'T NEED TO CATEGORIZE TO KNOW.
IN OTHER WORDS--ACCEPT UNKNOWN VARIABLES.
WHAM
SCRIBBLE
SCRIBBLE
NOT EXACTLY MY STRONG SUIT. AND HERE I AM, STUCK IN ONE PLACE. ONE TIME...
...TRYING TO BUILD A TIME TUNNEL WITHOUT THE PERSPECTIVE TO SCOUT THE DESTINATION.
AS IF THIS WERE A TUNNEL TO NEW JERSEY. BUT THIS ISN'T JUST TRANSIT. IT'S EXPLORATION.
TIME HASN'T BEEN MAPPED WE DON'T KNO WHERE WE'RE GOING--NOT FOR SURE.
IT'S DESTINATION UNKNOWN.
IT'S A GUESS, EDUCATED OR NO WE CAN'T SET A DESTINATION.
WE SET DIRECTION. WE SET DURATION OF TRAVEL...AND WE HOPE. WE GO BRAVELY.
IF THE DEVICE ISN'T TRYING TO SOLVE THE UNSOLVABLE, IT SHOULD STOP LOCKING AT IGNITION.
"IF." SO HERE WE ARE. ME AND AN ON-SWITCH. EVEN AFTER COUNTLESS FAILURES, I ALL BUT SHIVER...
SLAMP
...WITH ANTICIPATIO

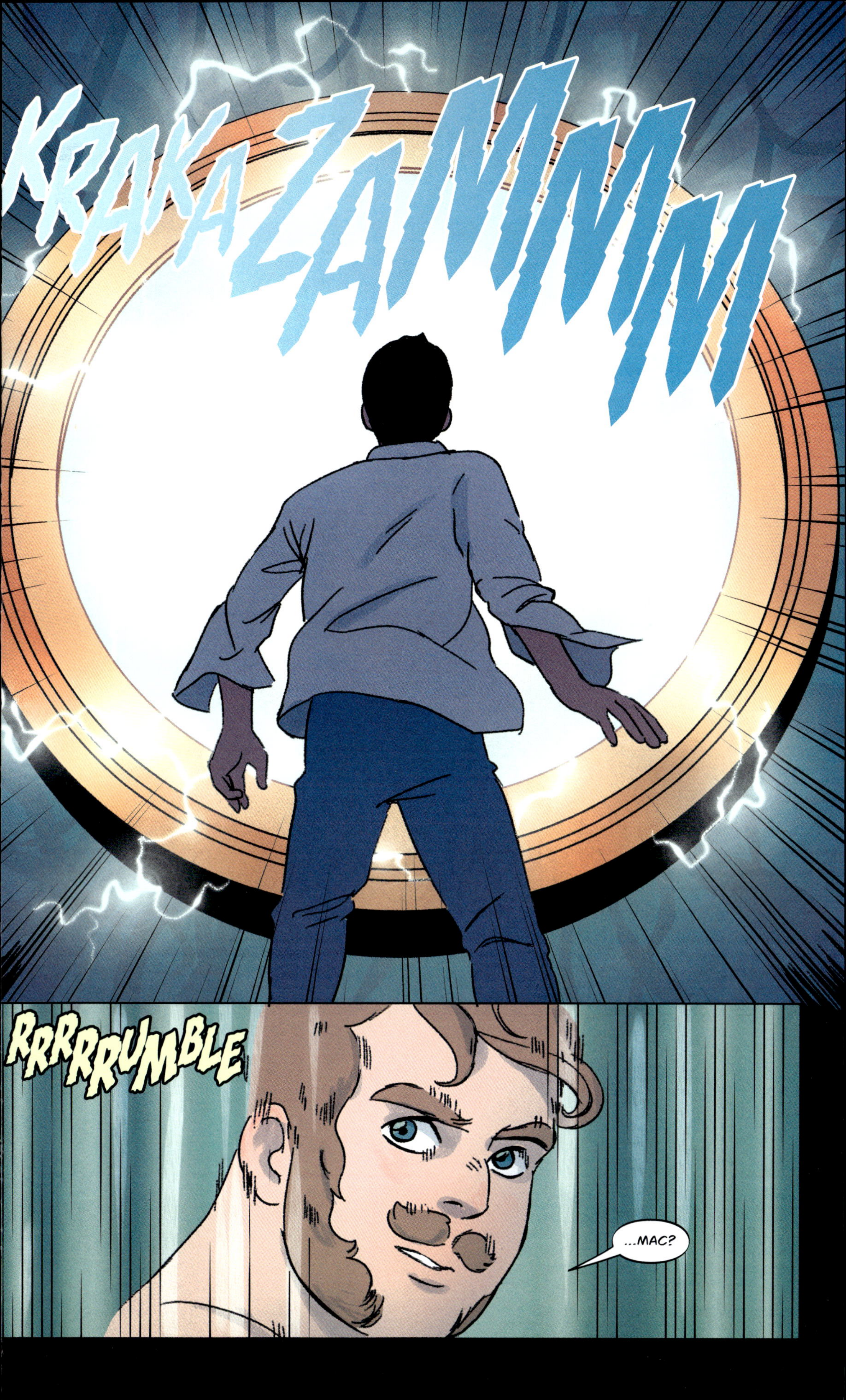
KRAKAZAMMM
RRRRRUMBLE
...MAC?

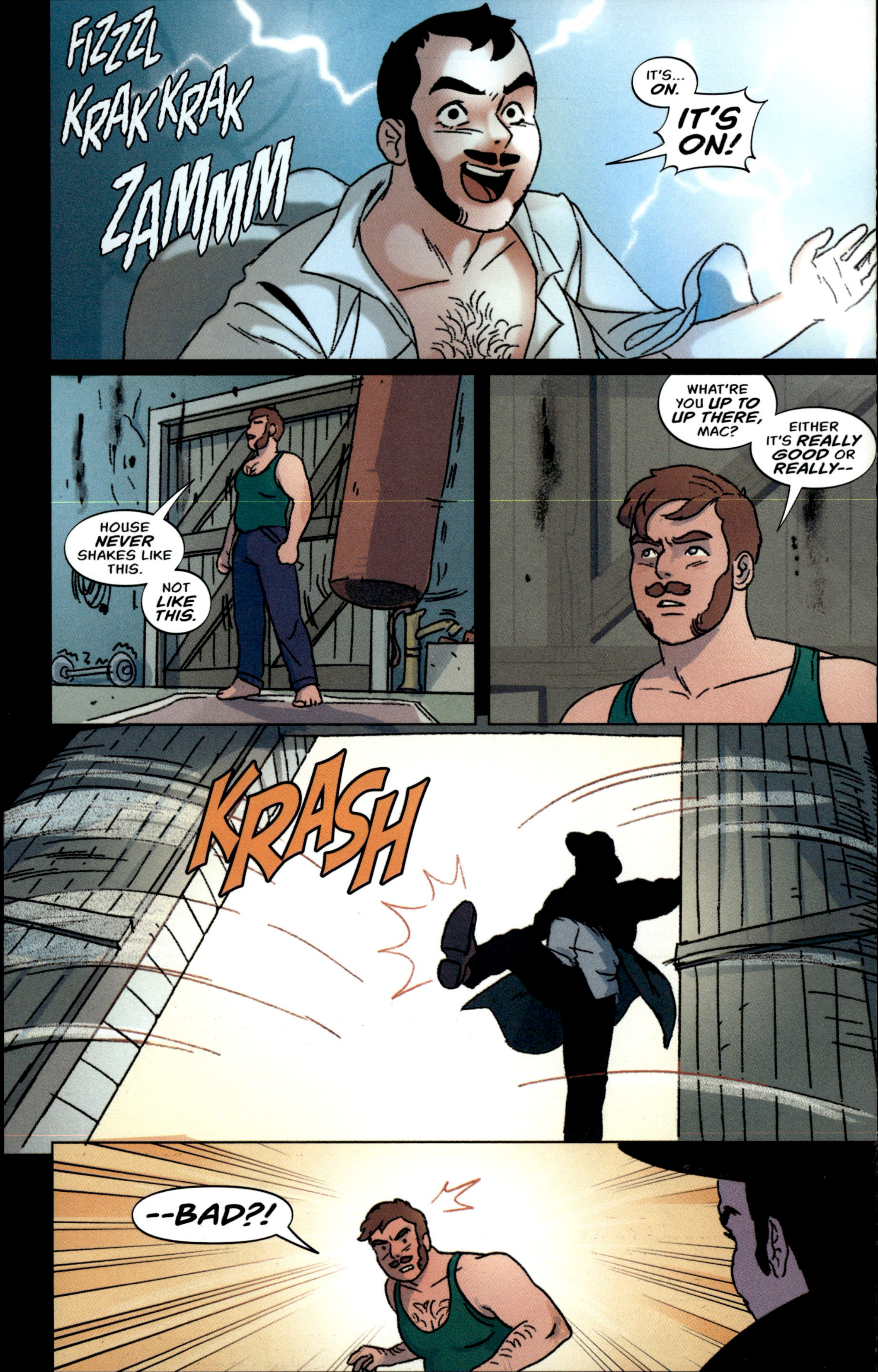
FIZZZL
KRAK KRAK
ZAMMM
IT'S... ON.
IT'S ON!
HOUSE NEVER SHAKES LIKE THIS.
NOT LIKE THIS.
WHAT'RE YOU UP TO UP THERE, MAC?
EITHER IT'S REALLY GOOD OR REALLY--
KRASH
--BAD?!

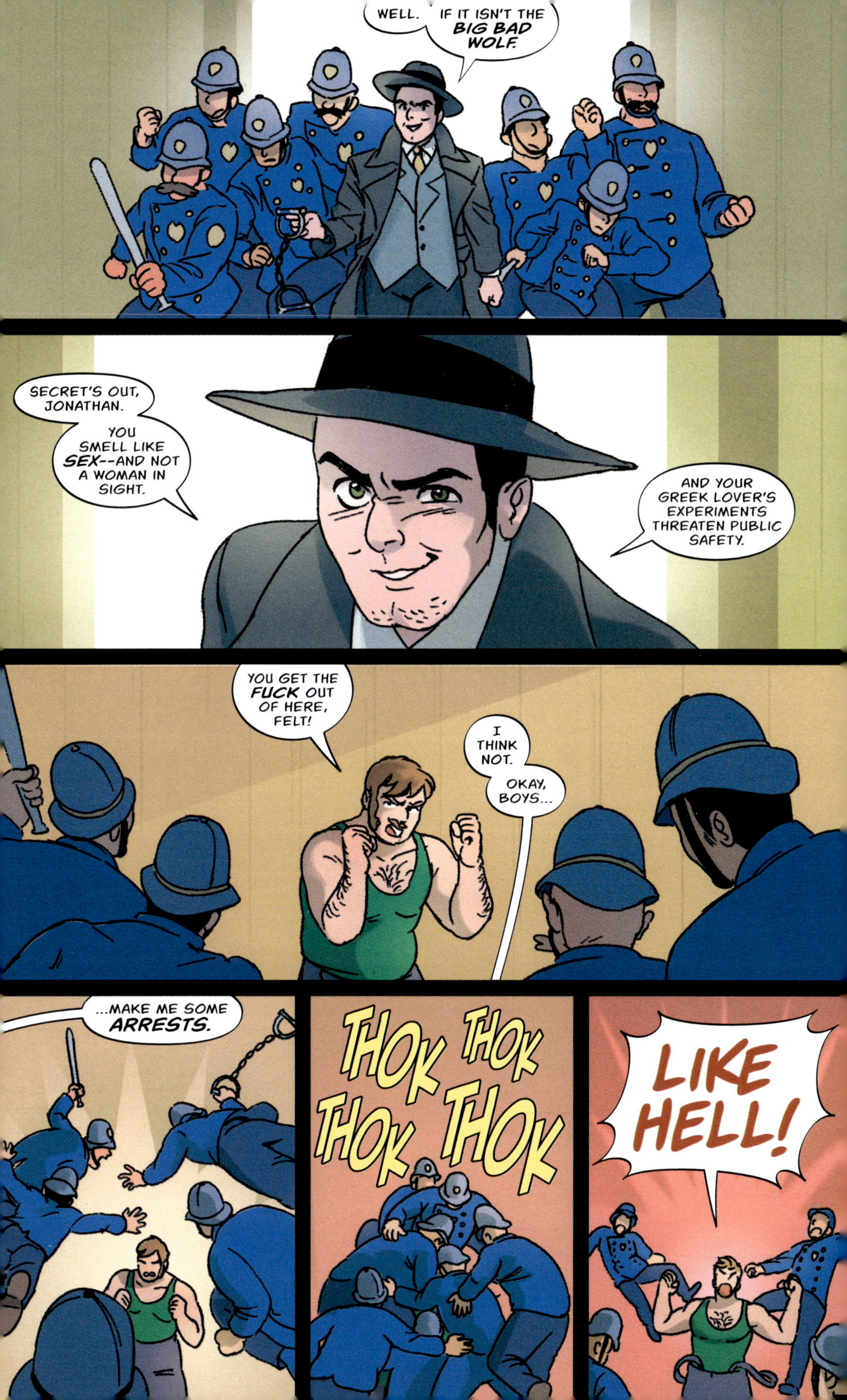
WELL. IF IT ISN'T THE BIG BAD WOLF.
SECRET'S OUT, JONATHAN.
YOU SMELL LIKE SEX--AND NOT A WOMAN IN SIGHT.
AND YOUR GREEK LOVER'S EXPERIMENTS THREATEN PUBLIC SAFETY.
YOU GET THE FUCK OUT OF HERE, FELT!
I THINK NOT.
OKAY, BOYS...
...MAKE ME SOME ARRESTS.
THOK THOK THOK THOK
LIKE HELL!

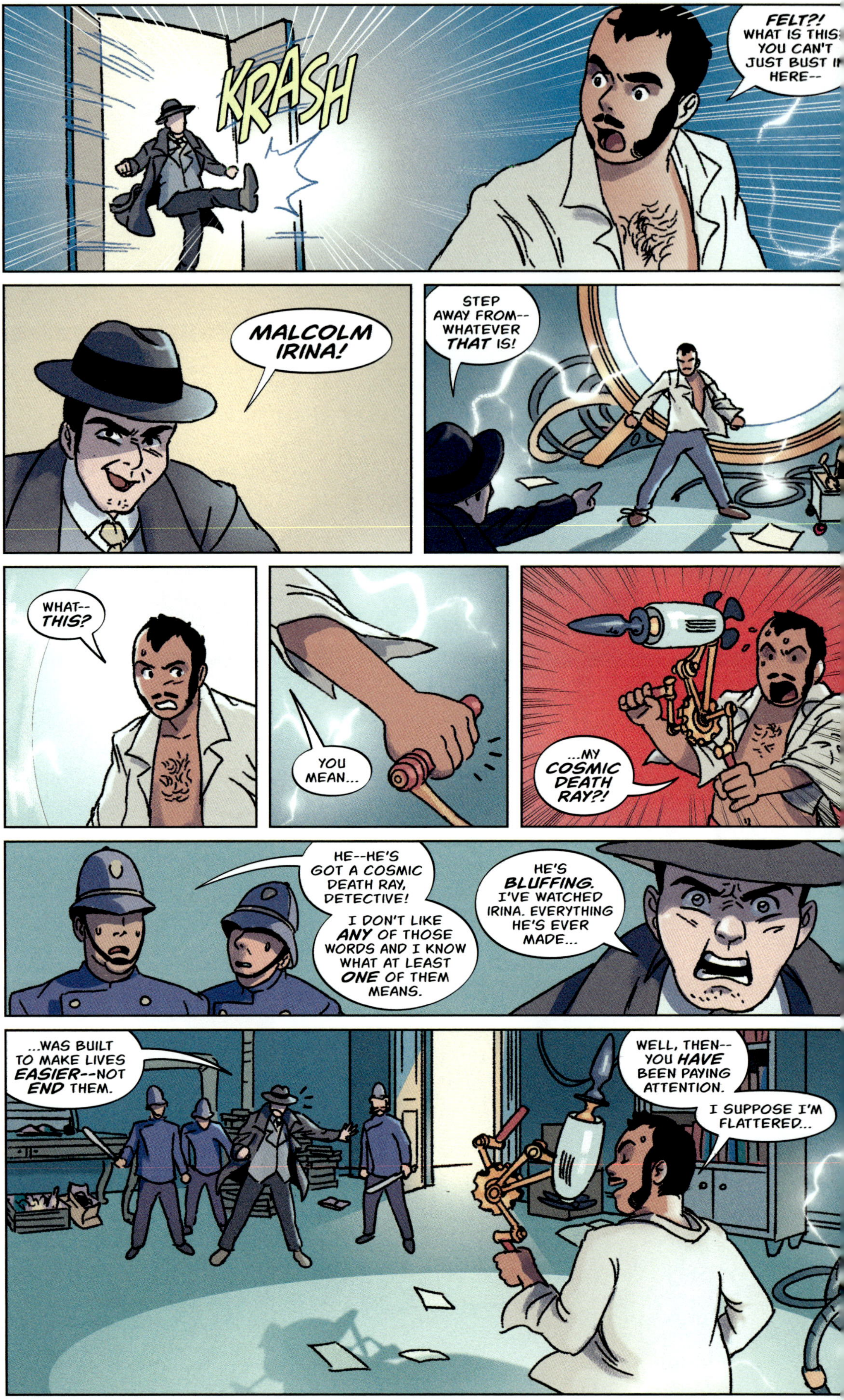
KRASH
FELT?! WHAT IS THIS? YOU CAN'T JUST BUST IN HERE--
MALCOLM IRINA!
STEP AWAY FROM-- WHATEVER THAT IS!
WHAT-- THIS?
YOU MEAN...
...MY COSMIC DEATH RAY?!
HE--HE'S GOT A COSMIC DEATH RAY, DETECTIVE!
I DON'T LIKE ANY OF THOSE WORDS AND I KNOW WHAT AT LEAST ONE OF THEM MEANS.
HE'S BLUFFING. I'VE WATCHED IRINA. EVERYTHING HE'S EVER MADE...
...WAS BUILT TO MAKE LIVES EASIER--NOT END THEM.
WELL, THEN-- YOU HAVE BEEN PAYING ATTENTION.
I SUPPOSE I'M FLATTERED...

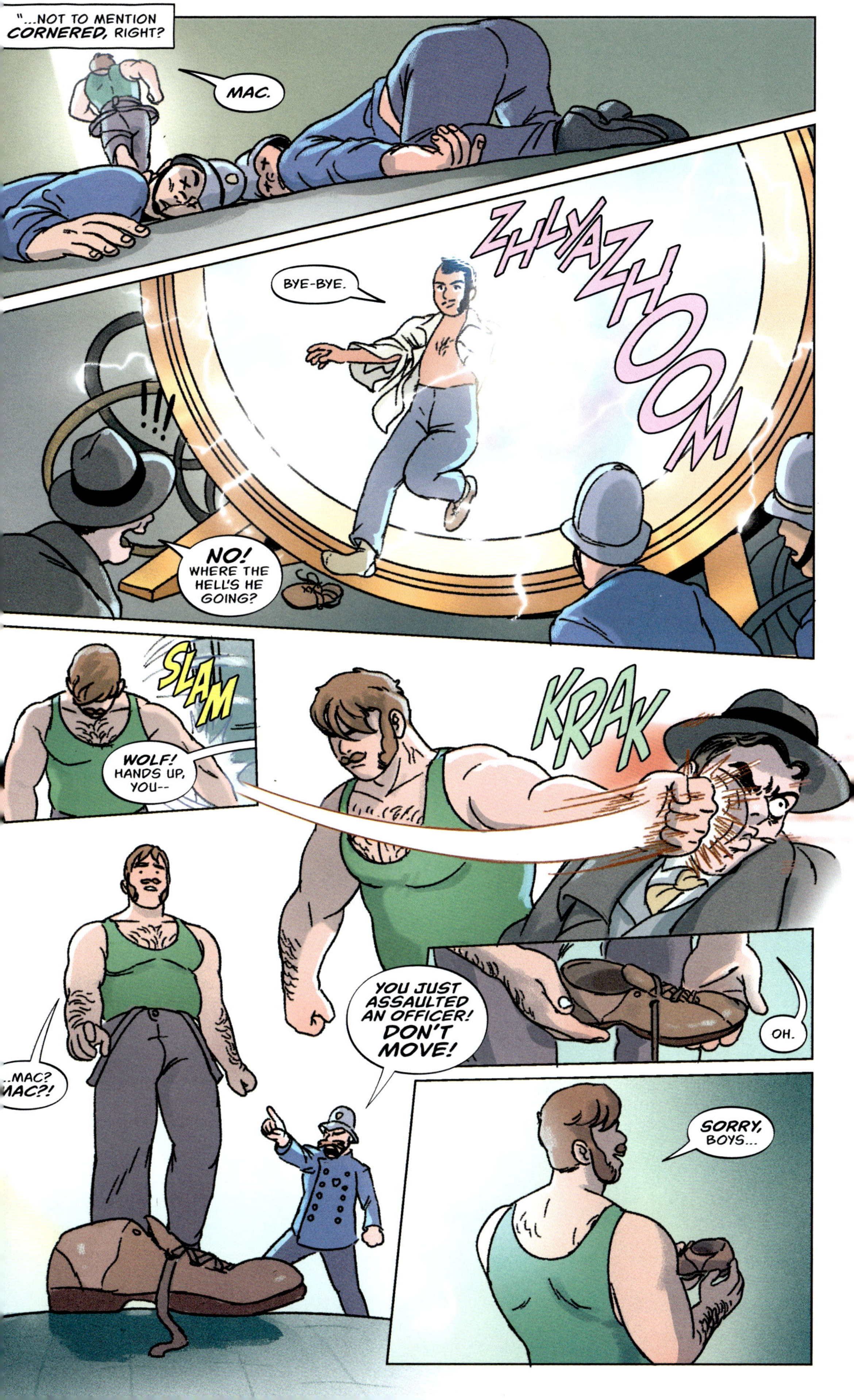
"...NOT TO MENTION CORNERED, RIGHT?
MAC.
BYE-BYE.
ZHLYAZHOOM
!!!
NO! WHERE THE HELL'S HE GOING?
SLAM
WOLF! HANDS UP, YOU--
KRAK
...MAC? MAC?!
YOU JUST ASSAULTED AN OFFICER! DON'T MOVE!
OH.
SORRY, BOYS...

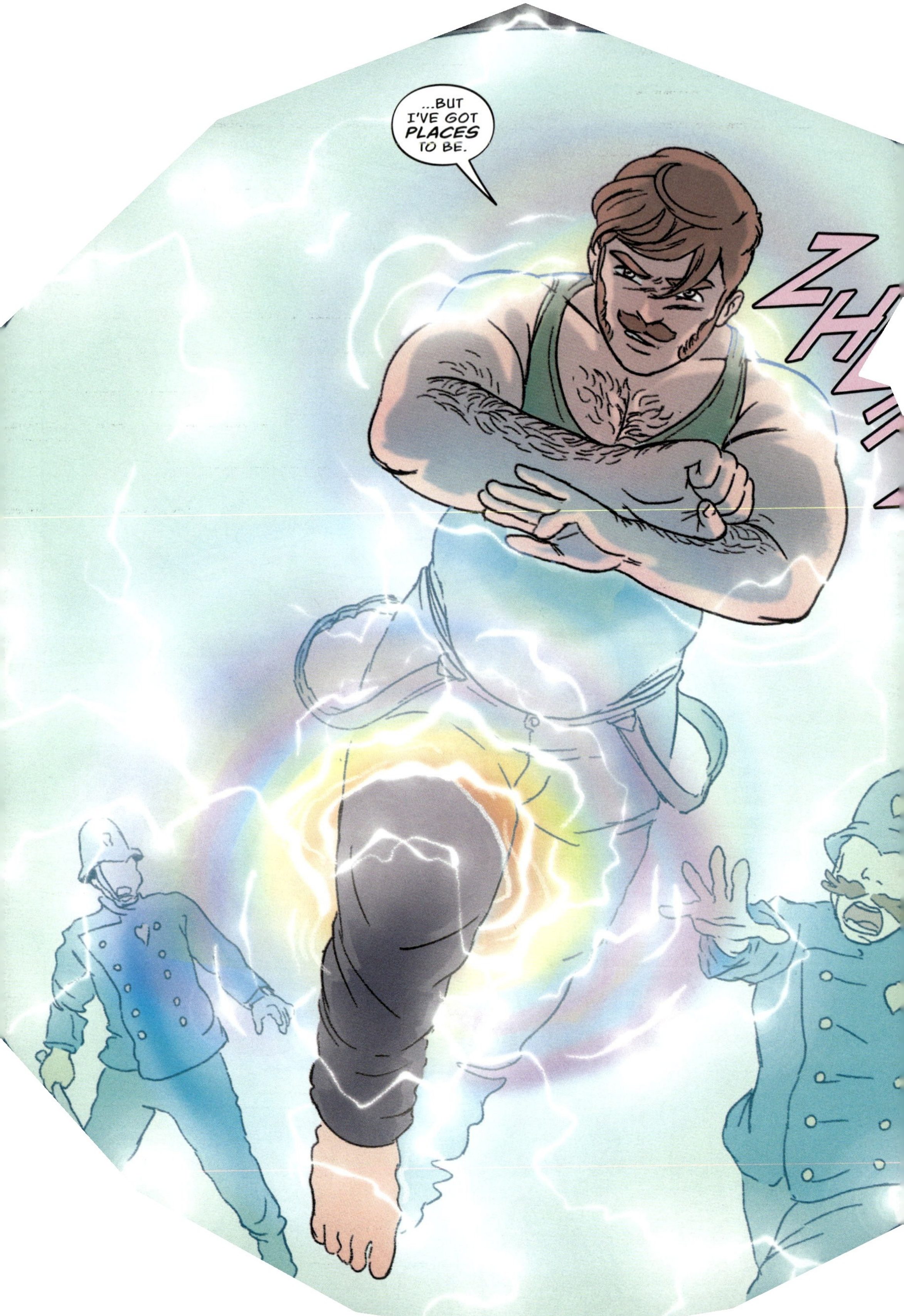
...BUT I'VE GOT PLACES TO BE.

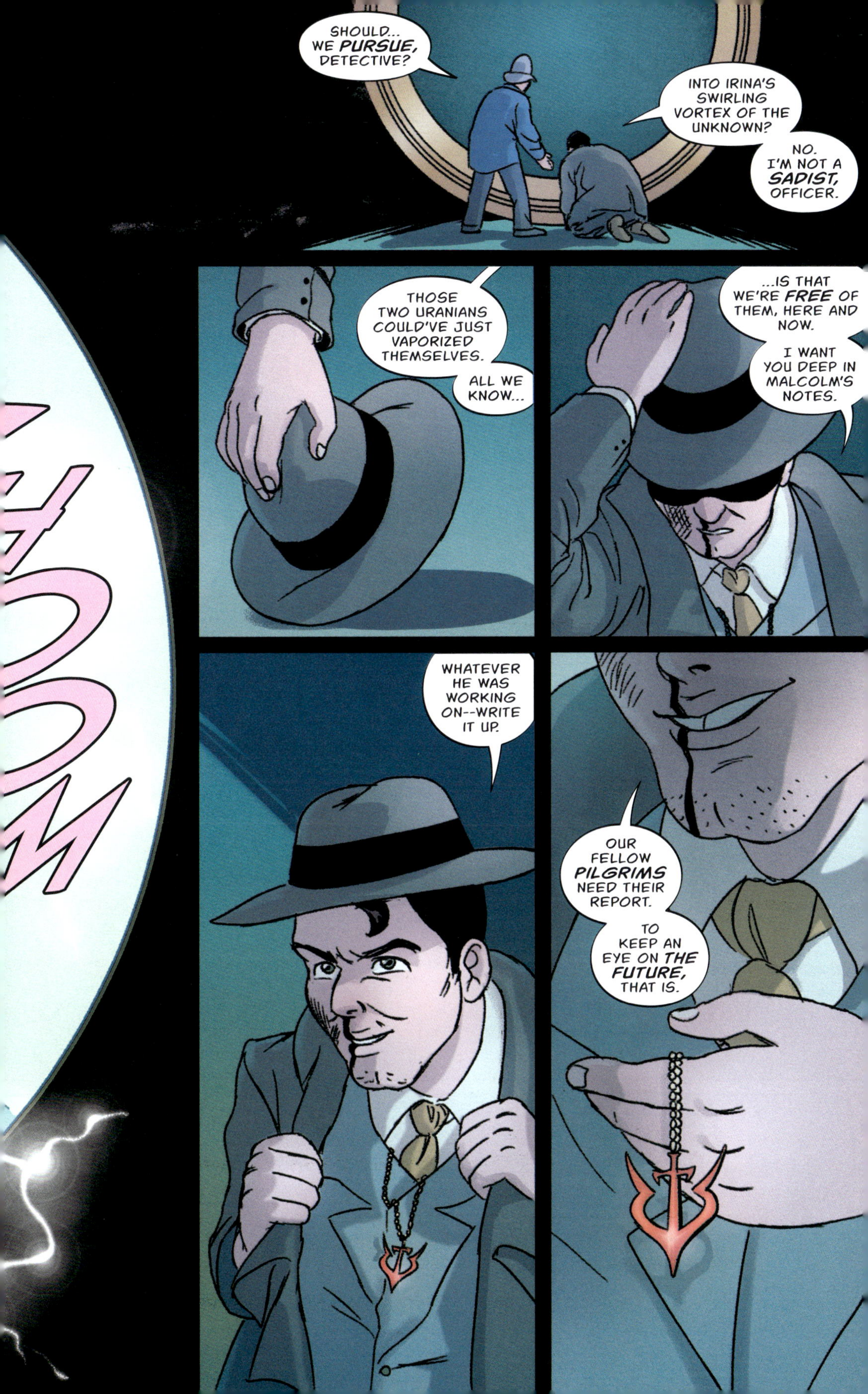
SHOULD... WE PURSUE, DETECTIVE?
INTO IRINA'S SWIRLING VORTEX OF THE UNKNOWN?
NO. I'M NOT A SADIST, OFFICER.
THOSE TWO URANIANS COULD'VE JUST VAPORIZED THEMSELVES.
ALL WE KNOW...
...IS THAT WE'RE FREE OF THEM, HERE AND NOW.
I WANT YOU DEEP IN MALCOLM'S NOTES.
WHATEVER HE WAS WORKING ON--WRITE IT UP.
OUR FELLOW PILGRIMS NEED THEIR REPORT.
TO KEEP AN EYE ON THE FUTURE, THAT IS.

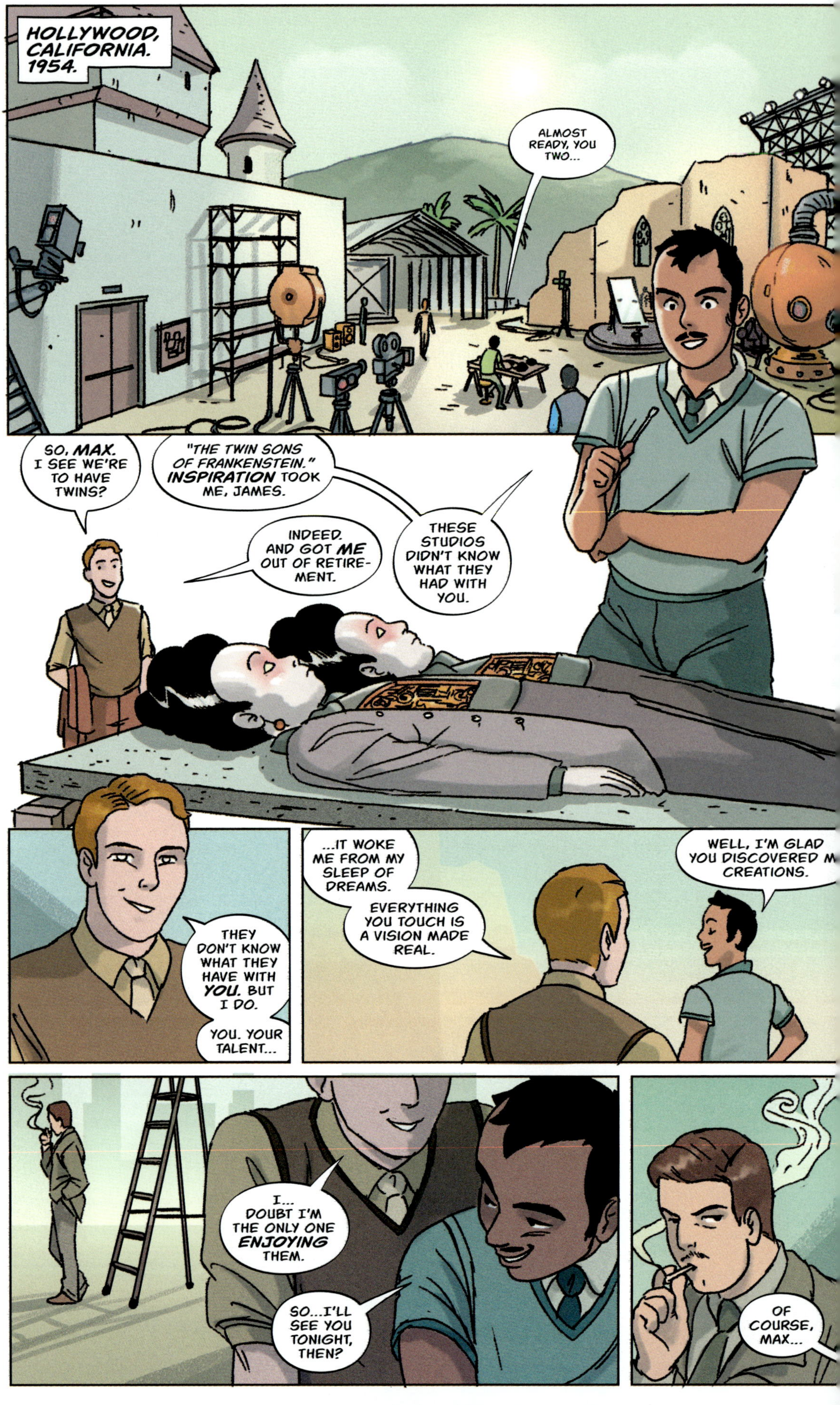
HOLLYWOOD, CALIFORNIA. 1954.
ALMOST READY, YOU TWO...
SO, MAX. I SEE WE'RE TO HAVE TWINS?
"THE TWIN SONS OF FRANKENSTEIN." INSPIRATION TOOK ME, JAMES.
THESE STUDIOS DIDN'T KNOW WHAT THEY HAD WITH YOU.
INDEED. AND GOT ME OUT OF RETIRE-MENT.
THEY DON'T KNOW WHAT THEY HAVE WITH YOU. BUT I DO.
YOU. YOUR TALENT...
...IT WOKE ME FROM MY SLEEP OF DREAMS.
EVERYTHING YOU TOUCH IS A VISION MADE REAL.
WELL, I'M GLAD YOU DISCOVERED M CREATIONS.
I... DOUBT I'M THE ONLY ONE ENJOYING THEM.
SO...I'LL SEE YOU TONIGHT, THEN?
OF COURSE, MAX...

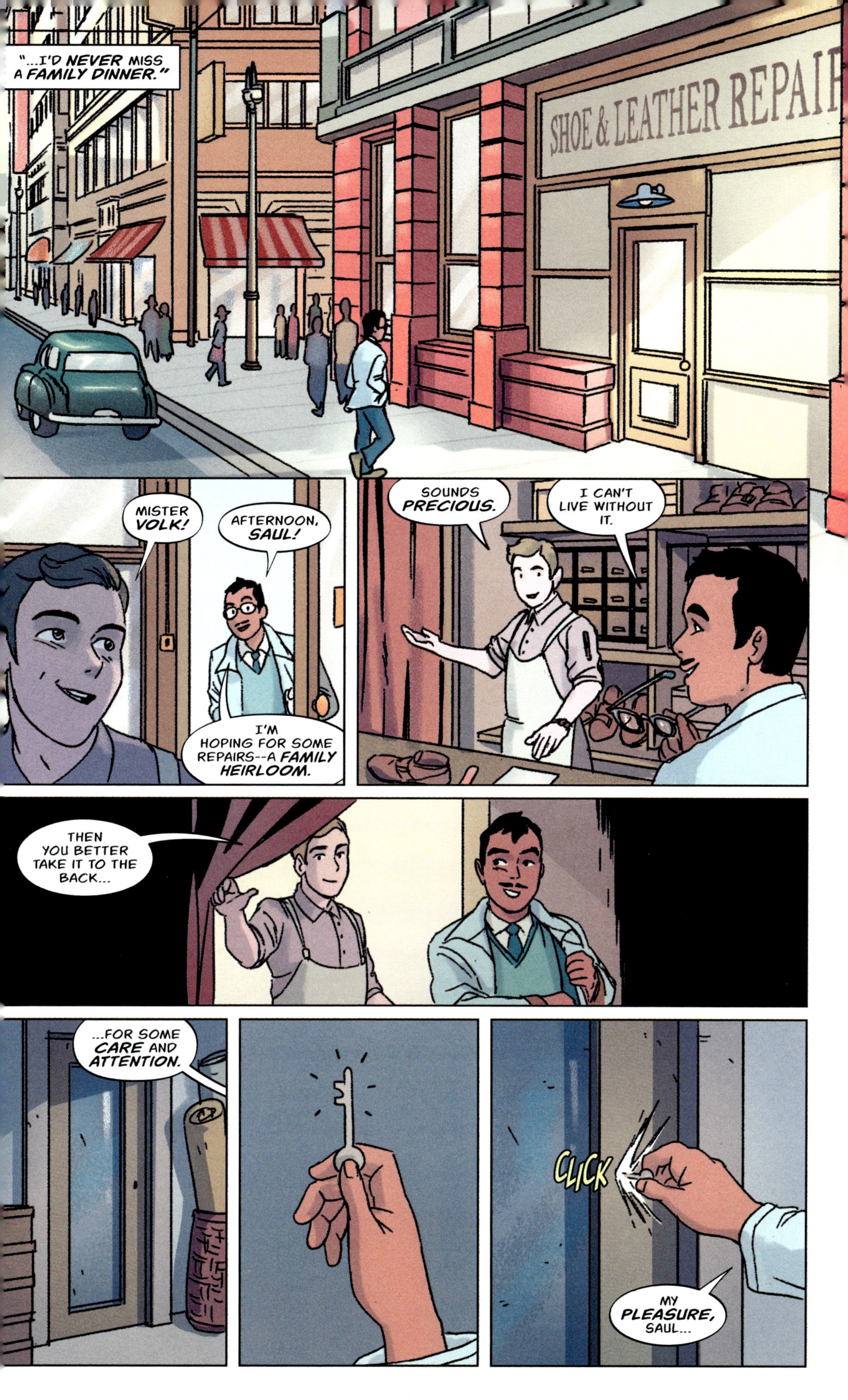
"...I'D NEVER MISS A FAMILY DINNER."
SHOE & LEATHER REPAIR
MISTER VOLK!
AFTERNOON, SAUL!
I'M HOPING FOR SOME REPAIRS--A FAMILY HEIRLOOM.
SOUNDS PRECIOUS.
I CAN'T LIVE WITHOUT IT.
THEN YOU BETTER TAKE IT TO THE BACK...
...FOR SOME CARE AND ATTENTION.
CLICK
MY PLEASURE, SAUL...

"...MY **PLEASURE.**"

GOOD TO SEE YOU, OSCAR. HOW'RE TODAY'S NUMBERS?

ONLY A FEW TABLES LEFT OPEN UP HERE, BOSS. UPSTAIRS IS BOOKED.

THE **CHRONO-SHUNT** IS STRONG. THE WHOLE SITE'S HOLDING STEADY-- ONE SECOND OUT OF TIME.

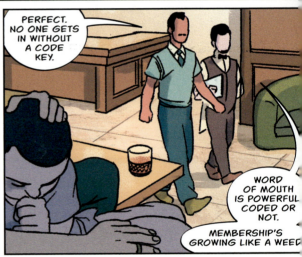

PERFECT. NO ONE GETS IN WITHOUT A CODE KEY.

WORD OF MOUTH IS POWERFUL CODED OR NOT.

MEMBERSHIP'S GROWING LIKE A WEED

SAFETY WILL DO THAT--TO **BE** WHO YOU WANT AND **BE WITH** WHO YOU WANT.

AS FOR YOUR **PRIVATE** PROJECT--

THAT STAYS BETWEEN US. AND, ANYWAY, YOU LEFT OUT THE **DOWNSTAIRS** NUMBERS.

THE BATHS ARE PACKED LIKE ALWAYS. IN FACT...

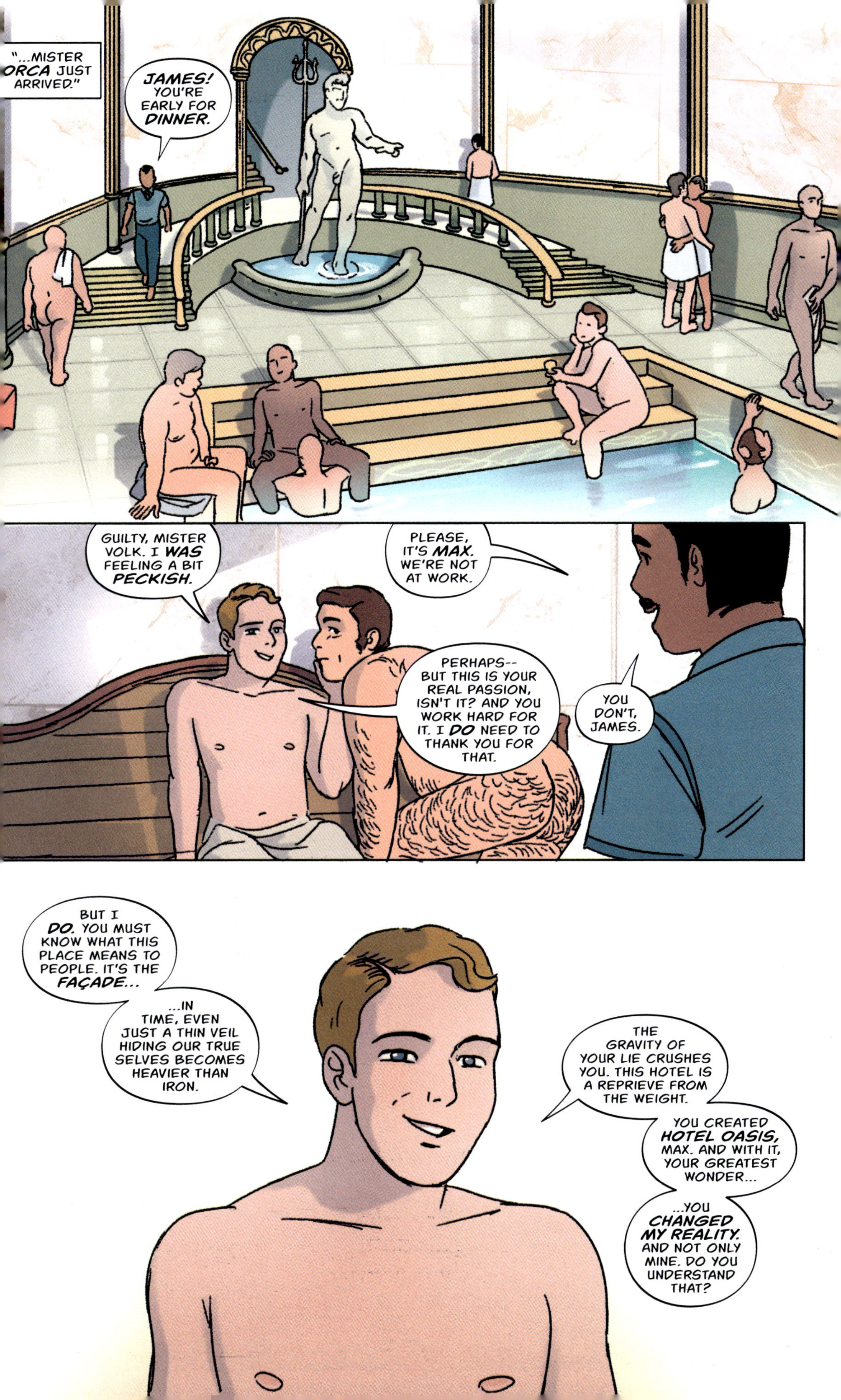

"...MISTER ORCA JUST ARRIVED."
JAMES! YOU'RE EARLY FOR DINNER.
GUILTY, MISTER VOLK. I WAS FEELING A BIT PECKISH.
PLEASE, IT'S MAX. WE'RE NOT AT WORK.
PERHAPS-- BUT THIS IS YOUR REAL PASSION, ISN'T IT? AND YOU WORK HARD FOR IT. I DO NEED TO THANK YOU FOR THAT.
YOU DON'T, JAMES.
BUT I DO. YOU MUST KNOW WHAT THIS PLACE MEANS TO PEOPLE. IT'S THE FAÇADE...
...IN TIME, EVEN JUST A THIN VEIL HIDING OUR TRUE SELVES BECOMES HEAVIER THAN IRON.
THE GRAVITY OF YOUR LIE CRUSHES YOU. THIS HOTEL IS A REPRIEVE FROM THE WEIGHT.
YOU CREATED HOTEL OASIS, MAX. AND WITH IT, YOUR GREATEST WONDER...
...YOU CHANGED MY REALITY. AND NOT ONLY MINE. DO YOU UNDERSTAND THAT?

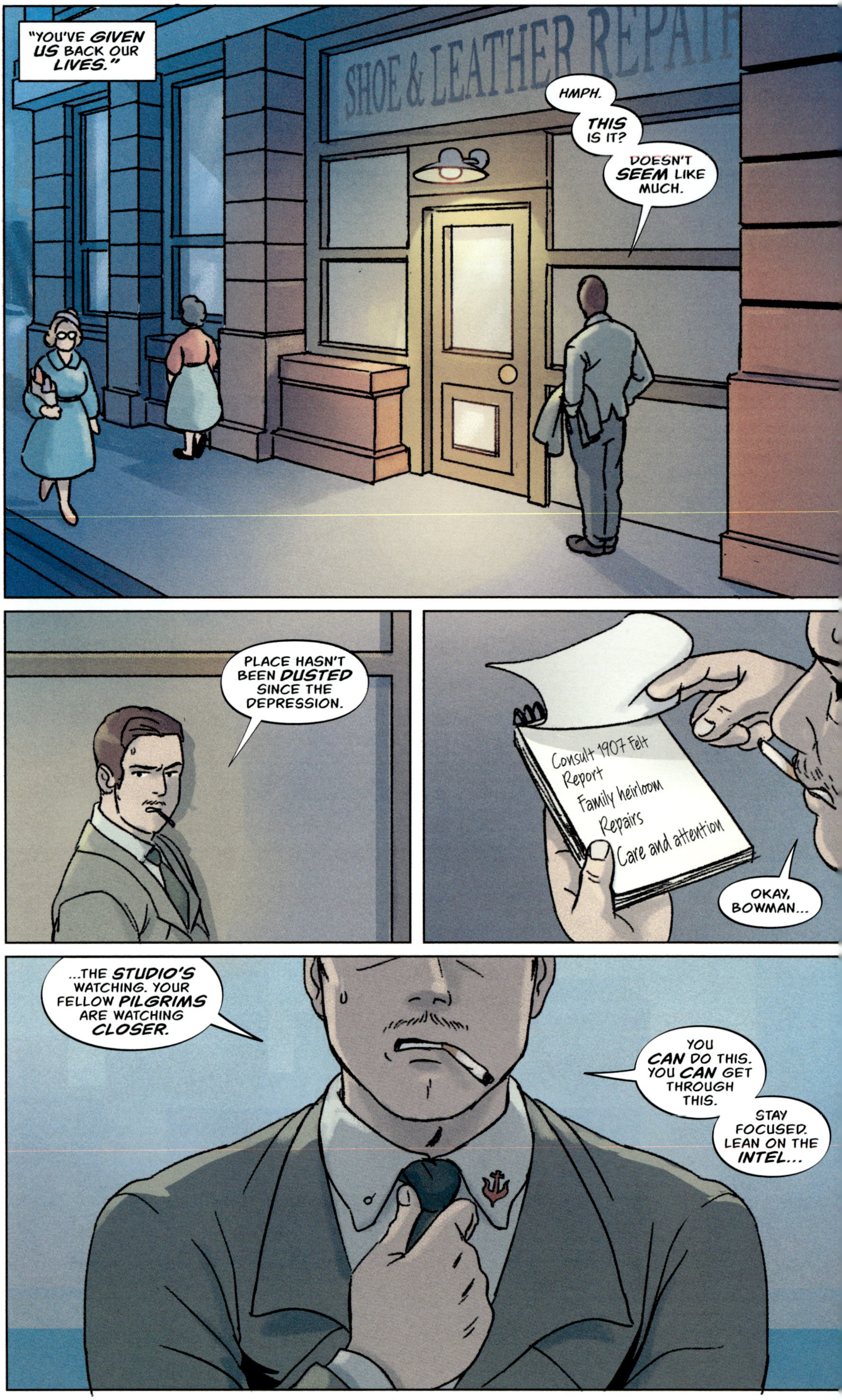
"YOU'VE GIVEN US BACK OUR LIVES."
SHOE & LEATHER REPAIR
HMPH.
THIS IS IT?
DOESN'T SEEM LIKE MUCH.
PLACE HASN'T BEEN DUSTED SINCE THE DEPRESSION.
Consult 1907 Felt Report
Family heirloom
Repairs
Care and attention
OKAY, BOWMAN...
...THE STUDIO'S WATCHING. YOUR FELLOW PILGRIMS ARE WATCHING CLOSER.
YOU CAN DO THIS. YOU CAN GET THROUGH THIS.
STAY FOCUSED. LEAN ON THE INTEL...

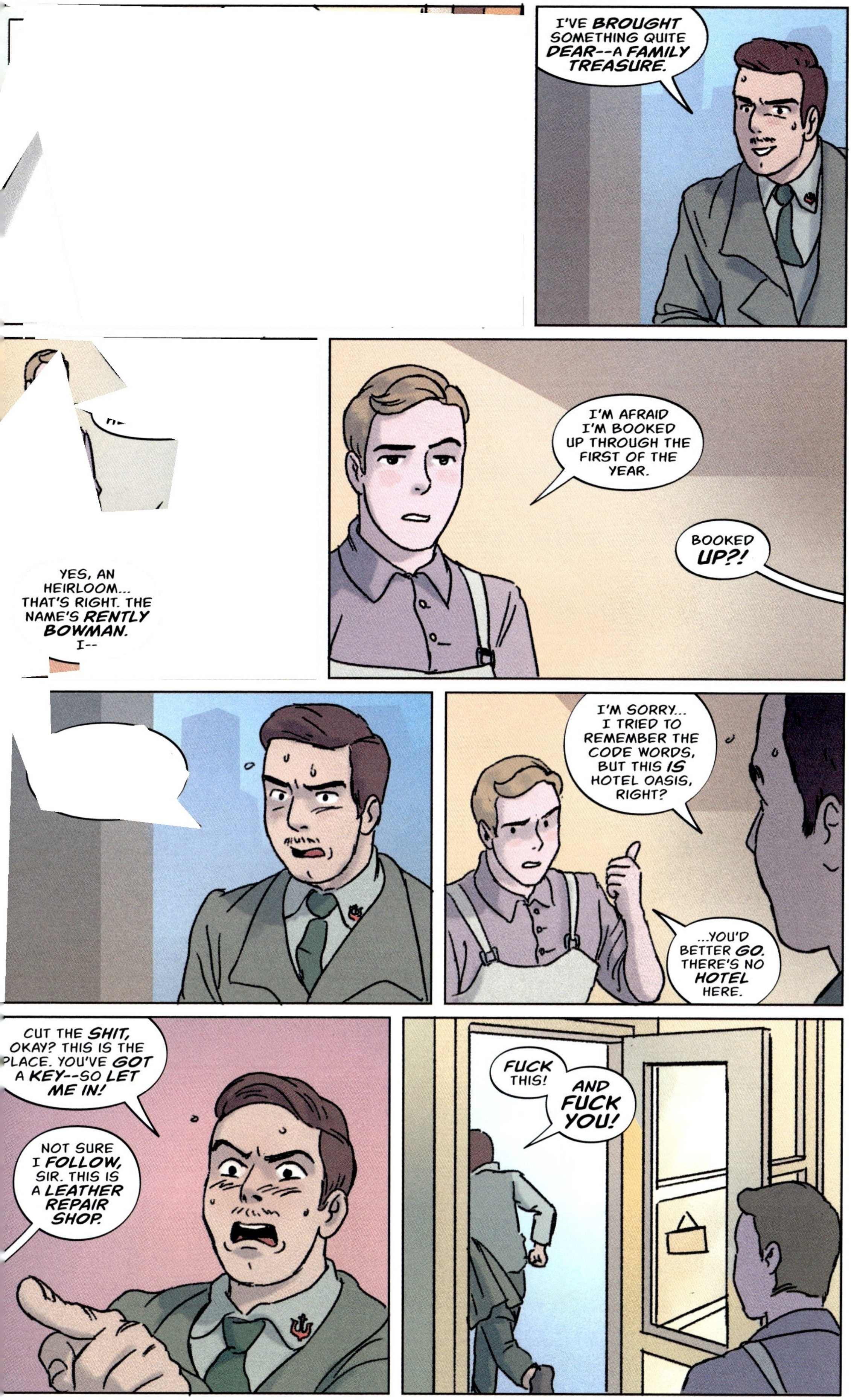

I'VE BROUGHT SOMETHING QUITE DEAR--A FAMILY TREASURE.
YES, AN HEIRLOOM... THAT'S RIGHT. THE NAME'S RENTLY BOWMAN. I--
I'M AFRAID I'M BOOKED UP THROUGH THE FIRST OF THE YEAR.
BOOKED UP?!
I'M SORRY... I TRIED TO REMEMBER THE CODE WORDS, BUT THIS IS HOTEL OASIS, RIGHT?
...YOU'D BETTER GO. THERE'S NO HOTEL HERE.
CUT THE SHIT, OKAY? THIS IS THE PLACE. YOU'VE GOT A KEY--SO LET ME IN!
NOT SURE I FOLLOW, SIR. THIS IS A LEATHER REPAIR SHOP.
FUCK THIS!
AND FUCK YOU!

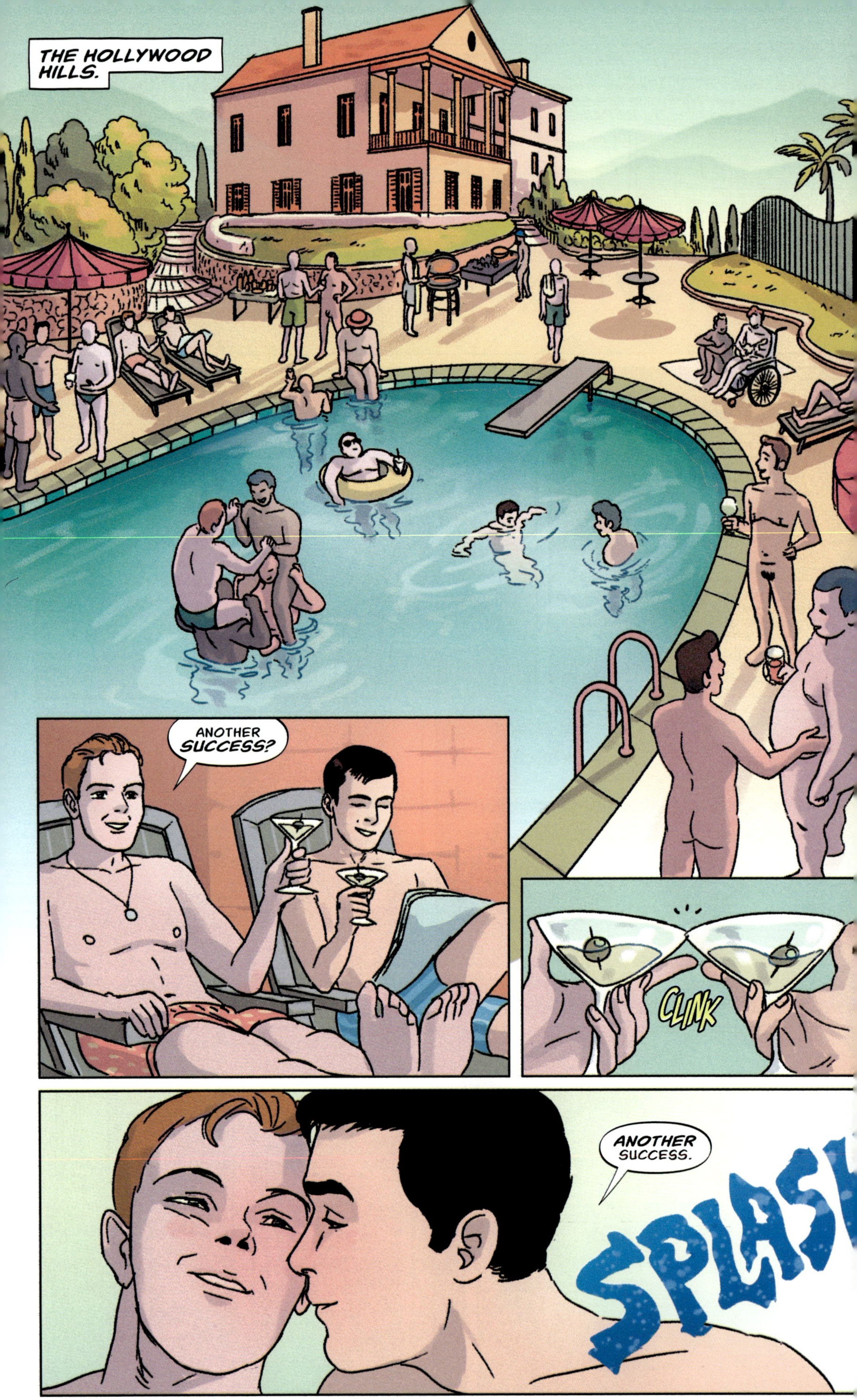
THE HOLLYWOOD HILLS.
ANOTHER SUCCESS?
CLINK
ANOTHER SUCCESS.
SPLAS

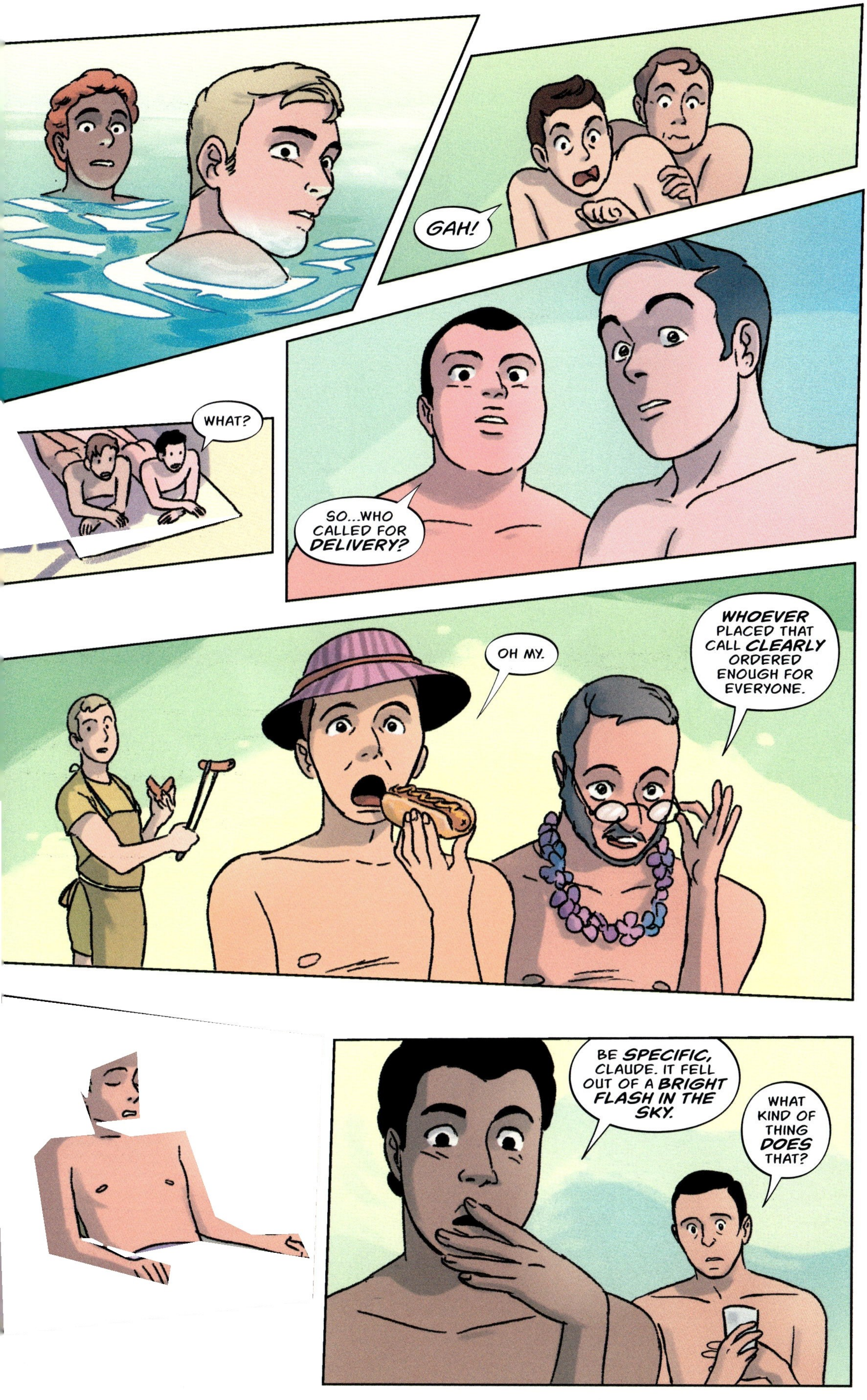
GAH!
WHAT?
SO...WHO CALLED FOR DELIVERY?
OH MY.
WHOEVER PLACED THAT CALL CLEARLY ORDERED ENOUGH FOR EVERYONE.
BE SPECIFIC, CLAUDE. IT FELL OUT OF A BRIGHT FLASH IN THE SKY.
WHAT KIND OF THING DOES THAT?

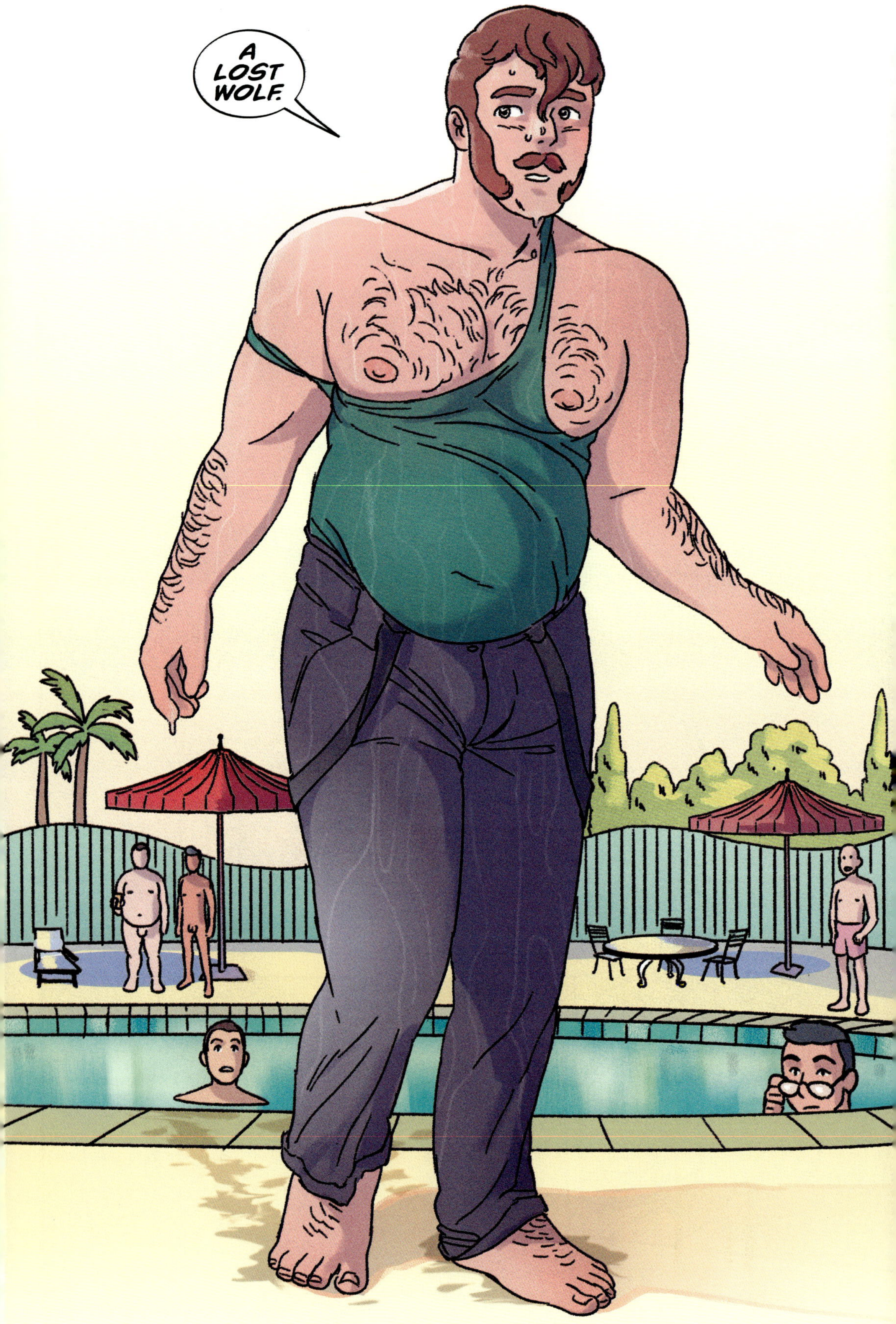
A LOST WOLF.

THAT'S NO WOLF.

HEH.

SLUHP

THERE. YOU'RE WET.

SPLASHING DOWN FROM THE SKY WILL DO THAT.

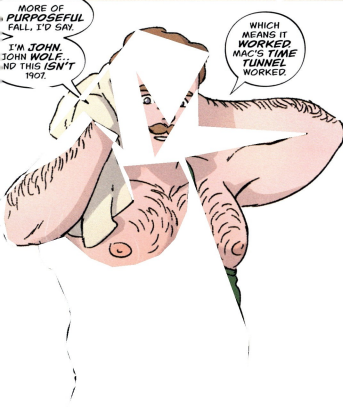

MORE OF PURPOSEFUL FALL, I'D SAY.

I'M JOHN. JOHN WOLF... AND THIS ISN'T 1907.

WHICH MEANS IT WORKED. MAC'S TIME TUNNEL WORKED.

"TIME TUNNEL"? SOUNDS SERIOUS.

I'M ART. THIS IS TONY. IT'S MY PLACE. OUR PARTY.

THIS IS 1954. AND YOU NEED SOME FRESH CLOTHES.

RIGHT NOW?

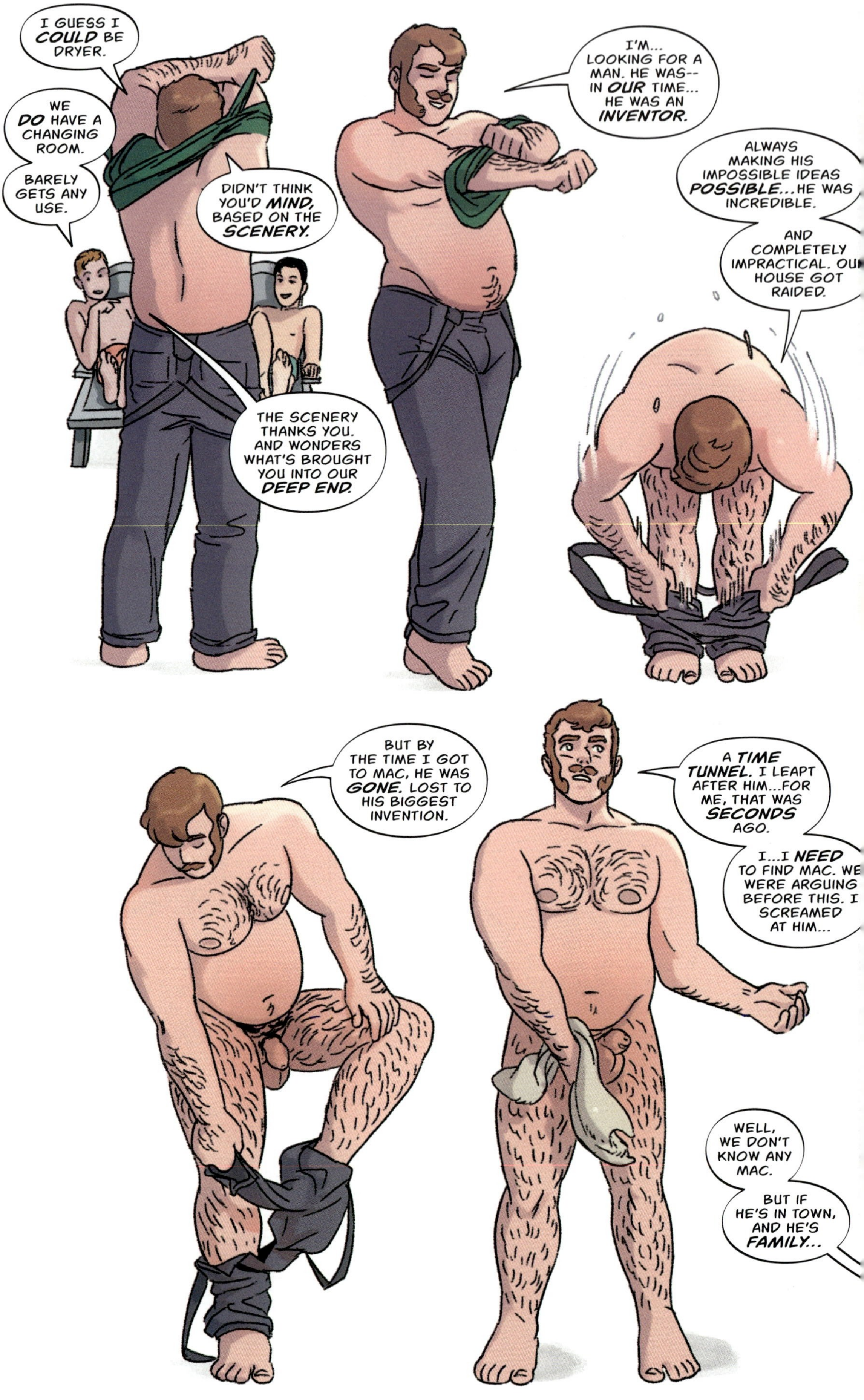

I GUESS I COULD BE DRYER.
WE DO HAVE A CHANGING ROOM.
BARELY GETS ANY USE.
DIDN'T THINK YOU'D MIND, BASED ON THE SCENERY.
THE SCENERY THANKS YOU. AND WONDERS WHAT'S BROUGHT YOU INTO OUR DEEP END.
I'M... LOOKING FOR A MAN. HE WAS-- IN OUR TIME... HE WAS AN INVENTOR.
ALWAYS MAKING HIS IMPOSSIBLE IDEAS POSSIBLE... HE WAS INCREDIBLE.
AND COMPLETELY IMPRACTICAL. OU HOUSE GOT RAIDED.
BUT BY THE TIME I GOT TO MAC, HE WAS GONE. LOST TO HIS BIGGEST INVENTION.
A TIME TUNNEL. I LEAPT AFTER HIM...FOR ME, THAT WAS SECONDS AGO.
I...I NEED TO FIND MAC. WE WERE ARGUING BEFORE THIS. I SCREAMED AT HIM...
WELL, WE DON'T KNOW ANY MAC.
BUT IF HE'S IN TOWN, AND HE'S FAMILY...

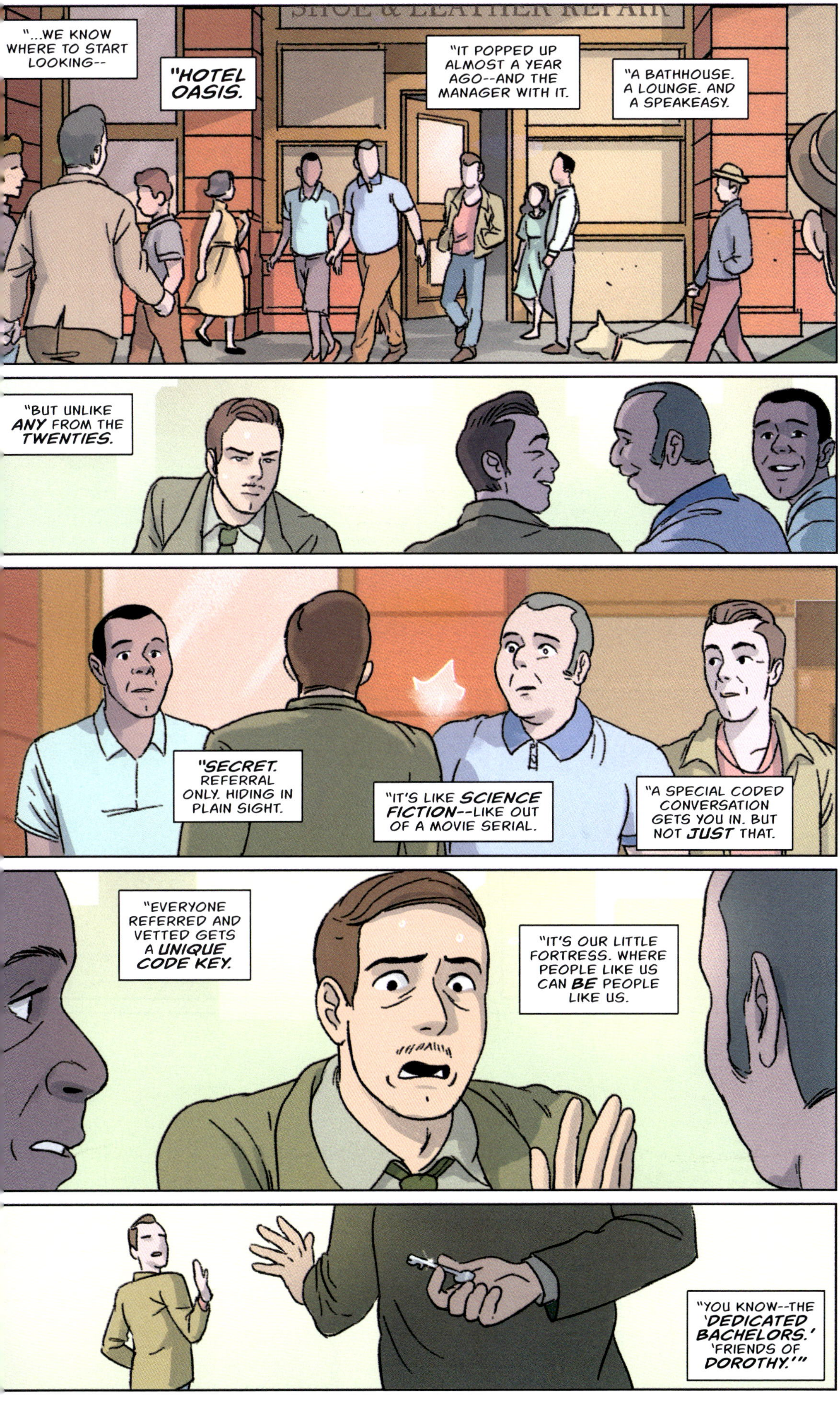
SHOE & LEATHER REPAIR
"...WE KNOW WHERE TO START LOOKING--
"HOTEL OASIS.
"IT POPPED UP ALMOST A YEAR AGO--AND THE MANAGER WITH IT.
"A BATHHOUSE. A LOUNGE. AND A SPEAKEASY.
"BUT UNLIKE ANY FROM THE TWENTIES.
"SECRET. REFERRAL ONLY. HIDING IN PLAIN SIGHT.
"IT'S LIKE SCIENCE FICTION--LIKE OUT OF A MOVIE SERIAL.
"A SPECIAL CODED CONVERSATION GETS YOU IN. BUT NOT JUST THAT.
"EVERYONE REFERRED AND VETTED GETS A UNIQUE CODE KEY.
"IT'S OUR LITTLE FORTRESS. WHERE PEOPLE LIKE US CAN BE PEOPLE LIKE US.
"YOU KNOW--THE 'DEDICATED BACHELORS.' 'FRIENDS OF DOROTHY.'"

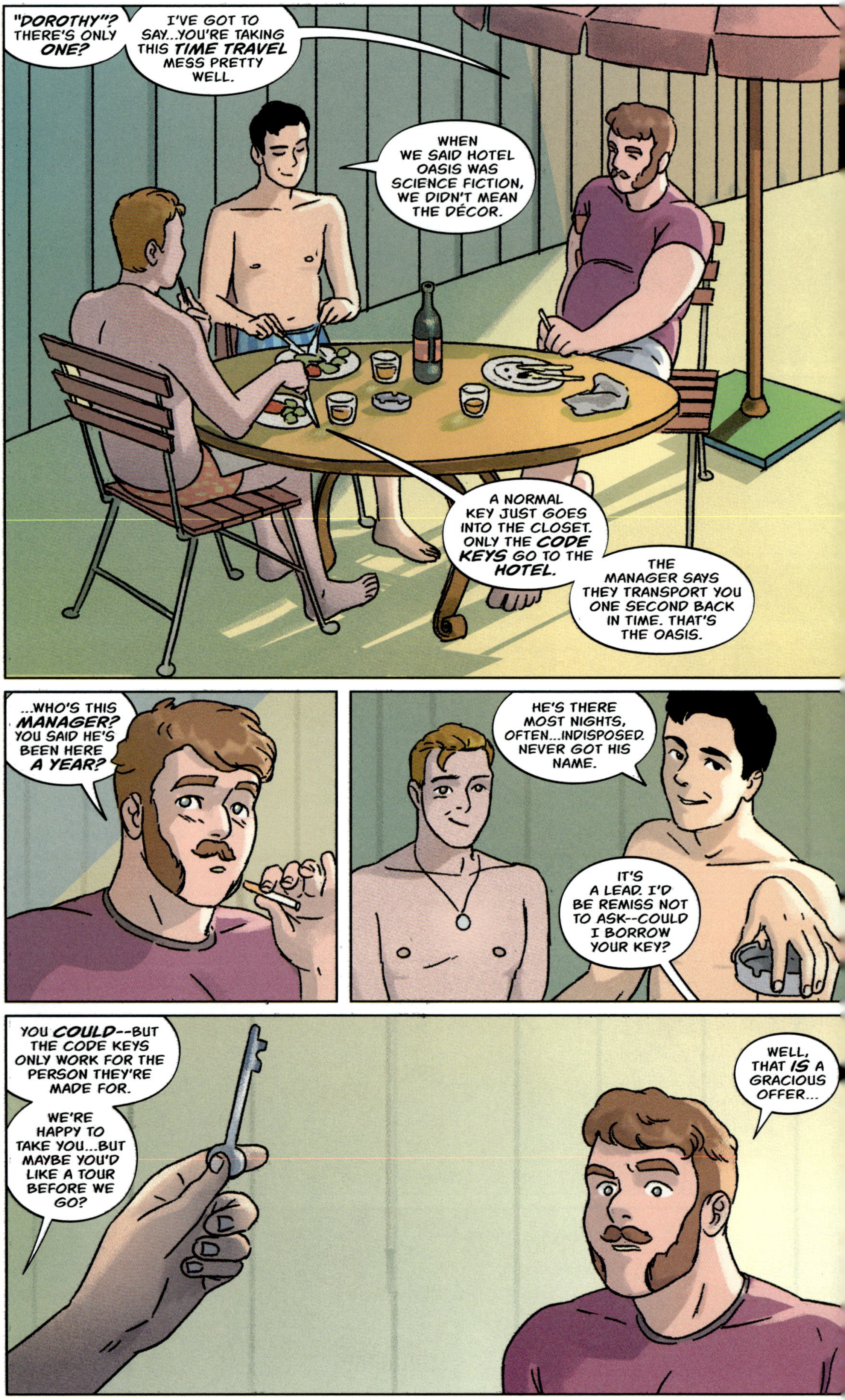
"DOROTHY"? THERE'S ONLY ONE?
I'VE GOT TO SAY...YOU'RE TAKING THIS TIME TRAVEL MESS PRETTY WELL.
WHEN WE SAID HOTEL OASIS WAS SCIENCE FICTION, WE DIDN'T MEAN THE DÉCOR.
A NORMAL KEY JUST GOES INTO THE CLOSET. ONLY THE CODE KEYS GO TO THE HOTEL.
THE MANAGER SAYS THEY TRANSPORT YOU ONE SECOND BACK IN TIME. THAT'S THE OASIS.
...WHO'S THIS MANAGER? YOU SAID HE'S BEEN HERE A YEAR?
HE'S THERE MOST NIGHTS, OFTEN...INDISPOSED. NEVER GOT HIS NAME.
IT'S A LEAD. I'D BE REMISS NOT TO ASK--COULD I BORROW YOUR KEY?
YOU COULD--BUT THE CODE KEYS ONLY WORK FOR THE PERSON THEY'RE MADE FOR.
WE'RE HAPPY TO TAKE YOU...BUT MAYBE YOU'D LIKE A TOUR BEFORE WE GO?
WELL, THAT IS A GRACIOUS OFFER...

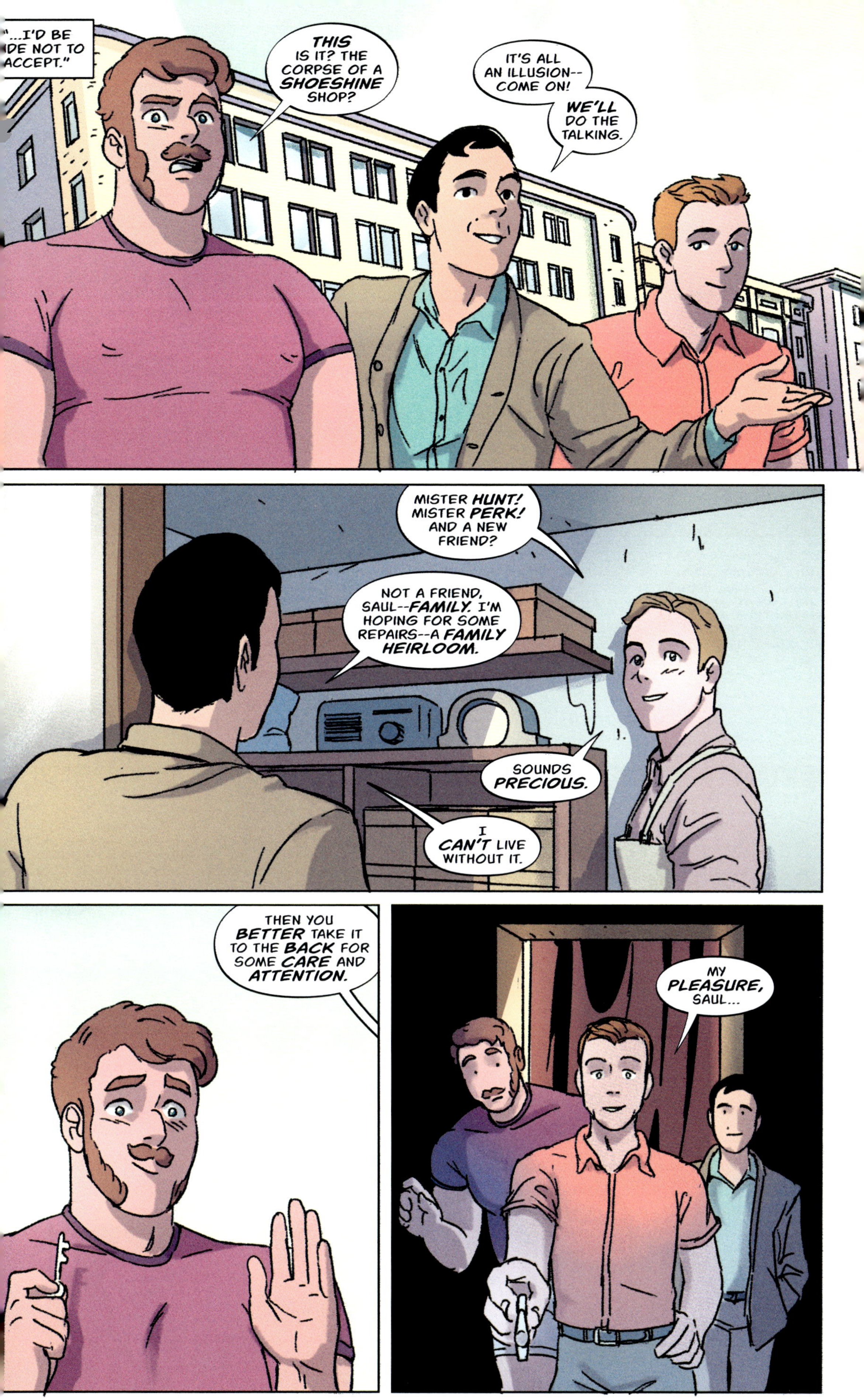
"...I'D BE
DE NOT TO
ACCEPT."
THIS IS IT? THE CORPSE OF A SHOESHINE SHOP?
IT'S ALL AN ILLUSION-- COME ON!
WE'LL DO THE TALKING.
MISTER HUNT! MISTER PERK! AND A NEW FRIEND?
NOT A FRIEND, SAUL--FAMILY. I'M HOPING FOR SOME REPAIRS--A FAMILY HEIRLOOM.
SOUNDS PRECIOUS.
I CAN'T LIVE WITHOUT IT.
THEN YOU BETTER TAKE IT TO THE BACK FOR SOME CARE AND ATTENTION.
MY PLEASURE, SAUL...

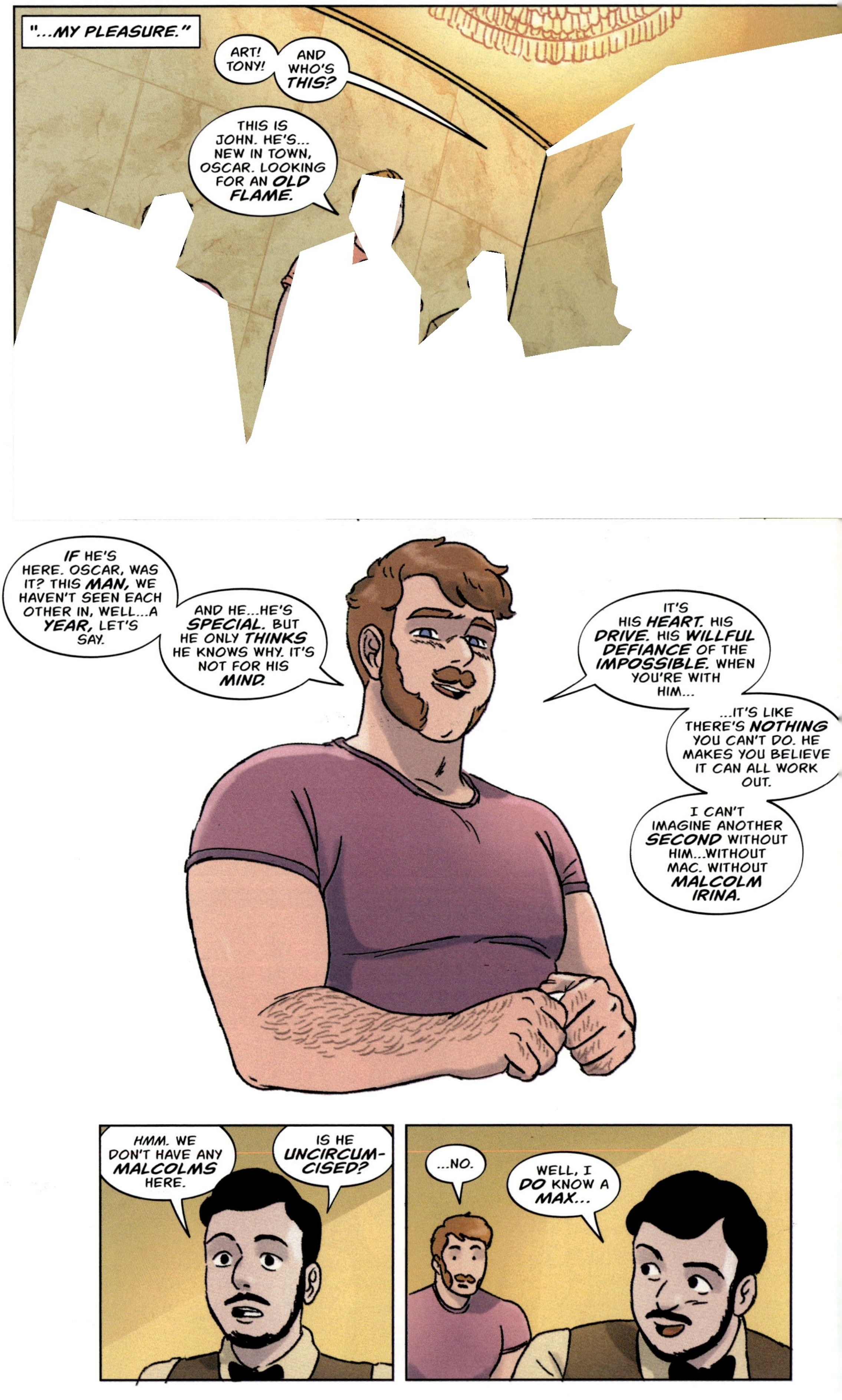
"...MY PLEASURE."
ART! TONY!
AND WHO'S THIS?
THIS IS JOHN. HE'S... NEW IN TOWN, OSCAR. LOOKING FOR AN OLD FLAME.
IF HE'S HERE. OSCAR, WAS IT? THIS MAN, WE HAVEN'T SEEN EACH OTHER IN, WELL...A YEAR, LET'S SAY.
AND HE...HE'S SPECIAL. BUT HE ONLY THINKS HE KNOWS WHY. IT'S NOT FOR HIS MIND.
IT'S HIS HEART. HIS DRIVE. HIS WILLFUL DEFIANCE OF THE IMPOSSIBLE. WHEN YOU'RE WITH HIM...
...IT'S LIKE THERE'S NOTHING YOU CAN'T DO. HE MAKES YOU BELIEVE IT CAN ALL WORK OUT.
I CAN'T IMAGINE ANOTHER SECOND WITHOUT HIM...WITHOUT MAC. WITHOUT MALCOLM IRINA.
HMM. WE DON'T HAVE ANY MALCOLMS HERE.
IS HE UNCIRCUM-CISED?
...NO.
WELL, I DO KNOW A MAX...

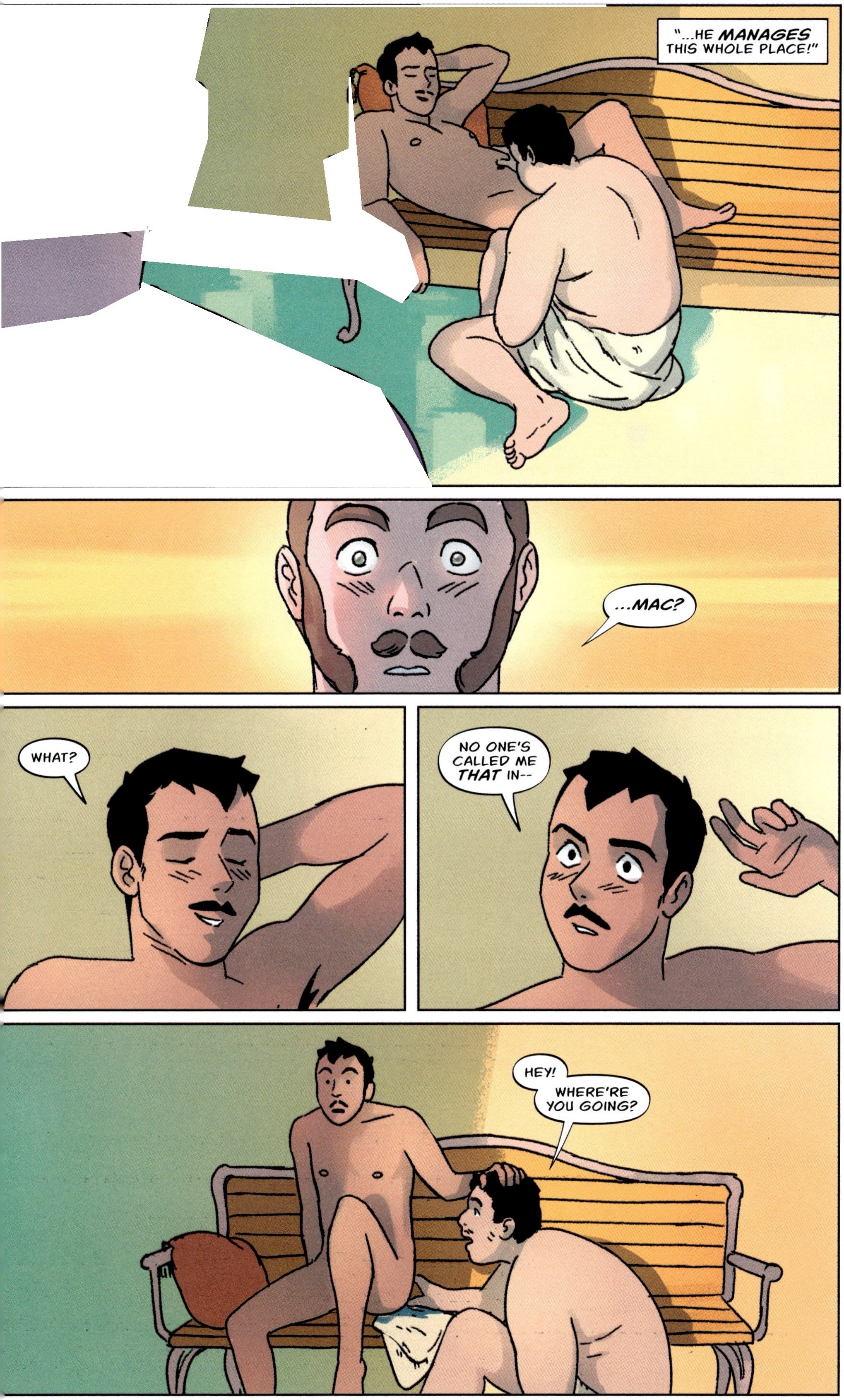
"...HE MANAGES THIS WHOLE PLACE!"
...MAC?
WHAT?
NO ONE'S CALLED ME THAT IN--
HEY!
WHERE'RE YOU GOING?

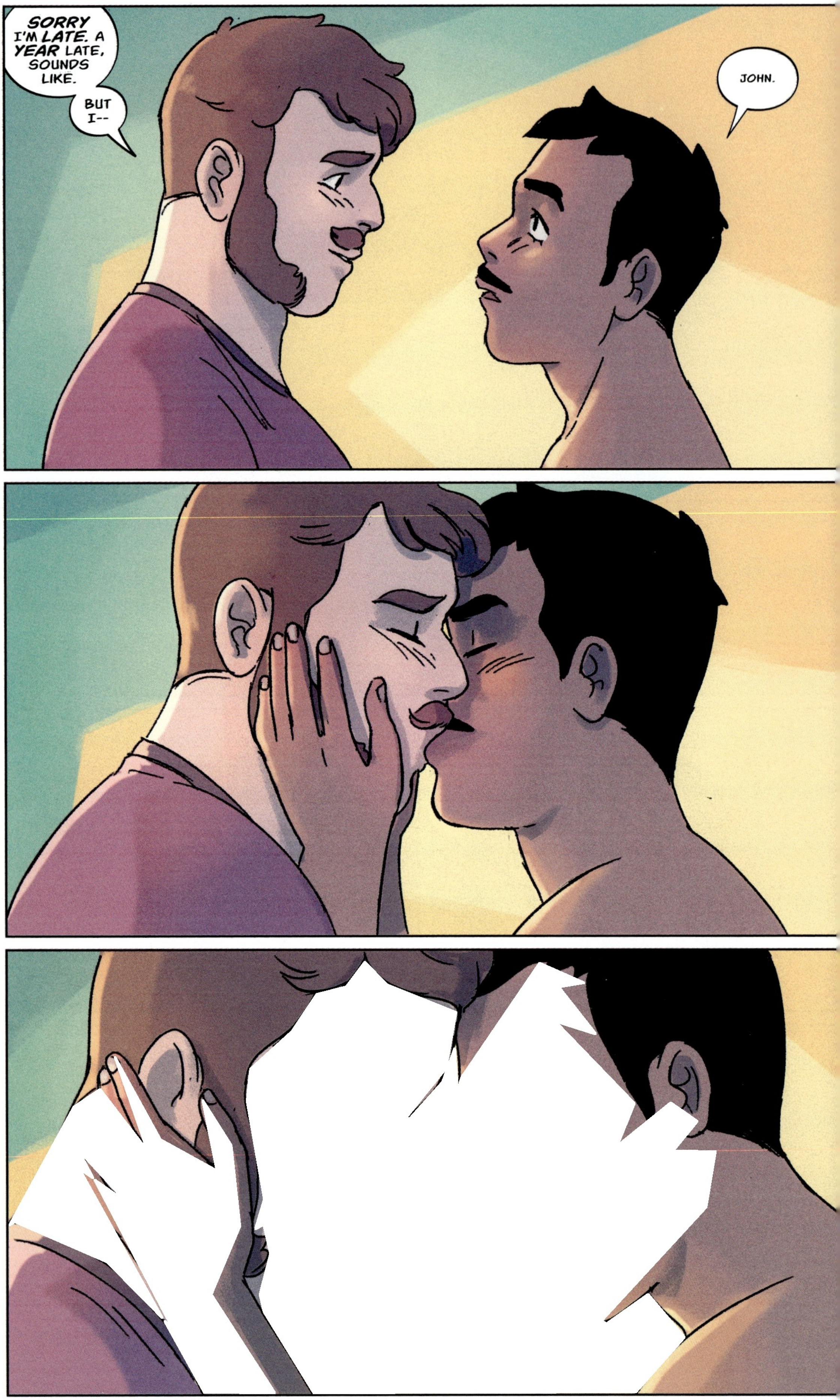
SORRY I'M LATE. A YEAR LATE, SOUNDS LIKE.
BUT I--
JOHN.

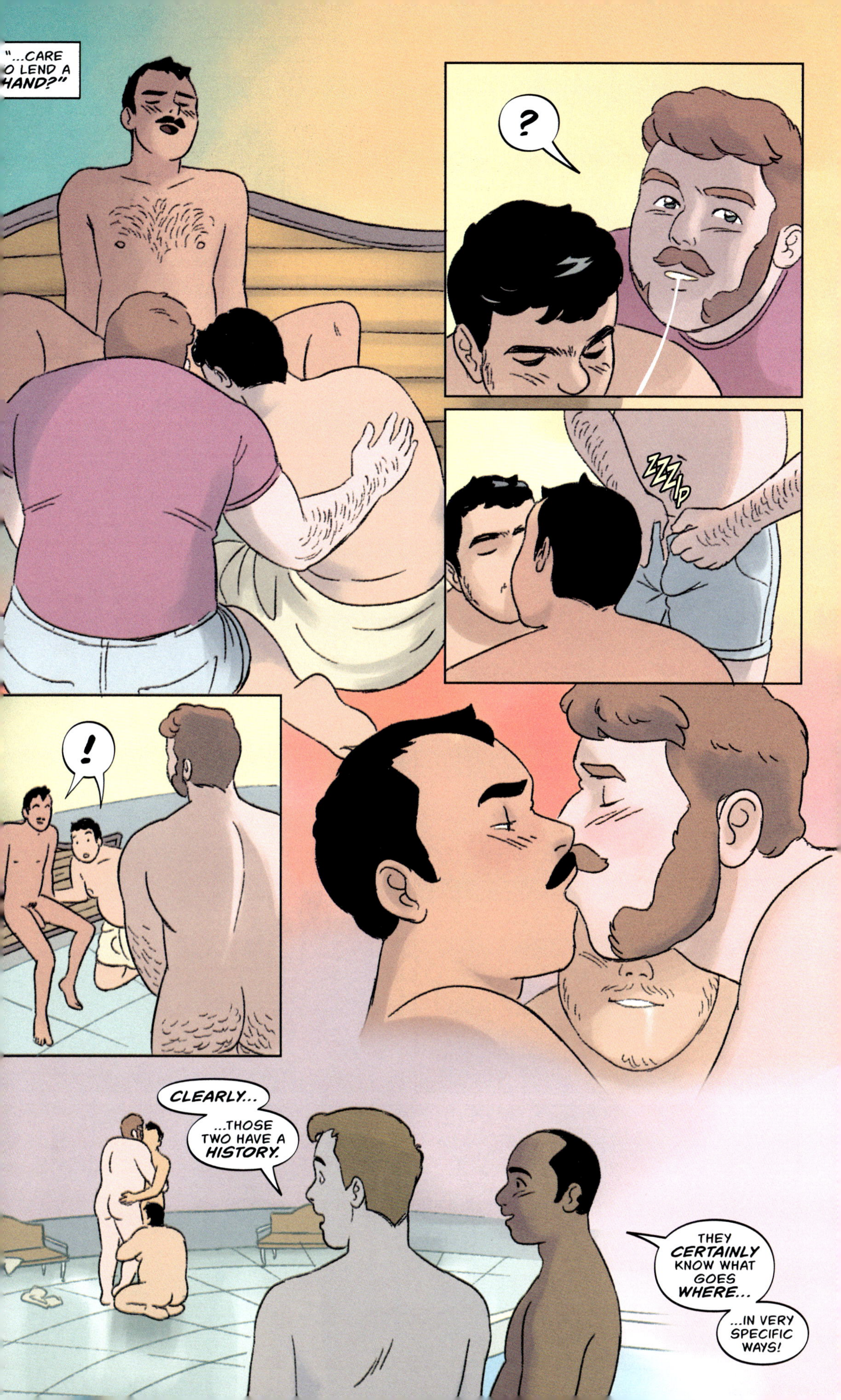
"...CARE
O LEND A
HAND?"
?
ZZZIP
!
CLEARLY...
...THOSE TWO HAVE A HISTORY.
THEY CERTAINLY KNOW WHAT GOES WHERE...
...IN VERY SPECIFIC WAYS!

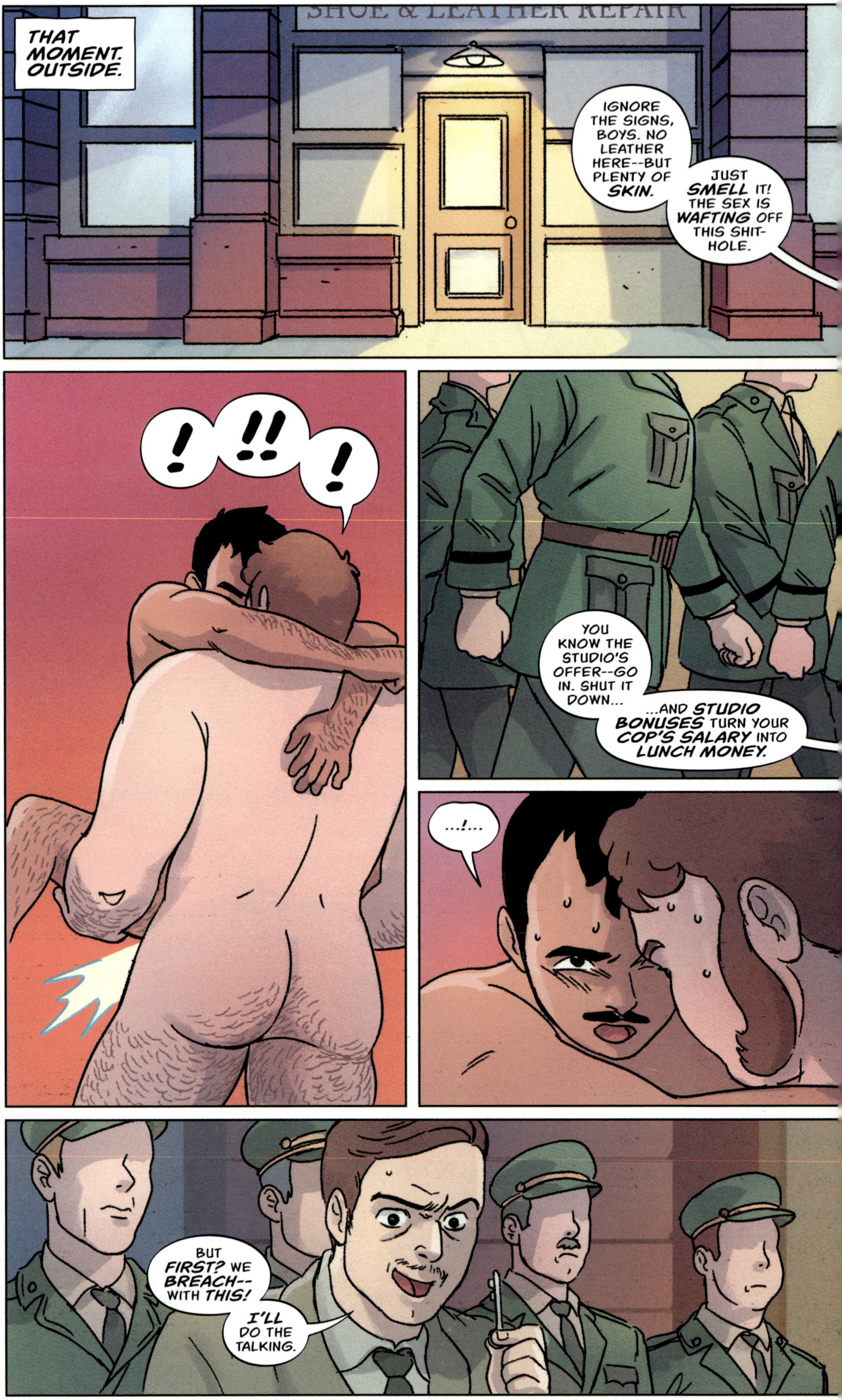
SHOE & LEATHER REPAIR
THAT MOMENT. OUTSIDE.
IGNORE THE SIGNS, BOYS. NO LEATHER HERE--BUT PLENTY OF SKIN.
JUST SMELL IT! THE SEX IS WAFTING OFF THIS SHIT-HOLE.
!
!!
!
YOU KNOW THE STUDIO'S OFFER--GO IN. SHUT IT DOWN...
...AND STUDIO BONUSES TURN YOUR COP'S SALARY INTO LUNCH MONEY.
...!...
BUT FIRST? WE BREACH--WITH THIS!
I'LL DO THE TALKING.

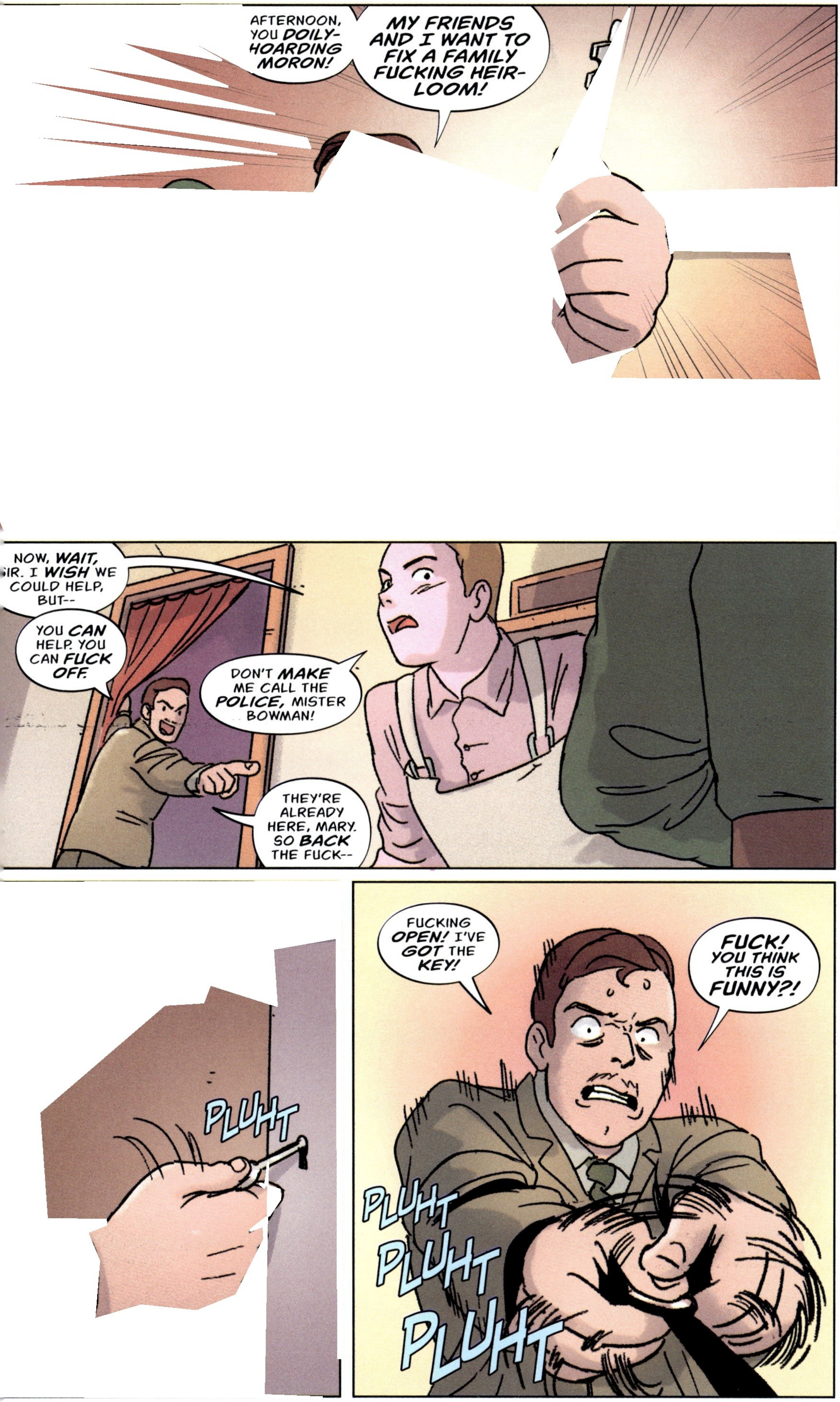

AFTERNOON, YOU DOILY-HOARDING MORON!
MY FRIENDS AND I WANT TO FIX A FAMILY FUCKING HEIR-LOOM!
NOW, WAIT, SIR. I WISH WE COULD HELP, BUT--
YOU CAN HELP. YOU CAN FUCK OFF.
DON'T MAKE ME CALL THE POLICE, MISTER BOWMAN!
THEY'RE ALREADY HERE, MARY. SO BACK THE FUCK--
PLUHT
FUCKING OPEN! I'VE GOT THE KEY!
FUCK! YOU THINK THIS IS FUNNY?!
PLUHT
PLUHT
PLUHT

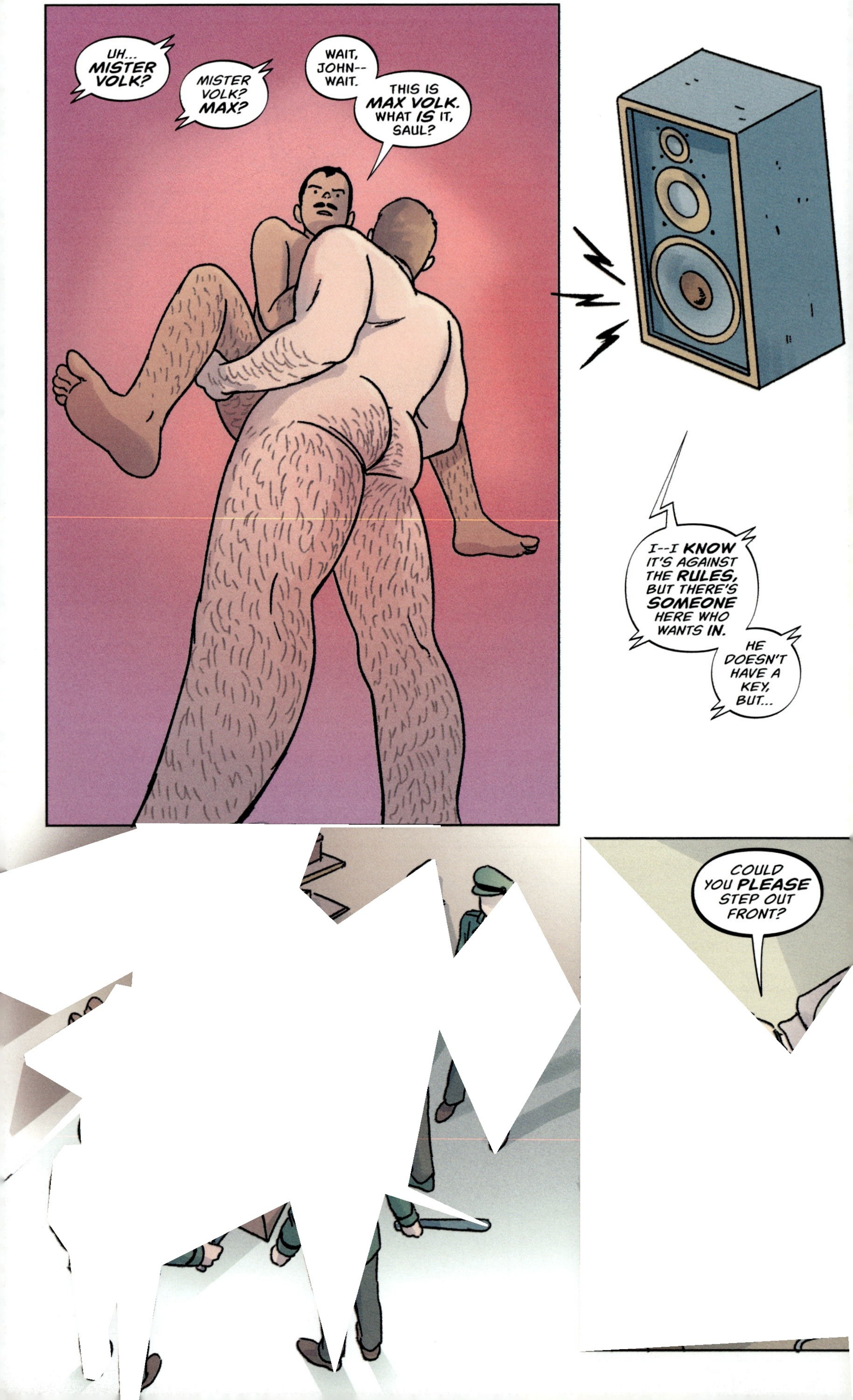
UH... MISTER VOLK?
MISTER VOLK? MAX?
WAIT, JOHN-- WAIT.
THIS IS MAX VOLK. WHAT IS IT, SAUL?
I--I KNOW IT'S AGAINST THE RULES, BUT THERE'S SOMEONE HERE WHO WANTS IN.
HE DOESN'T HAVE A KEY, BUT...
COULD YOU PLEASE STEP OUT FRONT?

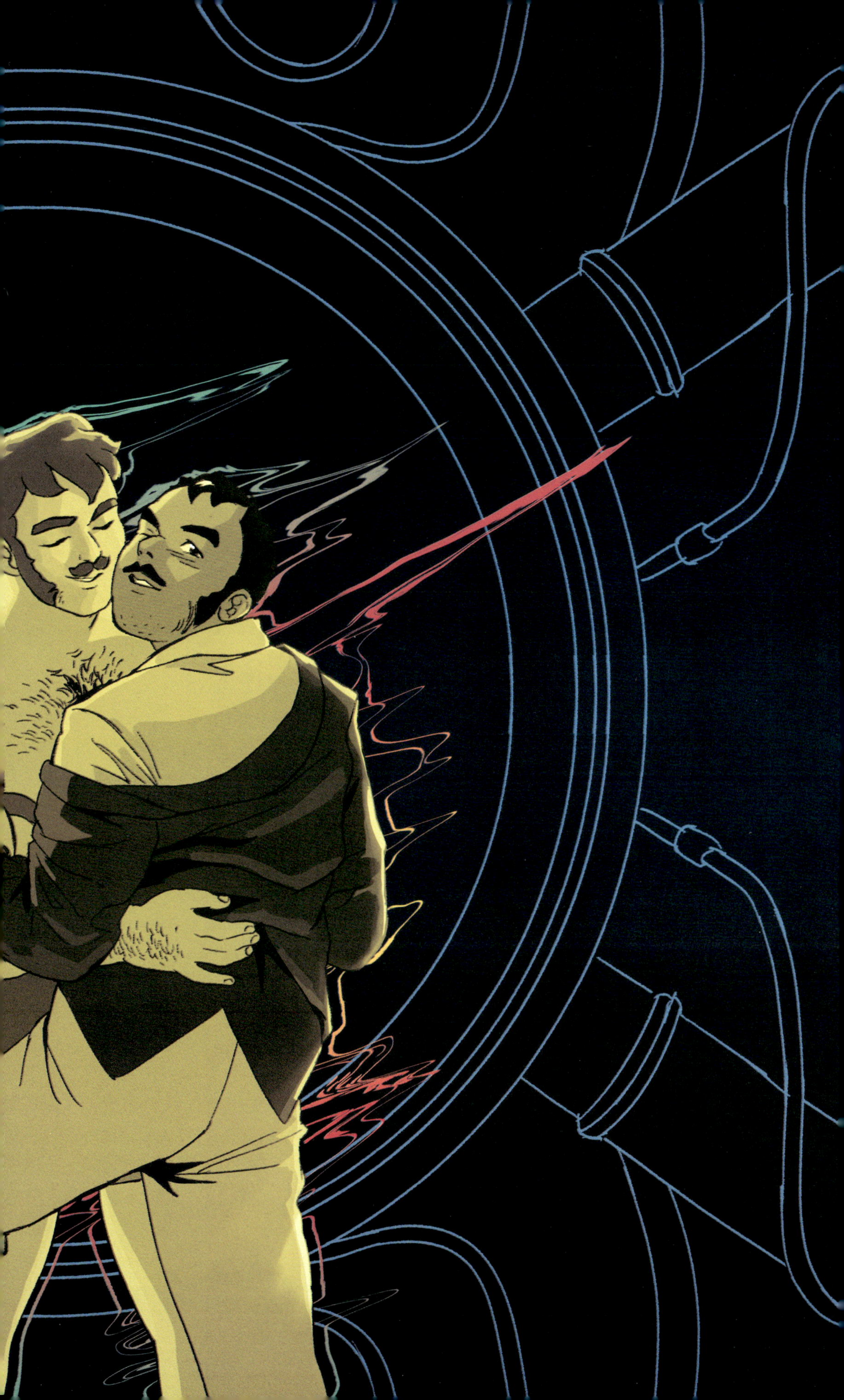

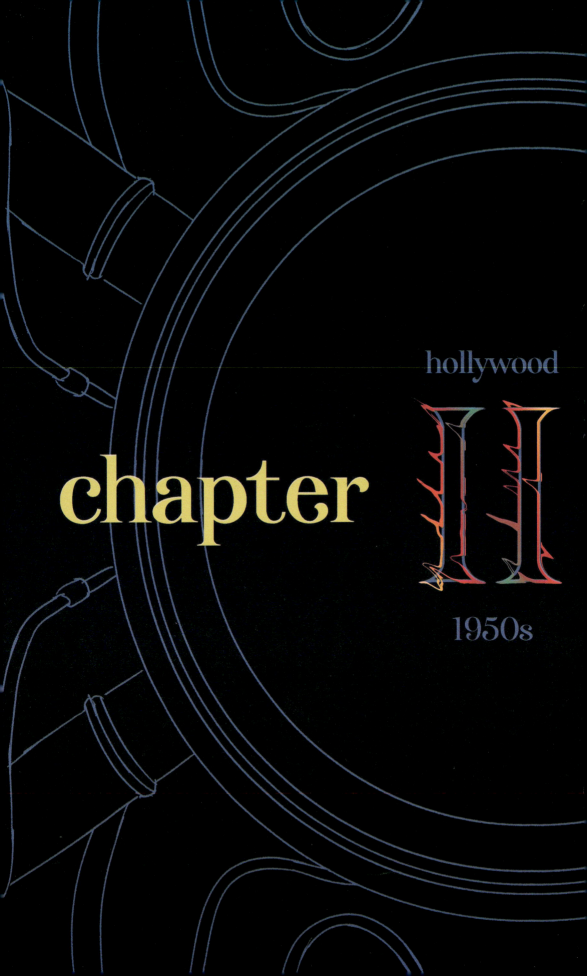

chapter II

hollywood

1950s

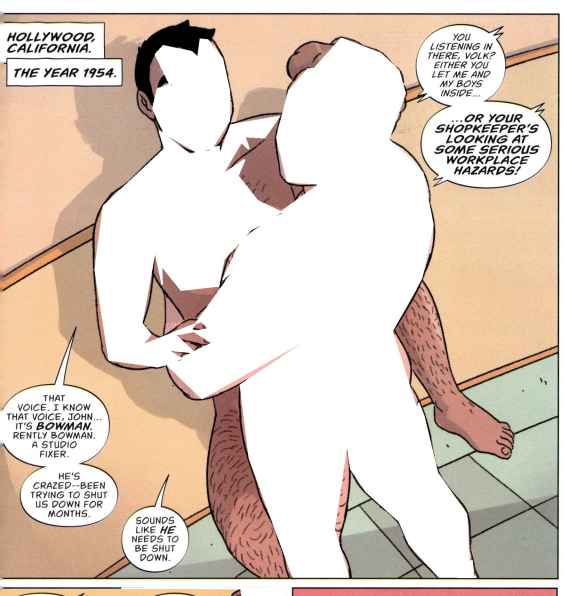

HOLLYWOOD, CALIFORNIA.

THE YEAR 1954.

YOU LISTENING IN THERE, VOLK? EITHER YOU LET ME AND MY BOYS INSIDE...

...OR YOUR SHOPKEEPER'S LOOKING AT SOME SERIOUS WORKPLACE HAZARDS!

THAT VOICE. I KNOW THAT VOICE, JOHN... IT'S *BOWMAN.* RENTLY BOWMAN. A STUDIO FIXER.

HE'S CRAZED--BEEN TRYING TO SHUT US DOWN FOR MONTHS.

SOUNDS LIKE *HE* NEEDS TO BE SHUT DOWN.

SILENCE BR... VIOLENCE, VOLK. WHAT'... IT

SAUL!

YOU GOING TO OPEN YOUR SECRET DOOR?

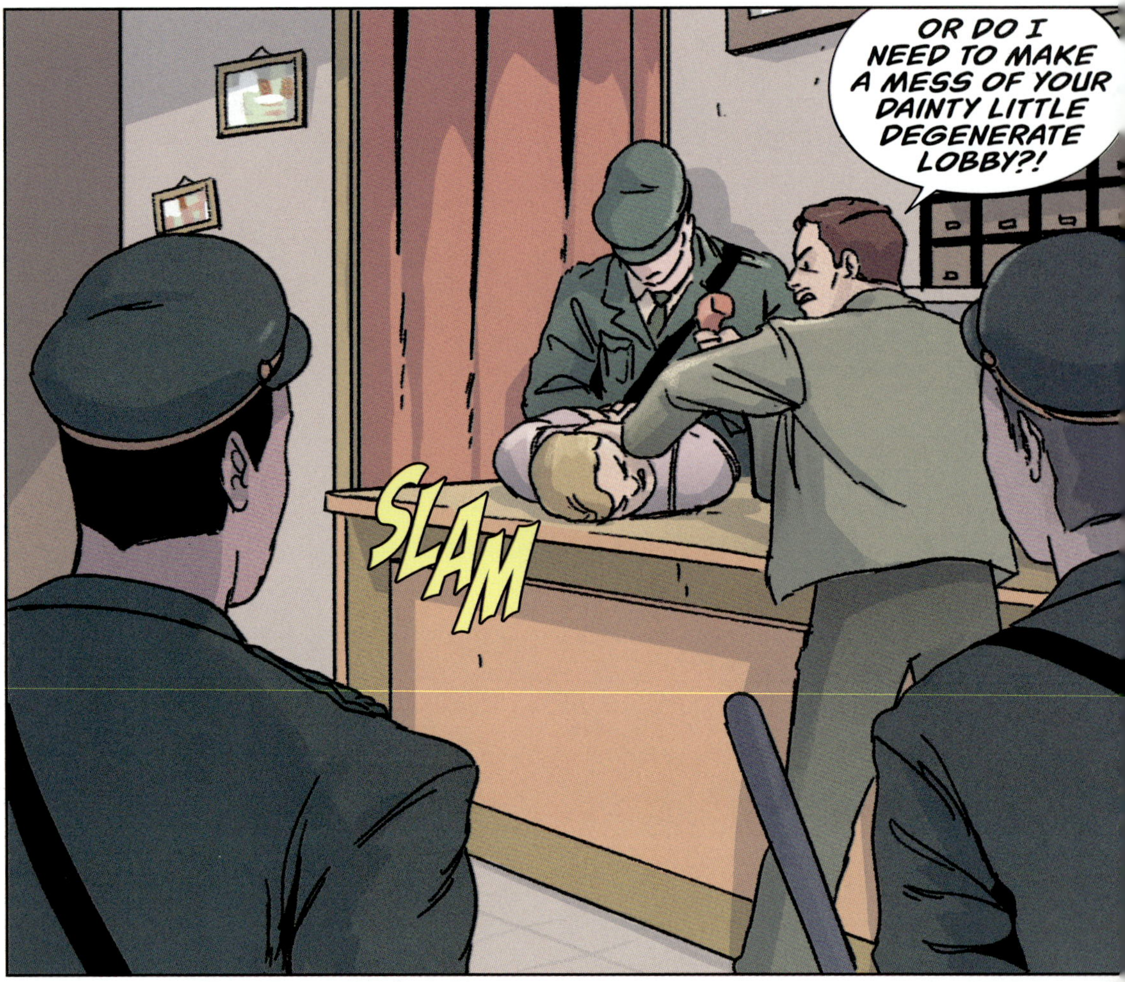
OR DO I NEED TO MAKE A MESS OF YOUR DAINTY LITTLE DEGENERATE LOBBY?!
SLAM

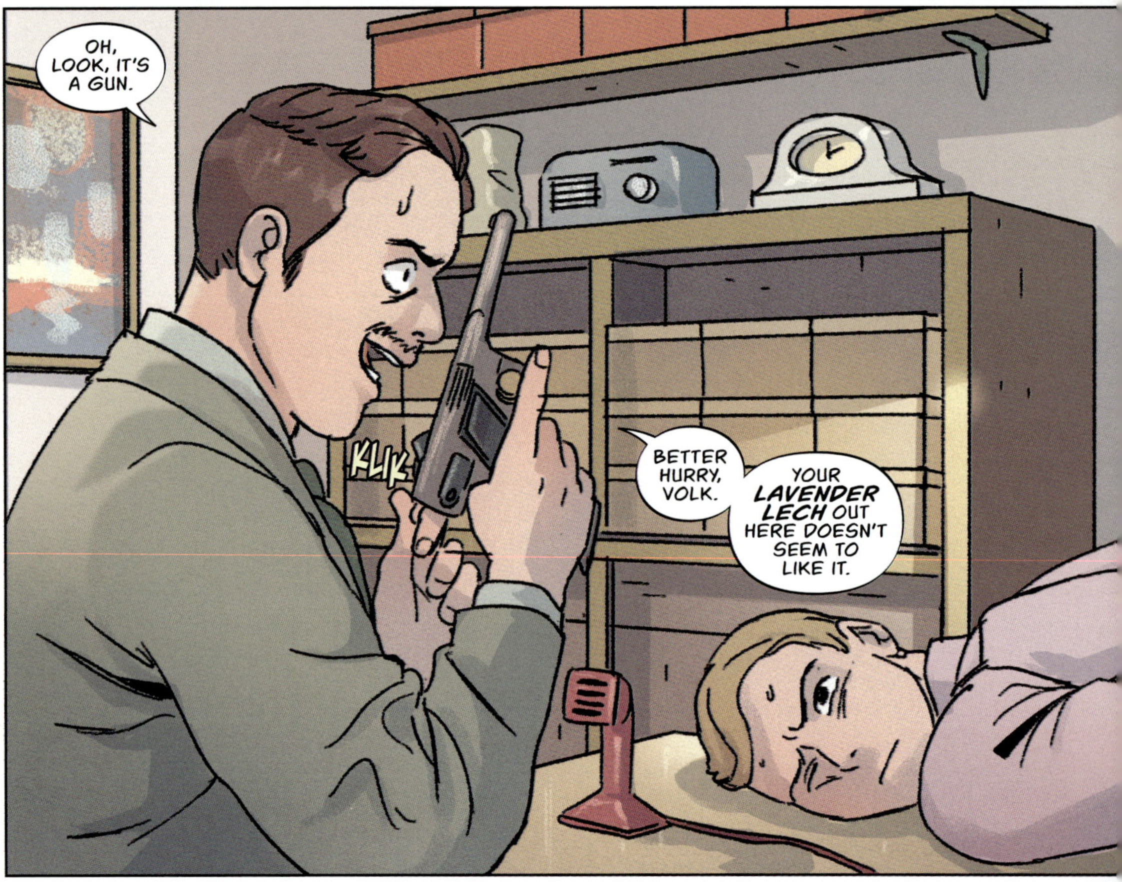
OH, LOOK, IT'S A GUN.
KLIK
BETTER HURRY, VOLK.
YOUR LAVENDER LECH OUT HERE DOESN'T SEEM TO LIKE IT.

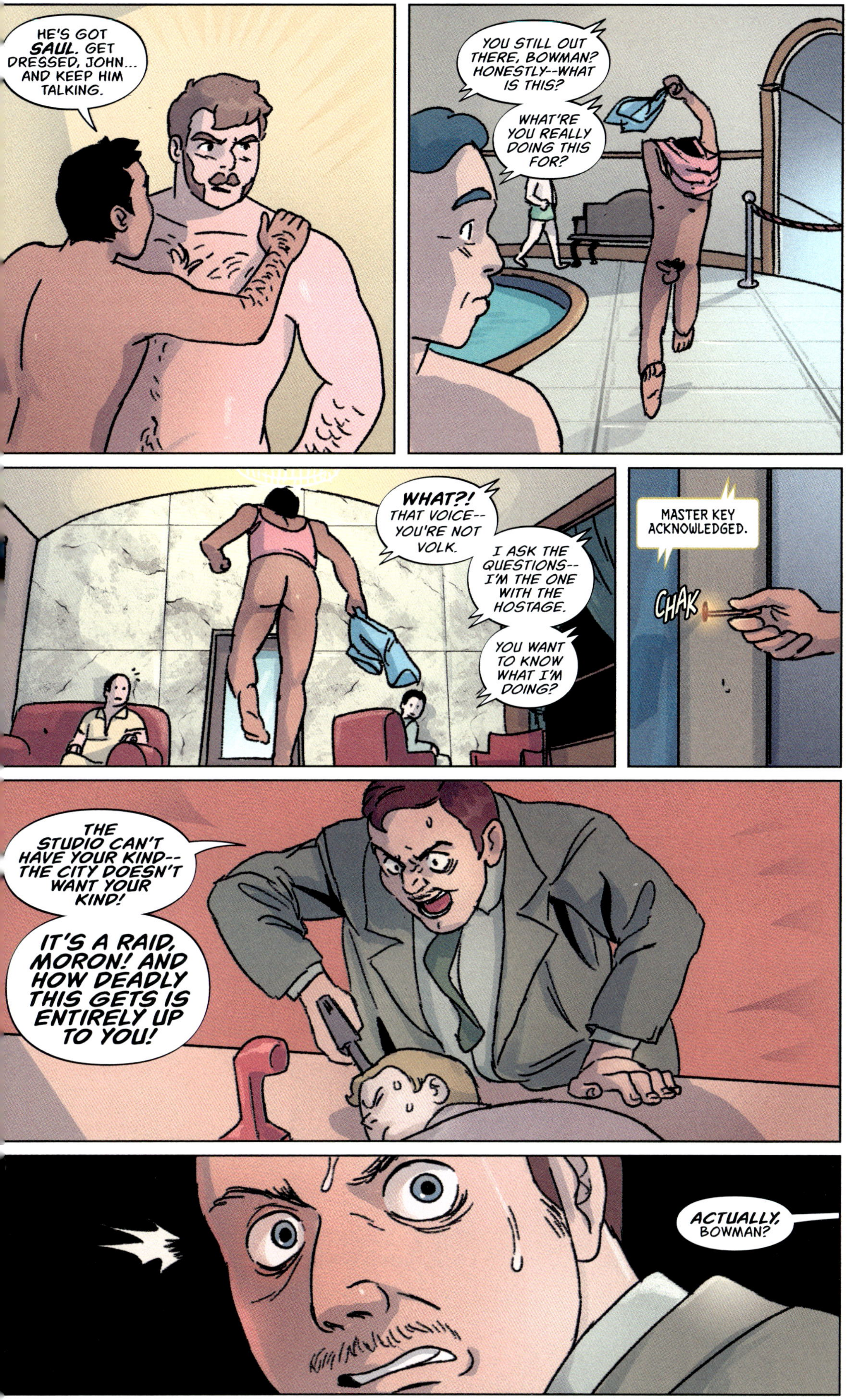
HE'S GOT **SAUL**. GET DRESSED, JOHN... AND KEEP HIM TALKING.
YOU STILL OUT THERE, BOWMAN? HONESTLY--WHAT IS THIS?
WHAT'RE YOU REALLY DOING THIS FOR?
WHAT?! THAT VOICE-- YOU'RE NOT VOLK.
I ASK THE QUESTIONS-- I'M THE ONE WITH THE HOSTAGE.
YOU WANT TO KNOW WHAT I'M DOING?
MASTER KEY ACKNOWLEDGED.
CHAK
THE STUDIO CAN'T HAVE YOUR KIND-- THE CITY DOESN'T WANT YOUR KIND!
IT'S A RAID, MORON! AND HOW DEADLY THIS GETS IS ENTIRELY UP TO YOU!
ACTUALLY, BOWMAN?

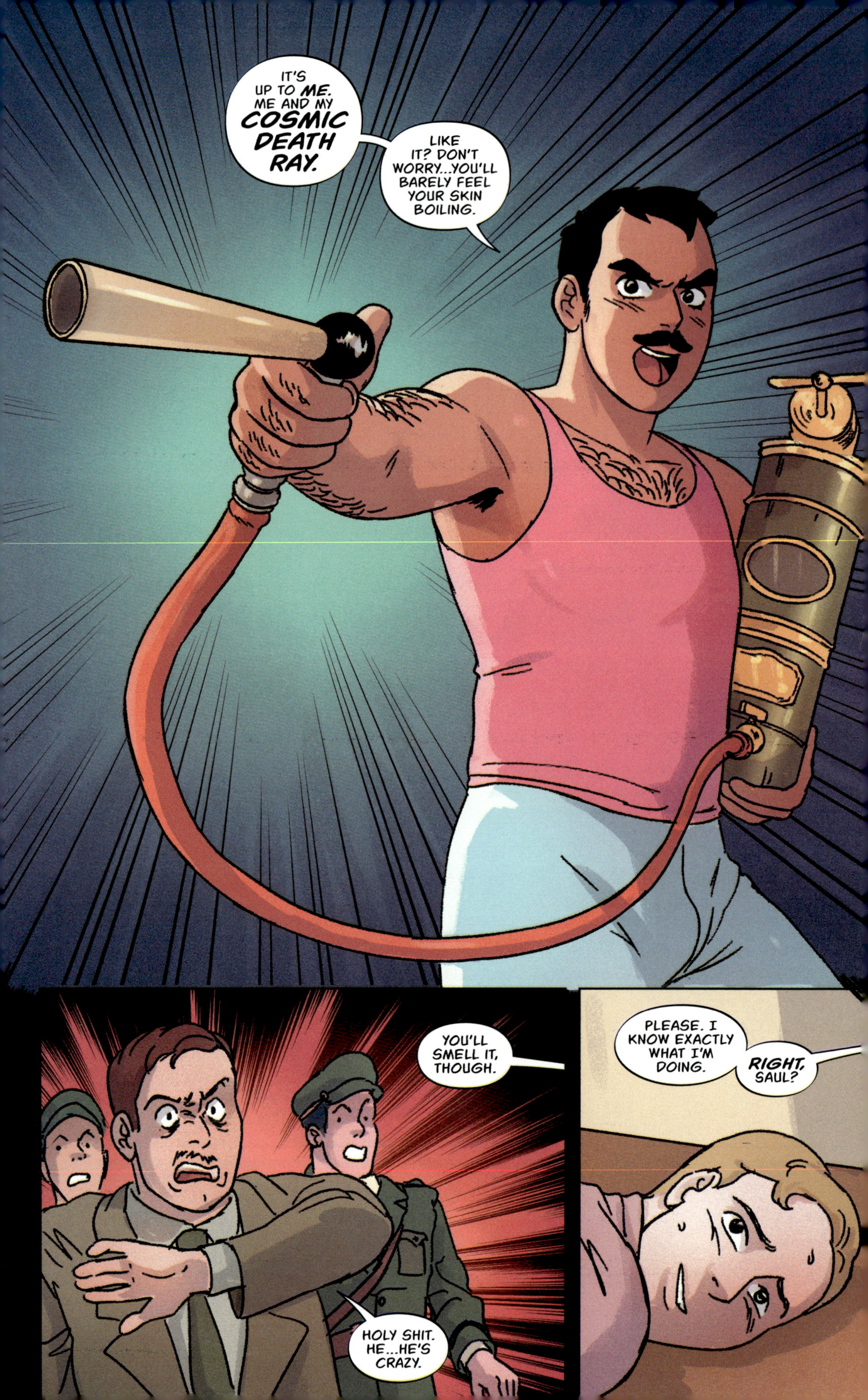
IT'S UP TO ME. ME AND MY COSMIC DEATH RAY.
LIKE IT? DON'T WORRY...YOU'LL BARELY FEEL YOUR SKIN BOILING.
YOU'LL SMELL IT, THOUGH.
HOLY SHIT. HE...HE'S CRAZY.
PLEASE. I KNOW EXACTLY WHAT I'M DOING.
RIGHT, SAUL?

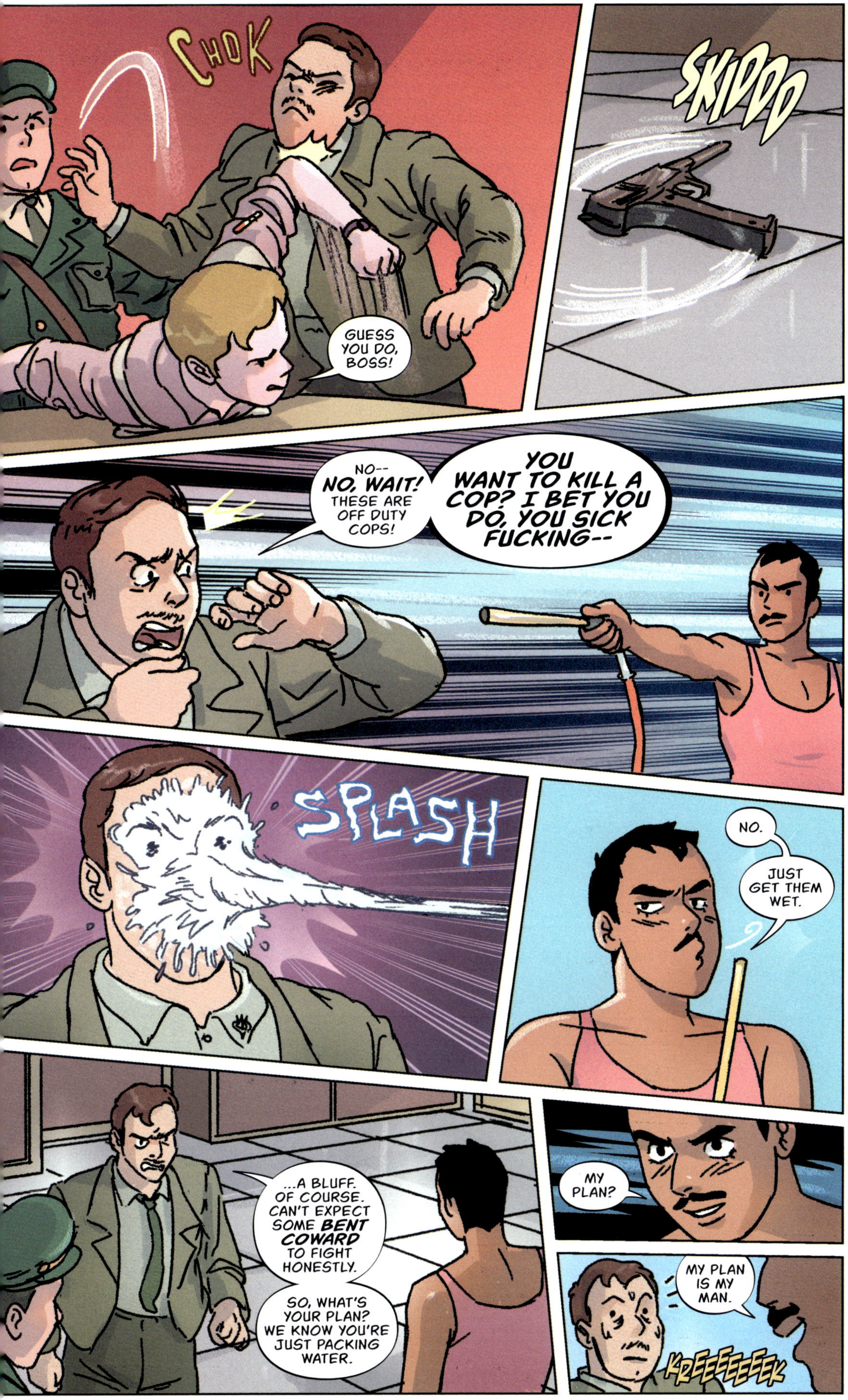
CHOK
SKIDDD
GUESS YOU DO, BOSS!
YOU WANT TO KILL A COP? I BET YOU DO, YOU SICK FUCKING--
NO-- NO, WAIT! THESE ARE OFF DUTY COPS!
SPLASH
NO.
JUST GET THEM WET.
...A BLUFF. OF COURSE. CAN'T EXPECT SOME BENT COWARD TO FIGHT HONESTLY.
SO, WHAT'S YOUR PLAN? WE KNOW YOU'RE JUST PACKING WATER.
MY PLAN?
MY PLAN IS MY MAN.
KREEEEEEEK

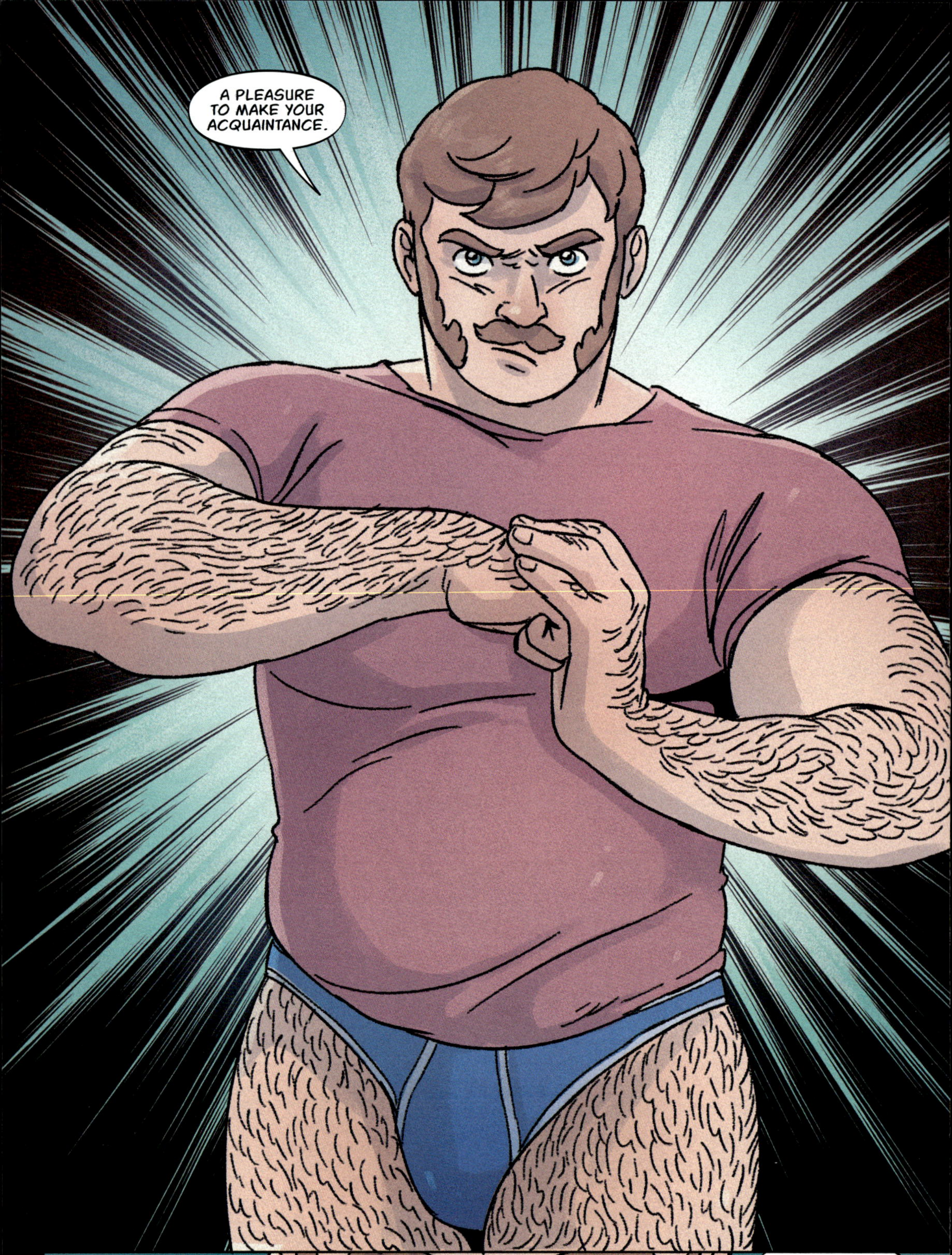
A PLEASURE TO MAKE YOUR ACQUAINTANCE.
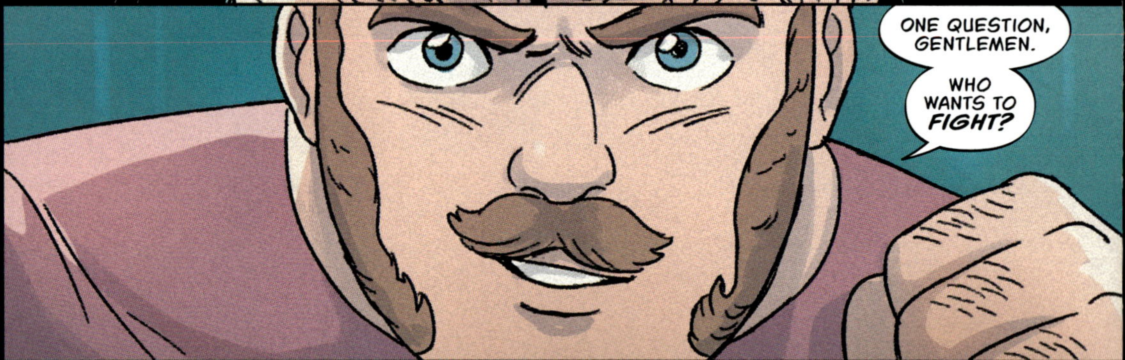
ONE QUESTION, GENTLEMEN.
WHO WANTS TO *FIGHT?*

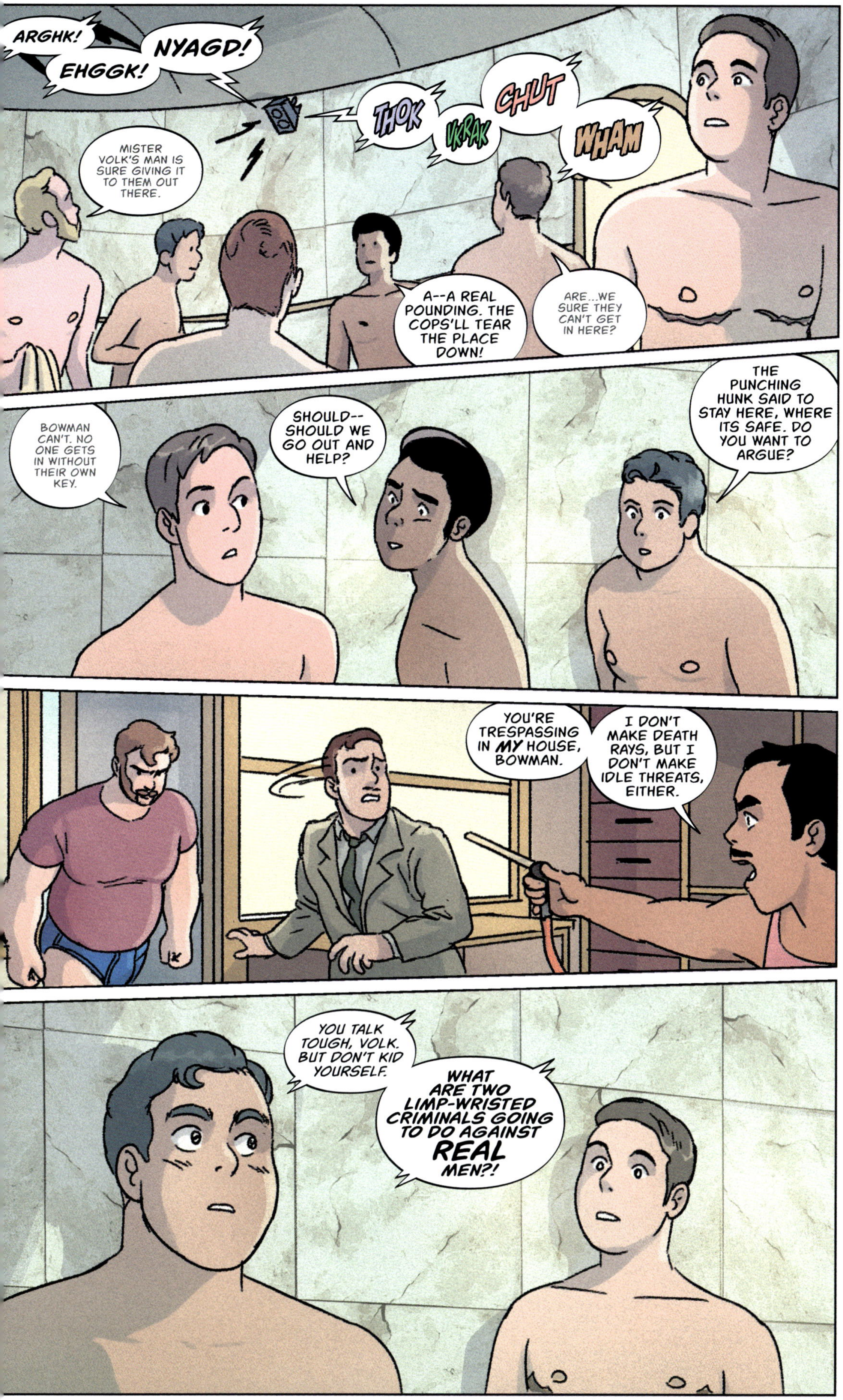

ARGHK!
EHGGK!
NYAGD!
THOK
VKRAK
CHUT
WHAM
MISTER VOLK'S MAN IS SURE GIVING IT TO THEM OUT THERE.
A--A REAL POUNDING. THE COPS'LL TEAR THE PLACE DOWN!
ARE...WE SURE THEY CAN'T GET IN HERE?
BOWMAN CAN'T. NO ONE GETS IN WITHOUT THEIR OWN KEY.
SHOULD--SHOULD WE GO OUT AND HELP?
THE PUNCHING HUNK SAID TO STAY HERE, WHERE ITS SAFE. DO YOU WANT TO ARGUE?
YOU'RE TRESPASSING IN MY HOUSE, BOWMAN.
I DON'T MAKE DEATH RAYS, BUT I DON'T MAKE IDLE THREATS, EITHER.
YOU TALK TOUGH, VOLK. BUT DON'T KID YOURSELF.
WHAT ARE TWO LIMP-WRISTED CRIMINALS GOING TO DO AGAINST REAL MEN?!

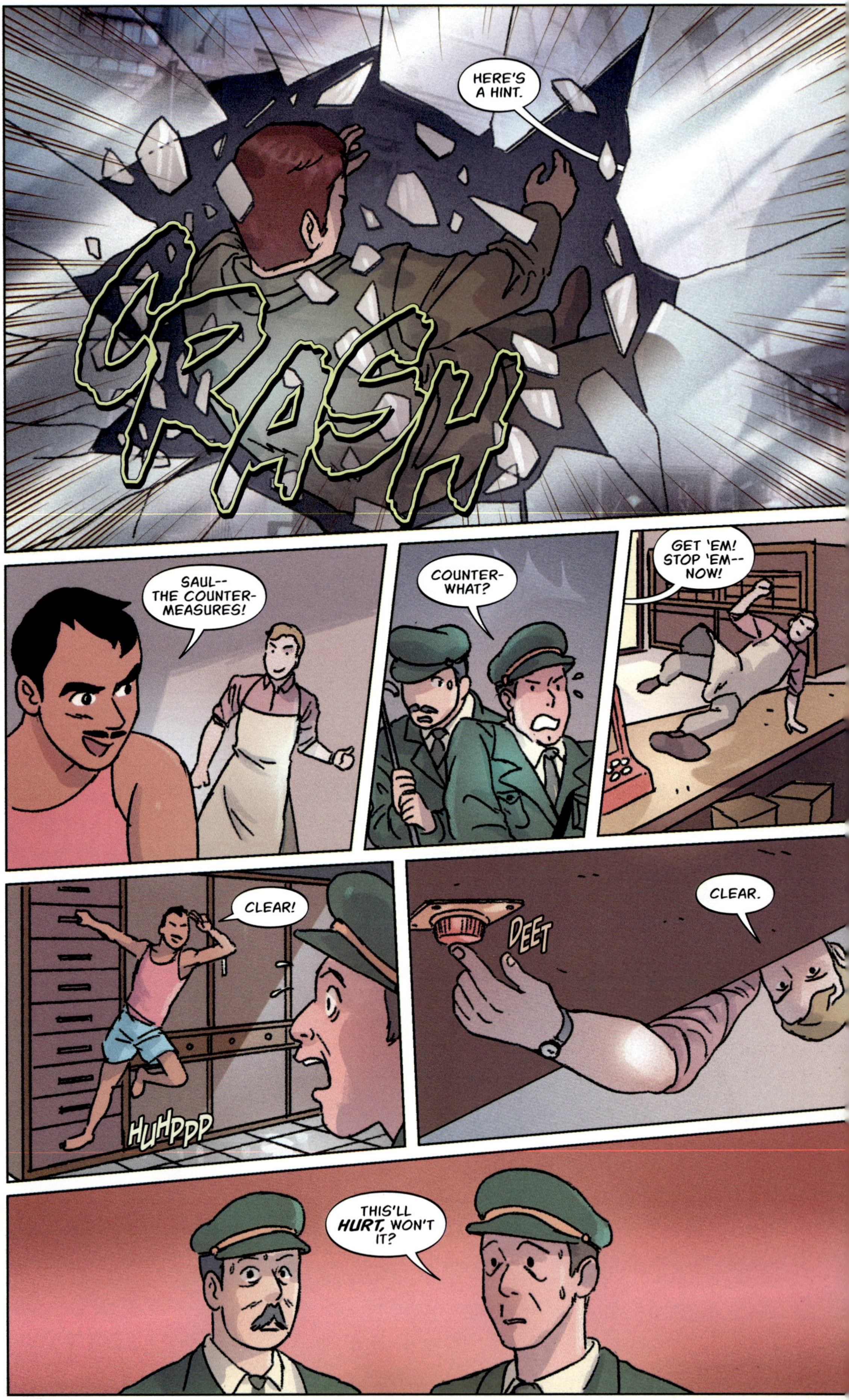
HERE'S A HINT.
CRASH
SAUL-- THE COUNTER-MEASURES!
COUNTER-WHAT?
GET 'EM! STOP 'EM-- NOW!
CLEAR!
HUHPPP
CLEAR.
DEET
THIS'LL *HURT,* WON'T IT?

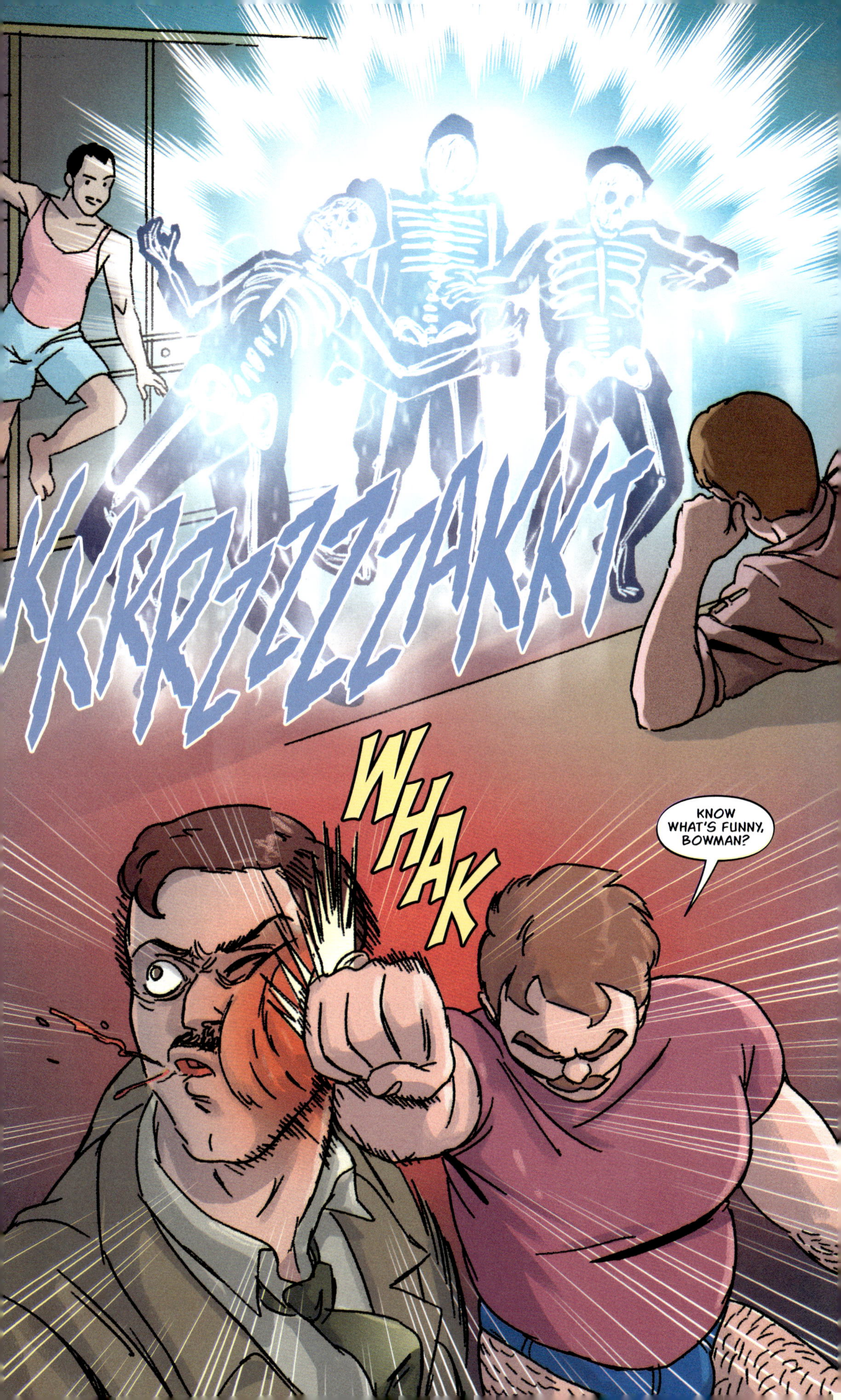
KKRZZZZAKKT
WHAK
KNOW WHAT'S FUNNY, BOWMAN?

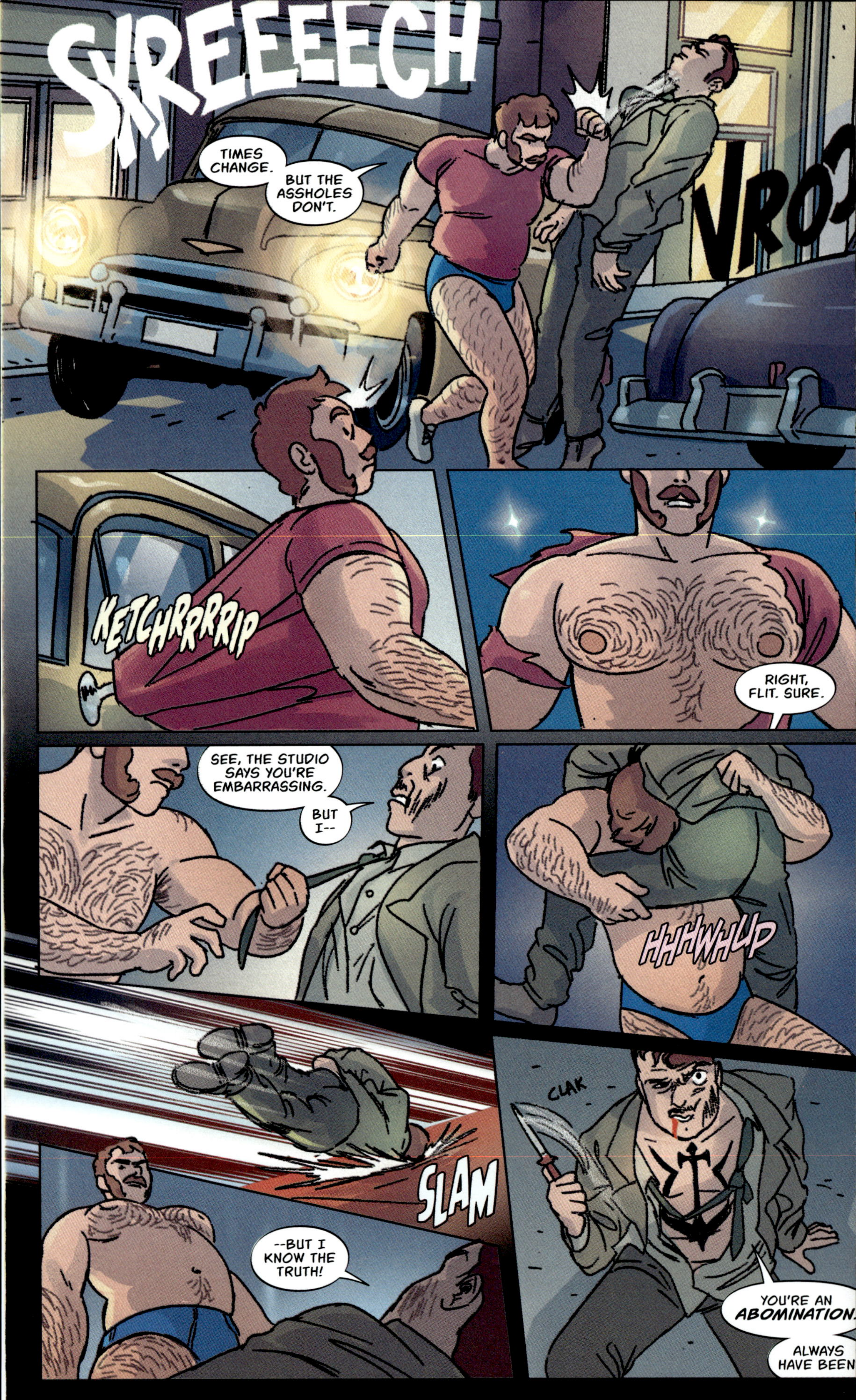
SKREEEECH
TIMES CHANGE.
BUT THE ASSHOLES DON'T.
VROO
KETCHRRRRIP
RIGHT, FLIT. SURE.
SEE, THE STUDIO SAYS YOU'RE EMBARRASSING.
BUT I--
HHHWHUP
SLAM
--BUT I KNOW THE TRUTH!
CLAK
YOU'RE AN ABOMINATION.
ALWAYS HAVE BEEN

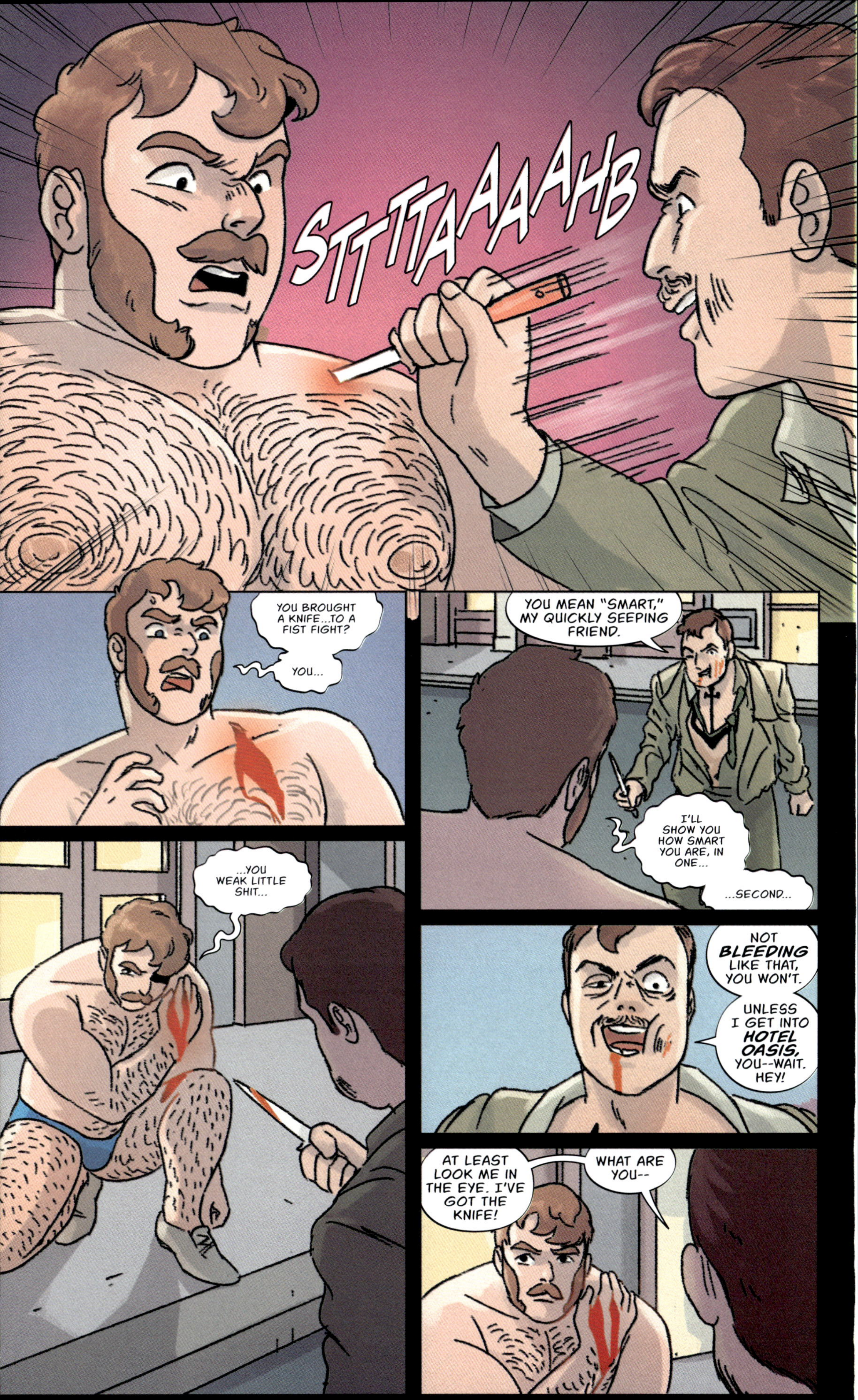
STTTTAAAAHB
YOU BROUGHT A KNIFE...TO A FIST FIGHT?
YOU...
YOU MEAN "SMART," MY QUICKLY SEEPING FRIEND.
I'LL SHOW YOU HOW SMART YOU ARE, IN ONE...
...SECOND...
...YOU WEAK LITTLE SHIT...
NOT BLEEDING LIKE THAT, YOU WON'T.
UNLESS I GET INTO HOTEL OASIS, YOU--WAIT. HEY!
AT LEAST LOOK ME IN THE EYE. I'VE GOT THE KNIFE!
WHAT ARE YOU--

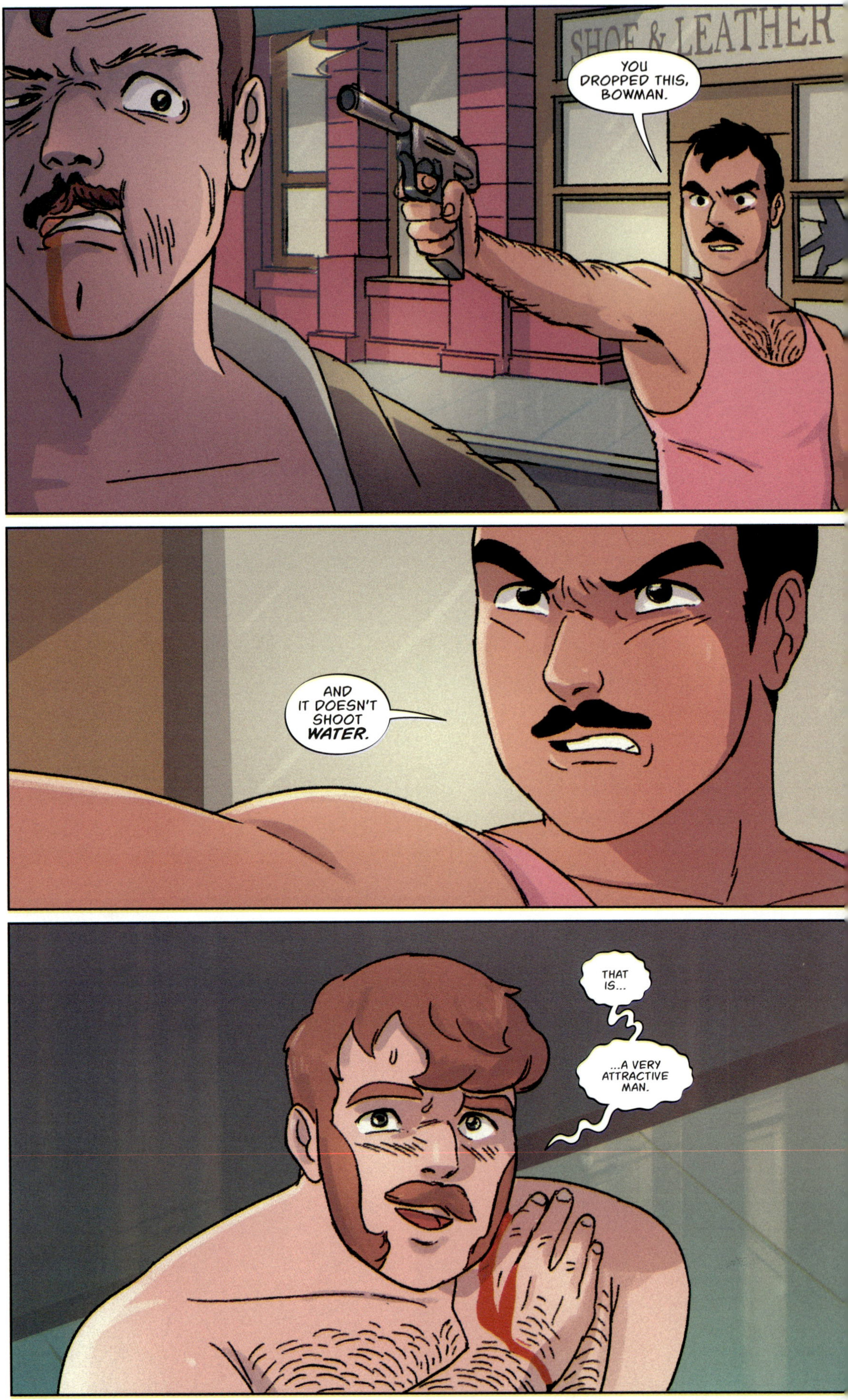
SHOE & LEATHER
YOU DROPPED THIS, BOWMAN.
AND IT DOESN'T SHOOT WATER.
THAT IS...
...A VERY ATTRACTIVE MAN.

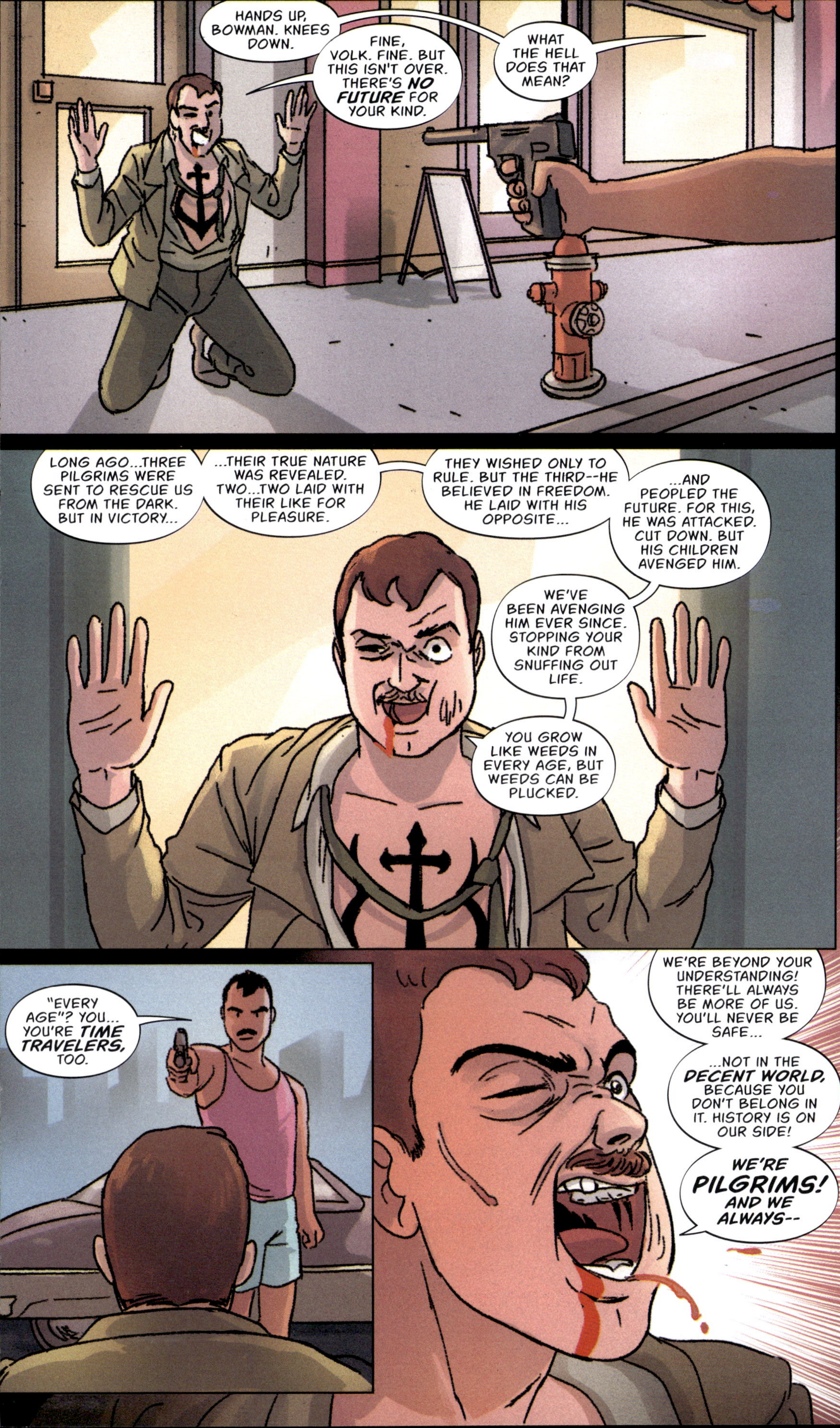
HANDS UP, BOWMAN. KNEES DOWN.
FINE, VOLK. FINE. BUT THIS ISN'T OVER. THERE'S **NO FUTURE** FOR YOUR KIND.
WHAT THE HELL DOES THAT MEAN?
LONG AGO...THREE PILGRIMS WERE SENT TO RESCUE US FROM THE DARK. BUT IN VICTORY...
...THEIR TRUE NATURE WAS REVEALED. TWO...TWO LAID WITH THEIR LIKE FOR PLEASURE.
THEY WISHED ONLY TO RULE. BUT THE THIRD--HE BELIEVED IN FREEDOM. HE LAID WITH HIS OPPOSITE...
...AND PEOPLED THE FUTURE. FOR THIS, HE WAS ATTACKED. CUT DOWN. BUT HIS CHILDREN AVENGED HIM.
WE'VE BEEN AVENGING HIM EVER SINCE. STOPPING YOUR KIND FROM SNUFFING OUT LIFE.
YOU GROW LIKE WEEDS IN EVERY AGE, BUT WEEDS CAN BE PLUCKED.
"EVERY AGE"? YOU... YOU'RE ***TIME TRAVELERS,*** TOO.
WE'RE BEYOND YOUR UNDERSTANDING! THERE'LL ALWAYS BE MORE OF US. YOU'LL NEVER BE SAFE...
...NOT IN THE ***DECENT WORLD,*** BECAUSE YOU DON'T BELONG IN IT. HISTORY IS ON OUR SIDE!
WE'RE PILGRIMS! AND WE ALWAYS--

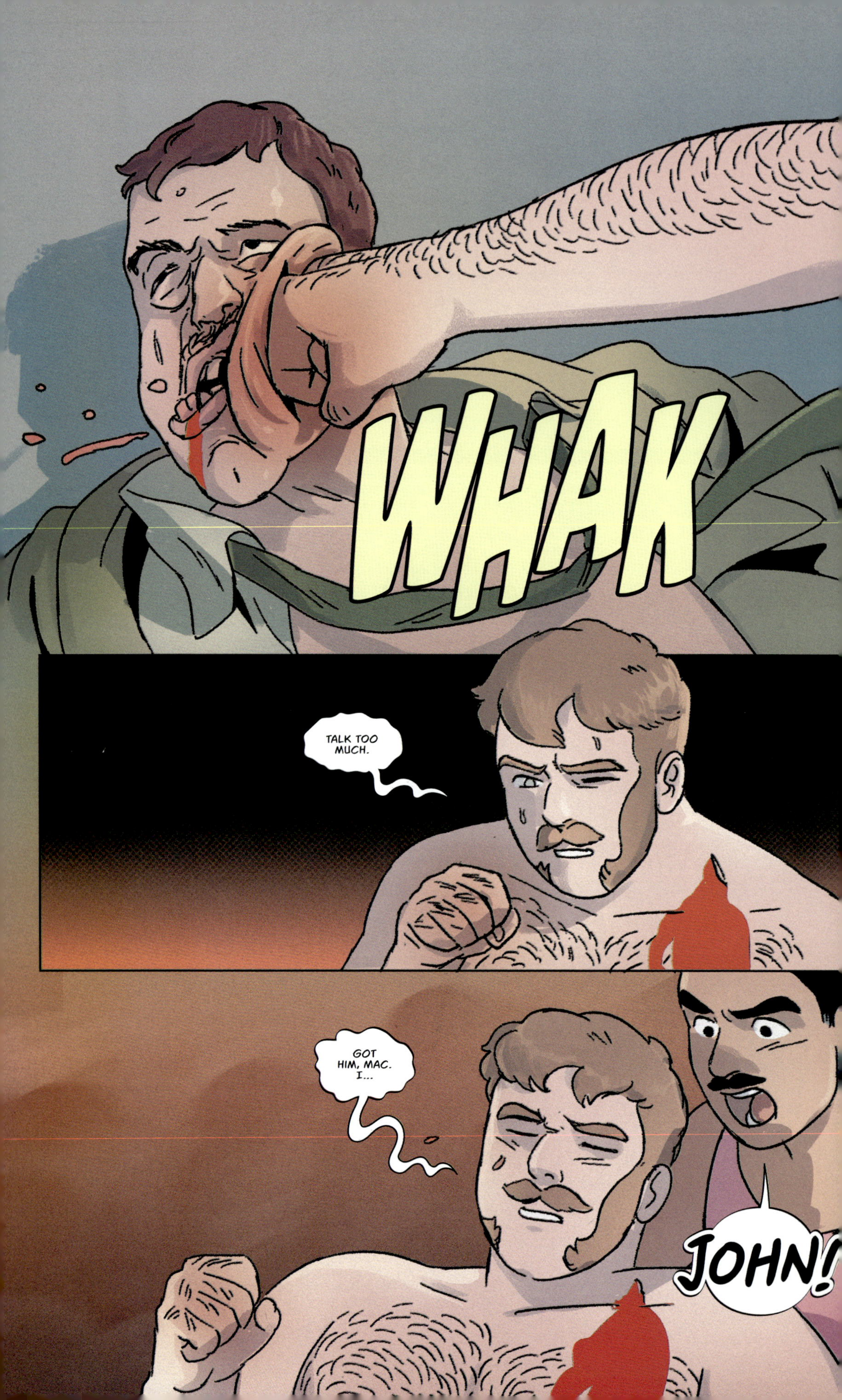
WHAK
TALK TOO MUCH.
GOT HIM, MAC. I...
JOHN!

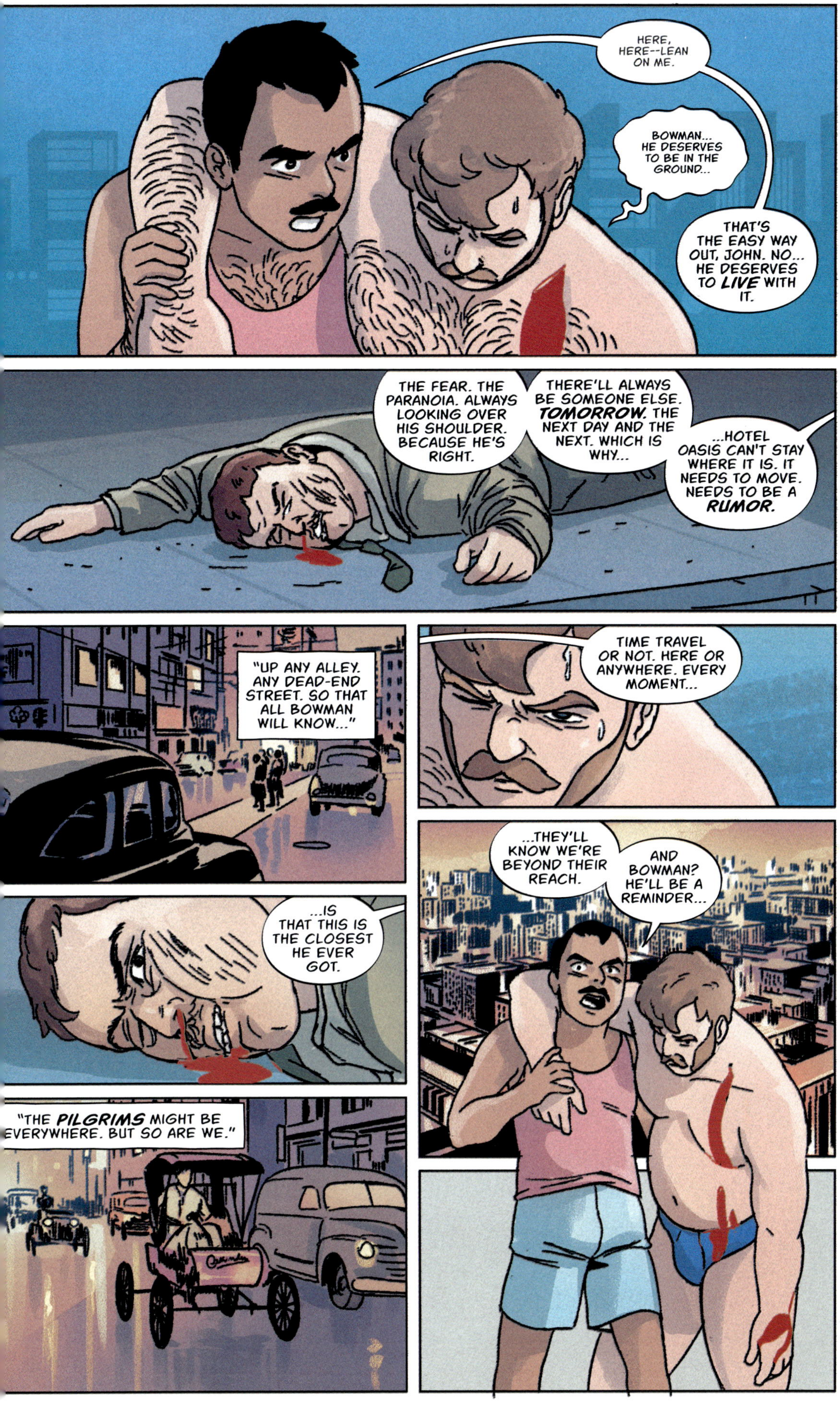
HERE, HERE--LEAN ON ME.
BOWMAN... HE DESERVES TO BE IN THE GROUND...
THAT'S THE EASY WAY OUT, JOHN. NO... HE DESERVES TO LIVE WITH IT.
THE FEAR. THE PARANOIA. ALWAYS LOOKING OVER HIS SHOULDER. BECAUSE HE'S RIGHT.
THERE'LL ALWAYS BE SOMEONE ELSE. TOMORROW. THE NEXT DAY AND THE NEXT. WHICH IS WHY...
...HOTEL OASIS CAN'T STAY WHERE IT IS. IT NEEDS TO MOVE. NEEDS TO BE A RUMOR.
"UP ANY ALLEY. ANY DEAD-END STREET. SO THAT ALL BOWMAN WILL KNOW..."
TIME TRAVEL OR NOT. HERE OR ANYWHERE. EVERY MOMENT...
...IS THAT THIS IS THE CLOSEST HE EVER GOT.
...THEY'LL KNOW WE'RE BEYOND THEIR REACH.
AND BOWMAN? HE'LL BE A REMINDER...
"THE PILGRIMS MIGHT BE EVERYWHERE. BUT SO ARE WE."

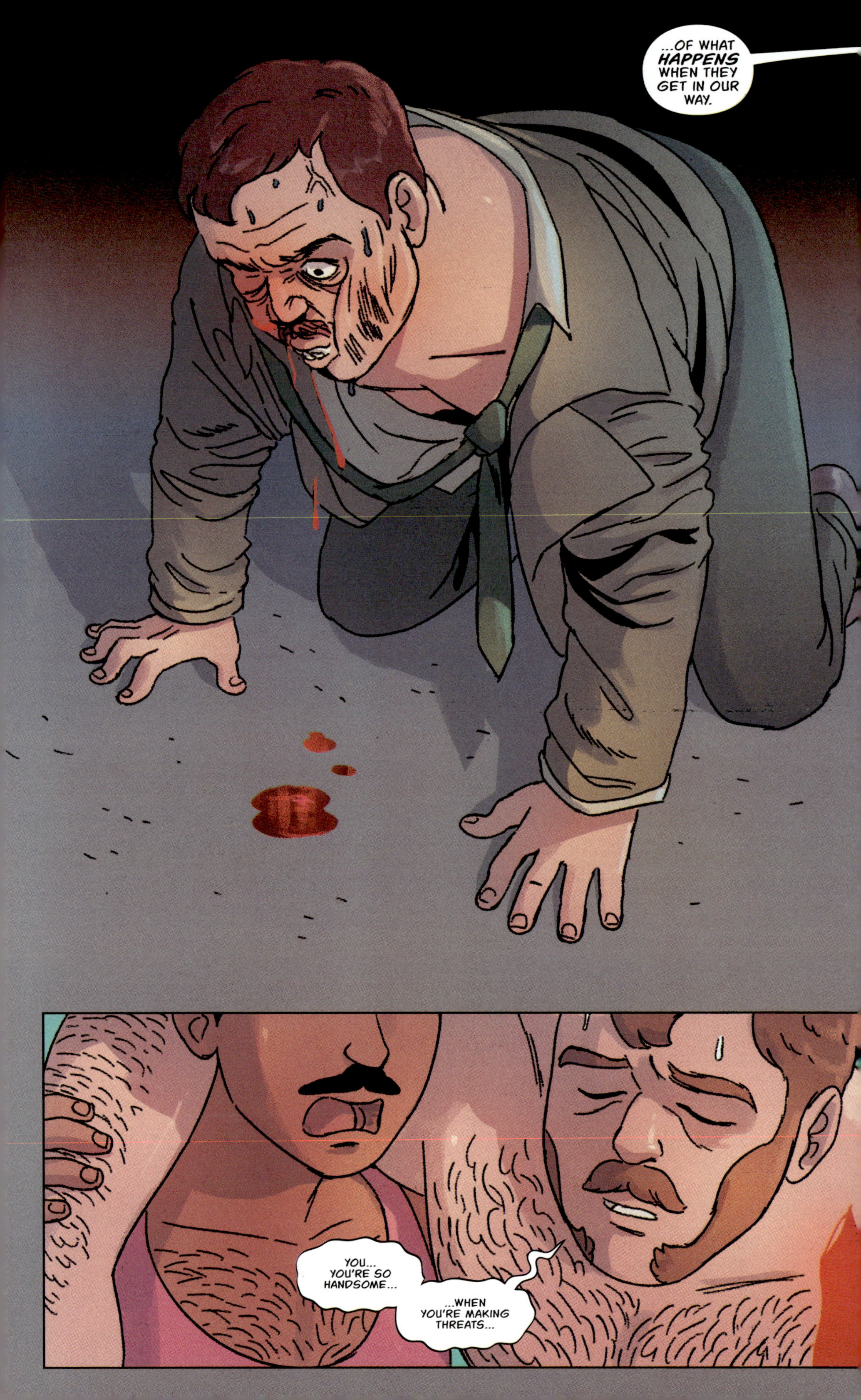
...OF WHAT HAPPENS WHEN THEY GET IN OUR WAY.
YOU... YOU'RE SO HANDSOME...
...WHEN YOU'RE MAKING THREATS...

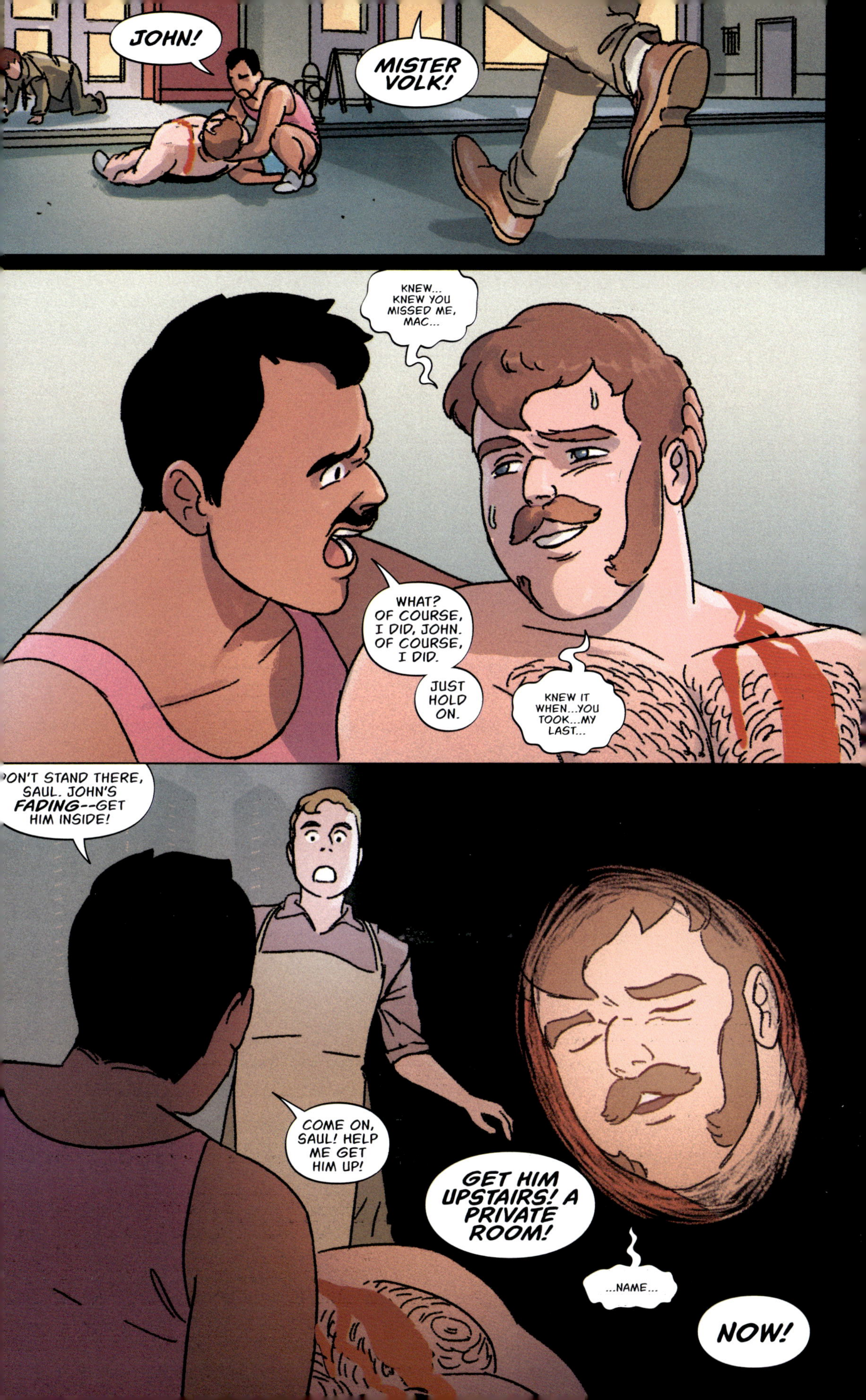
JOHN!
MISTER VOLK!
KNEW... KNEW YOU MISSED ME, MAC...
WHAT? OF COURSE, I DID, JOHN. OF COURSE, I DID.
JUST HOLD ON.
KNEW IT WHEN...YOU TOOK...MY LAST...
ON'T STAND THERE, SAUL. JOHN'S FADING--GET HIM INSIDE!
COME ON, SAUL! HELP ME GET HIM UP!
GET HIM UPSTAIRS! A PRIVATE ROOM!
...NAME...
NOW!

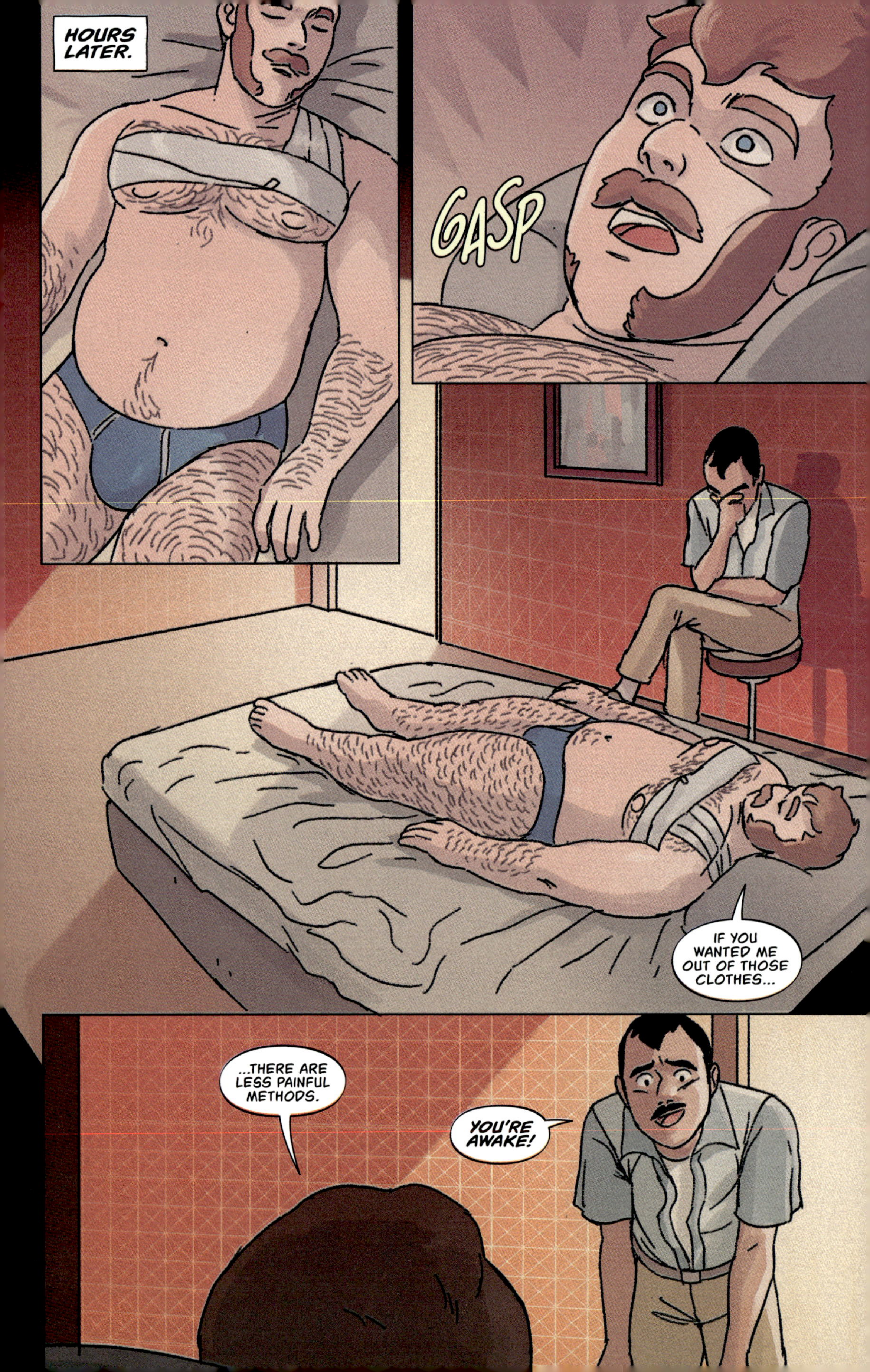
HOURS LATER.
GASP
IF YOU WANTED ME OUT OF THOSE CLOTHES...
...THERE ARE LESS PAINFUL METHODS.
YOU'RE AWAKE!

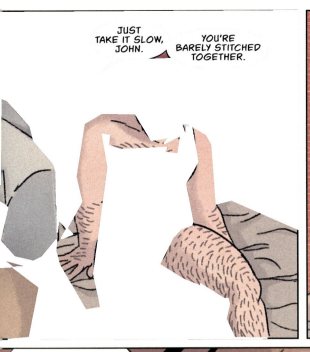

JUST TAKE IT SLOW, JOHN. YOU'RE BARELY STITCHED TOGETHER.

I'D SAY YOU'VE EARNED ONE.

ME? MAC...I'M ONLY HERE BECAUSE OF YOUR *CHRONOCORRIDOR.* NOW HERE I AM...

...SEWN UP IN THIS HAVEN YOU'VE CREATED-- THIS PARADISE. IN WHAT, A *YEAR?* IT'S AMAZING.

A YEAR...CAN BE A LONG TIME, JOHN. ESPECIALLY WITH HOW WE LEFT THINGS.

WE'RE HERE, MAC. WE'RE ALIVE. FOR NOW, THAT'S ENOUGH. AND, ANYWAY...

...DON'T YOU HAVE A HOTEL TO MOVE? *OASIS* NEEDS A NEW HOME.

THAT'S TOMORROW. I'VE CALLED A BRUNCH TO SOFTEN THE NEWS.

BUT *TONIGHT?*

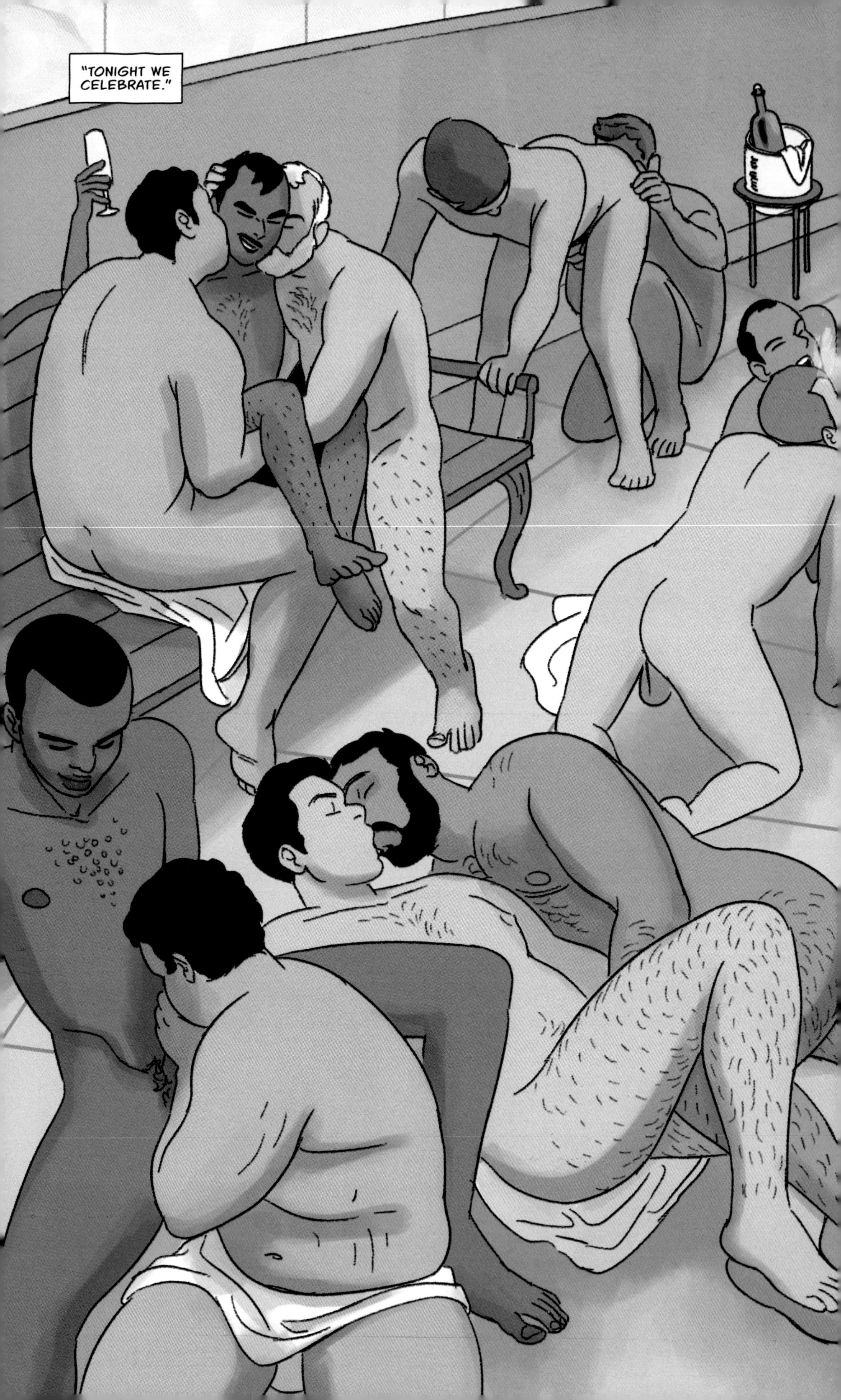
"TONIGHT WE CELEBRATE."

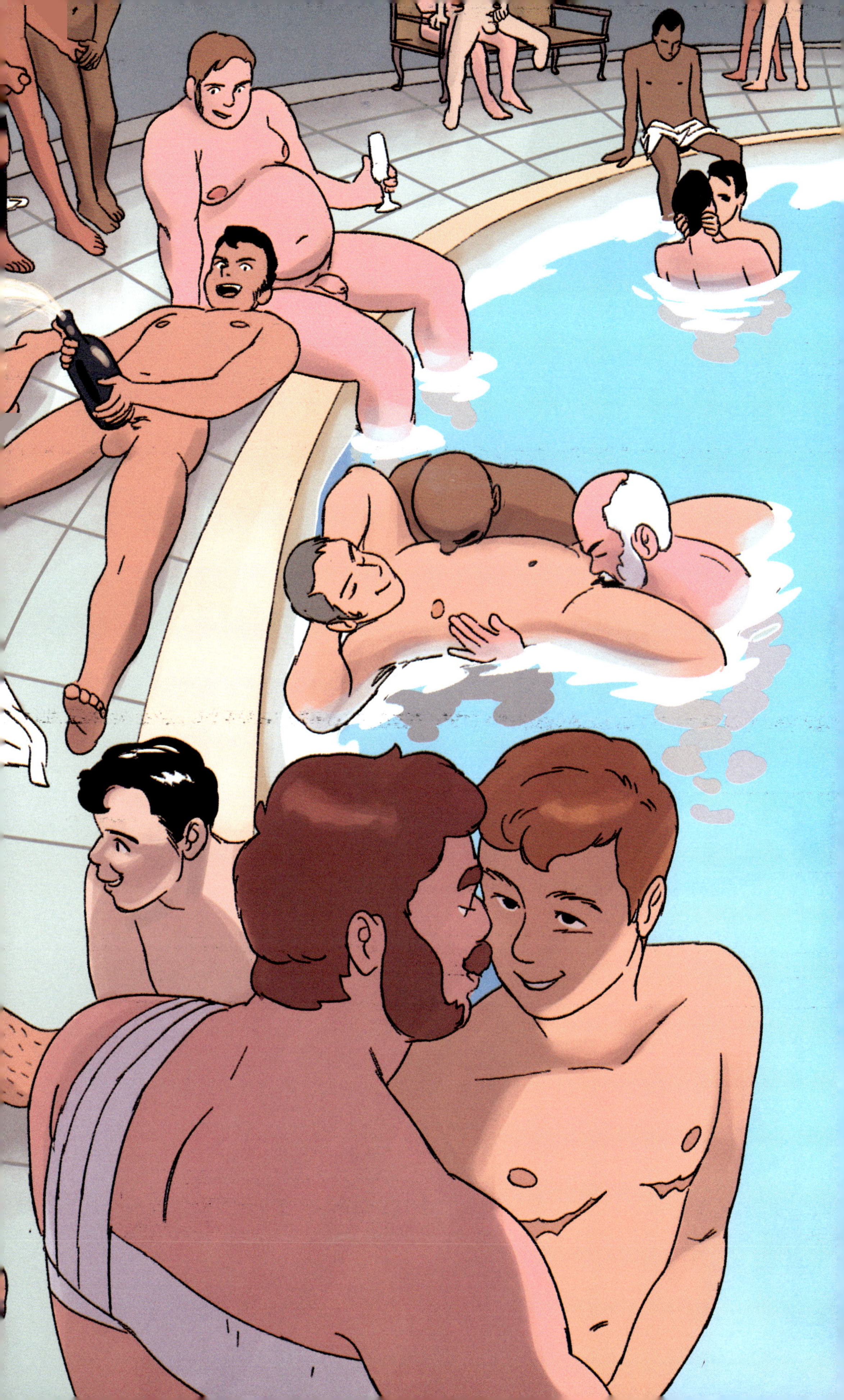

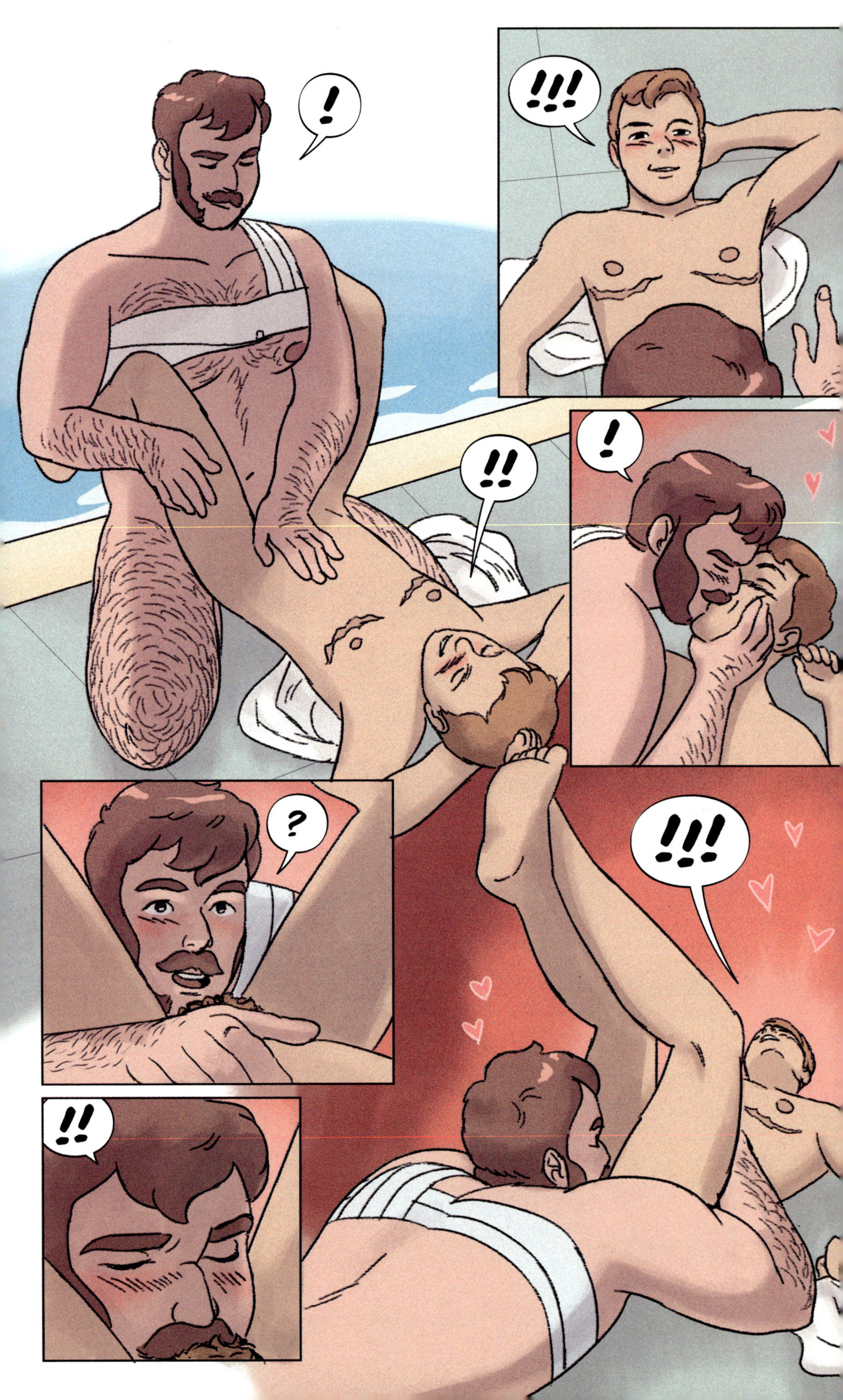
!
!!!
!!
!
?
!!!
!!

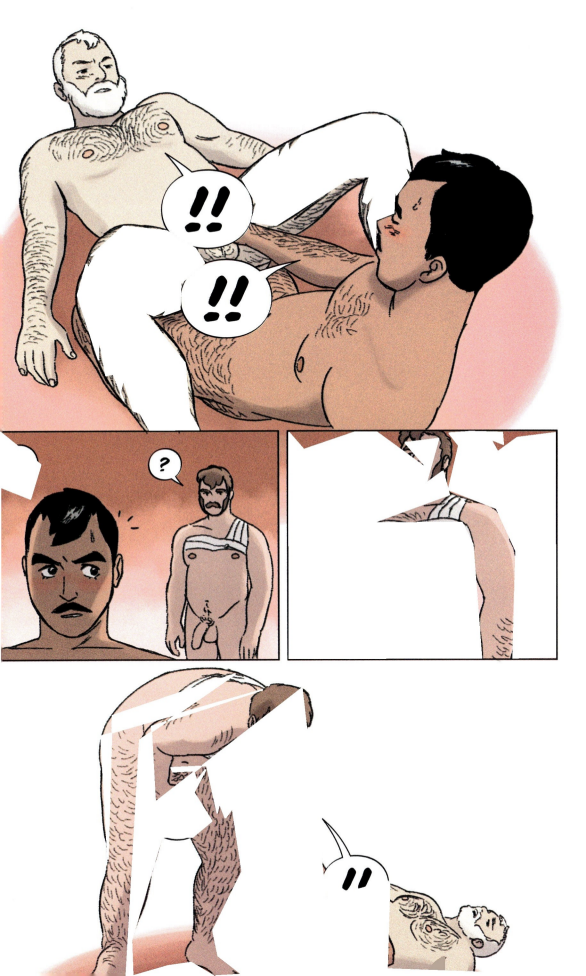

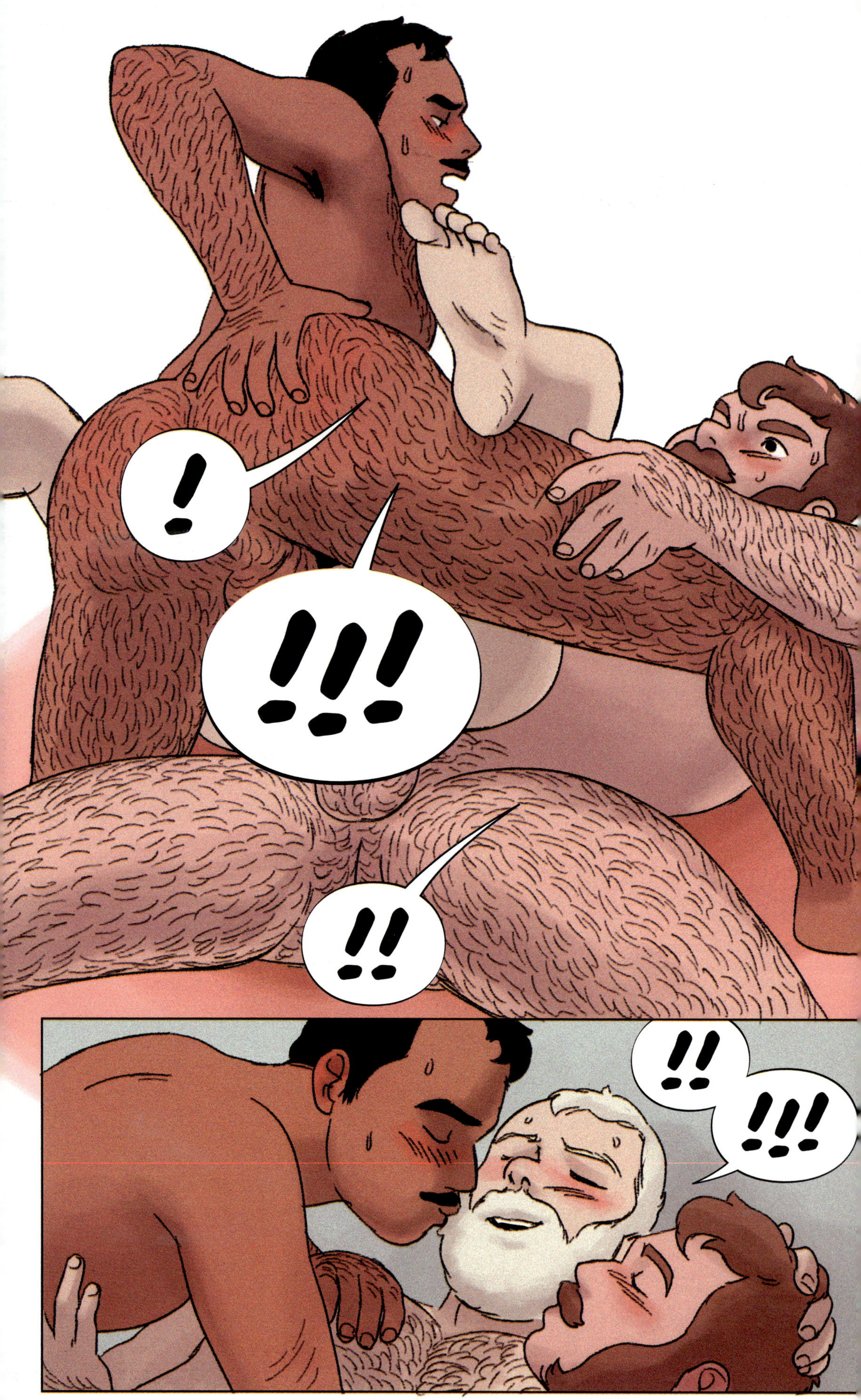
!
!!!
!!
!!
!!!

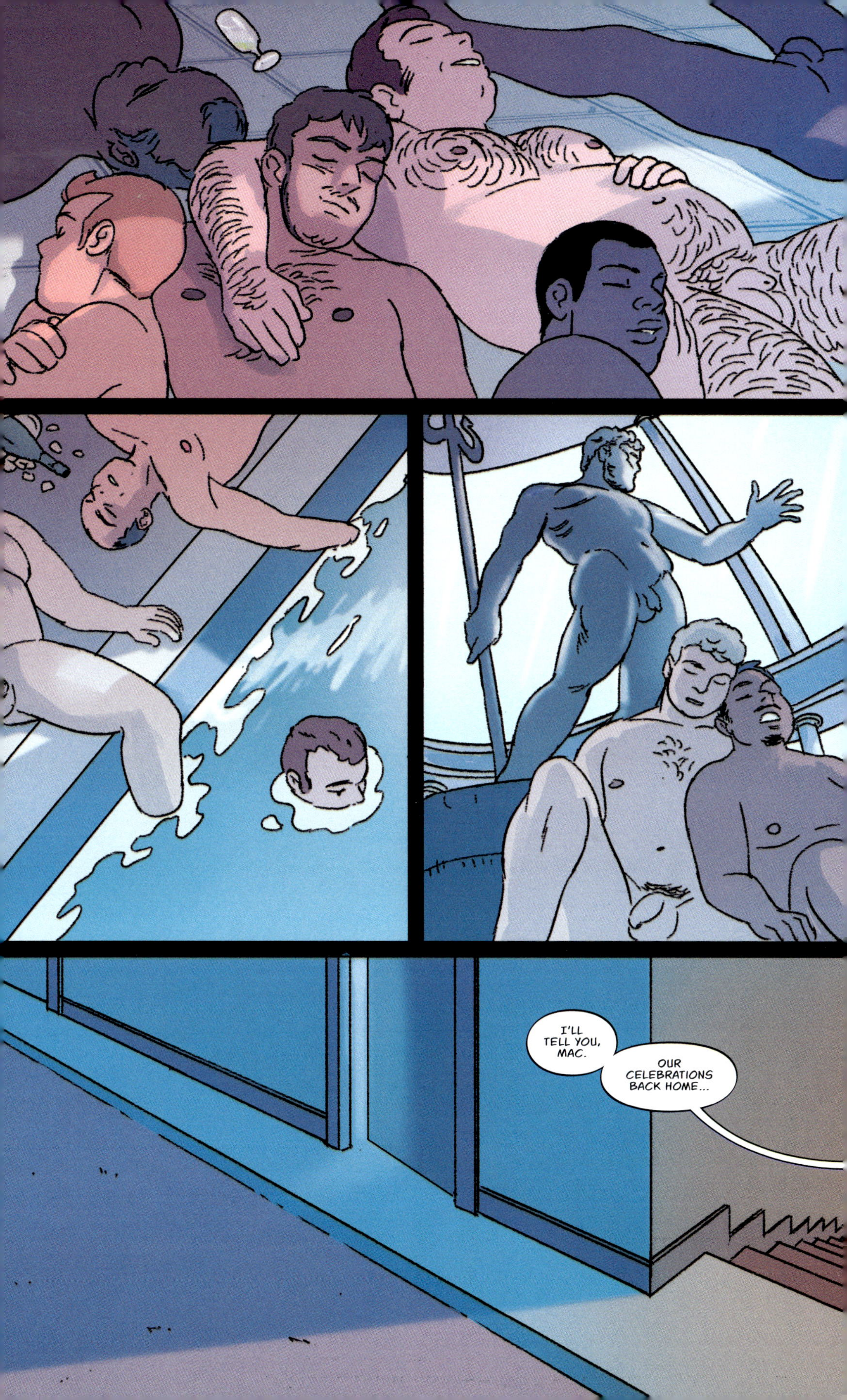
I'LL TELL YOU, MAC.
OUR CELEBRATIONS BACK HOME...

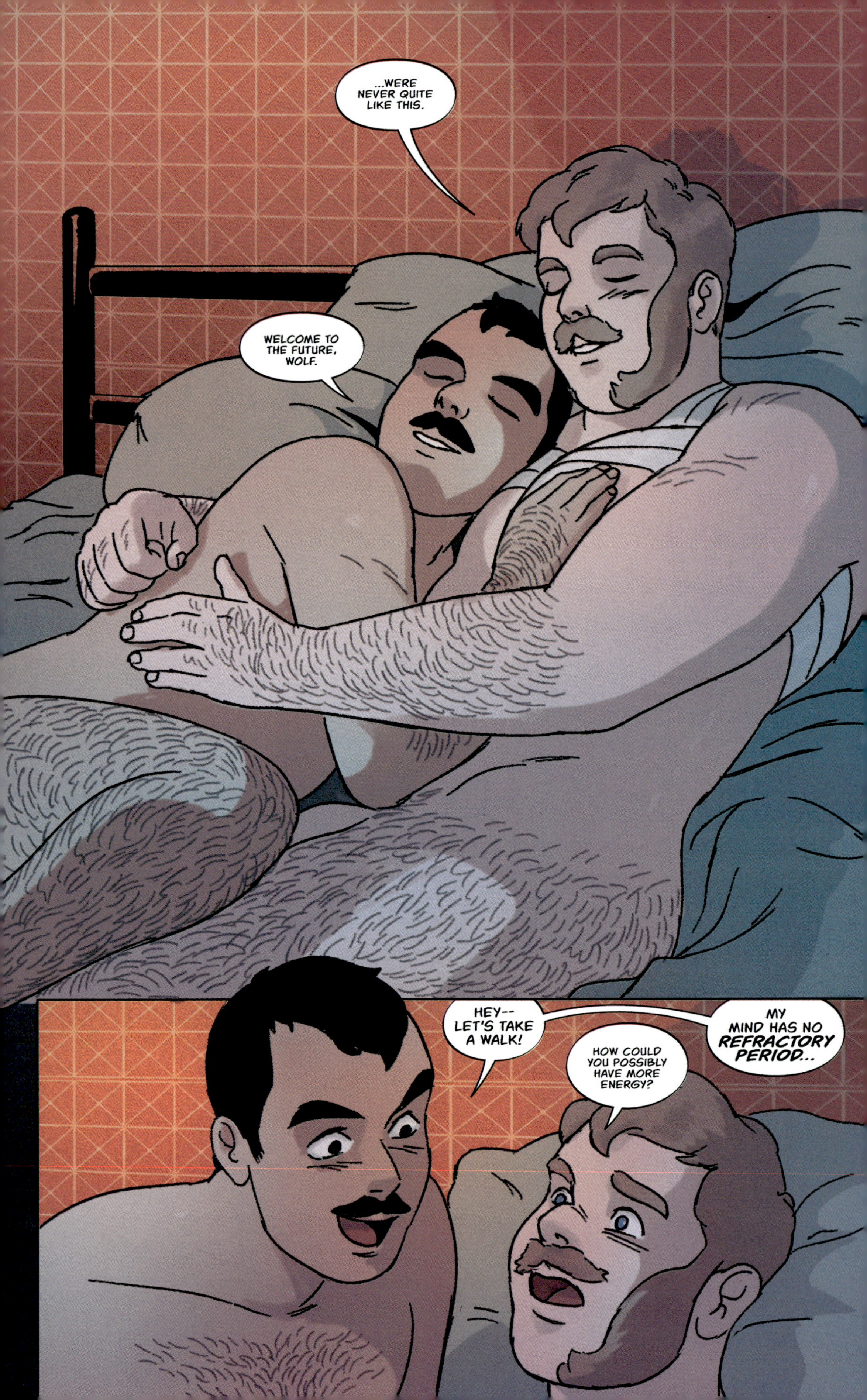
...WERE NEVER QUITE LIKE THIS.
WELCOME TO THE FUTURE, WOLF.
HEY-- LET'S TAKE A WALK!
HOW COULD YOU POSSIBLY HAVE MORE ENERGY?
MY MIND HAS NO *REFRACTORY PERIOD...*

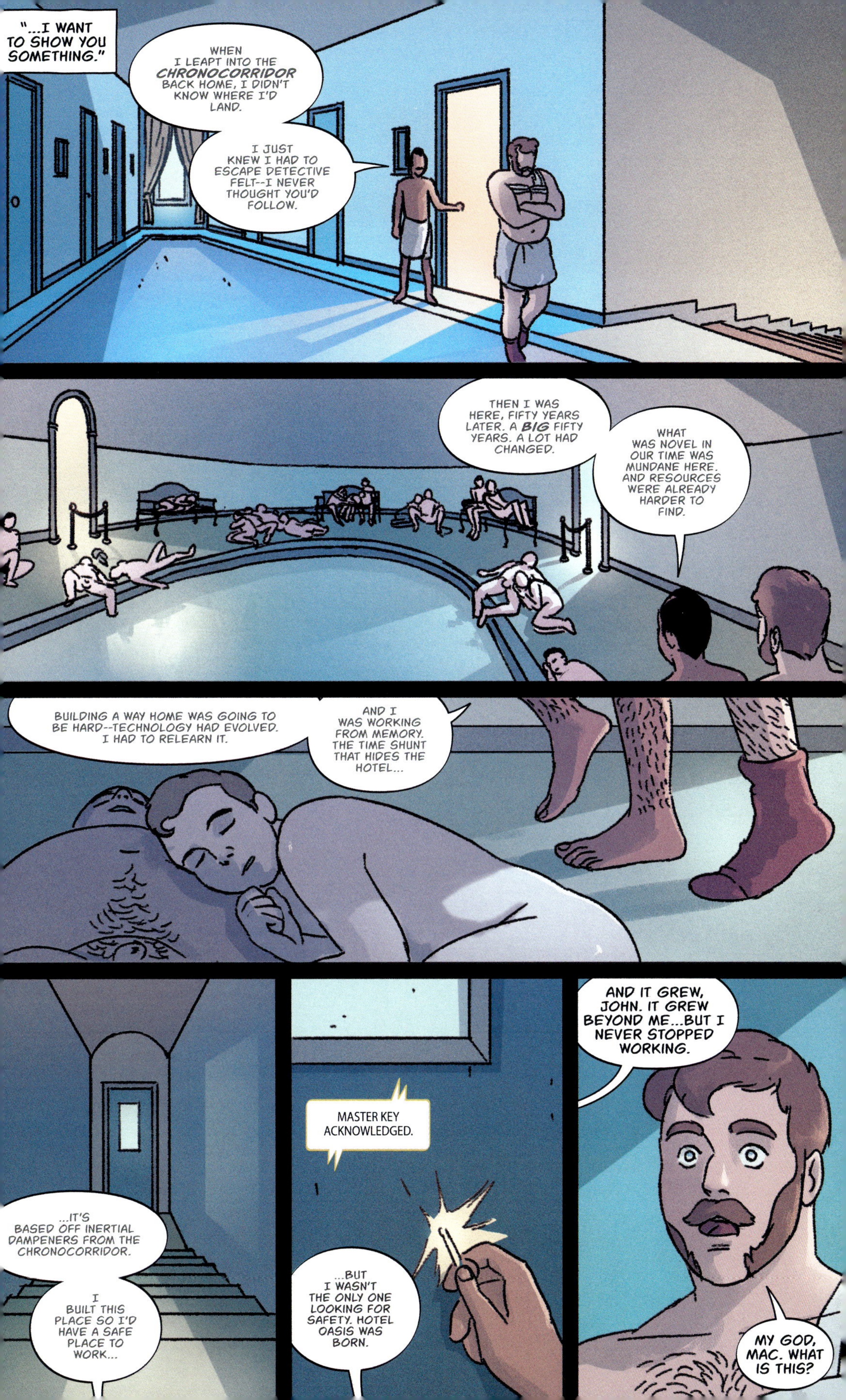
"...I WANT TO SHOW YOU SOMETHING."
WHEN I LEAPT INTO THE *CHRONOCORRIDOR* BACK HOME, I DIDN'T KNOW WHERE I'D LAND.
I JUST KNEW I HAD TO ESCAPE DETECTIVE FELT--I NEVER THOUGHT YOU'D FOLLOW.
THEN I WAS HERE, FIFTY YEARS LATER. A *BIG* FIFTY YEARS. A LOT HAD CHANGED.
WHAT WAS NOVEL IN OUR TIME WAS MUNDANE HERE. AND RESOURCES WERE ALREADY HARDER TO FIND.
BUILDING A WAY HOME WAS GOING TO BE HARD--TECHNOLOGY HAD EVOLVED. I HAD TO RELEARN IT.
AND I WAS WORKING FROM MEMORY. THE TIME SHUNT THAT HIDES THE HOTEL...
...IT'S BASED OFF INERTIAL DAMPENERS FROM THE CHRONOCORRIDOR.
I BUILT THIS PLACE SO I'D HAVE A SAFE PLACE TO WORK...
MASTER KEY ACKNOWLEDGED.
...BUT I WASN'T THE ONLY ONE LOOKING FOR SAFETY. HOTEL OASIS WAS BORN.
AND IT GREW, JOHN. IT GREW BEYOND ME...BUT I NEVER STOPPED WORKING.
MY GOD, MAC. WHAT IS THIS?

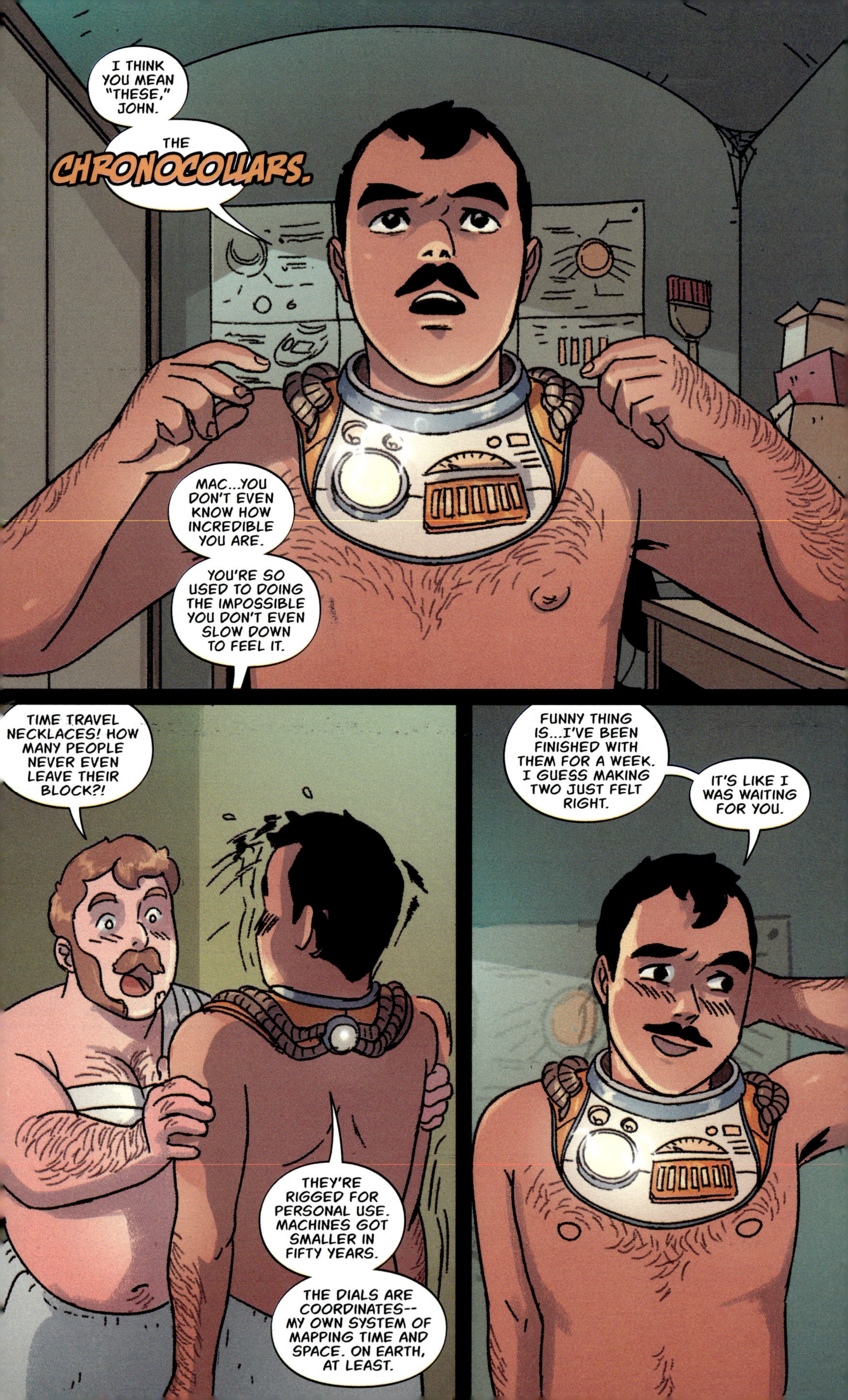
I THINK YOU MEAN "THESE," JOHN.
THE CHRONOCOLLARS.
MAC...YOU DON'T EVEN KNOW HOW INCREDIBLE YOU ARE.
YOU'RE SO USED TO DOING THE IMPOSSIBLE YOU DON'T EVEN SLOW DOWN TO FEEL IT.
TIME TRAVEL NECKLACES! HOW MANY PEOPLE NEVER EVEN LEAVE THEIR BLOCK?!
THEY'RE RIGGED FOR PERSONAL USE. MACHINES GOT SMALLER IN FIFTY YEARS.
THE DIALS ARE COORDINATES-- MY OWN SYSTEM OF MAPPING TIME AND SPACE. ON EARTH, AT LEAST.
FUNNY THING IS...I'VE BEEN FINISHED WITH THEM FOR A WEEK. I GUESS MAKING TWO JUST FELT RIGHT.
IT'S LIKE I WAS WAITING FOR YOU.

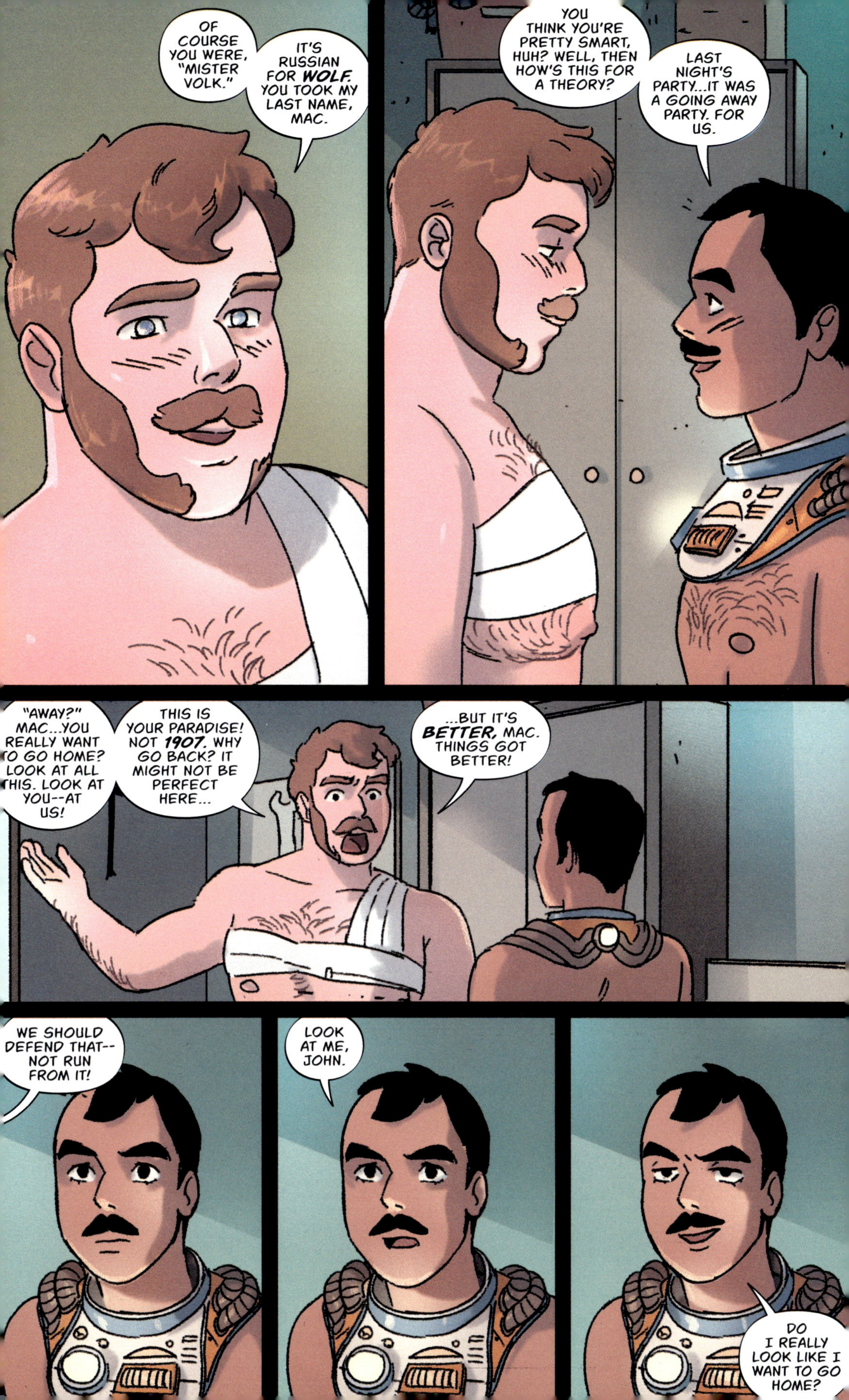
OF COURSE YOU WERE, "MISTER VOLK."
IT'S RUSSIAN FOR WOLF. YOU TOOK MY LAST NAME, MAC.
YOU THINK YOU'RE PRETTY SMART, HUH? WELL, THEN HOW'S THIS FOR A THEORY?
LAST NIGHT'S PARTY...IT WAS A GOING AWAY PARTY. FOR US.
"AWAY?" MAC...YOU REALLY WANT TO GO HOME? LOOK AT ALL THIS. LOOK AT YOU--AT US!
THIS IS YOUR PARADISE! NOT 1907. WHY GO BACK? IT MIGHT NOT BE PERFECT HERE...
...BUT IT'S BETTER, MAC. THINGS GOT BETTER!
WE SHOULD DEFEND THAT--NOT RUN FROM IT!
LOOK AT ME, JOHN.
DO I REALLY LOOK LIKE I WANT TO GO HOME?

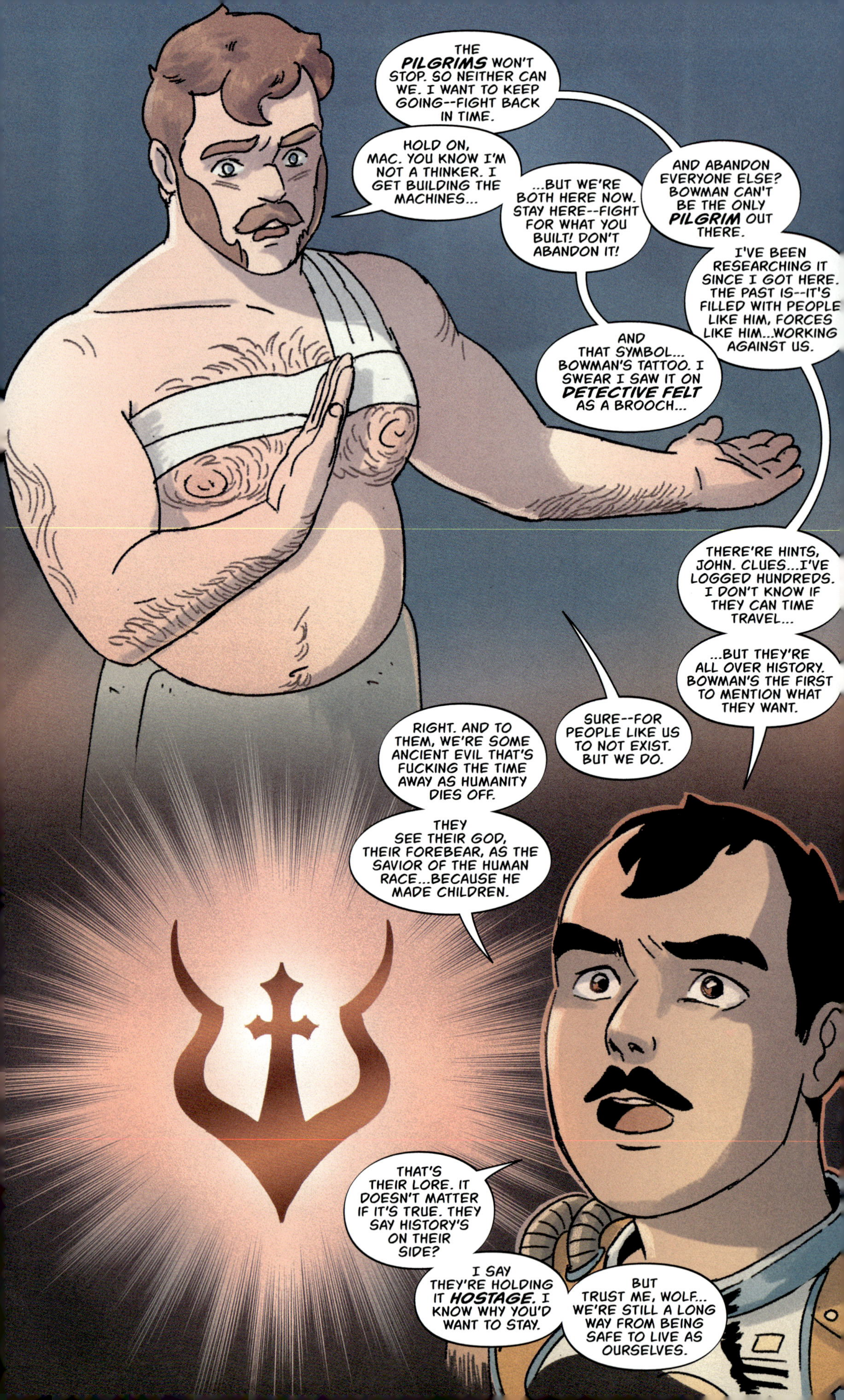
THE PILGRIMS WON'T STOP. SO NEITHER CAN WE. I WANT TO KEEP GOING--FIGHT BACK IN TIME.
AND ABANDON EVERYONE ELSE? BOWMAN CAN'T BE THE ONLY PILGRIM OUT THERE.
HOLD ON, MAC. YOU KNOW I'M NOT A THINKER. I GET BUILDING THE MACHINES...
...BUT WE'RE BOTH HERE NOW. STAY HERE--FIGHT FOR WHAT YOU BUILT! DON'T ABANDON IT!
I'VE BEEN RESEARCHING IT SINCE I GOT HERE. THE PAST IS--IT'S FILLED WITH PEOPLE LIKE HIM, FORCES LIKE HIM...WORKING AGAINST US.
AND THAT SYMBOL... BOWMAN'S TATTOO. I SWEAR I SAW IT ON DETECTIVE FELT AS A BROOCH...
THERE'RE HINTS, JOHN. CLUES...I'VE LOGGED HUNDREDS. I DON'T KNOW IF THEY CAN TIME TRAVEL...
...BUT THEY'RE ALL OVER HISTORY. BOWMAN'S THE FIRST TO MENTION WHAT THEY WANT.
SURE--FOR PEOPLE LIKE US TO NOT EXIST. BUT WE DO.
RIGHT. AND TO THEM, WE'RE SOME ANCIENT EVIL THAT'S FUCKING THE TIME AWAY AS HUMANITY DIES OFF.
THEY SEE THEIR GOD, THEIR FOREBEAR, AS THE SAVIOR OF THE HUMAN RACE...BECAUSE HE MADE CHILDREN.
THAT'S THEIR LORE. IT DOESN'T MATTER IF IT'S TRUE. THEY SAY HISTORY'S ON THEIR SIDE?
I SAY THEY'RE HOLDING IT HOSTAGE. I KNOW WHY YOU'D WANT TO STAY.
BUT TRUST ME, WOLF... WE'RE STILL A LONG WAY FROM BEING SAFE TO LIVE AS OURSELVES.

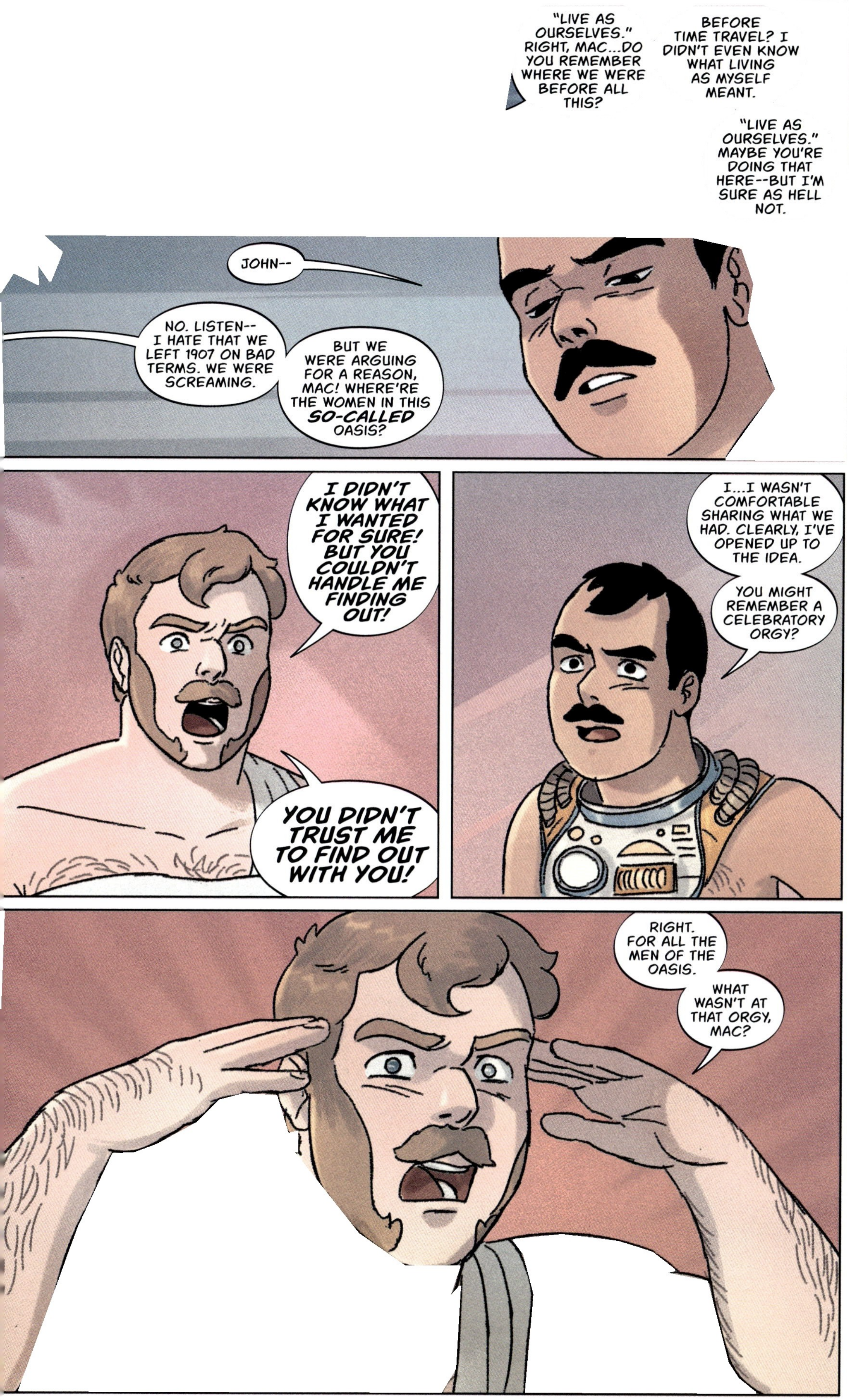
"LIVE AS OURSELVES." RIGHT, MAC...DO YOU REMEMBER WHERE WE WERE BEFORE ALL THIS?
BEFORE TIME TRAVEL? I DIDN'T EVEN KNOW WHAT LIVING AS MYSELF MEANT.
"LIVE AS OURSELVES." MAYBE YOU'RE DOING THAT HERE--BUT I'M SURE AS HELL NOT.
JOHN--
NO. LISTEN-- I HATE THAT WE LEFT 1907 ON BAD TERMS. WE WERE SCREAMING.
BUT WE WERE ARGUING FOR A REASON, MAC! WHERE'RE THE WOMEN IN THIS SO-CALLED OASIS?
I DIDN'T KNOW WHAT I WANTED FOR SURE! BUT YOU COULDN'T HANDLE ME FINDING OUT!
YOU DIDN'T TRUST ME TO FIND OUT WITH YOU!
I...I WASN'T COMFORTABLE SHARING WHAT WE HAD. CLEARLY, I'VE OPENED UP TO THE IDEA.
YOU MIGHT REMEMBER A CELEBRATORY ORGY?
RIGHT. FOR ALL THE MEN OF THE OASIS.
WHAT WASN'T AT THAT ORGY, MAC?

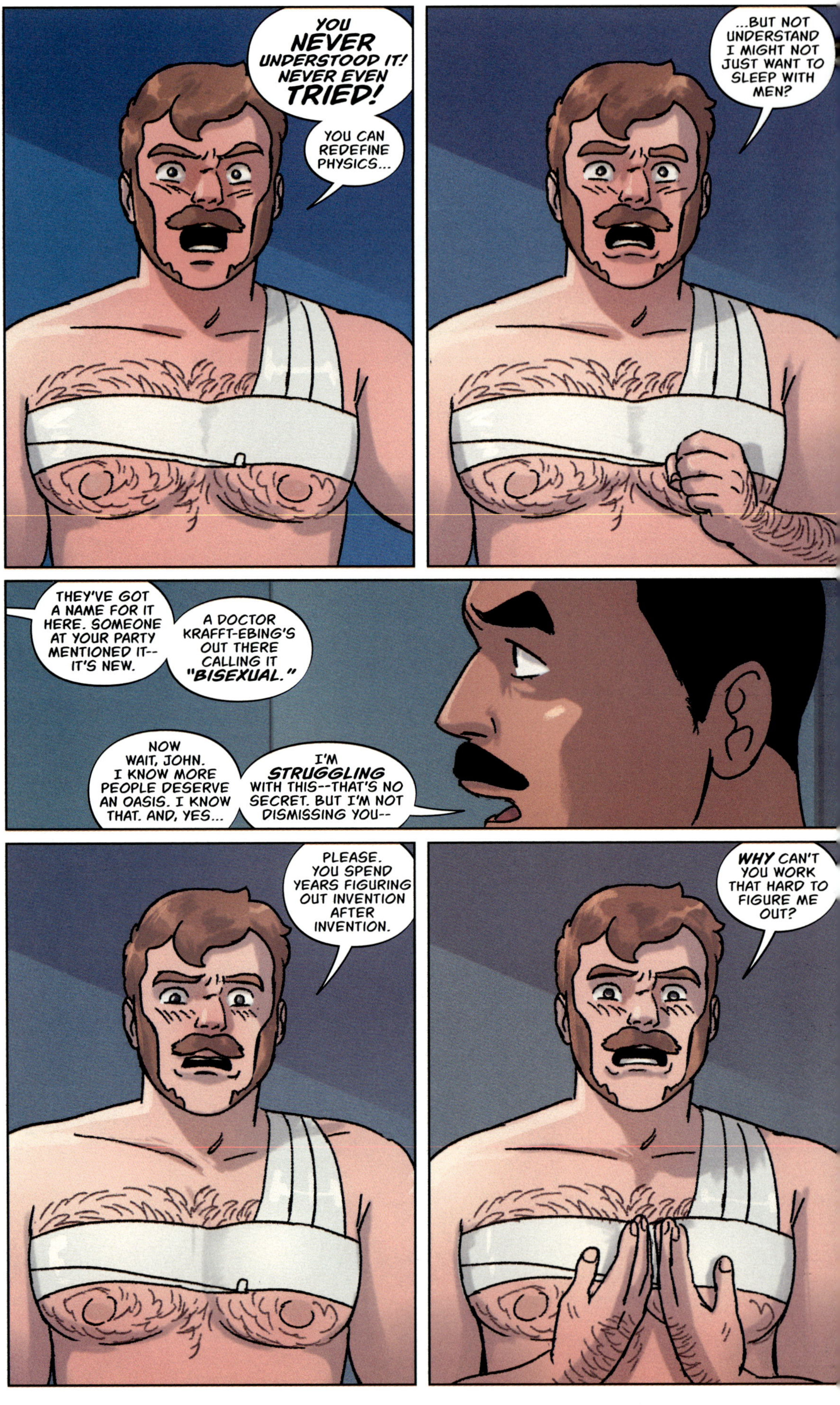
YOU NEVER UNDERSTOOD IT! NEVER EVEN TRIED!
YOU CAN REDEFINE PHYSICS...
...BUT NOT UNDERSTAND I MIGHT NOT JUST WANT TO SLEEP WITH MEN?
THEY'VE GOT A NAME FOR IT HERE. SOMEONE AT YOUR PARTY MENTIONED IT--IT'S NEW.
A DOCTOR KRAFFT-EBING'S OUT THERE CALLING IT "BISEXUAL."
NOW WAIT, JOHN. I KNOW MORE PEOPLE DESERVE AN OASIS. I KNOW THAT. AND, YES...
I'M STRUGGLING WITH THIS--THAT'S NO SECRET. BUT I'M NOT DISMISSING YOU--
PLEASE. YOU SPEND YEARS FIGURING OUT INVENTION AFTER INVENTION.
WHY CAN'T YOU WORK THAT HARD TO FIGURE ME OUT?

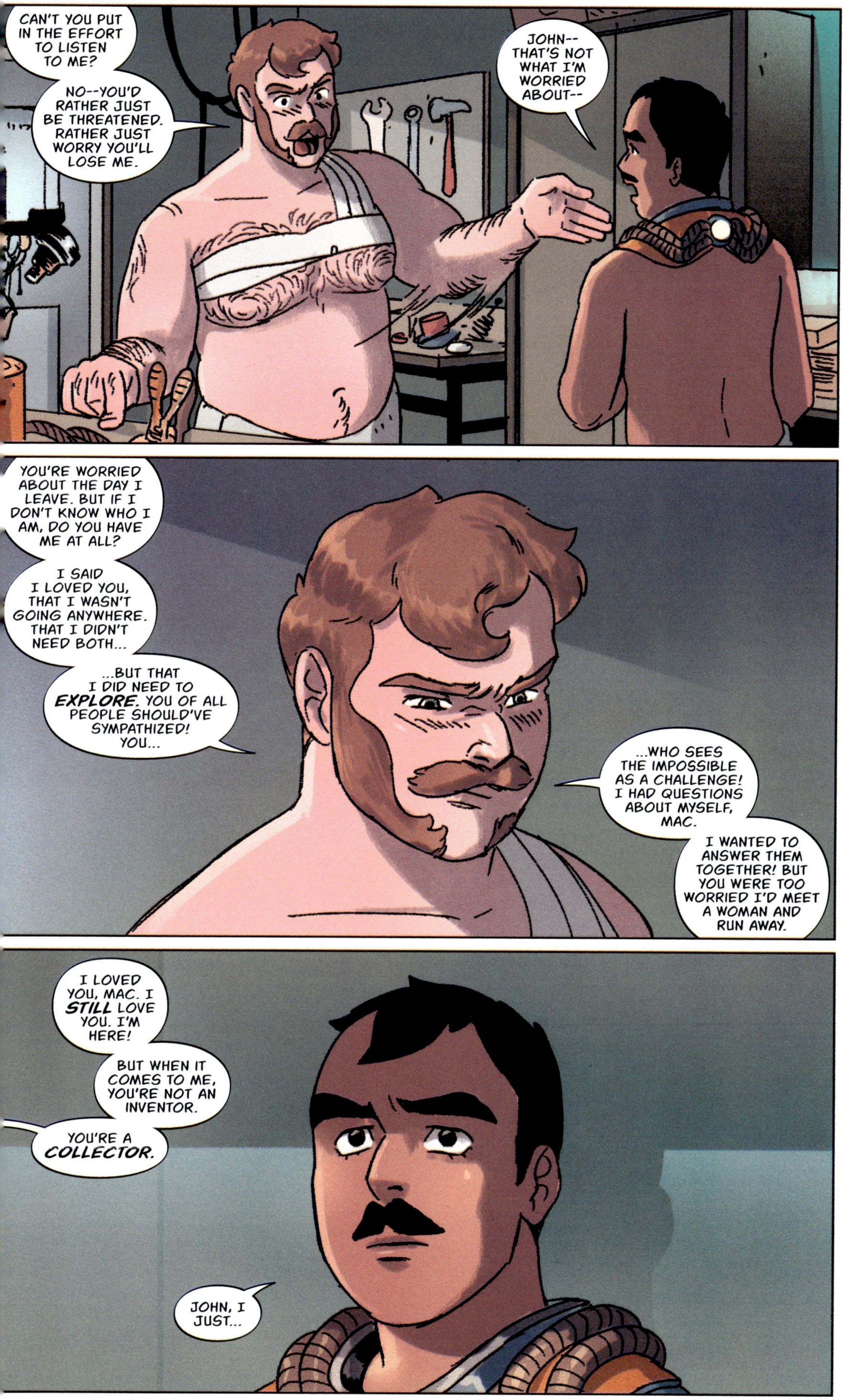
CAN'T YOU PUT IN THE EFFORT TO LISTEN TO ME?
NO--YOU'D RATHER JUST BE THREATENED. RATHER JUST WORRY YOU'LL LOSE ME.
JOHN-- THAT'S NOT WHAT I'M WORRIED ABOUT--
YOU'RE WORRIED ABOUT THE DAY I LEAVE. BUT IF I DON'T KNOW WHO I AM, DO YOU HAVE ME AT ALL?
I SAID I LOVED YOU, THAT I WASN'T GOING ANYWHERE. THAT I DIDN'T NEED BOTH...
...BUT THAT I DID NEED TO EXPLORE. YOU OF ALL PEOPLE SHOULD'VE SYMPATHIZED! YOU...
...WHO SEES THE IMPOSSIBLE AS A CHALLENGE! I HAD QUESTIONS ABOUT MYSELF, MAC.
I WANTED TO ANSWER THEM TOGETHER! BUT YOU WERE TOO WORRIED I'D MEET A WOMAN AND RUN AWAY.
I LOVED YOU, MAC. I STILL LOVE YOU. I'M HERE!
BUT WHEN IT COMES TO ME, YOU'RE NOT AN INVENTOR.
YOU'RE A COLLECTOR.
JOHN, I JUST...

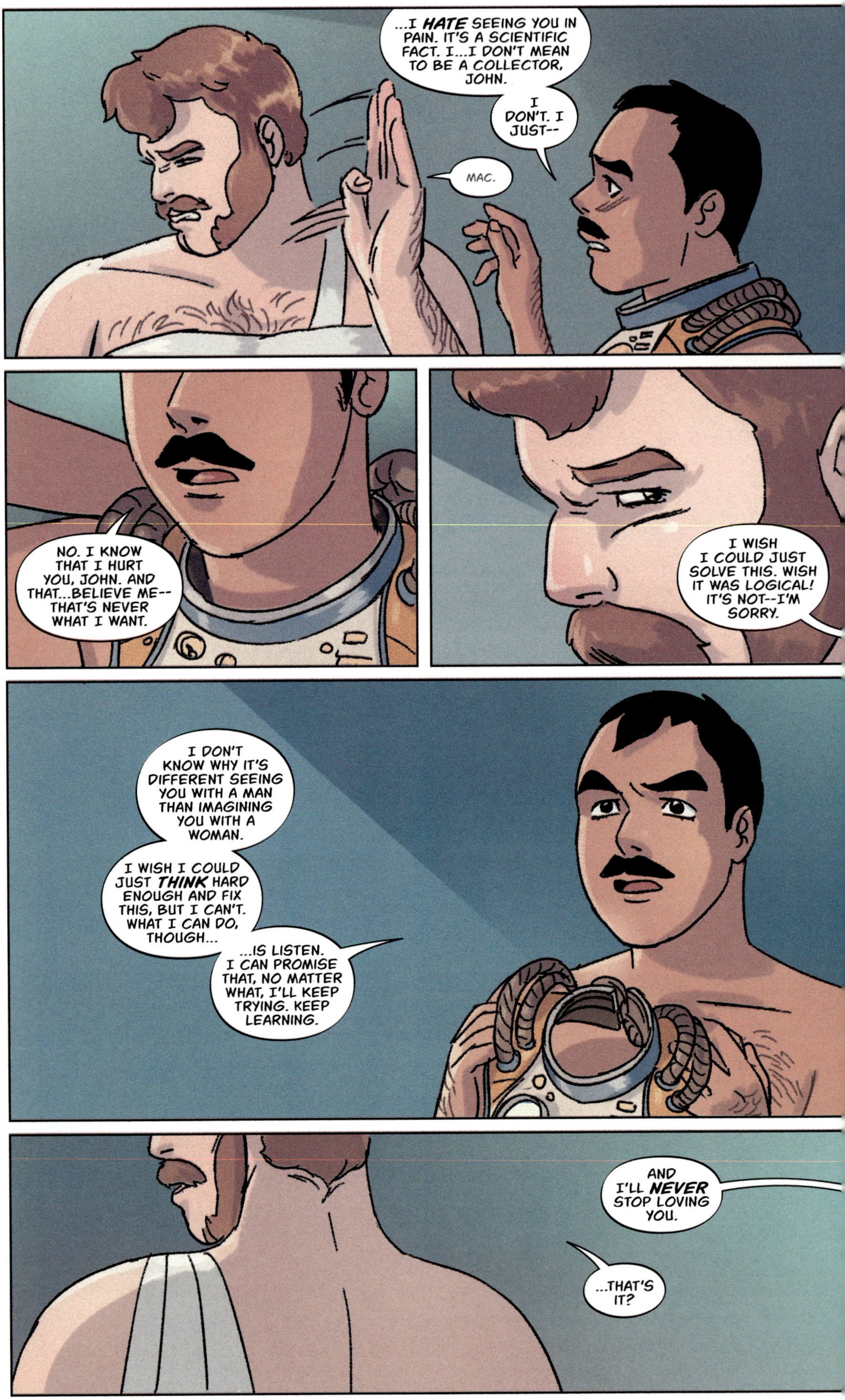
...I HATE SEEING YOU IN PAIN. IT'S A SCIENTIFIC FACT. I...I DON'T MEAN TO BE A COLLECTOR, JOHN.
I DON'T. I JUST--
MAC.
NO. I KNOW THAT I HURT YOU, JOHN. AND THAT...BELIEVE ME--THAT'S NEVER WHAT I WANT.
I WISH I COULD JUST SOLVE THIS. WISH IT WAS LOGICAL! IT'S NOT--I'M SORRY.
I DON'T KNOW WHY IT'S DIFFERENT SEEING YOU WITH A MAN THAN IMAGINING YOU WITH A WOMAN.
I WISH I COULD JUST THINK HARD ENOUGH AND FIX THIS, BUT I CAN'T. WHAT I CAN DO, THOUGH...
...IS LISTEN. I CAN PROMISE THAT, NO MATTER WHAT, I'LL KEEP TRYING. KEEP LEARNING.
AND I'LL NEVER STOP LOVING YOU.
...THAT'S IT?

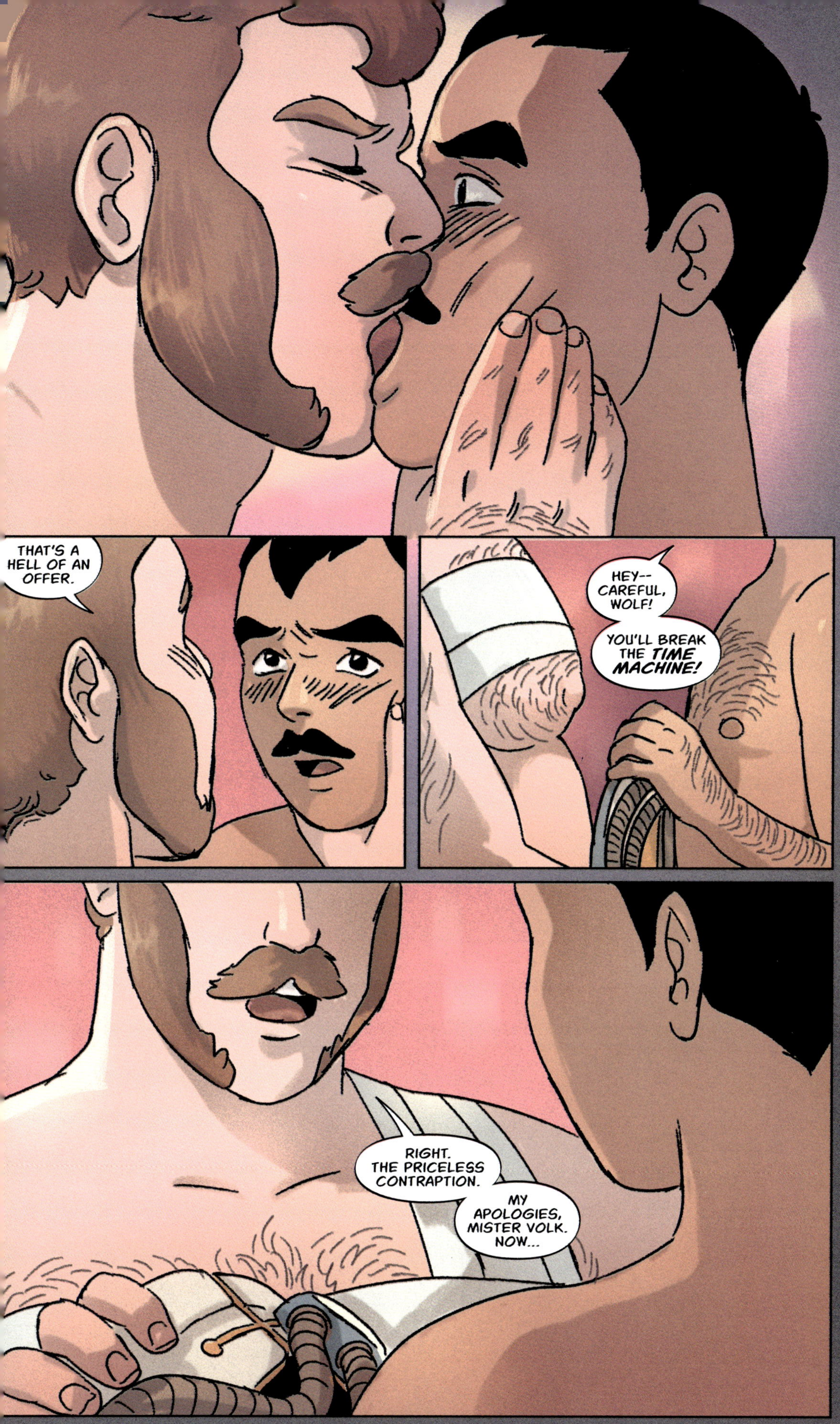
THAT'S A HELL OF AN OFFER.
HEY-- CAREFUL, WOLF!
YOU'LL BREAK THE *TIME MACHINE!*
RIGHT. THE PRICELESS CONTRAPTION.
MY APOLOGIES, MISTER VOLK. NOW...

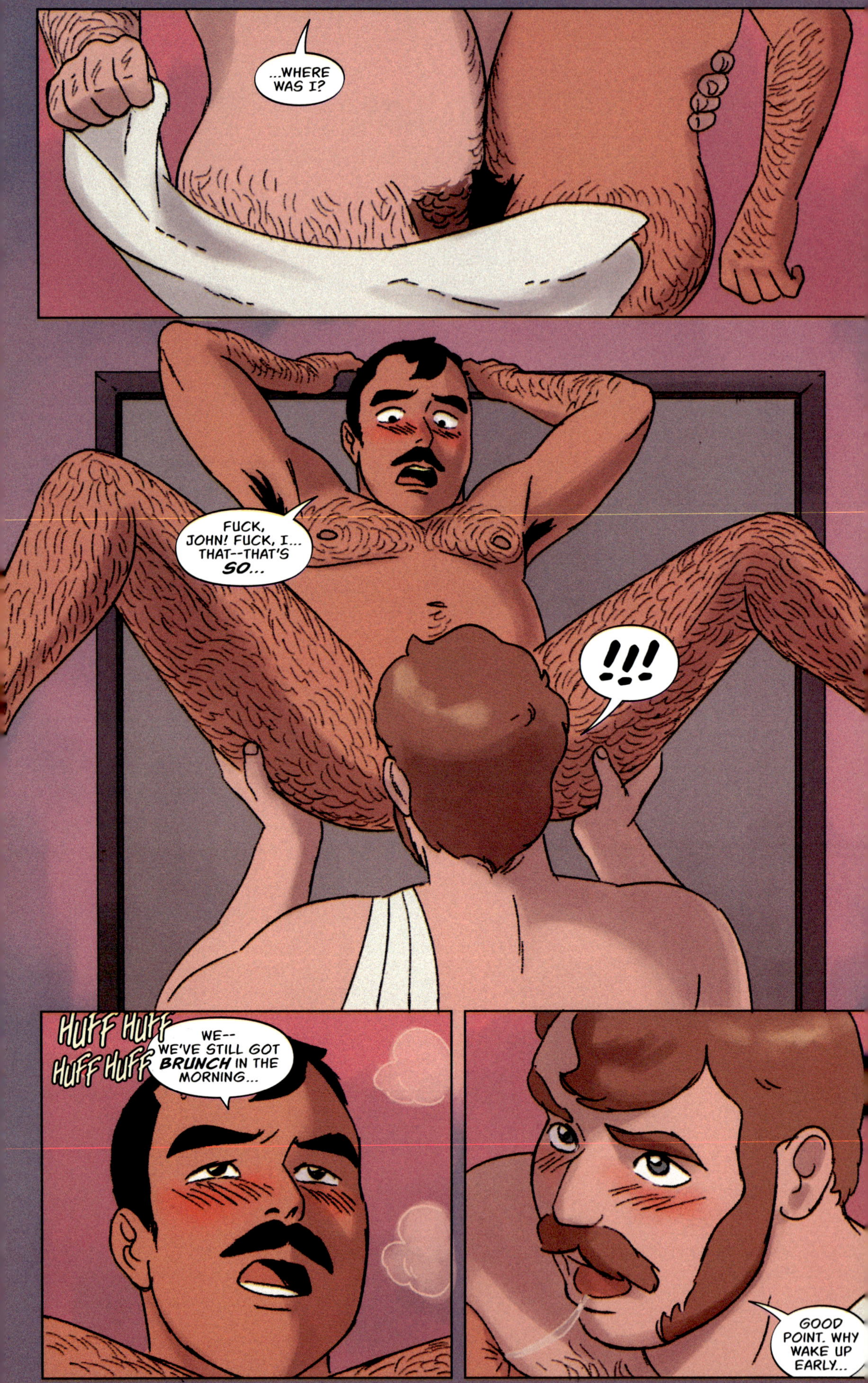
...WHERE WAS I?
FUCK, JOHN! FUCK, I... THAT--THAT'S SO...
!!!
HUFF HUFF HUFF HUFF
WE-- WE'VE STILL GOT BRUNCH IN THE MORNING...
GOOD POINT. WHY WAKE UP EARLY...

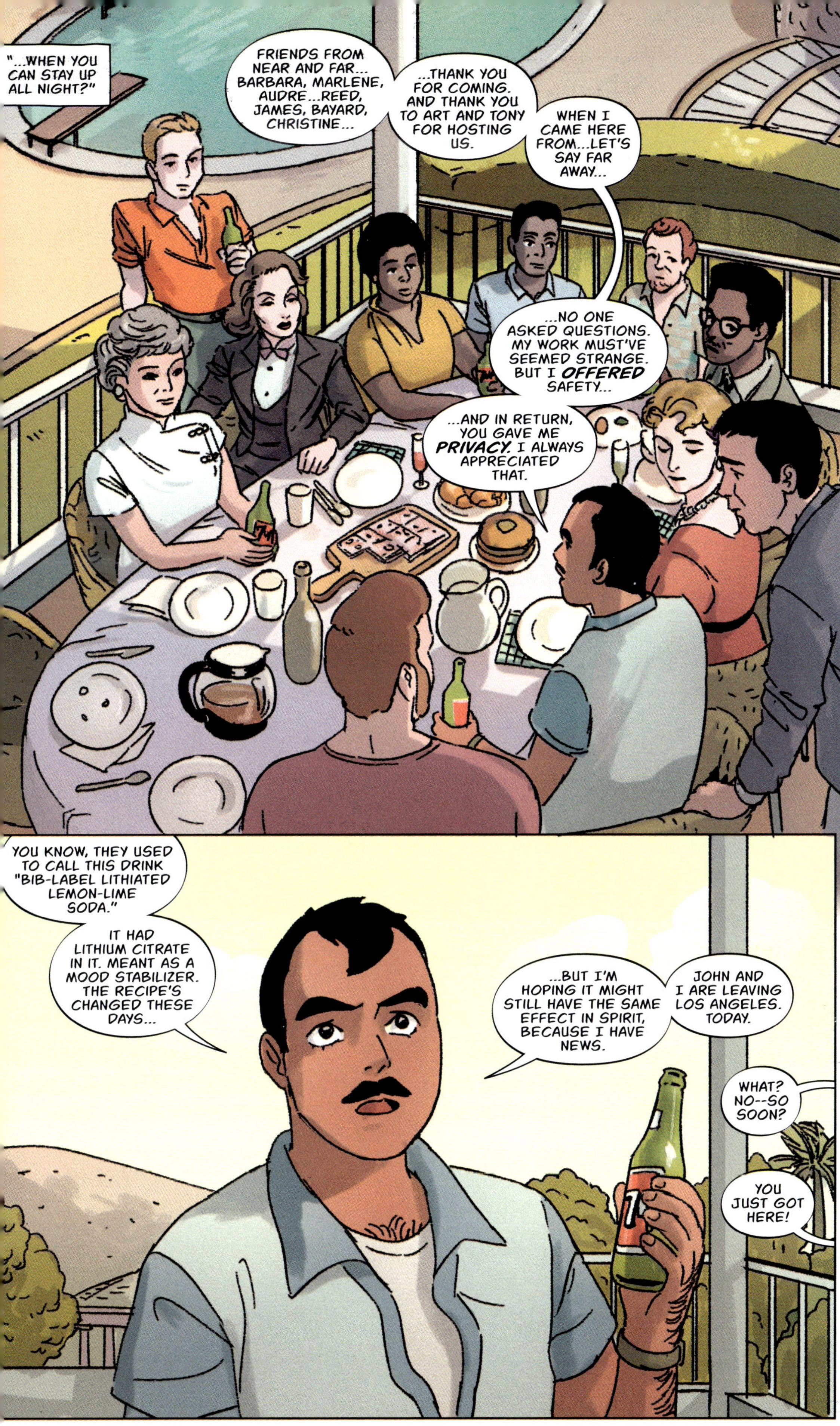
"...WHEN YOU CAN STAY UP ALL NIGHT?"
FRIENDS FROM NEAR AND FAR... BARBARA, MARLENE, AUDRE...REED, JAMES, BAYARD, CHRISTINE...
...THANK YOU FOR COMING. AND THANK YOU TO ART AND TONY FOR HOSTING US.
WHEN I CAME HERE FROM...LET'S SAY FAR AWAY...
...NO ONE ASKED QUESTIONS. MY WORK MUST'VE SEEMED STRANGE. BUT I OFFERED SAFETY...
...AND IN RETURN, YOU GAVE ME PRIVACY. I ALWAYS APPRECIATED THAT.
YOU KNOW, THEY USED TO CALL THIS DRINK "BIB-LABEL LITHIATED LEMON-LIME SODA."
IT HAD LITHIUM CITRATE IN IT. MEANT AS A MOOD STABILIZER. THE RECIPE'S CHANGED THESE DAYS...
...BUT I'M HOPING IT MIGHT STILL HAVE THE SAME EFFECT IN SPIRIT, BECAUSE I HAVE NEWS.
JOHN AND I ARE LEAVING LOS ANGELES. TODAY.
WHAT? NO--SO SOON?
YOU JUST GOT HERE!

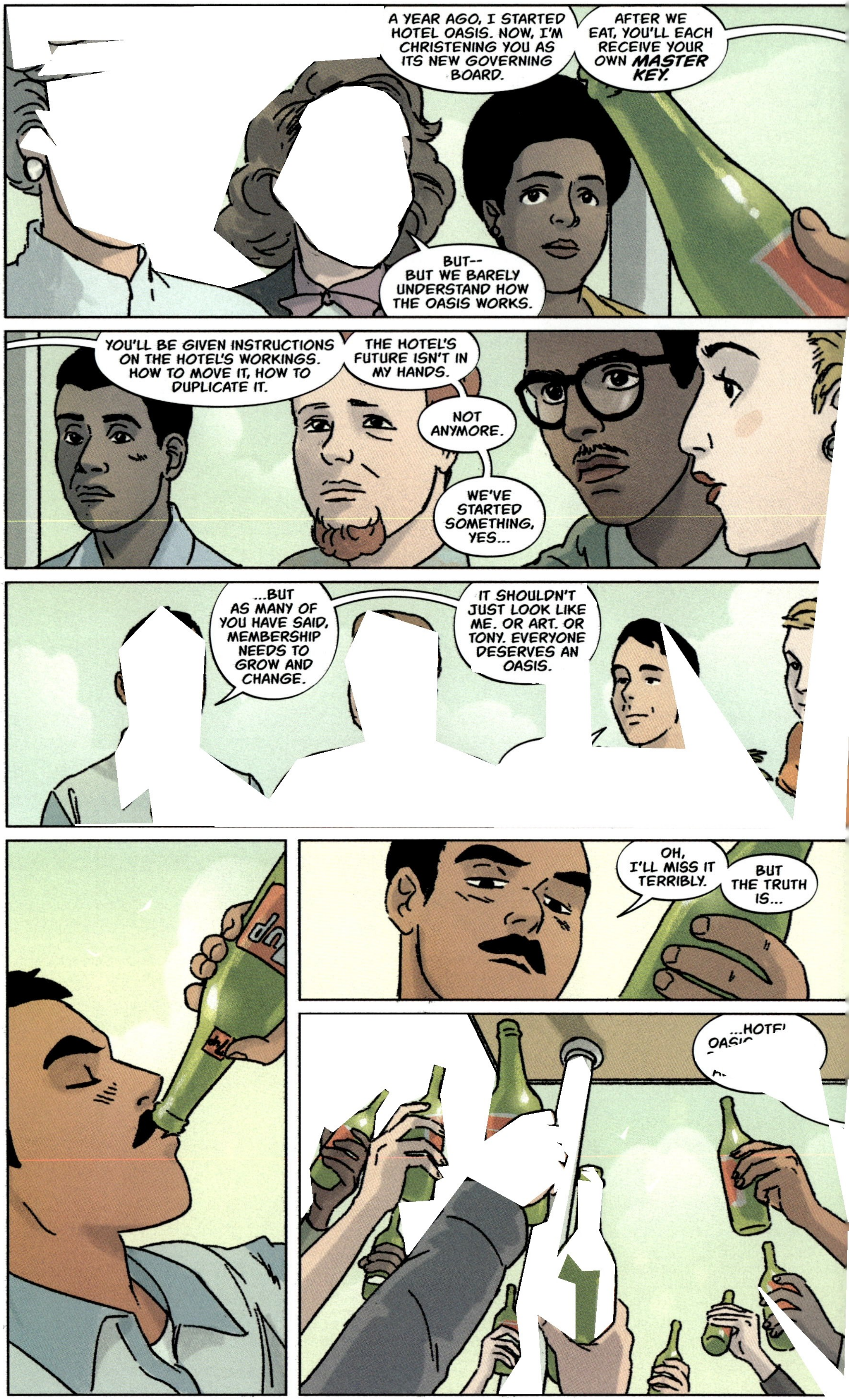
A YEAR AGO, I STARTED HOTEL OASIS. NOW, I'M CHRISTENING YOU AS ITS NEW GOVERNING BOARD.
AFTER WE EAT, YOU'LL EACH RECEIVE YOUR OWN MASTER KEY.
BUT-- BUT WE BARELY UNDERSTAND HOW THE OASIS WORKS.
YOU'LL BE GIVEN INSTRUCTIONS ON THE HOTEL'S WORKINGS. HOW TO MOVE IT, HOW TO DUPLICATE IT.
THE HOTEL'S FUTURE ISN'T IN MY HANDS.
NOT ANYMORE.
WE'VE STARTED SOMETHING, YES...
...BUT AS MANY OF YOU HAVE SAID, MEMBERSHIP NEEDS TO GROW AND CHANGE.
IT SHOULDN'T JUST LOOK LIKE ME. OR ART. OR TONY. EVERYONE DESERVES AN OASIS.
OH, I'LL MISS IT TERRIBLY.
BUT THE TRUTH IS...

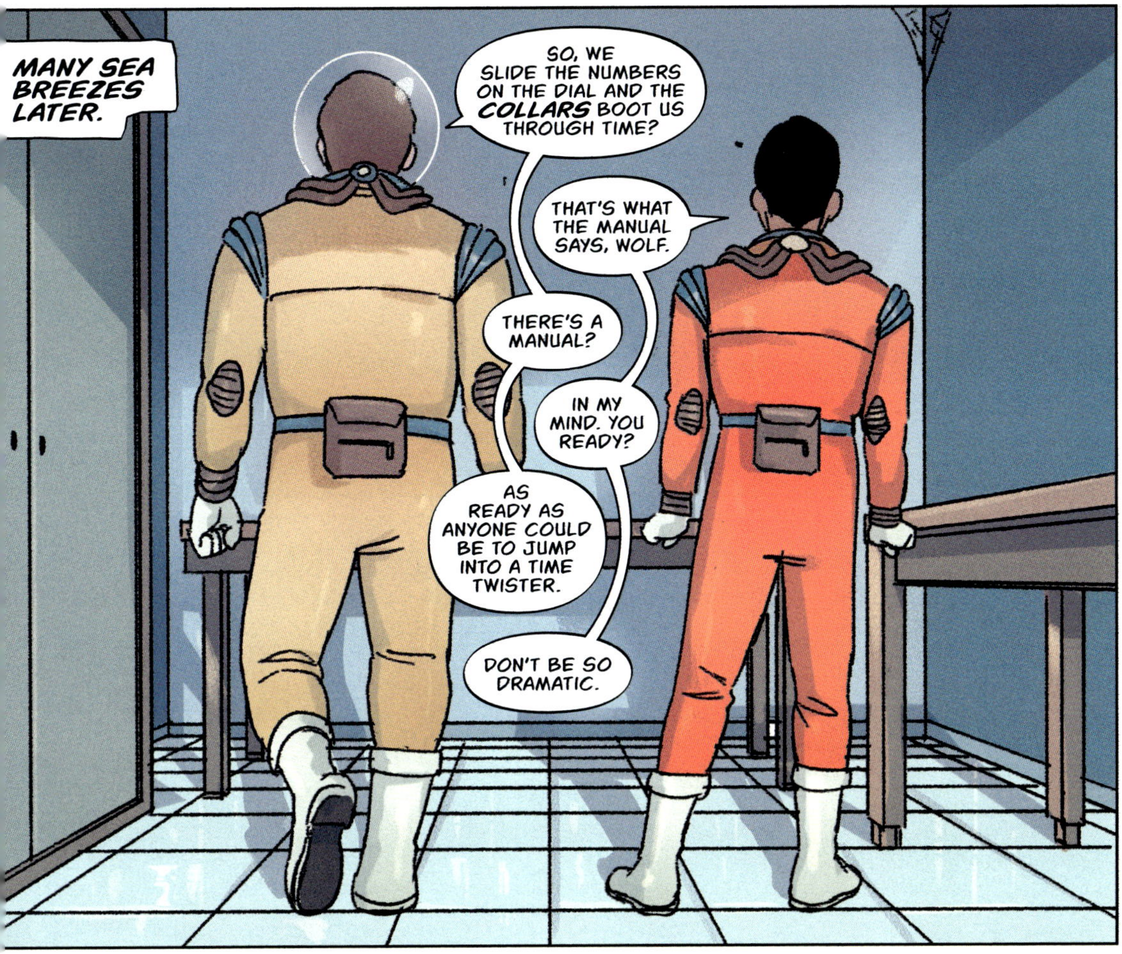
MANY SEA BREEZES LATER.
SO, WE SLIDE THE NUMBERS ON THE DIAL AND THE COLLARS BOOT US THROUGH TIME?
THAT'S WHAT THE MANUAL SAYS, WOLF.
THERE'S A MANUAL?
IN MY MIND. YOU READY?
AS READY AS ANYONE COULD BE TO JUMP INTO A TIME TWISTER.
DON'T BE SO DRAMATIC.

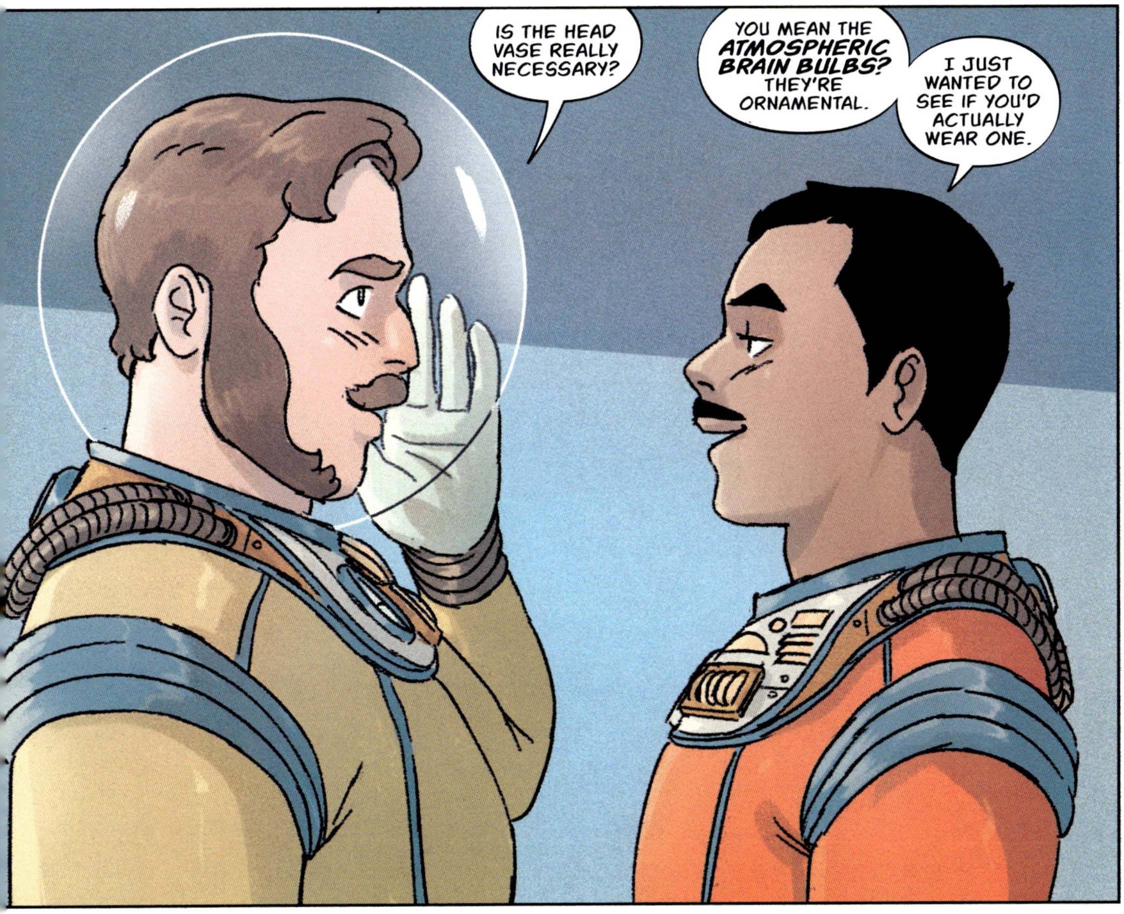
IS THE HEAD VASE REALLY NECESSARY?
YOU MEAN THE ATMOSPHERIC BRAIN BULBS? THEY'RE ORNAMENTAL.
I JUST WANTED TO SEE IF YOU'D ACTUALLY WEAR ONE.

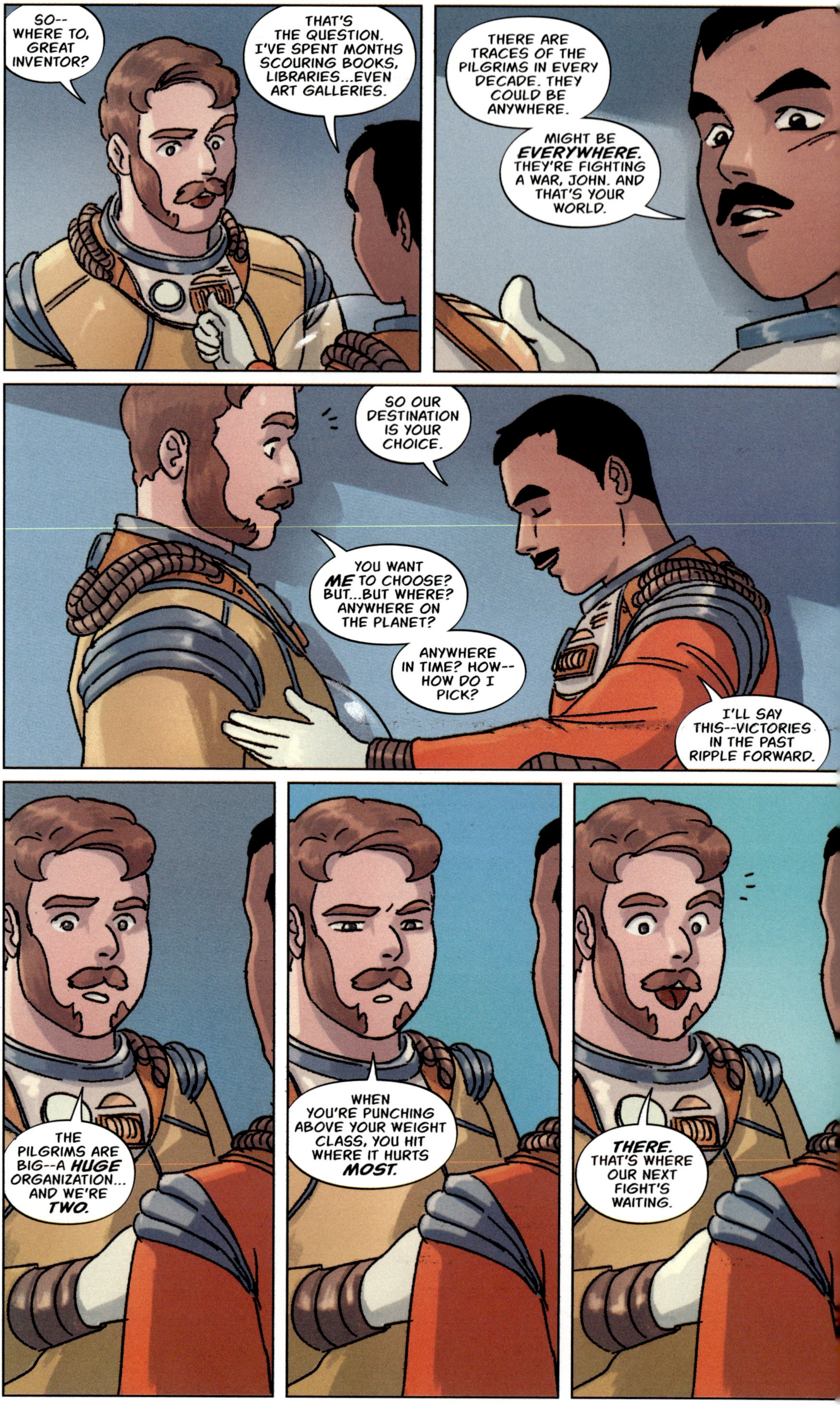
SO--WHERE TO, GREAT INVENTOR?
THAT'S THE QUESTION. I'VE SPENT MONTHS SCOURING BOOKS, LIBRARIES...EVEN ART GALLERIES.
THERE ARE TRACES OF THE PILGRIMS IN EVERY DECADE. THEY COULD BE ANYWHERE.
MIGHT BE EVERYWHERE. THEY'RE FIGHTING A WAR, JOHN. AND THAT'S YOUR WORLD.
SO OUR DESTINATION IS YOUR CHOICE.
YOU WANT ME TO CHOOSE? BUT...BUT WHERE? ANYWHERE ON THE PLANET?
ANYWHERE IN TIME? HOW--HOW DO I PICK?
I'LL SAY THIS--VICTORIES IN THE PAST RIPPLE FORWARD.
THE PILGRIMS ARE BIG--A HUGE ORGANIZATION... AND WE'RE TWO.
WHEN YOU'RE PUNCHING ABOVE YOUR WEIGHT CLASS, YOU HIT WHERE IT HURTS MOST.
THERE. THAT'S WHERE OUR NEXT FIGHT'S WAITING.

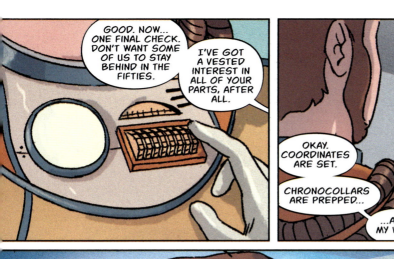

GOOD. NOW... ONE FINAL CHECK. DON'T WANT SOME OF US TO STAY BEHIND IN THE FIFTIES.

I'VE GOT A VESTED INTEREST IN ALL OF YOUR PARTS, AFTER ALL.

OKAY. COORDINATES ARE SET.

CHRONOCOLLARS ARE PREPPED...

...AS IS MY WOLF.

SO, WE'RE READY?

READY.

READY TO GO MAKE SOME *TROUBLE.*

FZWOOOSH

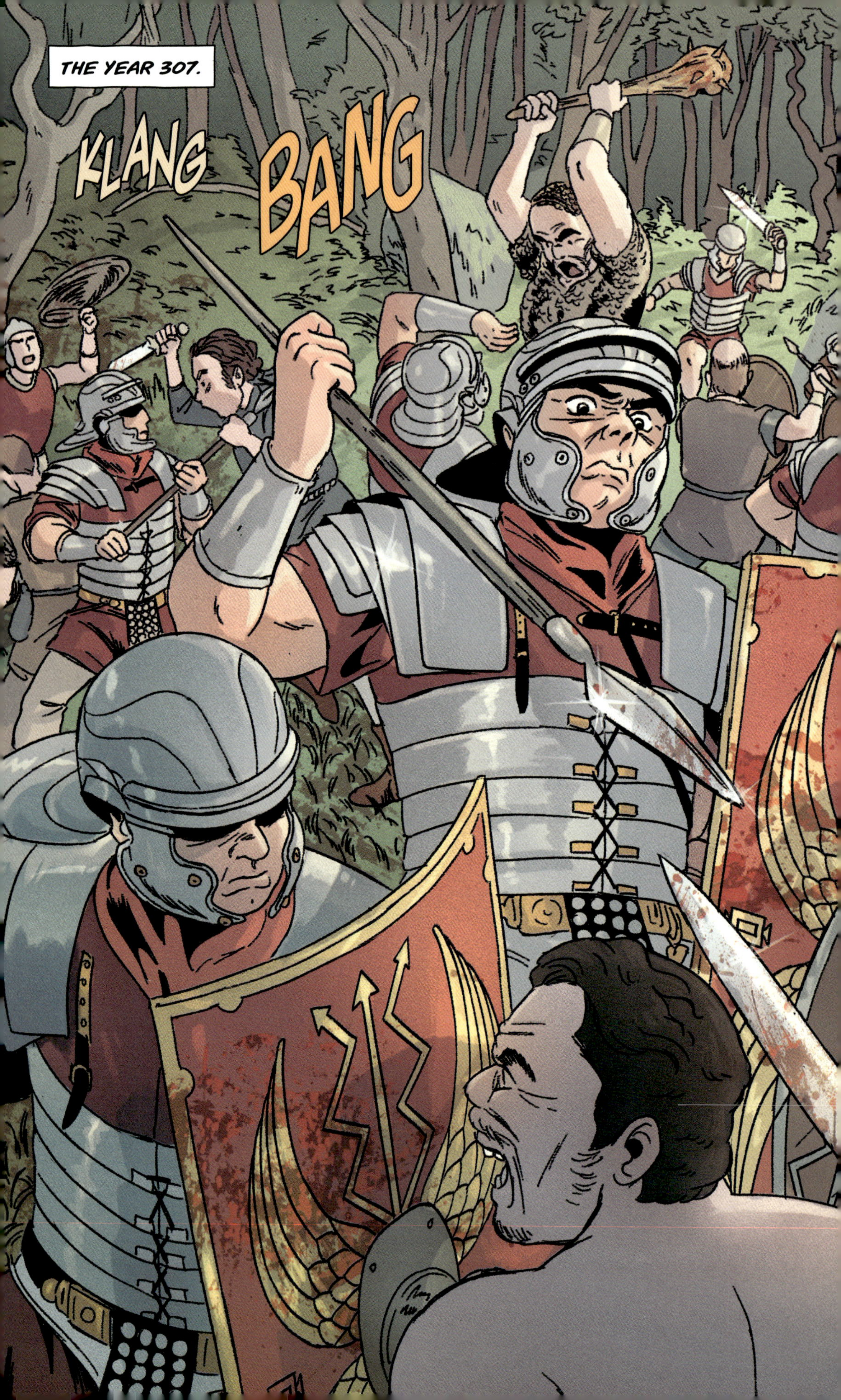
THE YEAR 307.
KLANG
BANG

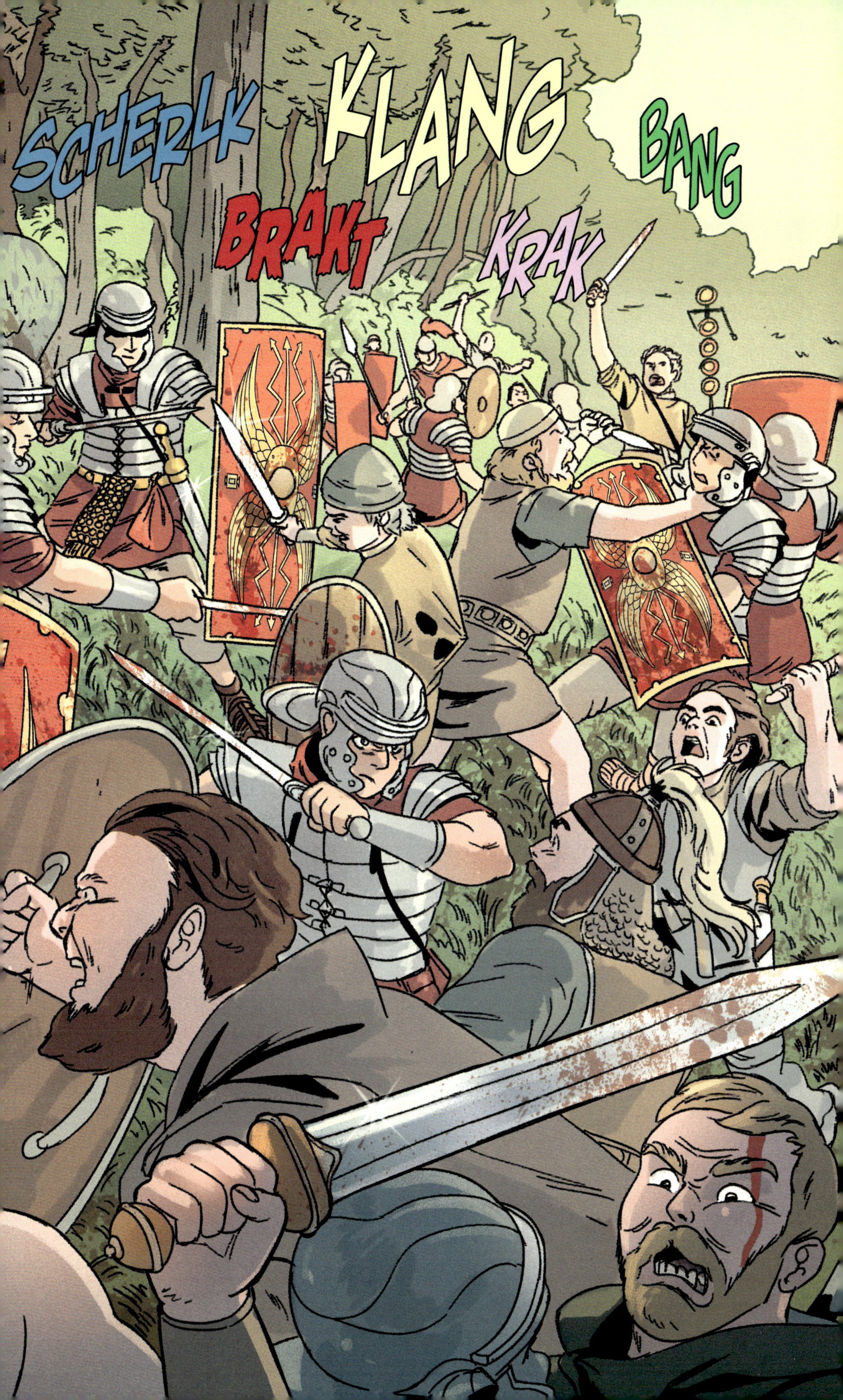
SCHERLK
KLANG
BANG
BRAKT
KRAK

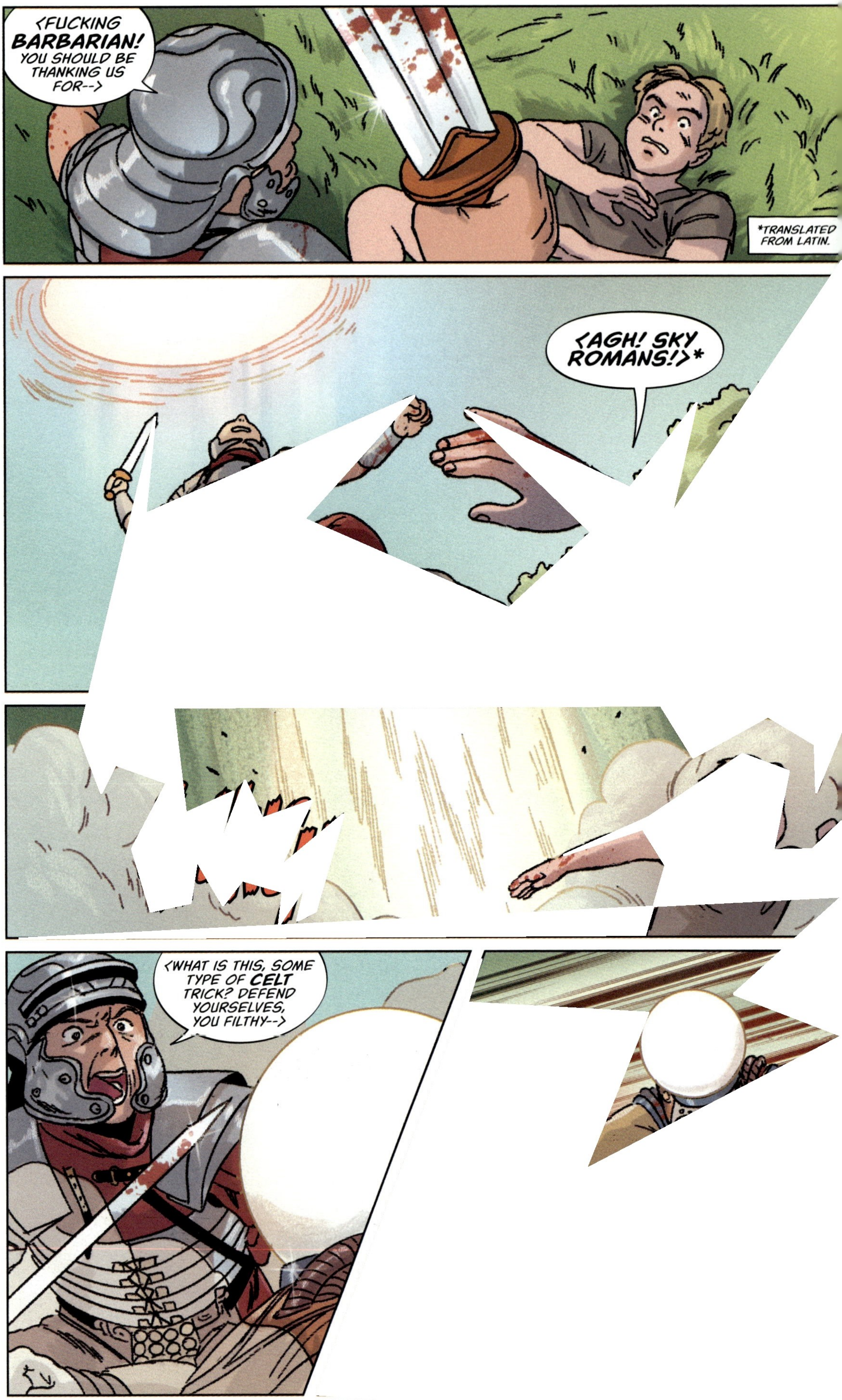

<FUCKING BARBARIAN! YOU SHOULD BE THANKING US FOR-->
*TRANSLATED FROM LATIN.
<AGH! SKY ROMANS!>*
<WHAT IS THIS, SOME TYPE OF CELT TRICK? DEFEND YOURSELVES, YOU FILTHY-->

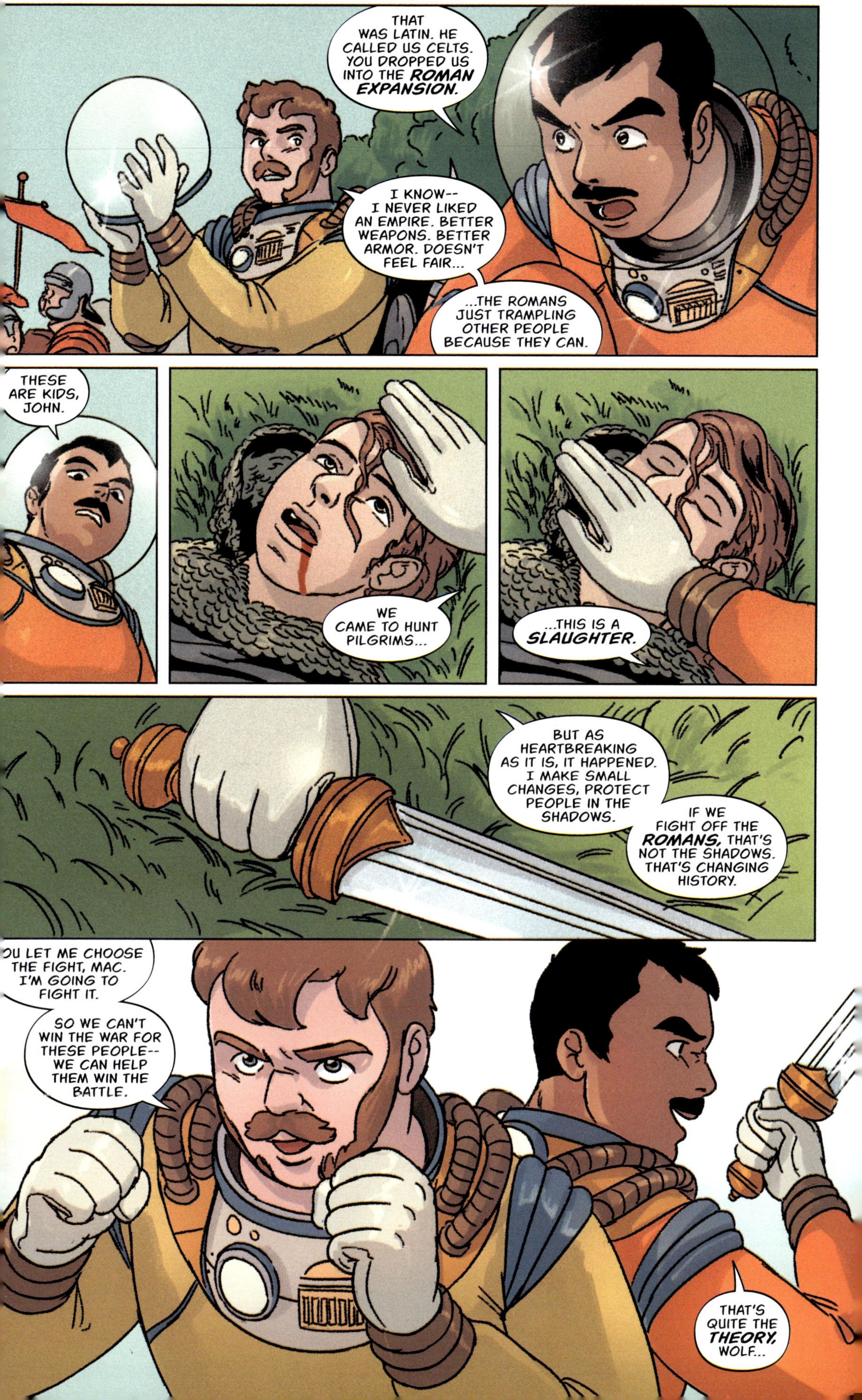

THAT WAS LATIN. HE CALLED US CELTS. YOU DROPPED US INTO THE **ROMAN EXPANSION.**
I KNOW-- I NEVER LIKED AN EMPIRE. BETTER WEAPONS. BETTER ARMOR. DOESN'T FEEL FAIR...
...THE ROMANS JUST TRAMPLING OTHER PEOPLE BECAUSE THEY CAN.
THESE ARE KIDS, JOHN.
WE CAME TO HUNT PILGRIMS...
...THIS IS A **SLAUGHTER.**
BUT AS HEARTBREAKING AS IT IS, IT HAPPENED. I MAKE SMALL CHANGES, PROTECT PEOPLE IN THE SHADOWS.
IF WE FIGHT OFF THE **ROMANS,** THAT'S NOT THE SHADOWS. THAT'S CHANGING HISTORY.
OU LET ME CHOOSE THE FIGHT, MAC. I'M GOING TO FIGHT IT.
SO WE CAN'T WIN THE WAR FOR THESE PEOPLE-- WE CAN HELP THEM WIN THE BATTLE.
THAT'S QUITE THE **THEORY,** WOLF...

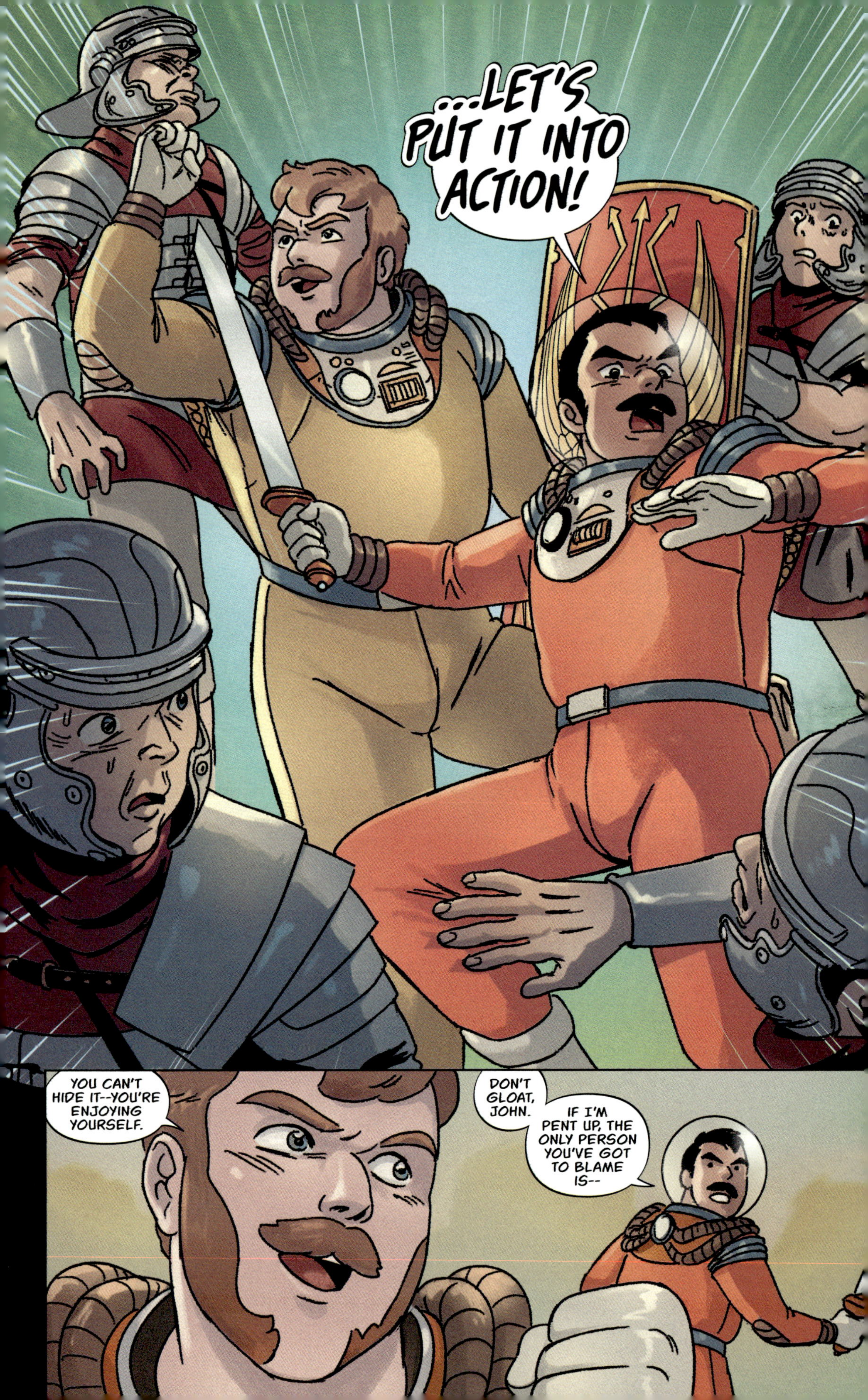
...LET'S PUT IT INTO ACTION!
YOU CAN'T HIDE IT--YOU'RE ENJOYING YOURSELF.
DON'T GLOAT, JOHN.
IF I'M PENT UP, THE ONLY PERSON YOU'VE GOT TO BLAME IS--

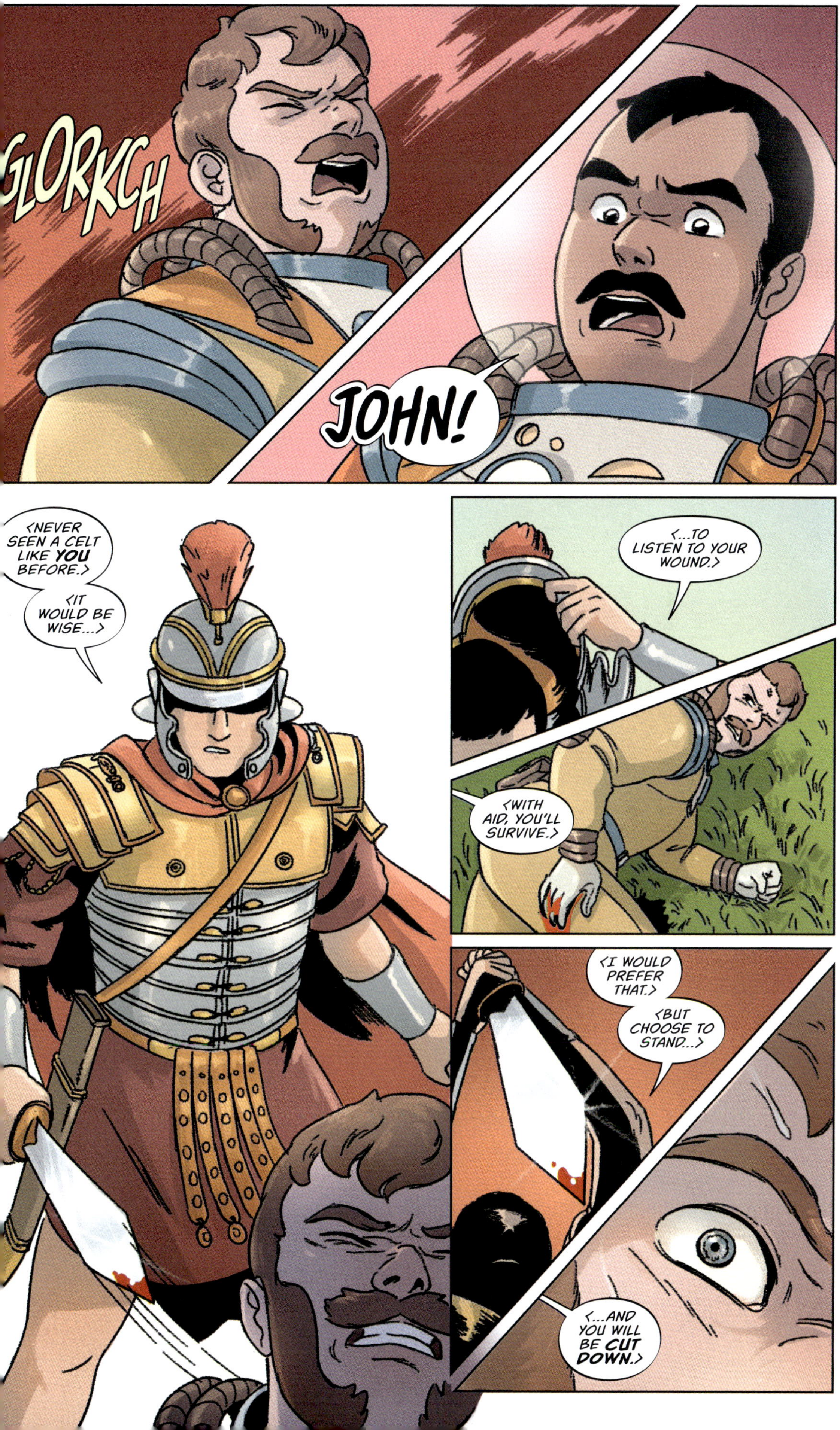
GLORKCH
JOHN!
<NEVER SEEN A CELT LIKE **YOU** BEFORE.>
<IT WOULD BE WISE...>
<...TO LISTEN TO YOUR WOUND.>
<WITH AID, YOU'LL SURVIVE.>
<I WOULD PREFER THAT.>
<BUT CHOOSE TO STAND...>
<...AND YOU WILL BE **CUT DOWN.**>

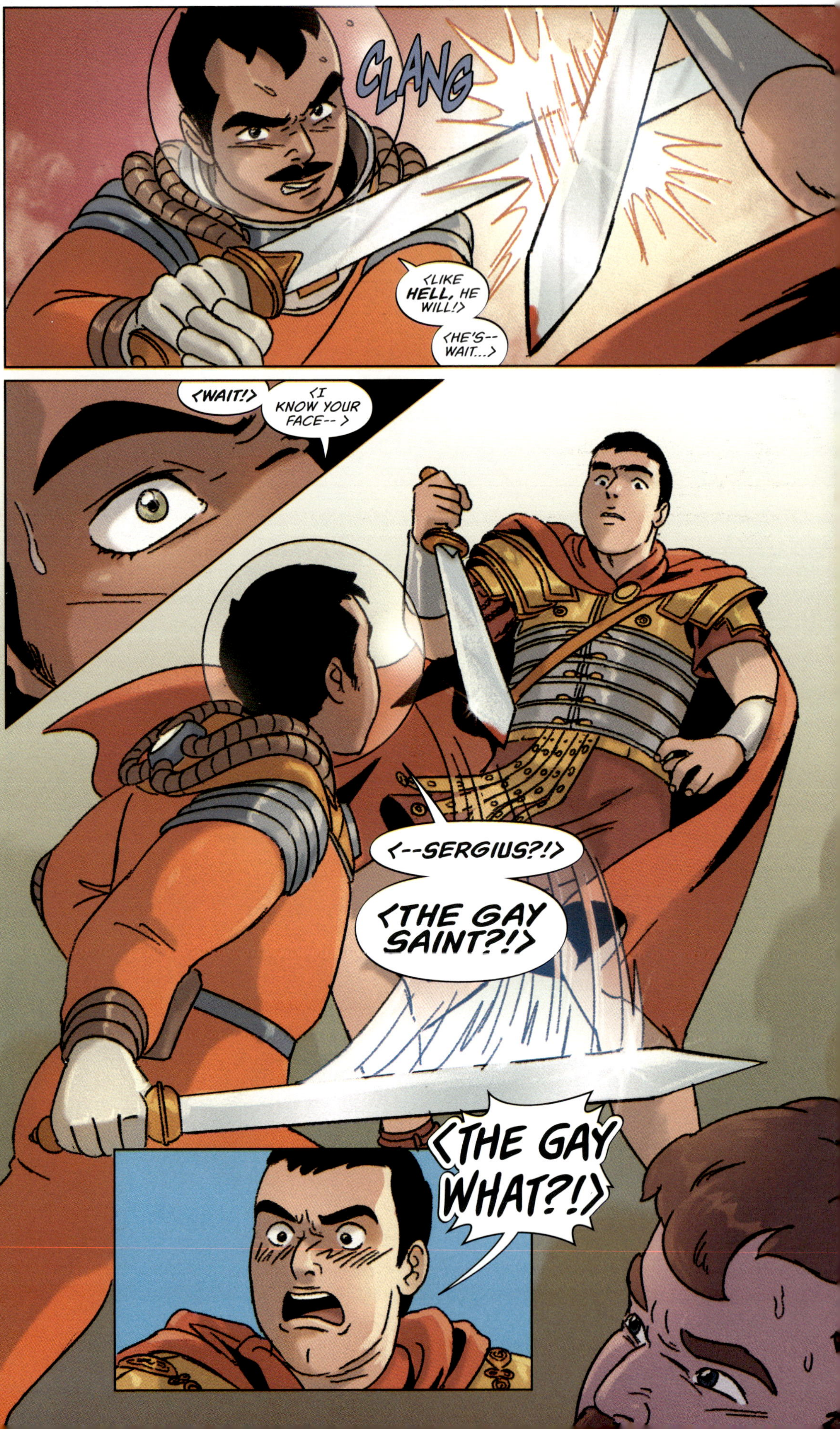
CLANG
<LIKE HELL, HE WILL!>
<HE'S-- WAIT...>
<WAIT!>
<I KNOW YOUR FACE-- >
<--SERGIUS?!>
<THE GAY SAINT?!>
<THE GAY WHAT?!>

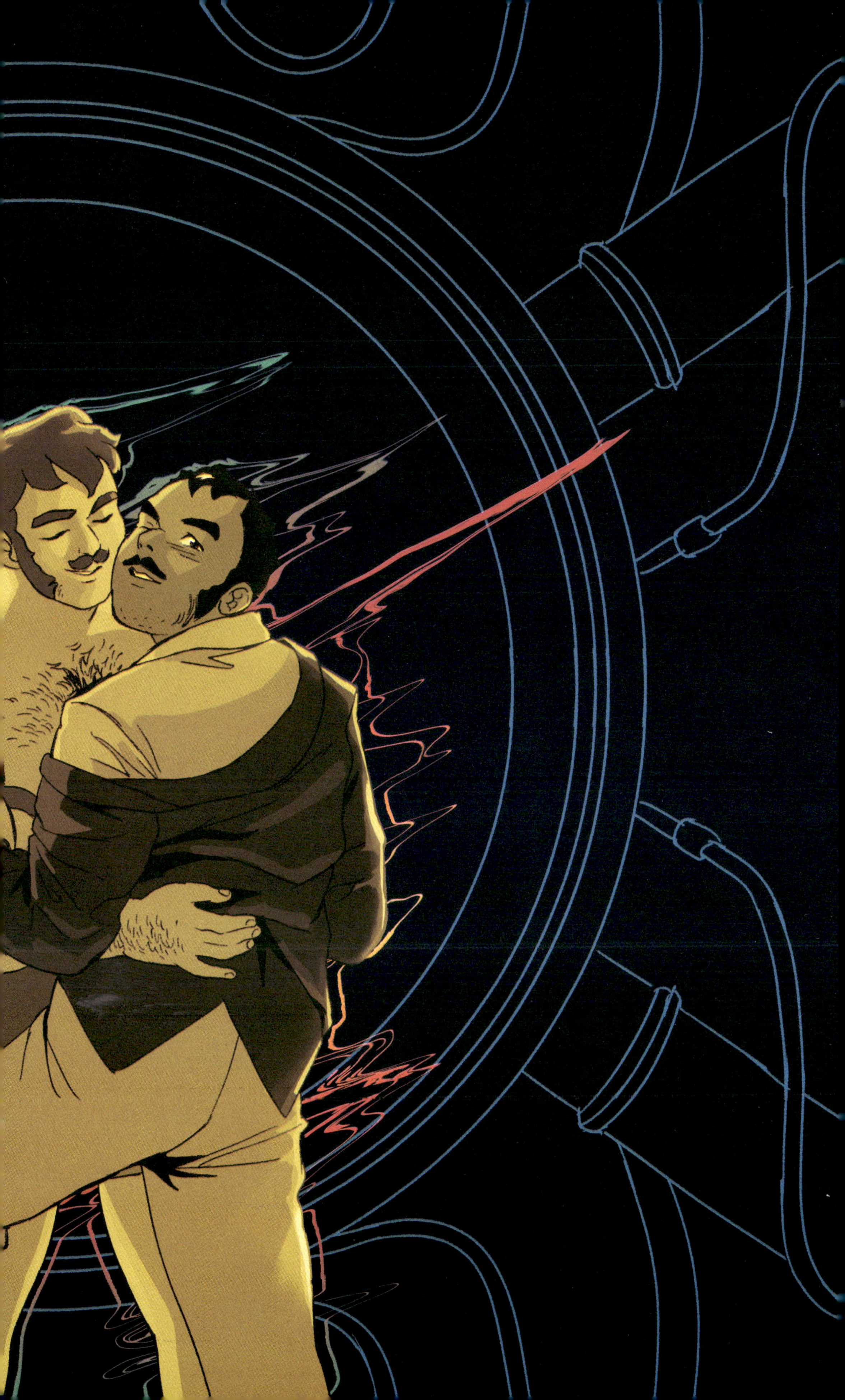

ancient

chapter III

rome

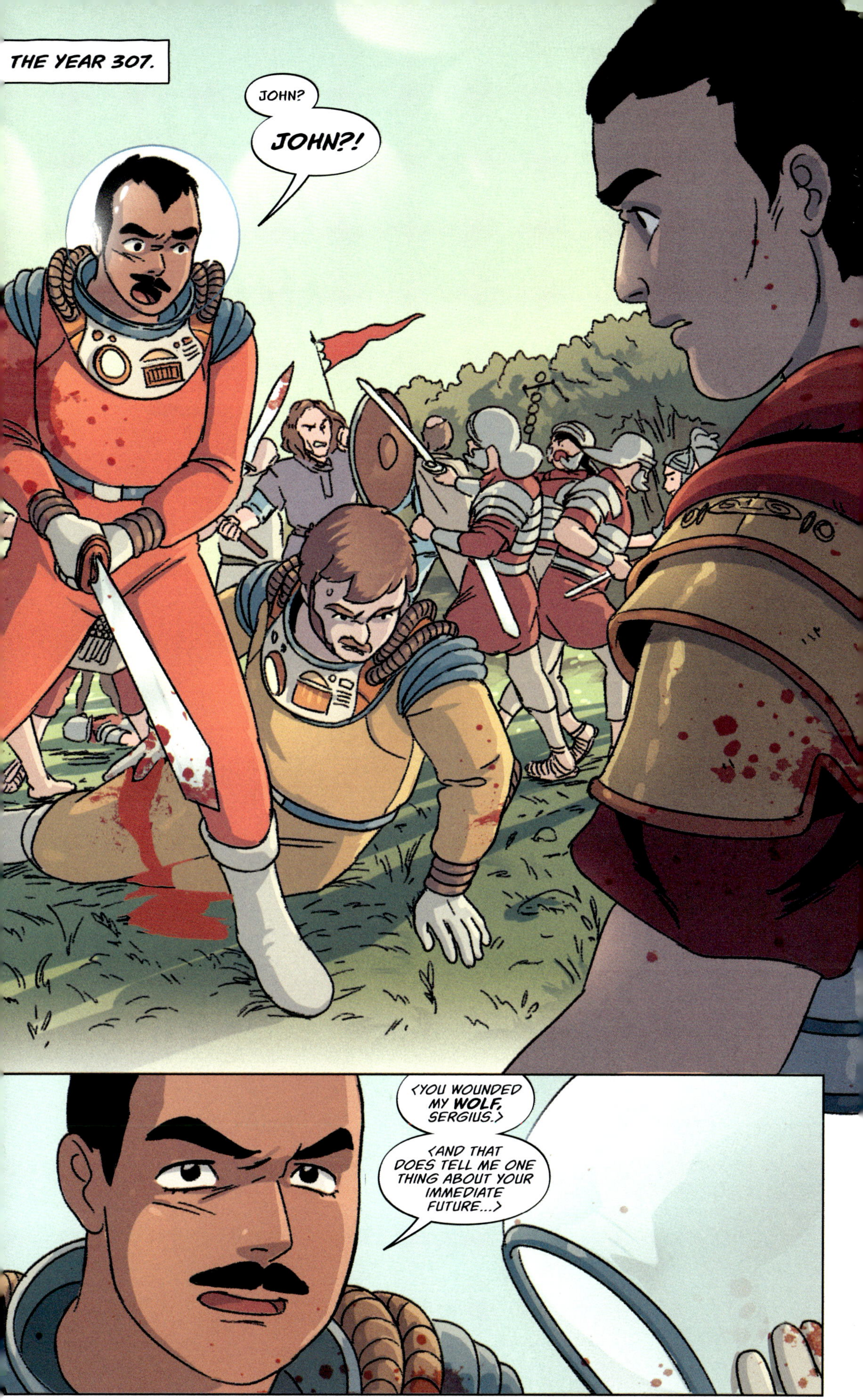

THE YEAR 307.
JOHN?
JOHN?!
<YOU WOUNDED MY WOLF, SERGIUS.>
<AND THAT DOES TELL ME ONE THING ABOUT YOUR IMMEDIATE FUTURE...>

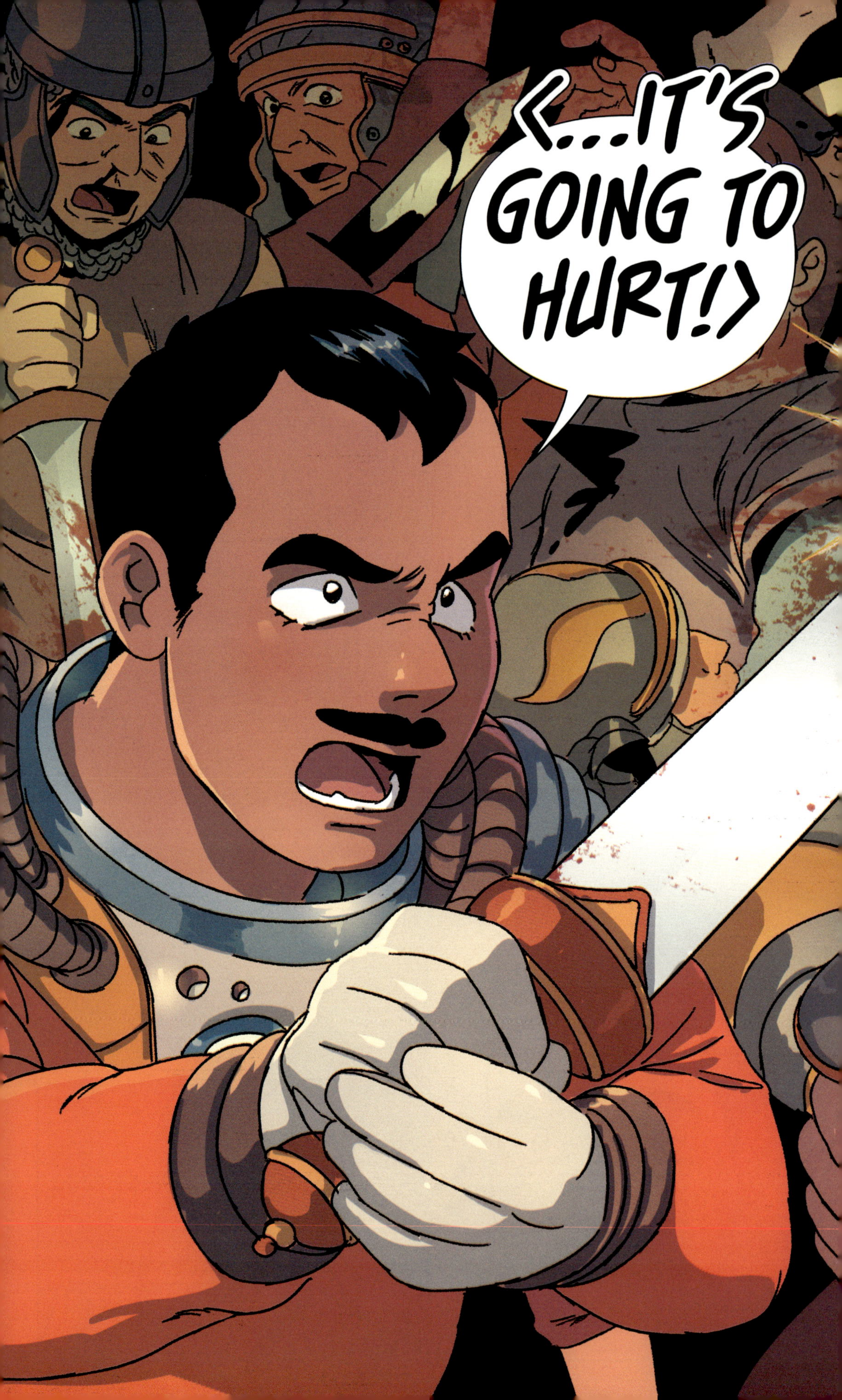
<...IT'S GOING TO HURT!>

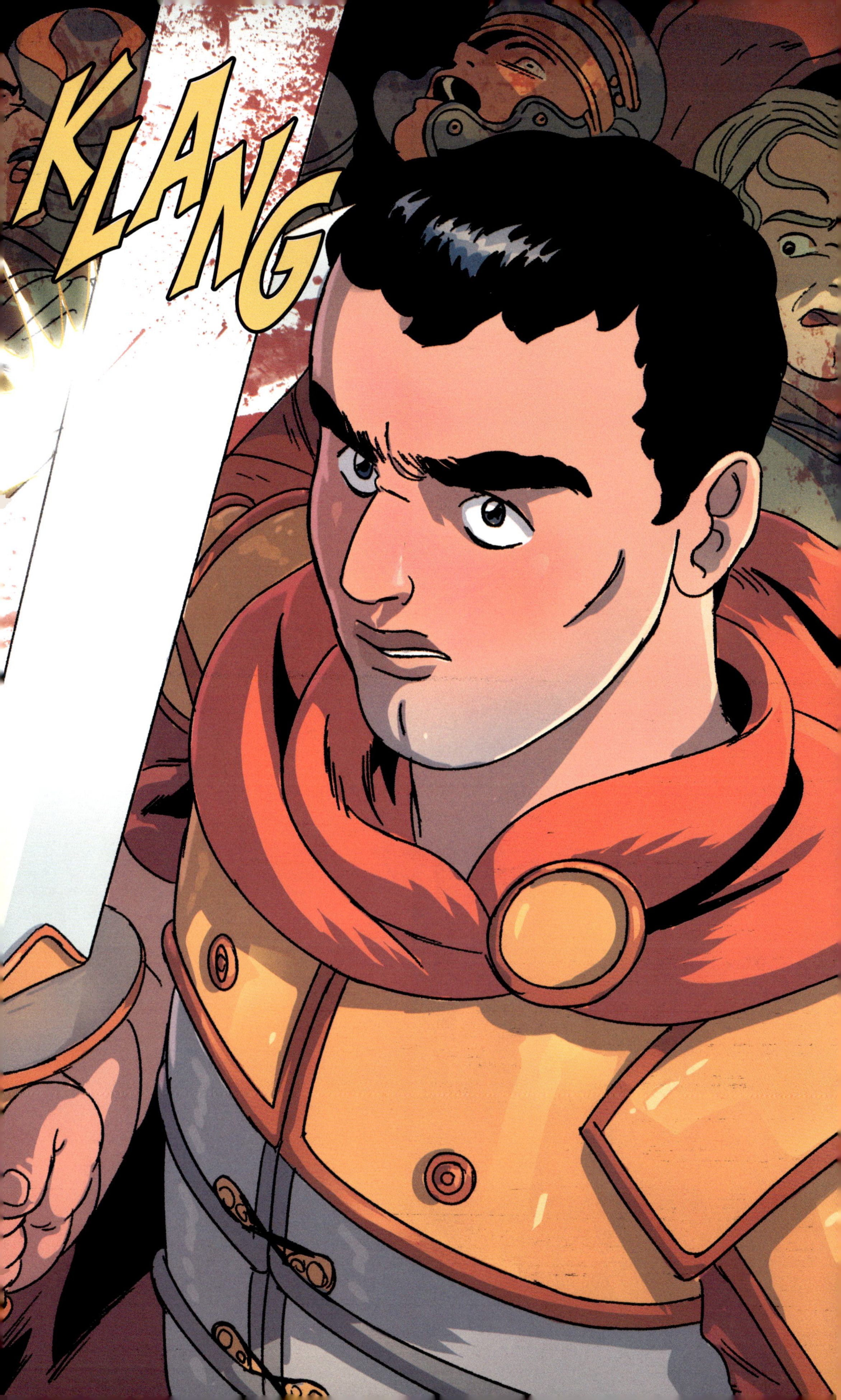
KLANG

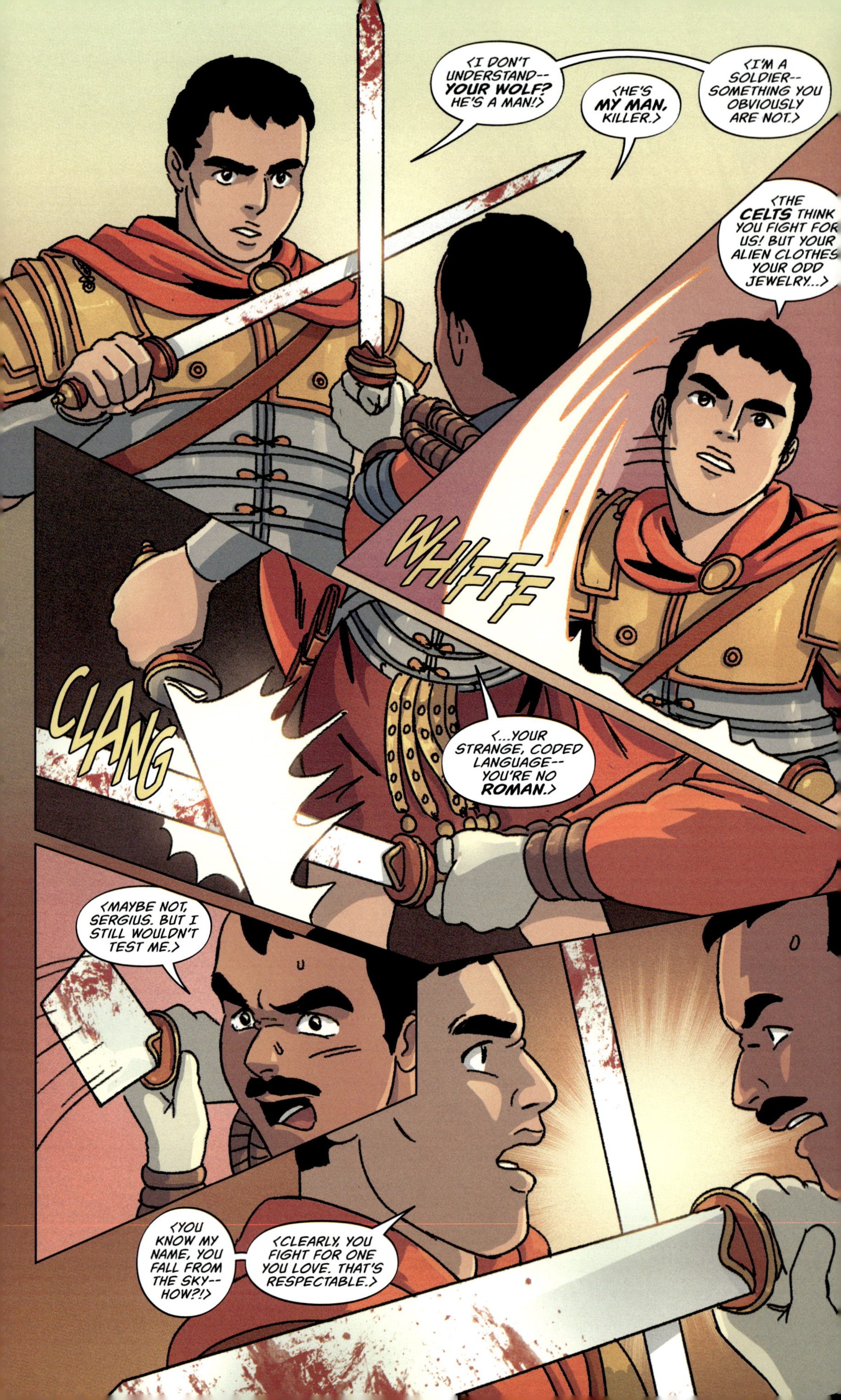

<I DON'T UNDERSTAND-- YOUR WOLF? HE'S A MAN!>
<HE'S MY MAN, KILLER.>
<I'M A SOLDIER-- SOMETHING YOU OBVIOUSLY ARE NOT.>
<THE CELTS THINK YOU FIGHT FOR US! BUT YOUR ALIEN CLOTHES, YOUR ODD JEWELRY...>
WHIFFF
CLANG
<...YOUR STRANGE, CODED LANGUAGE-- YOU'RE NO ROMAN.>
<MAYBE NOT, SERGIUS. BUT I STILL WOULDN'T TEST ME.>
<YOU KNOW MY NAME, YOU FALL FROM THE SKY-- HOW?!>
<CLEARLY, YOU FIGHT FOR ONE YOU LOVE. THAT'S RESPECTABLE.>

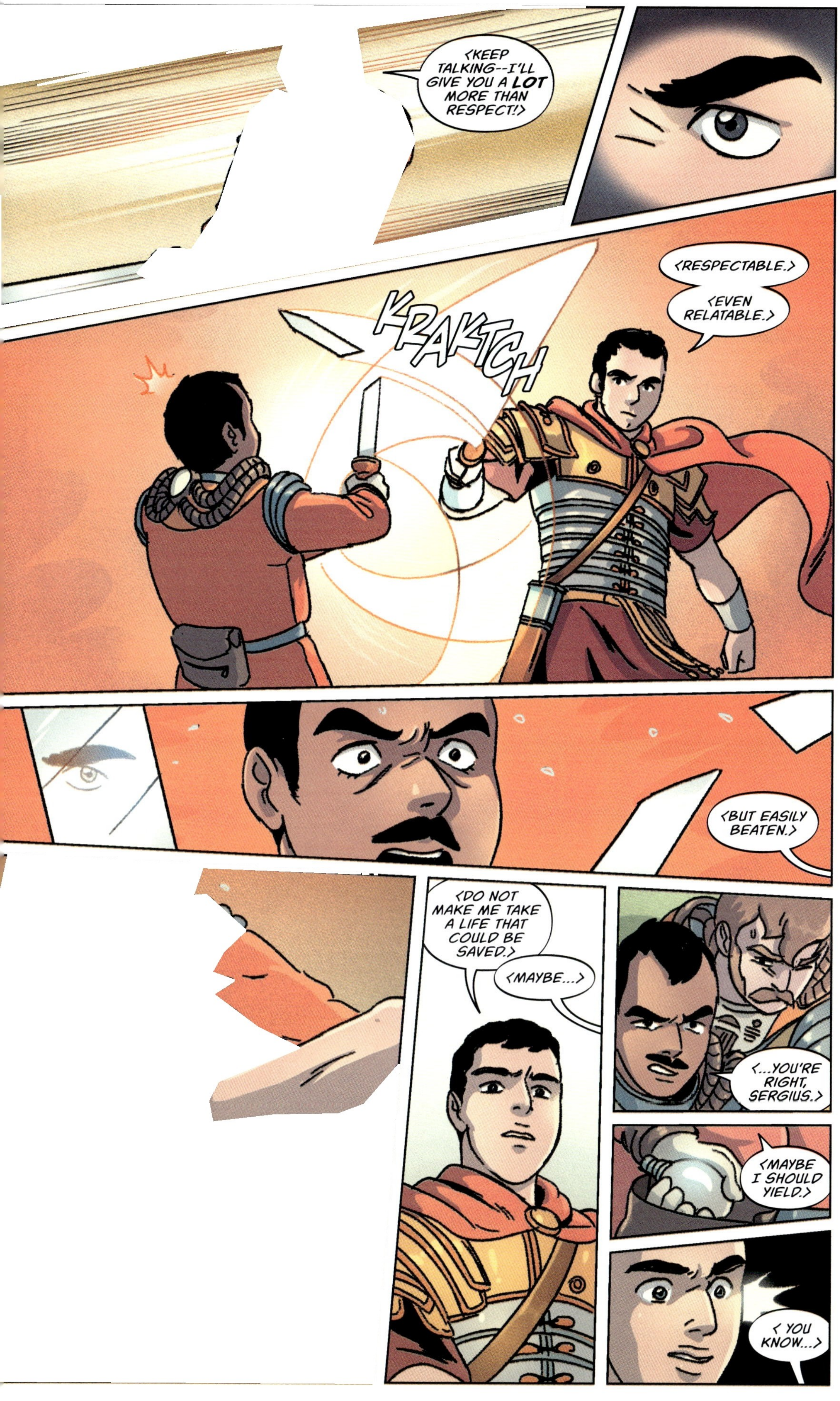
<KEEP TALKING--I'LL GIVE YOU A **LOT** MORE THAN RESPECT!>
<RESPECTABLE.>
<EVEN RELATABLE.>
KRAKTCH
<BUT EASILY BEATEN.>
<DO NOT MAKE ME TAKE A LIFE THAT COULD BE SAVED.>
<MAYBE...>
<...YOU'RE RIGHT, SERGIUS.>
<MAYBE I SHOULD YIELD.>
< YOU KNOW...>

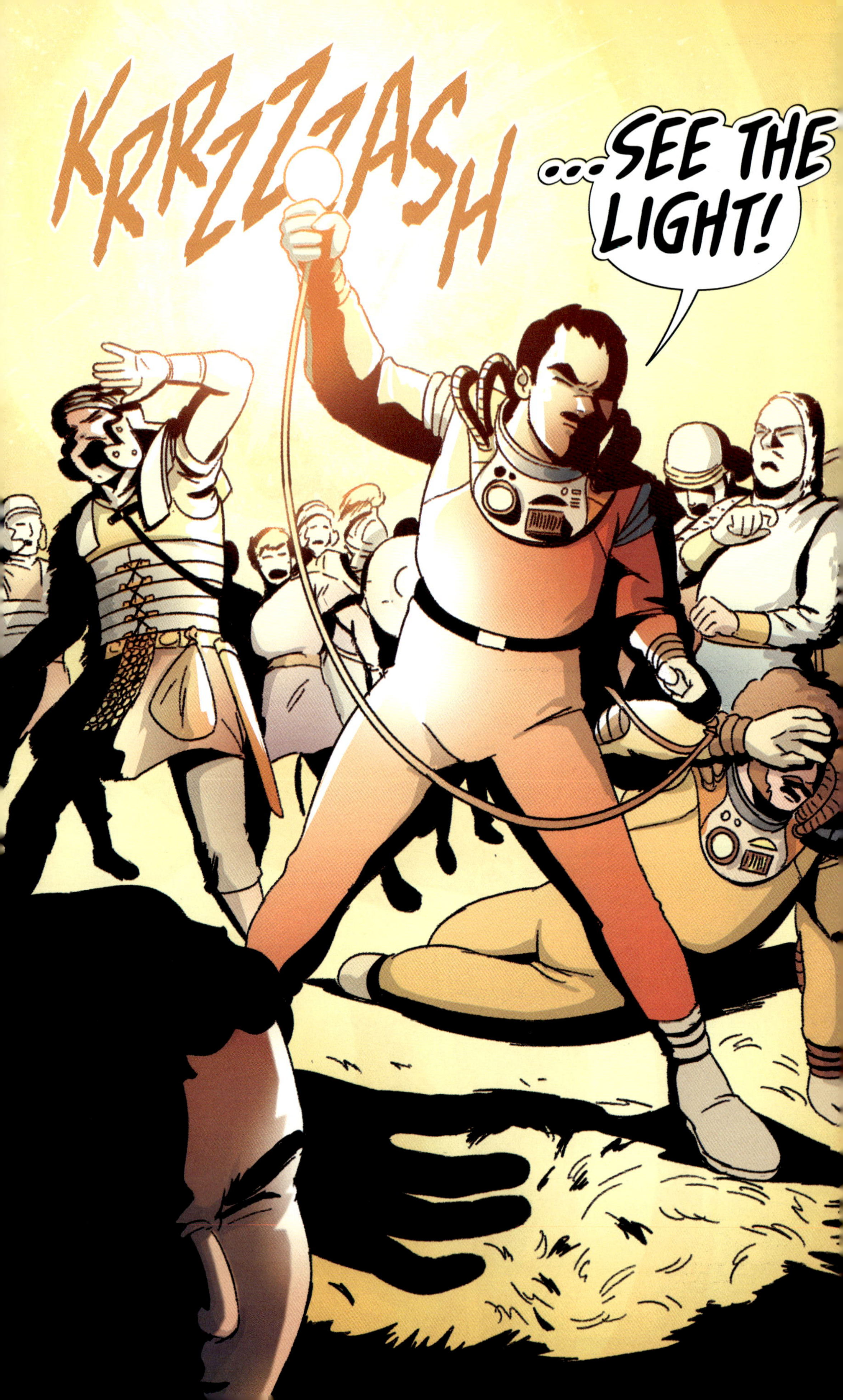
KRRZZZASH
...SEE THE LIGHT!

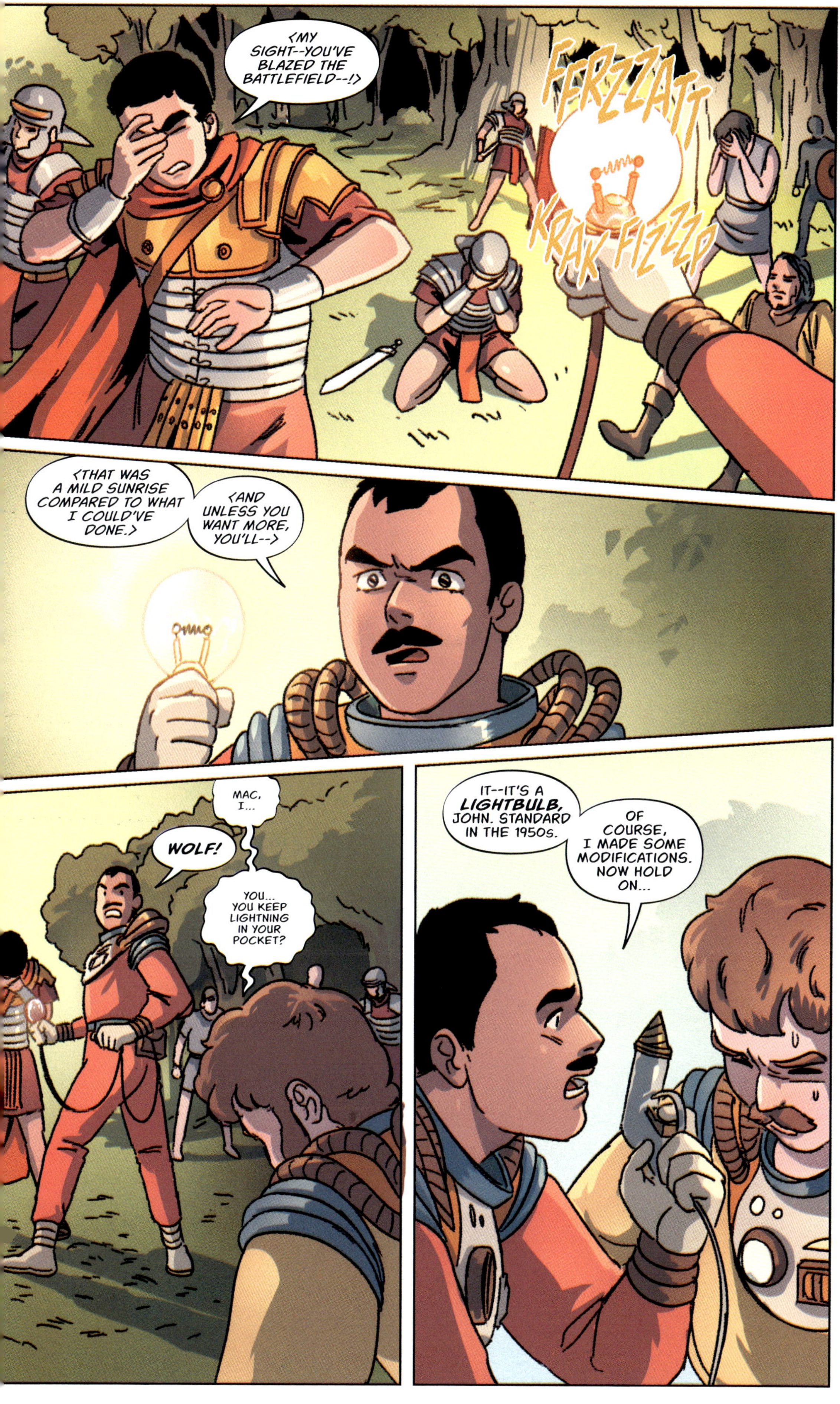
<MY SIGHT--YOU'VE BLAZED THE BATTLEFIELD--!>
FFERZZATT
KRAK FIZZZP
<THAT WAS A MILD SUNRISE COMPARED TO WHAT I COULD'VE DONE.>
<AND UNLESS YOU WANT MORE, YOU'LL-->
MAC, I...
WOLF!
YOU... YOU KEEP LIGHTNING IN YOUR POCKET?
IT--IT'S A LIGHTBULB, JOHN. STANDARD IN THE 1950s.
OF COURSE, I MADE SOME MODIFICATIONS. NOW HOLD ON...

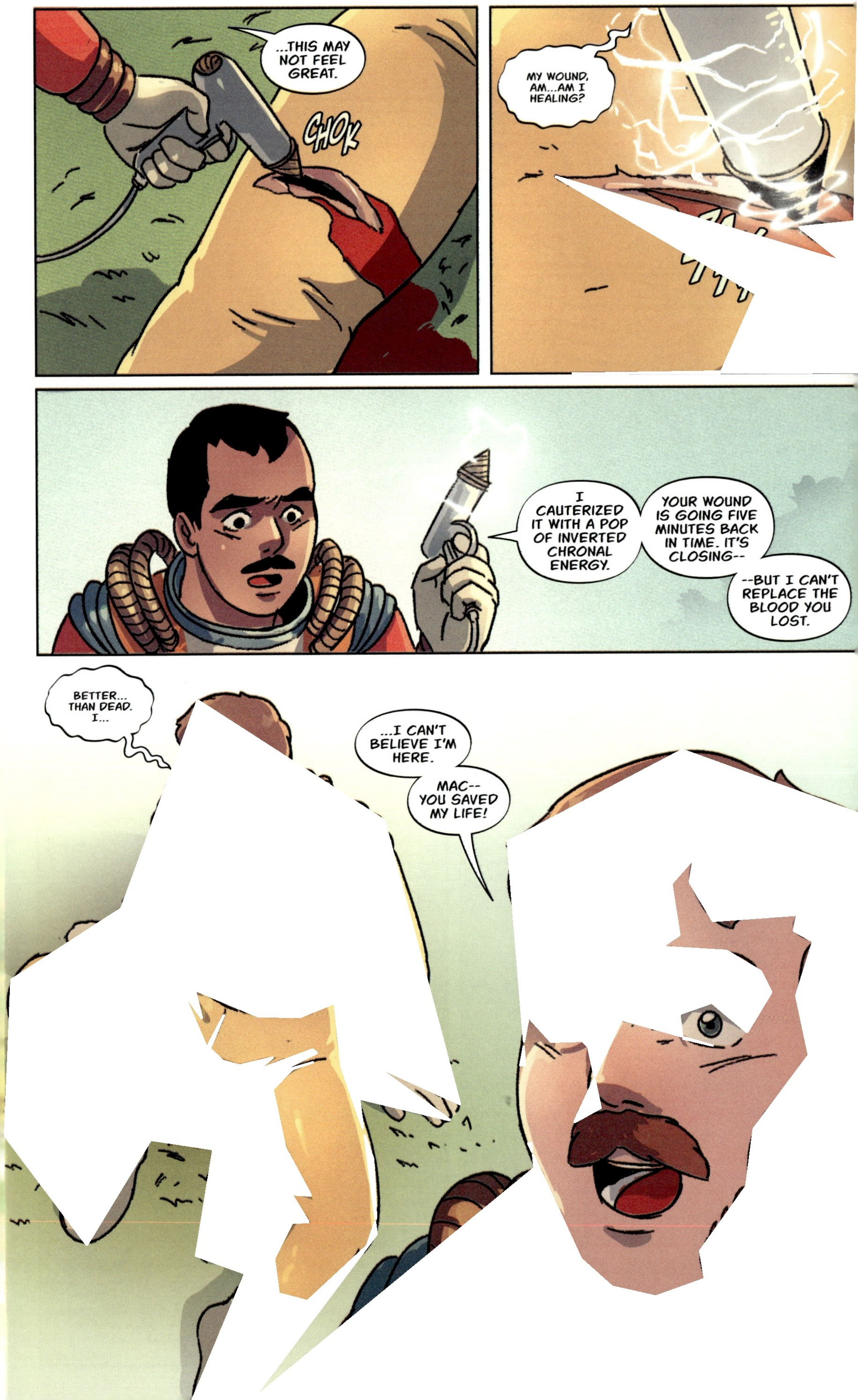
...THIS MAY NOT FEEL GREAT.
CHOK
MY WOUND, AM...AM I HEALING?
I CAUTERIZED IT WITH A POP OF INVERTED CHRONAL ENERGY.
YOUR WOUND IS GOING FIVE MINUTES BACK IN TIME. IT'S CLOSING--
--BUT I CAN'T REPLACE THE BLOOD YOU LOST.
BETTER... THAN DEAD. I...
...I CAN'T BELIEVE I'M HERE.
MAC-- YOU SAVED MY LIFE!

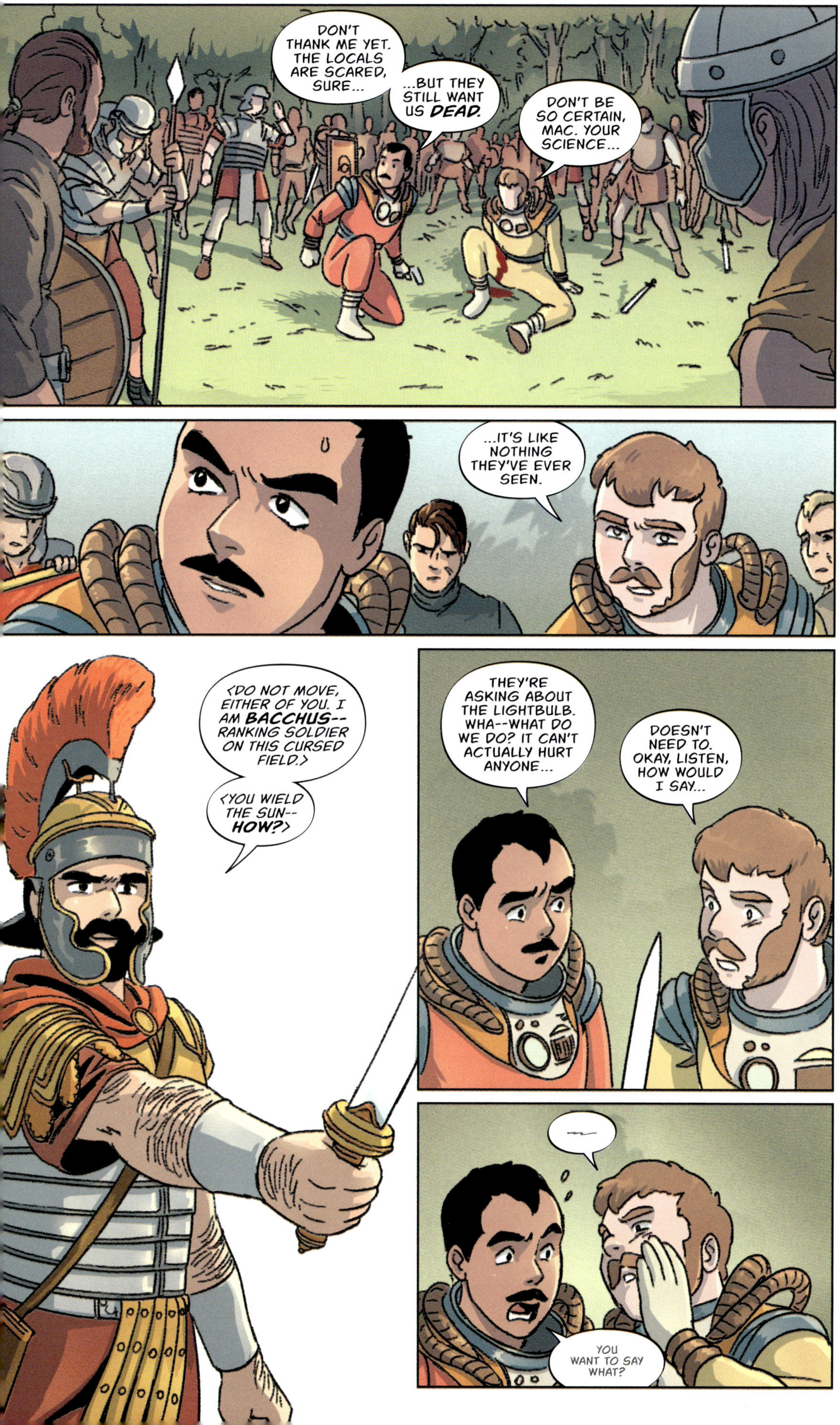
DON'T THANK ME YET. THE LOCALS ARE SCARED, SURE...
...BUT THEY STILL WANT US **DEAD.**
DON'T BE SO CERTAIN, MAC. YOUR SCIENCE...
...IT'S LIKE NOTHING THEY'VE EVER SEEN.
<DO NOT MOVE, EITHER OF YOU. I AM **BACCHUS--** RANKING SOLDIER ON THIS CURSED FIELD.>
<YOU WIELD THE SUN-- **HOW?**>
THEY'RE ASKING ABOUT THE LIGHTBULB. WHA--WHAT DO WE DO? IT CAN'T ACTUALLY HURT ANYONE...
DOESN'T NEED TO. OKAY, LISTEN, HOW WOULD I SAY...
YOU WANT TO SAY WHAT?

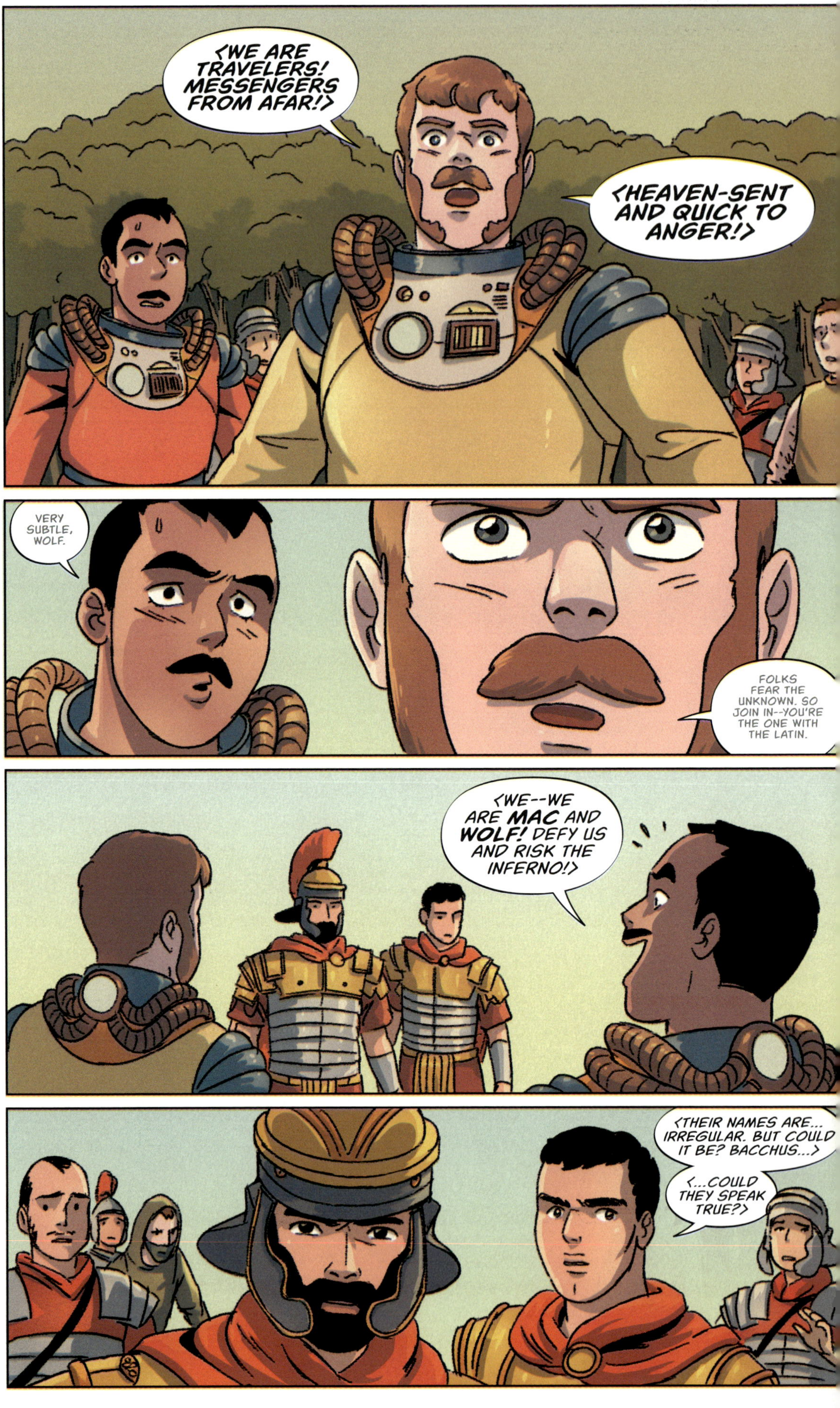

<WE ARE TRAVELERS! MESSENGERS FROM AFAR!>
<HEAVEN-SENT AND QUICK TO ANGER!>
VERY SUBTLE, WOLF.
FOLKS FEAR THE UNKNOWN. SO JOIN IN--YOU'RE THE ONE WITH THE LATIN.
<WE--WE ARE **MAC** AND **WOLF!** DEFY US AND RISK THE INFERNO!>
<THEIR NAMES ARE... IRREGULAR. BUT COULD IT BE? BACCHUS...>
<...COULD THEY SPEAK TRUE?>

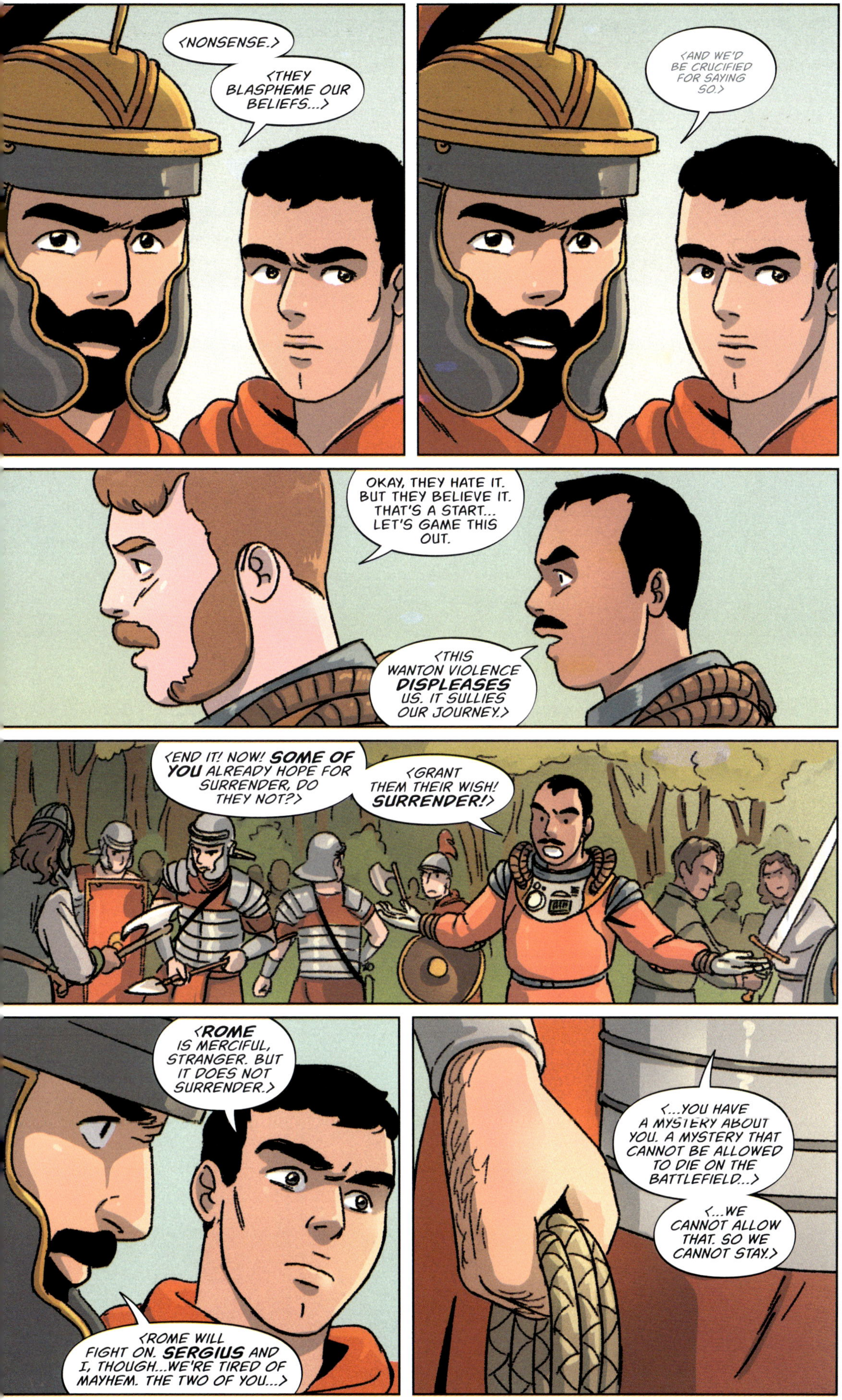

<NONSENSE.>
<THEY BLASPHEME OUR BELIEFS...>
<AND WE'D BE CRUCIFIED FOR SAYING SO.>
OKAY, THEY HATE IT. BUT THEY BELIEVE IT. THAT'S A START... LET'S GAME THIS OUT.
<THIS WANTON VIOLENCE **DISPLEASES** US. IT SULLIES OUR JOURNEY.>
<END IT! NOW! **SOME OF YOU** ALREADY HOPE FOR SURRENDER, DO THEY NOT?>
<GRANT THEM THEIR WISH! **SURRENDER!**>
<**ROME** IS MERCIFUL, STRANGER. BUT IT DOES NOT SURRENDER.>
<ROME WILL FIGHT ON. **SERGIUS** AND I, THOUGH... WE'RE TIRED OF MAYHEM. THE TWO OF YOU...>
<...YOU HAVE A MYSTERY ABOUT YOU. A MYSTERY THAT CANNOT BE ALLOWED TO DIE ON THE BATTLEFIELD...>
<...WE CANNOT ALLOW THAT. SO WE CANNOT STAY.>

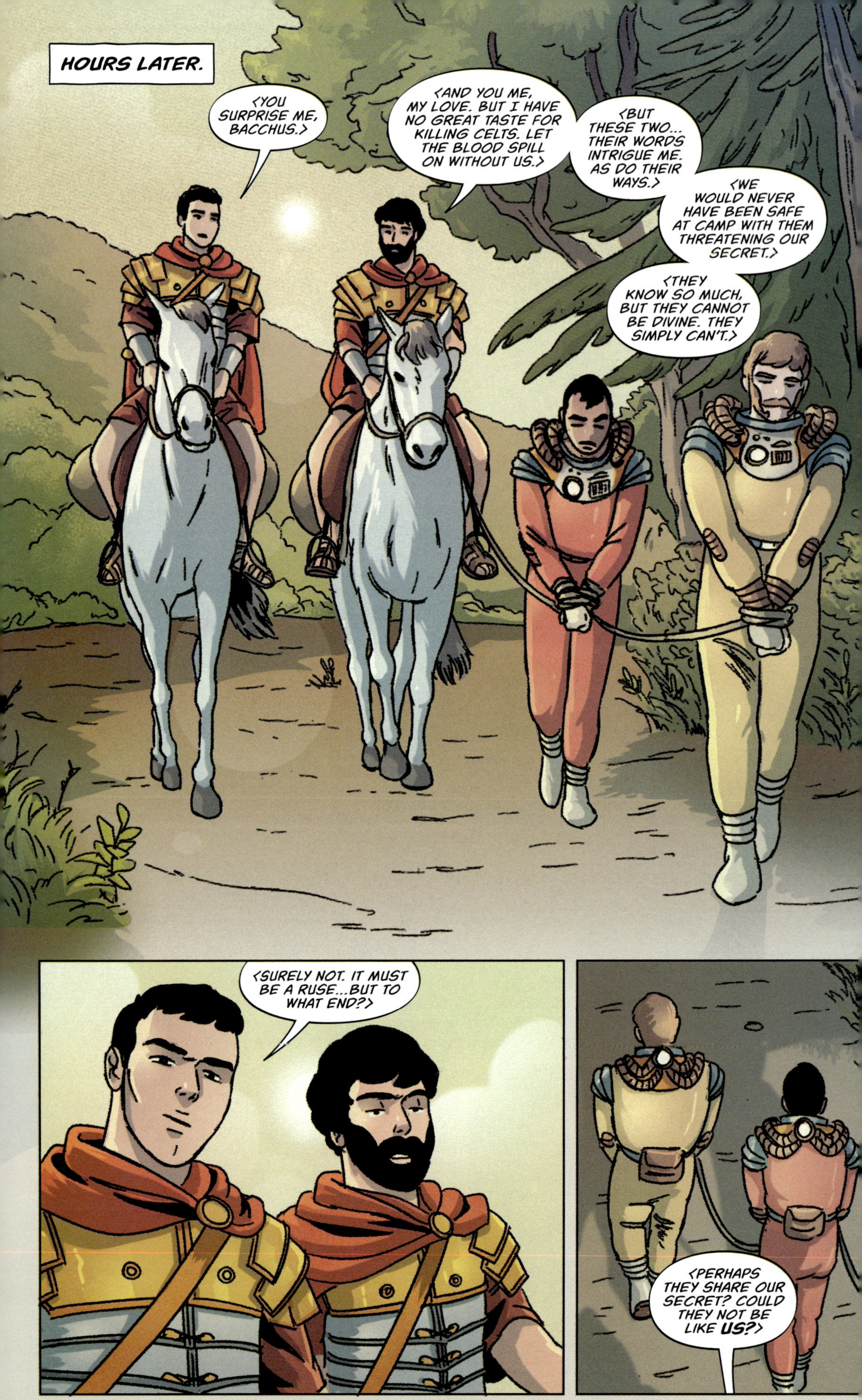
HOURS LATER.
<YOU SURPRISE ME, BACCHUS.>
<AND YOU ME, MY LOVE. BUT I HAVE NO GREAT TASTE FOR KILLING CELTS. LET THE BLOOD SPILL ON WITHOUT US.>
<BUT THESE TWO... THEIR WORDS INTRIGUE ME. AS DO THEIR WAYS.>
<WE WOULD NEVER HAVE BEEN SAFE AT CAMP WITH THEM THREATENING OUR SECRET.>
<THEY KNOW SO MUCH, BUT THEY CANNOT BE DIVINE. THEY SIMPLY CAN'T.>
<SURELY NOT. IT MUST BE A RUSE...BUT TO WHAT END?>
<PERHAPS THEY SHARE OUR SECRET? COULD THEY NOT BE LIKE US?>

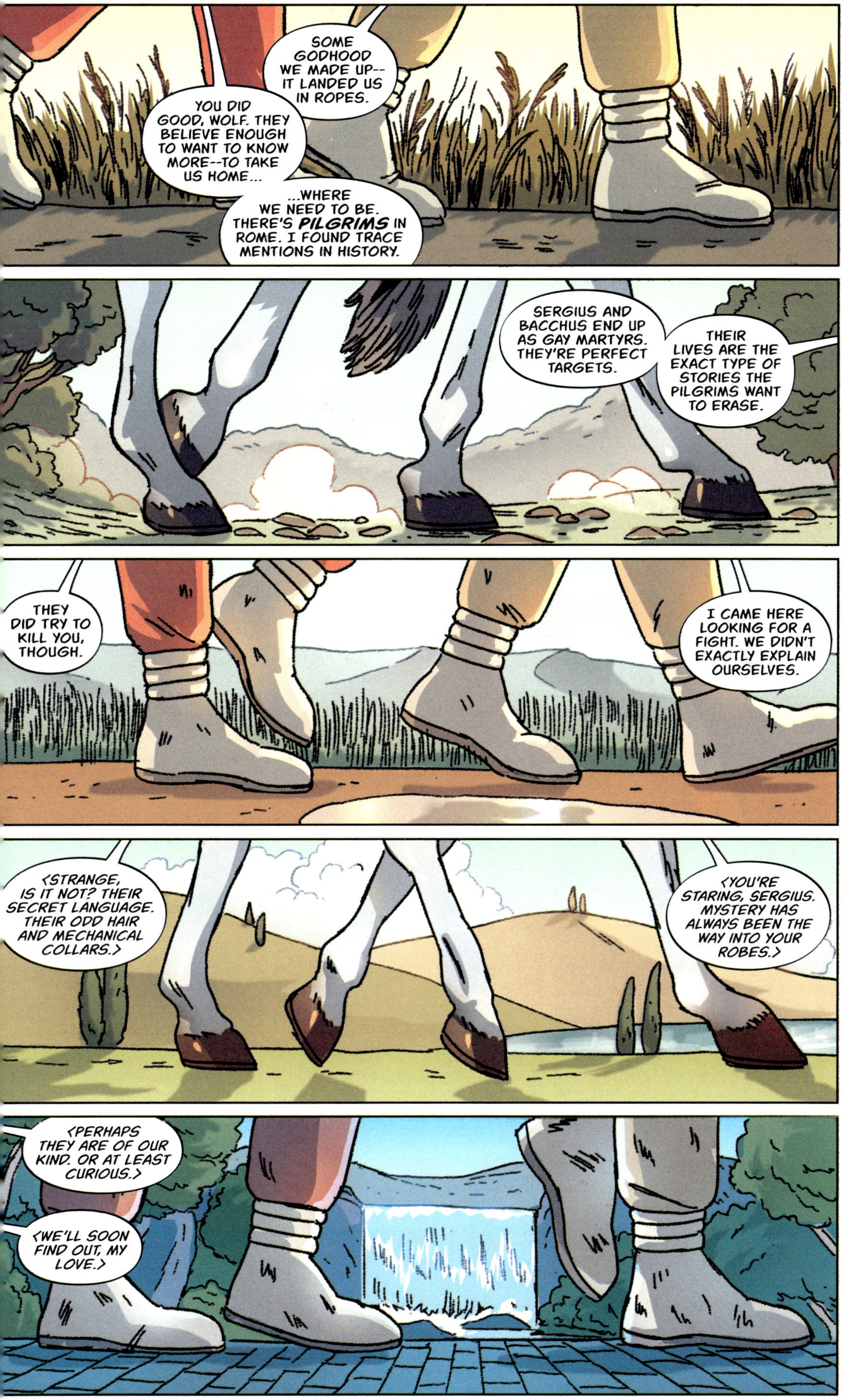
SOME GODHOOD WE MADE UP-- IT LANDED US IN ROPES.
YOU DID GOOD, WOLF. THEY BELIEVE ENOUGH TO WANT TO KNOW MORE--TO TAKE US HOME...
...WHERE WE NEED TO BE. THERE'S PILGRIMS IN ROME. I FOUND TRACE MENTIONS IN HISTORY.
SERGIUS AND BACCHUS END UP AS GAY MARTYRS. THEY'RE PERFECT TARGETS.
THEIR LIVES ARE THE EXACT TYPE OF STORIES THE PILGRIMS WANT TO ERASE.
THEY DID TRY TO KILL YOU, THOUGH.
I CAME HERE LOOKING FOR A FIGHT. WE DIDN'T EXACTLY EXPLAIN OURSELVES.
<STRANGE, IS IT NOT? THEIR SECRET LANGUAGE. THEIR ODD HAIR AND MECHANICAL COLLARS.>
<YOU'RE STARING, SERGIUS. MYSTERY HAS ALWAYS BEEN THE WAY INTO YOUR ROBES.>
<PERHAPS THEY ARE OF OUR KIND. OR AT LEAST CURIOUS.>
<WE'LL SOON FIND OUT, MY LOVE.>

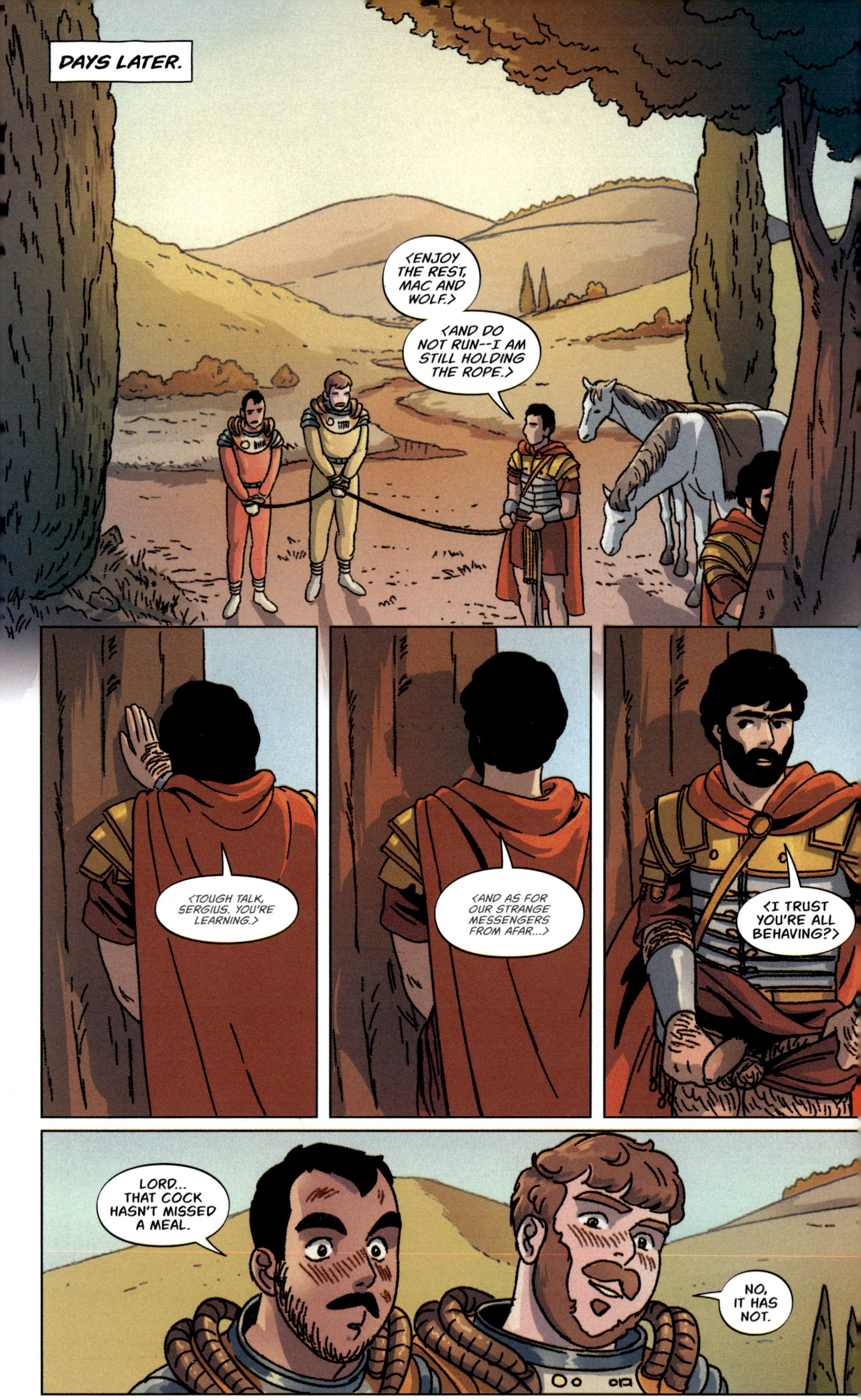
DAYS LATER.
<ENJOY THE REST, MAC AND WOLF.>
<AND DO NOT RUN--I AM STILL HOLDING THE ROPE.>
<TOUGH TALK, SERGIUS. YOU'RE LEARNING.>
<AND AS FOR OUR STRANGE MESSENGERS FROM AFAR...>
<I TRUST YOU'RE ALL BEHAVING?>
LORD... THAT COCK HASN'T MISSED A MEAL.
NO, IT HAS NOT.

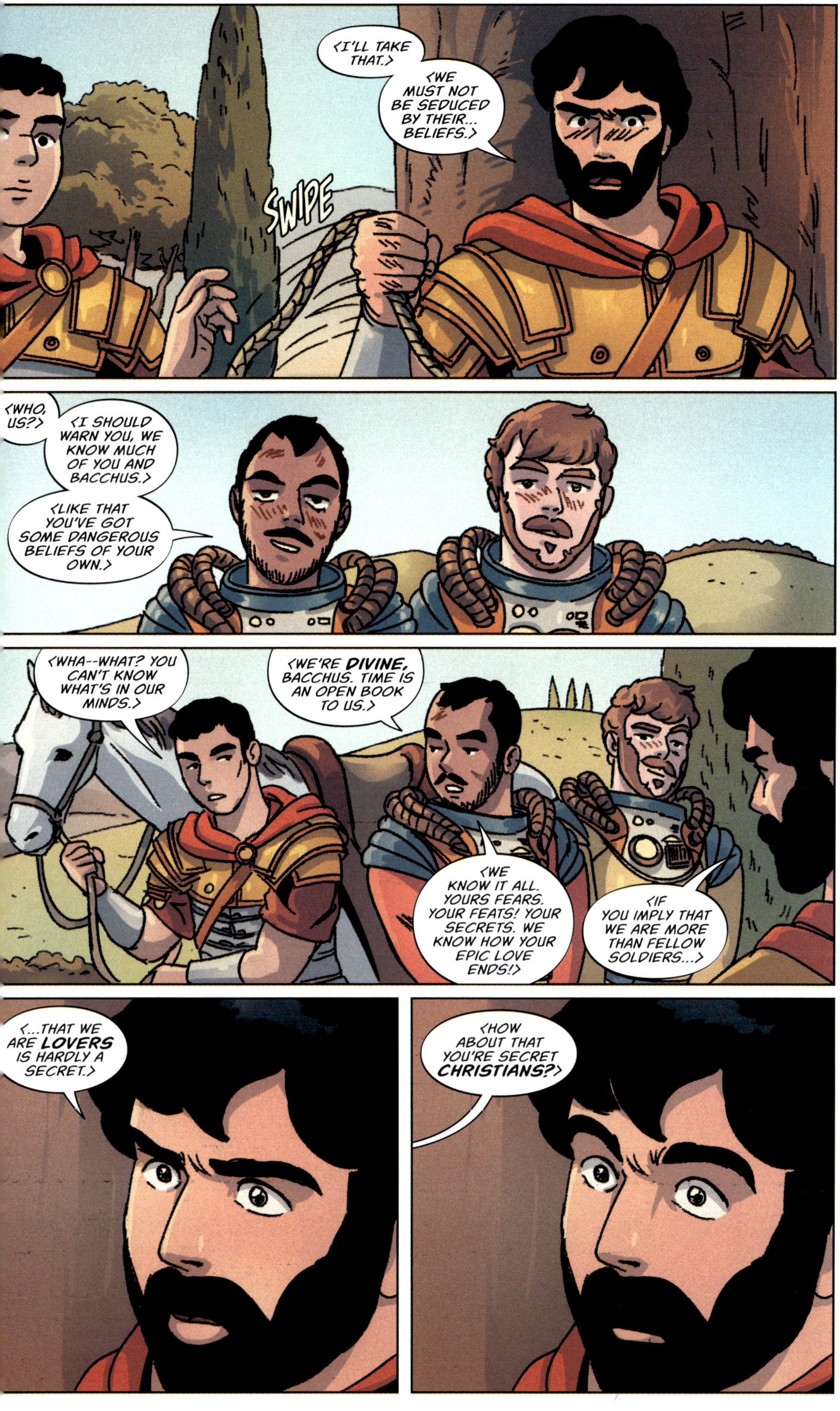
<I'LL TAKE THAT.>
<WE MUST NOT BE SEDUCED BY THEIR... BELIEFS.>
SWIPE
<WHO, US?>
<I SHOULD WARN YOU, WE KNOW MUCH OF YOU AND BACCHUS.>
<LIKE THAT YOU'VE GOT SOME DANGEROUS BELIEFS OF YOUR OWN.>
<WHA--WHAT? YOU CAN'T KNOW WHAT'S IN OUR MINDS.>
<WE'RE **DIVINE,** BACCHUS. TIME IS AN OPEN BOOK TO US.>
<WE KNOW IT ALL. YOURS FEARS. YOUR FEATS! YOUR SECRETS. WE KNOW HOW YOUR EPIC LOVE ENDS!>
<IF YOU IMPLY THAT WE ARE MORE THAN FELLOW SOLDIERS...>
<...THAT WE ARE **LOVERS** IS HARDLY A SECRET.>
<HOW ABOUT THAT YOU'RE SECRET **CHRISTIANS?**>

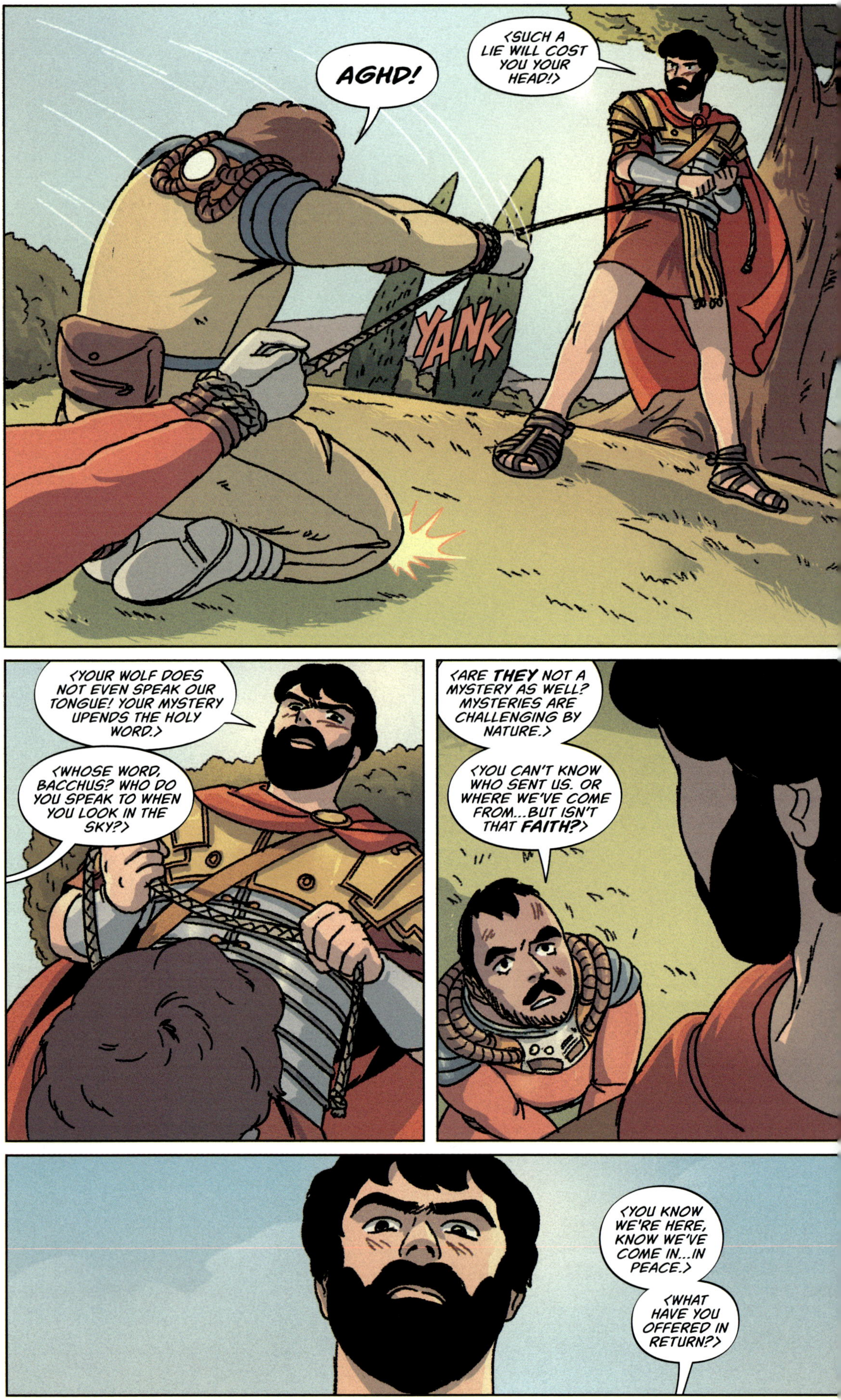
AGHD!
<SUCH A LIE WILL COST YOU YOUR HEAD!>
YANK
<YOUR WOLF DOES NOT EVEN SPEAK OUR TONGUE! YOUR MYSTERY UPENDS THE HOLY WORD.>
<WHOSE WORD, BACCHUS? WHO DO YOU SPEAK TO WHEN YOU LOOK IN THE SKY?>
<ARE THEY NOT A MYSTERY AS WELL? MYSTERIES ARE CHALLENGING BY NATURE.>
<YOU CAN'T KNOW WHO SENT US. OR WHERE WE'VE COME FROM...BUT ISN'T THAT FAITH?>
<YOU KNOW WE'RE HERE, KNOW WE'VE COME IN...IN PEACE.>
<WHAT HAVE YOU OFFERED IN RETURN?>

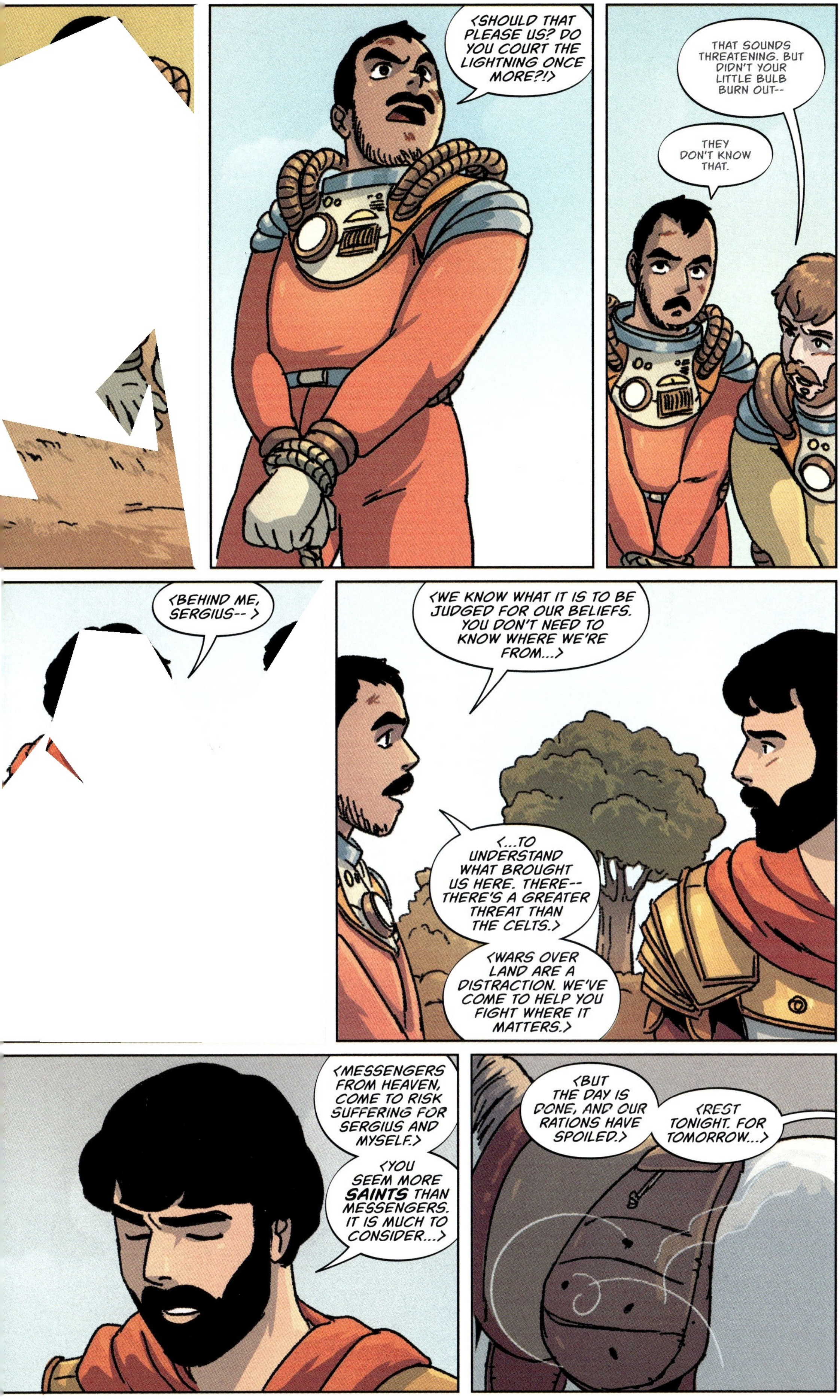

<SHOULD THAT PLEASE US? DO YOU COURT THE LIGHTNING ONCE MORE?!>
THAT SOUNDS THREATENING. BUT DIDN'T YOUR LITTLE BULB BURN OUT--
THEY DON'T KNOW THAT.
<BEHIND ME, SERGIUS-- >
<WE KNOW WHAT IT IS TO BE JUDGED FOR OUR BELIEFS. YOU DON'T NEED TO KNOW WHERE WE'RE FROM...>
<...TO UNDERSTAND WHAT BROUGHT US HERE. THERE-- THERE'S A GREATER THREAT THAN THE CELTS.>
<WARS OVER LAND ARE A DISTRACTION. WE'VE COME TO HELP YOU FIGHT WHERE IT MATTERS.>
<MESSENGERS FROM HEAVEN, COME TO RISK SUFFERING FOR SERGIUS AND MYSELF.>
<YOU SEEM MORE SAINTS THAN MESSENGERS. IT IS MUCH TO CONSIDER...>
<BUT THE DAY IS DONE, AND OUR RATIONS HAVE SPOILED.>
<REST TONIGHT. FOR TOMORROW...>

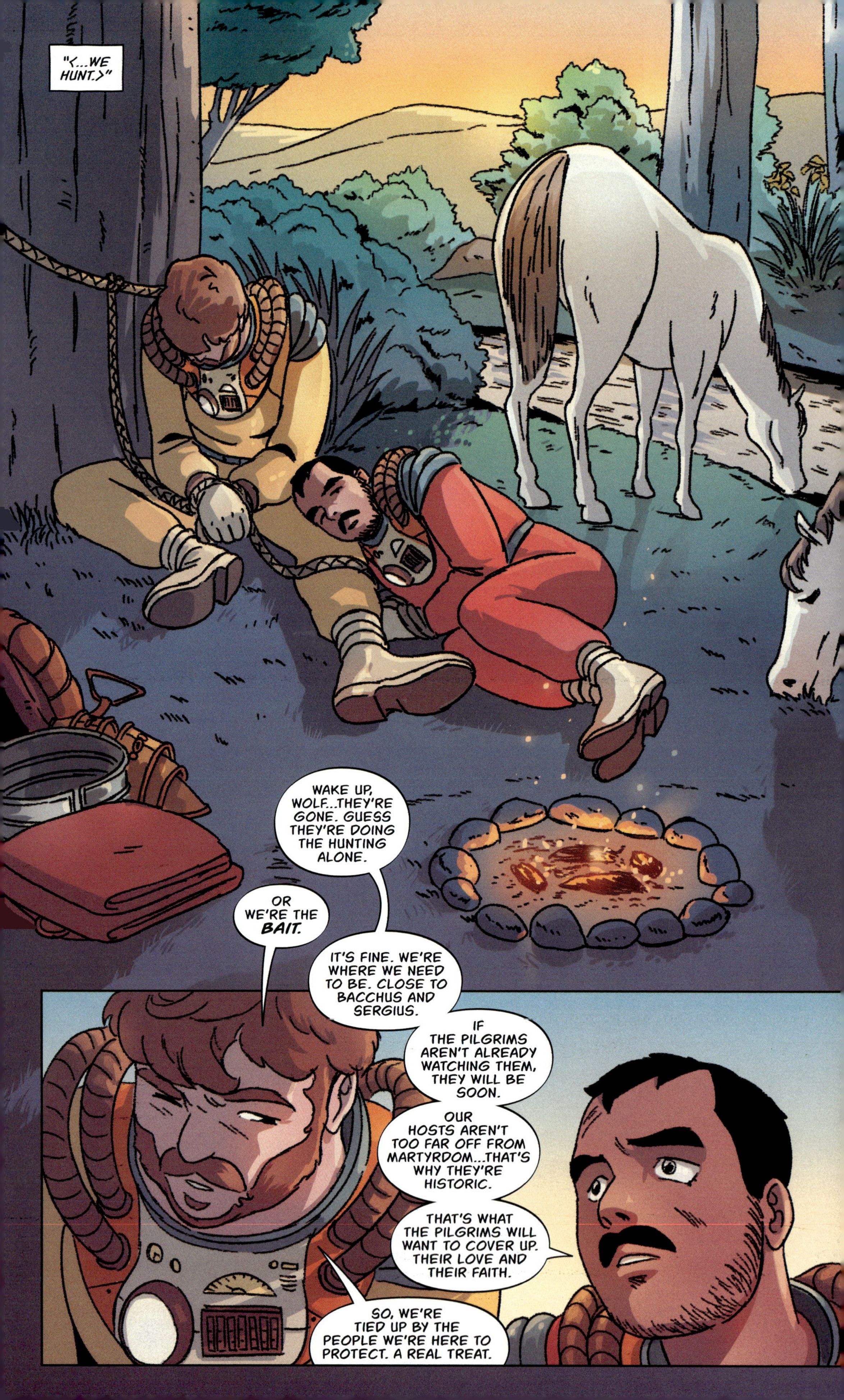
"<...WE HUNT.>"
WAKE UP, WOLF...THEY'RE GONE. GUESS THEY'RE DOING THE HUNTING ALONE.
OR WE'RE THE **BAIT.**
IT'S FINE. WE'RE WHERE WE NEED TO BE. CLOSE TO BACCHUS AND SERGIUS.
IF THE PILGRIMS AREN'T ALREADY WATCHING THEM, THEY WILL BE SOON.
OUR HOSTS AREN'T TOO FAR OFF FROM MARTYRDOM...THAT'S WHY THEY'RE HISTORIC.
THAT'S WHAT THE PILGRIMS WILL WANT TO COVER UP. THEIR LOVE AND THEIR FAITH.
SO, WE'RE TIED UP BY THE PEOPLE WE'RE HERE TO PROTECT. A REAL TREAT.

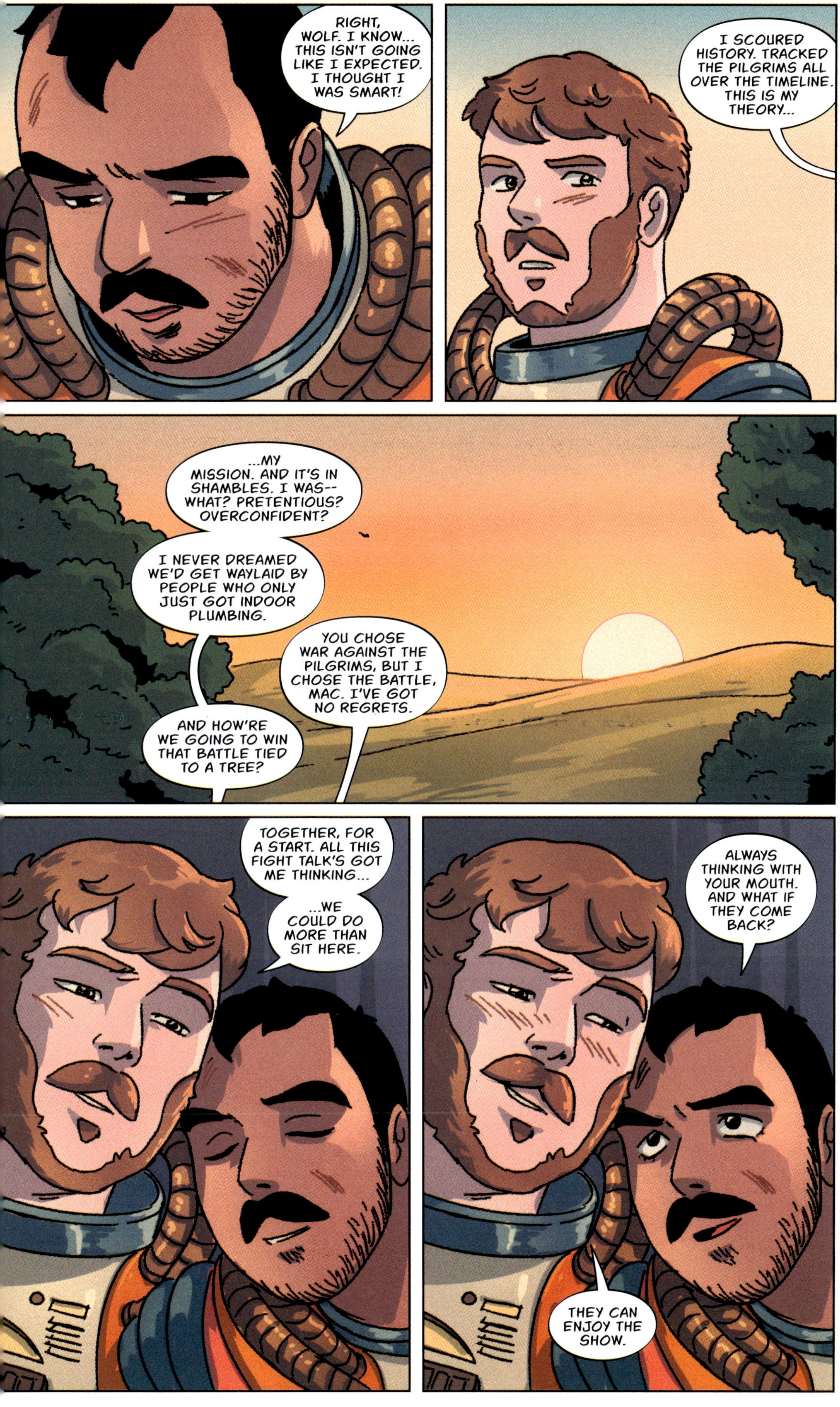
RIGHT, WOLF. I KNOW... THIS ISN'T GOING LIKE I EXPECTED. I THOUGHT I WAS SMART!
I SCOURED HISTORY. TRACKED THE PILGRIMS ALL OVER THE TIMELINE. THIS IS MY THEORY...
...MY MISSION. AND IT'S IN SHAMBLES. I WAS-- WHAT? PRETENTIOUS? OVERCONFIDENT?
I NEVER DREAMED WE'D GET WAYLAID BY PEOPLE WHO ONLY JUST GOT INDOOR PLUMBING.
YOU CHOSE WAR AGAINST THE PILGRIMS, BUT I CHOSE THE BATTLE, MAC. I'VE GOT NO REGRETS.
AND HOW'RE WE GOING TO WIN THAT BATTLE TIED TO A TREE?
TOGETHER, FOR A START. ALL THIS FIGHT TALK'S GOT ME THINKING...
...WE COULD DO MORE THAN SIT HERE.
ALWAYS THINKING WITH YOUR MOUTH. AND WHAT IF THEY COME BACK?
THEY CAN ENJOY THE SHOW.

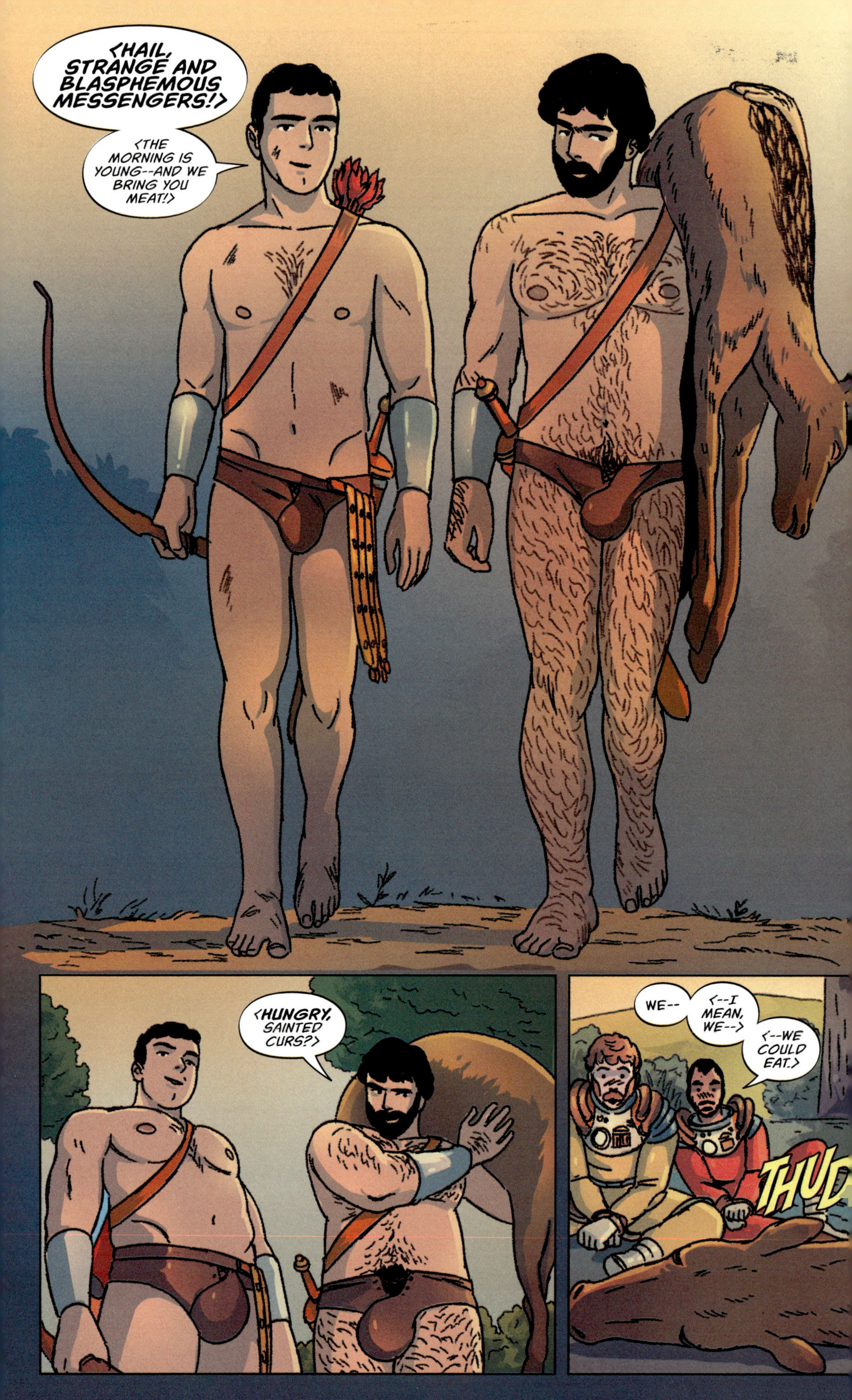
<HAIL, STRANGE AND BLASPHEMOUS MESSENGERS!>
<THE MORNING IS YOUNG--AND WE BRING YOU MEAT!>
<HUNGRY, SAINTED CURS?>
WE--
<--I MEAN, WE-->
<--WE COULD EAT.>
THUD

AN HOUR LATER.

SLOW DOWN, JOHN.

WOLF'S YOUR SURNAME...

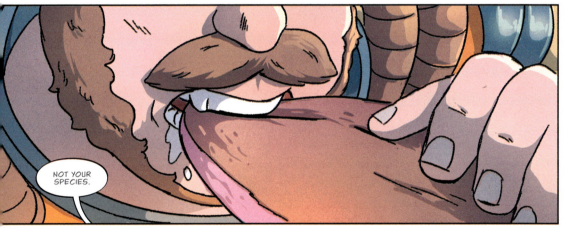

NOT YOUR SPECIES.

HAVE YOU EVER KNOWN ME TO ARGUE WITH A GOOD LEG?

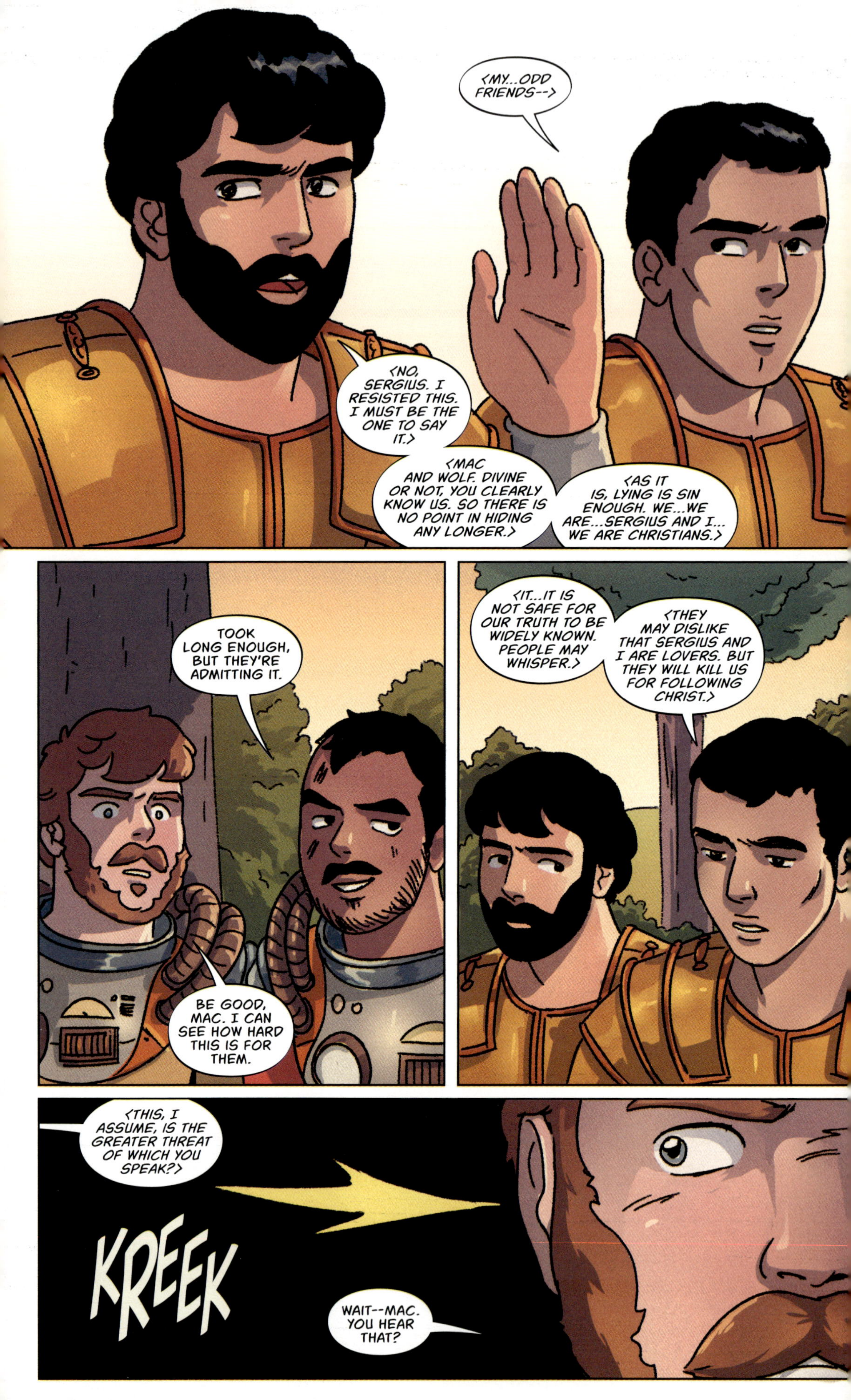
<MY...ODD FRIENDS-->
<NO, SERGIUS. I RESISTED THIS. I MUST BE THE ONE TO SAY IT.>
<MAC AND WOLF. DIVINE OR NOT, YOU CLEARLY KNOW US. SO THERE IS NO POINT IN HIDING ANY LONGER.>
<AS IT IS, LYING IS SIN ENOUGH. WE...WE ARE...SERGIUS AND I... WE ARE CHRISTIANS.>
TOOK LONG ENOUGH, BUT THEY'RE ADMITTING IT.
BE GOOD, MAC. I CAN SEE HOW HARD THIS IS FOR THEM.
<IT...IT IS NOT SAFE FOR OUR TRUTH TO BE WIDELY KNOWN. PEOPLE MAY WHISPER.>
<THEY MAY DISLIKE THAT SERGIUS AND I ARE LOVERS. BUT THEY WILL KILL US FOR FOLLOWING CHRIST.>
<THIS, I ASSUME, IS THE GREATER THREAT OF WHICH YOU SPEAK?>
KREEK
WAIT--MAC. YOU HEAR THAT?

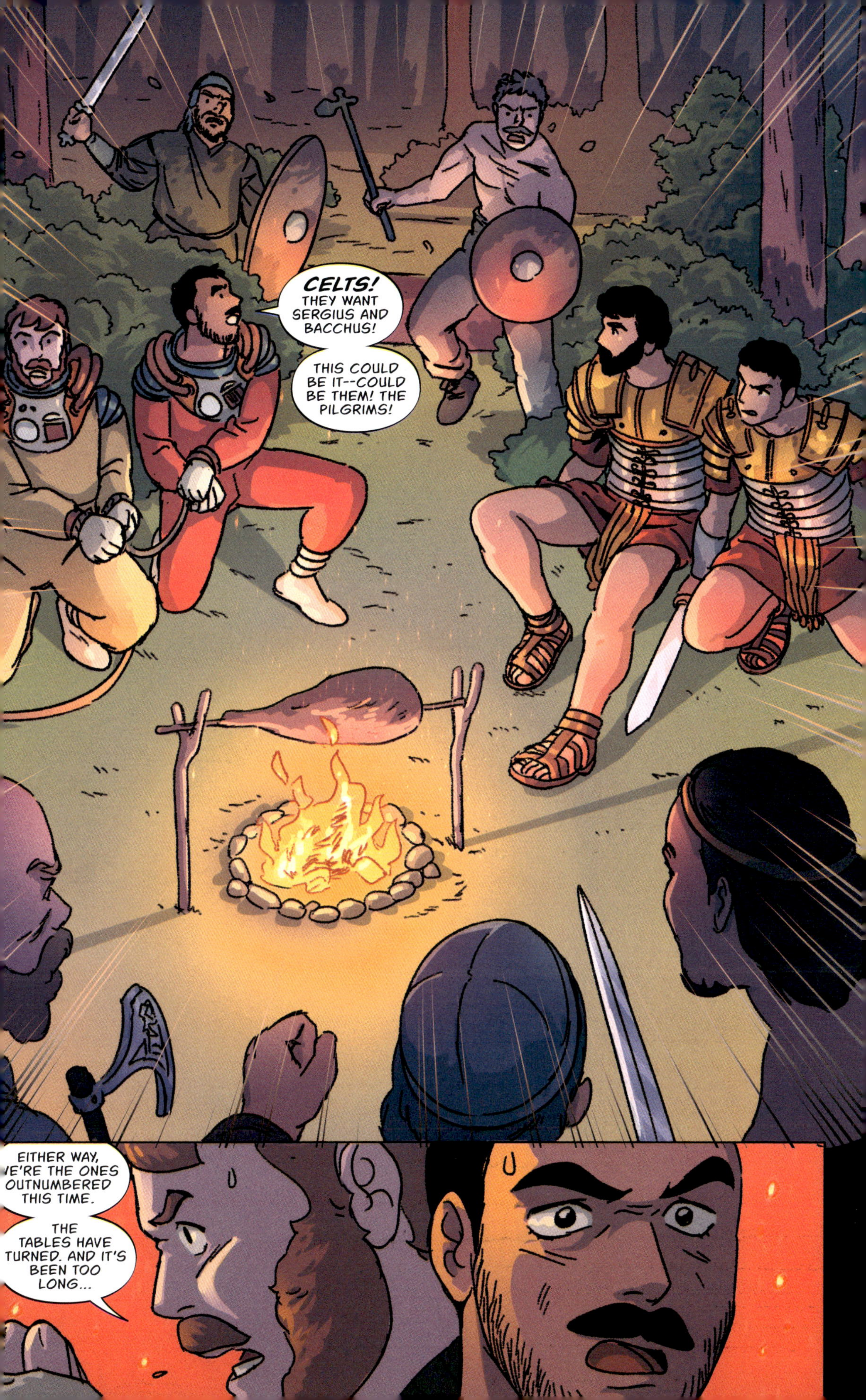
CELTS! THEY WANT SERGIUS AND BACCHUS!
THIS COULD BE IT--COULD BE THEM! THE PILGRIMS!
EITHER WAY, WE'RE THE ONES OUTNUMBERED THIS TIME.
THE TABLES HAVE TURNED. AND IT'S BEEN TOO LONG...

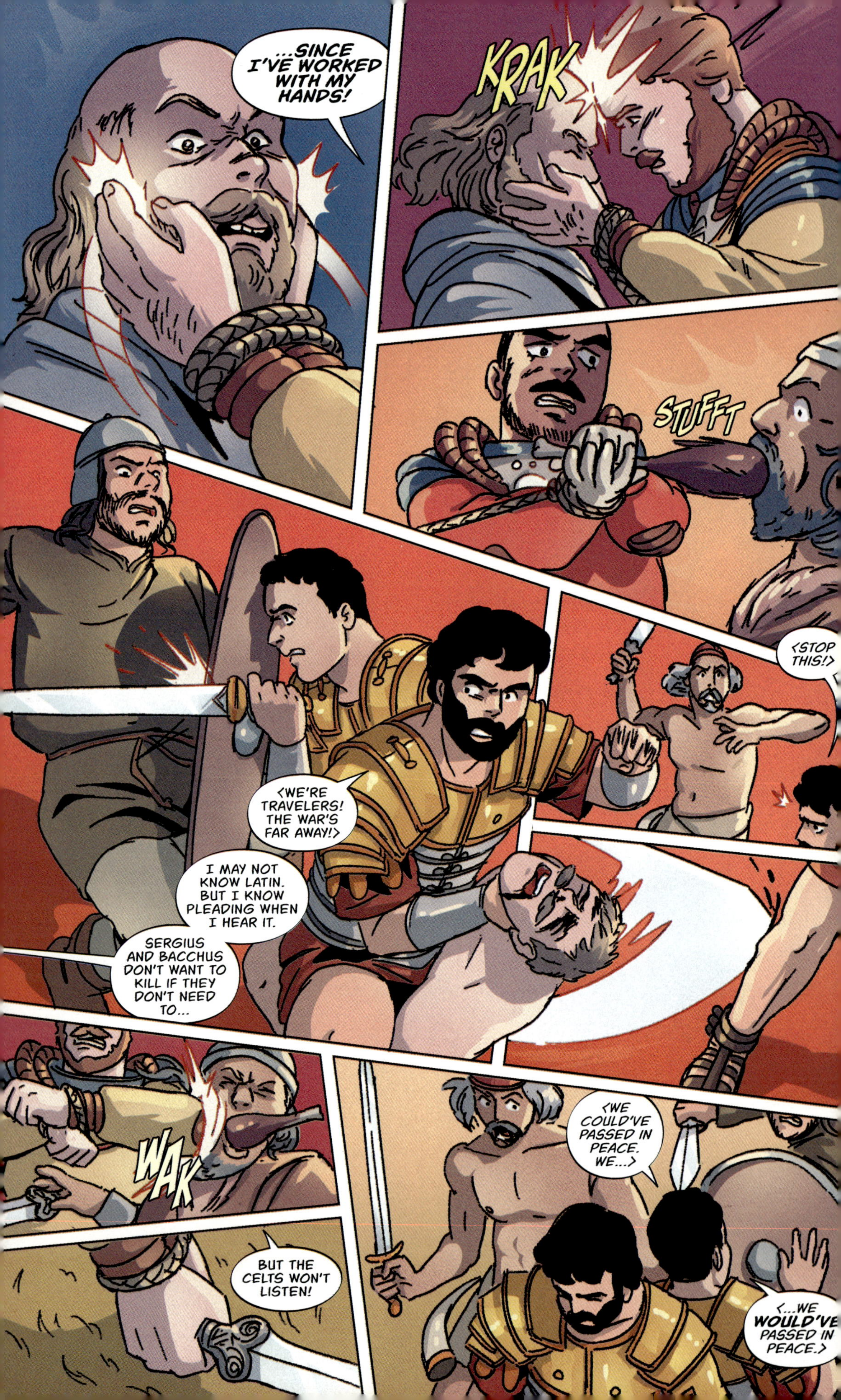
...SINCE I'VE WORKED WITH MY HANDS!
KRAK
STUFFT
<STOP THIS!>
<WE'RE TRAVELERS! THE WAR'S FAR AWAY!>
I MAY NOT KNOW LATIN. BUT I KNOW PLEADING WHEN I HEAR IT.
SERGIUS AND BACCHUS DON'T WANT TO KILL IF THEY DON'T NEED TO...
WAK
BUT THE CELTS WON'T LISTEN!
<WE COULD'VE PASSED IN PEACE. WE...>
<...WE WOULD'VE PASSED IN PEACE.>

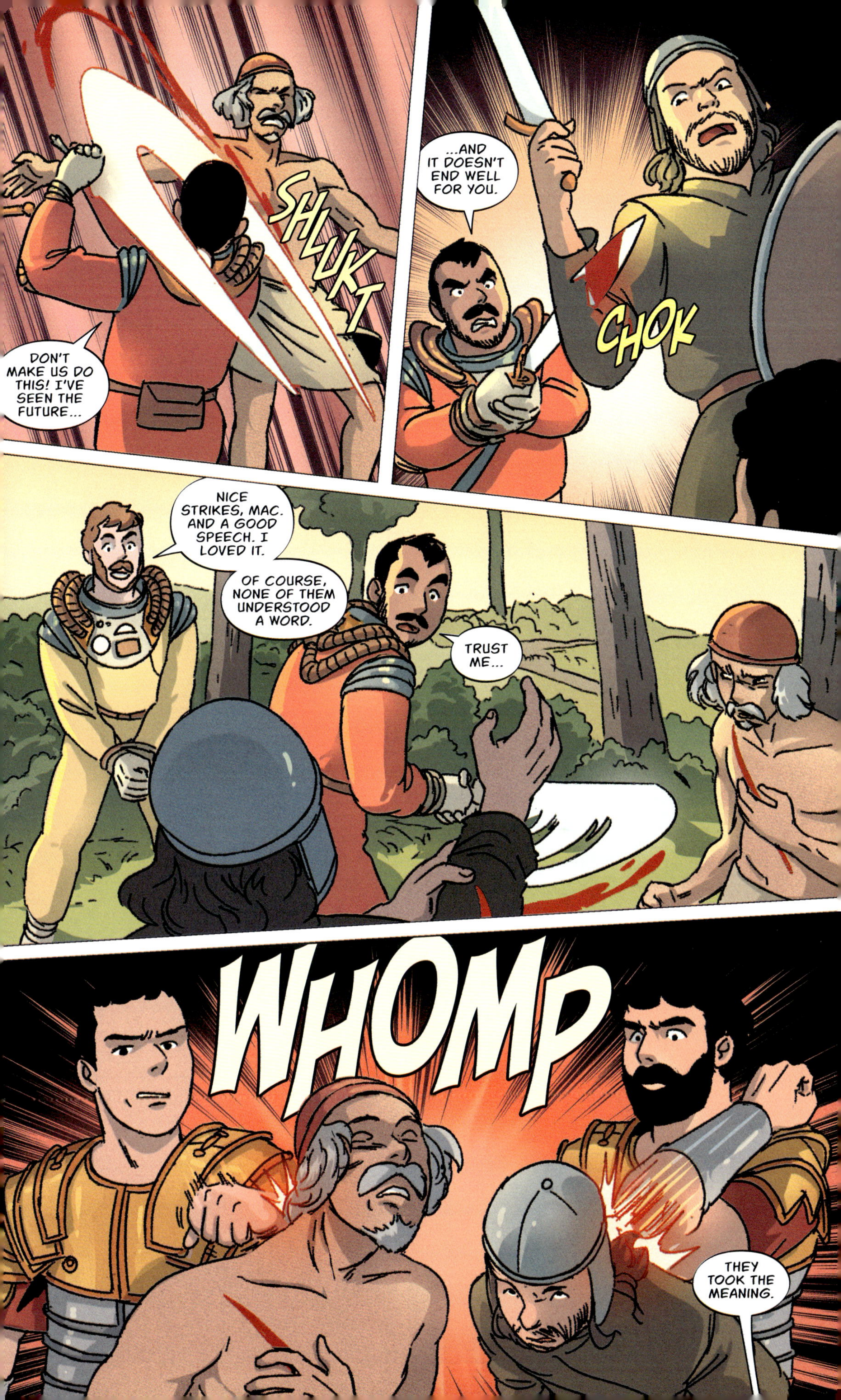
SHLUKT
DON'T MAKE US DO THIS! I'VE SEEN THE FUTURE...
...AND IT DOESN'T END WELL FOR YOU.
CHOK
NICE STRIKES, MAC. AND A GOOD SPEECH. I LOVED IT.
OF COURSE, NONE OF THEM UNDERSTOOD A WORD.
TRUST ME...
WHOMP
THEY TOOK THE MEANING.

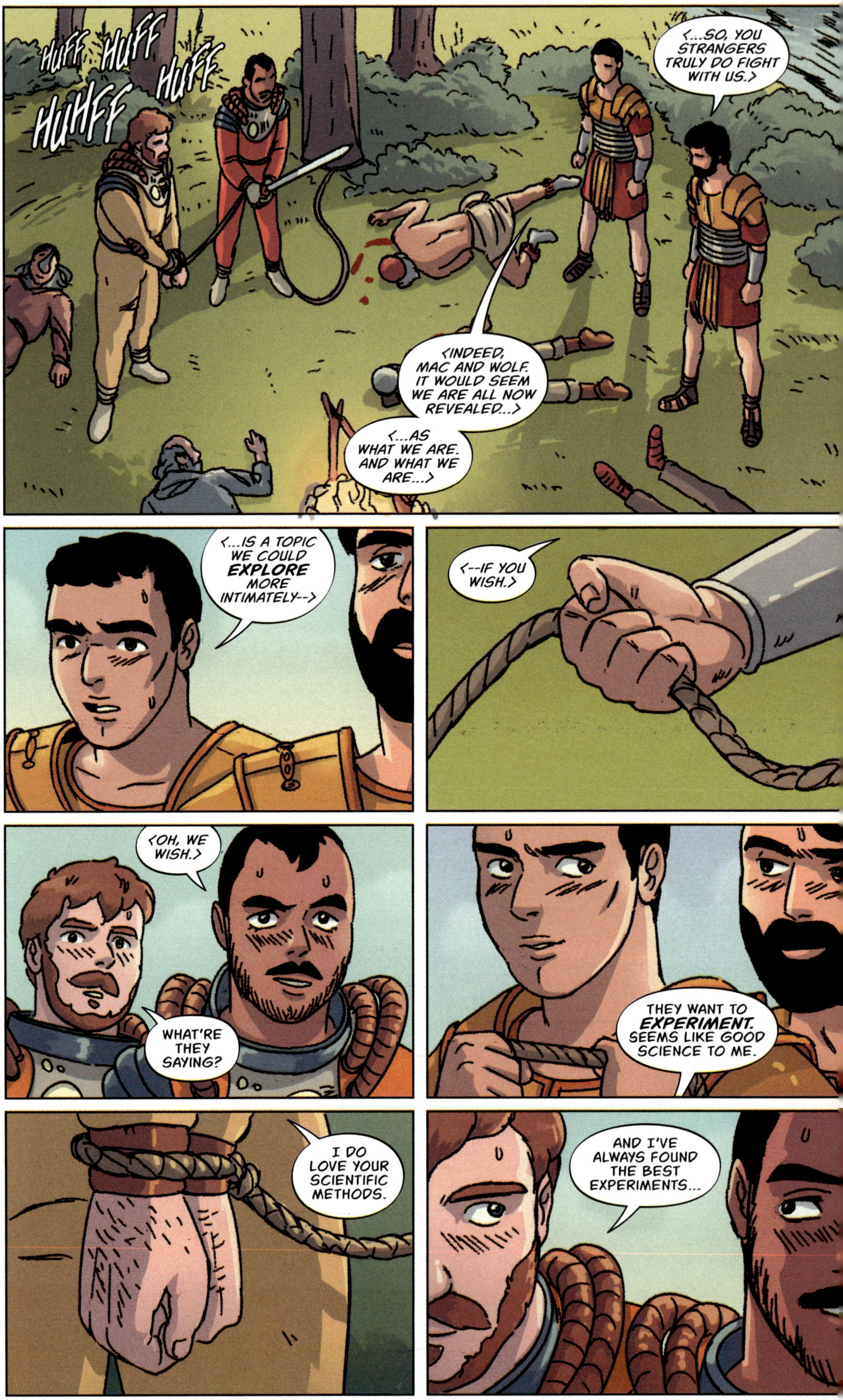
HUFF HUFF HUFF
HUHFF
<...SO, YOU STRANGERS TRULY DO FIGHT WITH US.>
<INDEED, MAC AND WOLF. IT WOULD SEEM WE ARE ALL NOW REVEALED...>
<...AS WHAT WE ARE. AND WHAT WE ARE...>
<...IS A TOPIC WE COULD EXPLORE MORE INTIMATELY-->
<--IF YOU WISH.>
<OH, WE WISH.>
WHAT'RE THEY SAYING?
THEY WANT TO EXPERIMENT. SEEMS LIKE GOOD SCIENCE TO ME.
I DO LOVE YOUR SCIENTIFIC METHODS.
AND I'VE ALWAYS FOUND THE BEST EXPERIMENTS...

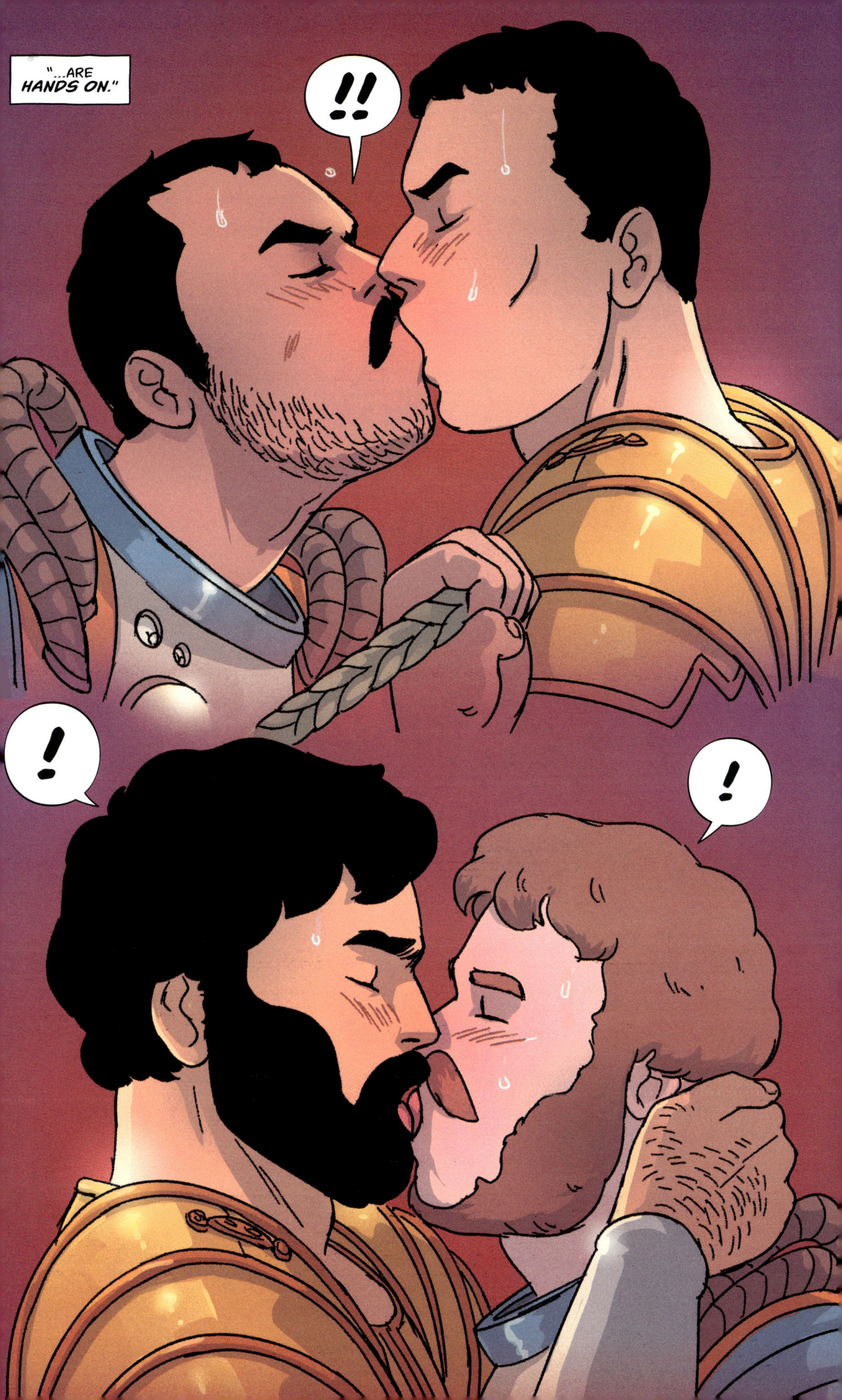
"...ARE HANDS ON."
!!
!
!

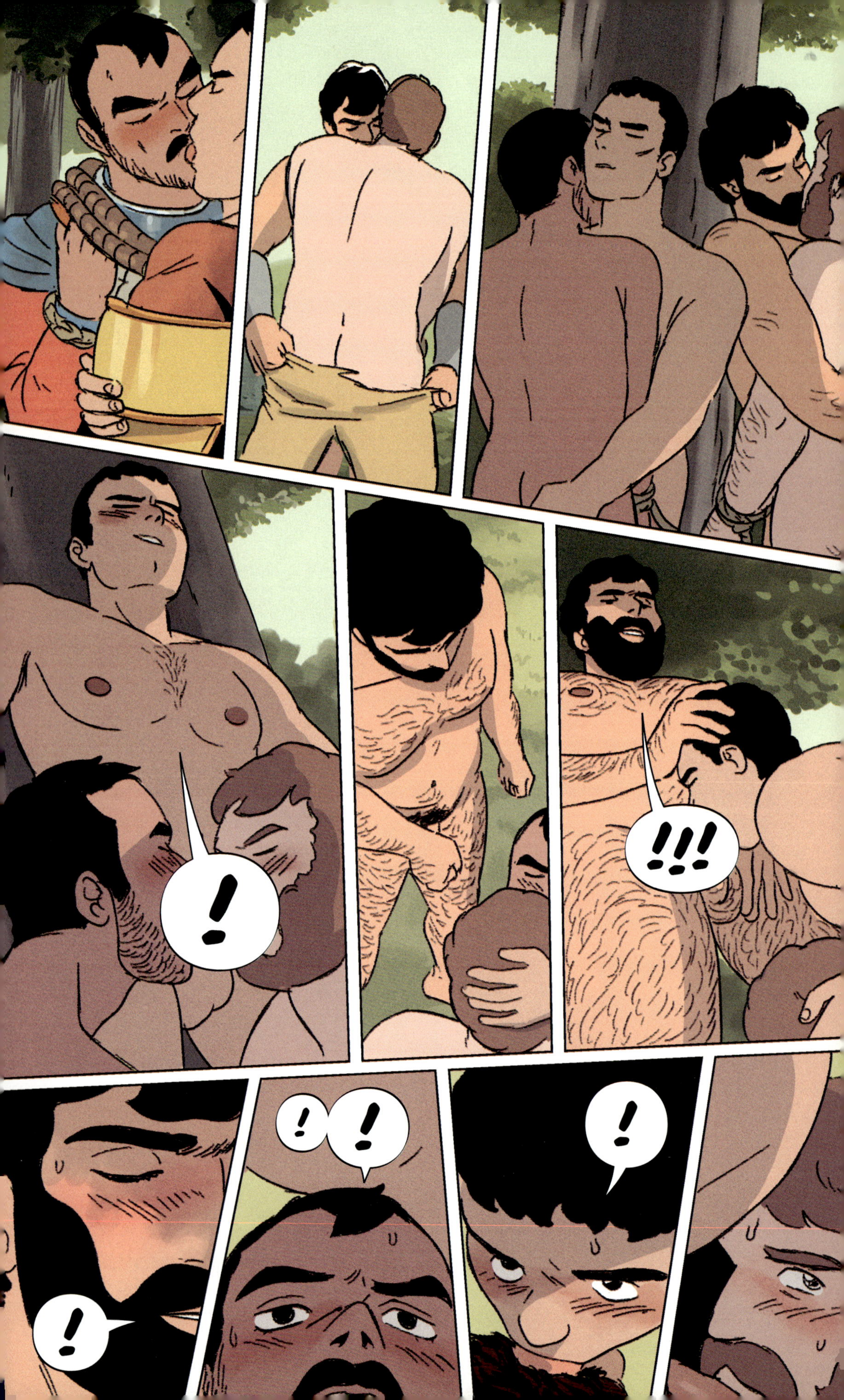
!
!!!
!
!
!
!

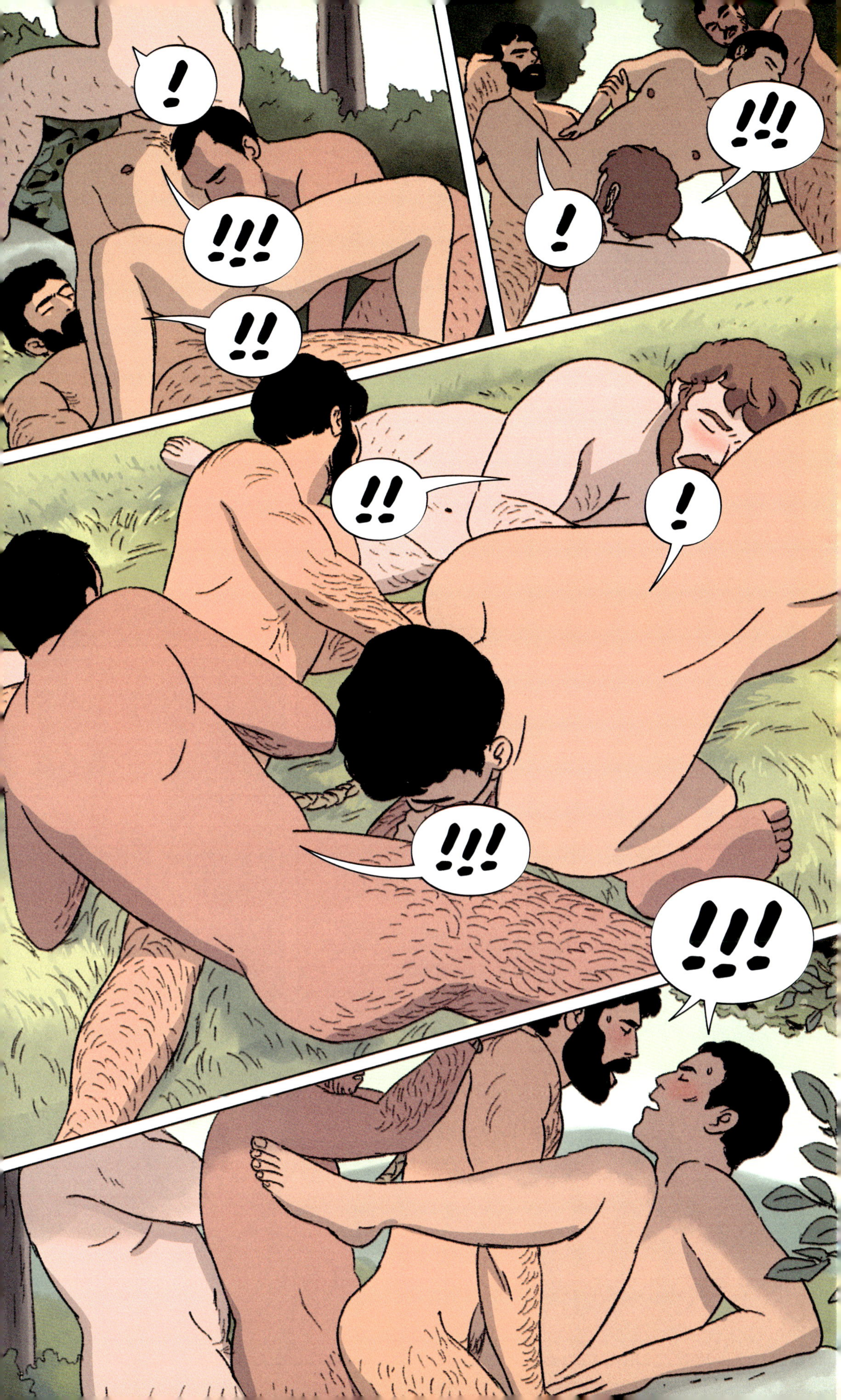
!
!!!
!!
!!!
!
!!
!
!!!
!!!

MORNING.

CHOK

CHOK

WHAT?

⟨WHAT--WHAT'S THIS?⟩

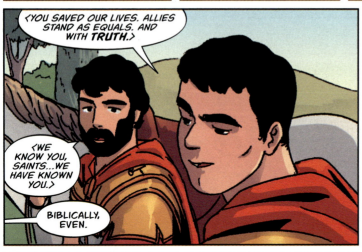

⟨YOU SAVED OUR LIVES. ALLIES STAND AS EQUALS. AND WITH **TRUTH**.⟩

⟨WE KNOW YOU, SAINTS...WE HAVE KNOWN YOU.⟩

BIBLICALLY, EVEN.

⟨BUT WE AREN'T FOOLS. YOU ARE NOT DIVINE--SO, WHAT ARE YOU?⟩

⟨WE'RE FELLOW TRAVELERS. FROM ANOTHER TIME AND PLACE...WE CAN'T SAY MORE.⟩

⟨AS FOR OUR ENEMIES... THEY HUNT US. THE **PILGRIMS** LOATHE LOVE LIKE OURS.⟩

⟨THESE DO SOUND LIKE MEN I'D ENJOY KILLING. GATHER YOURSELVES...⟩

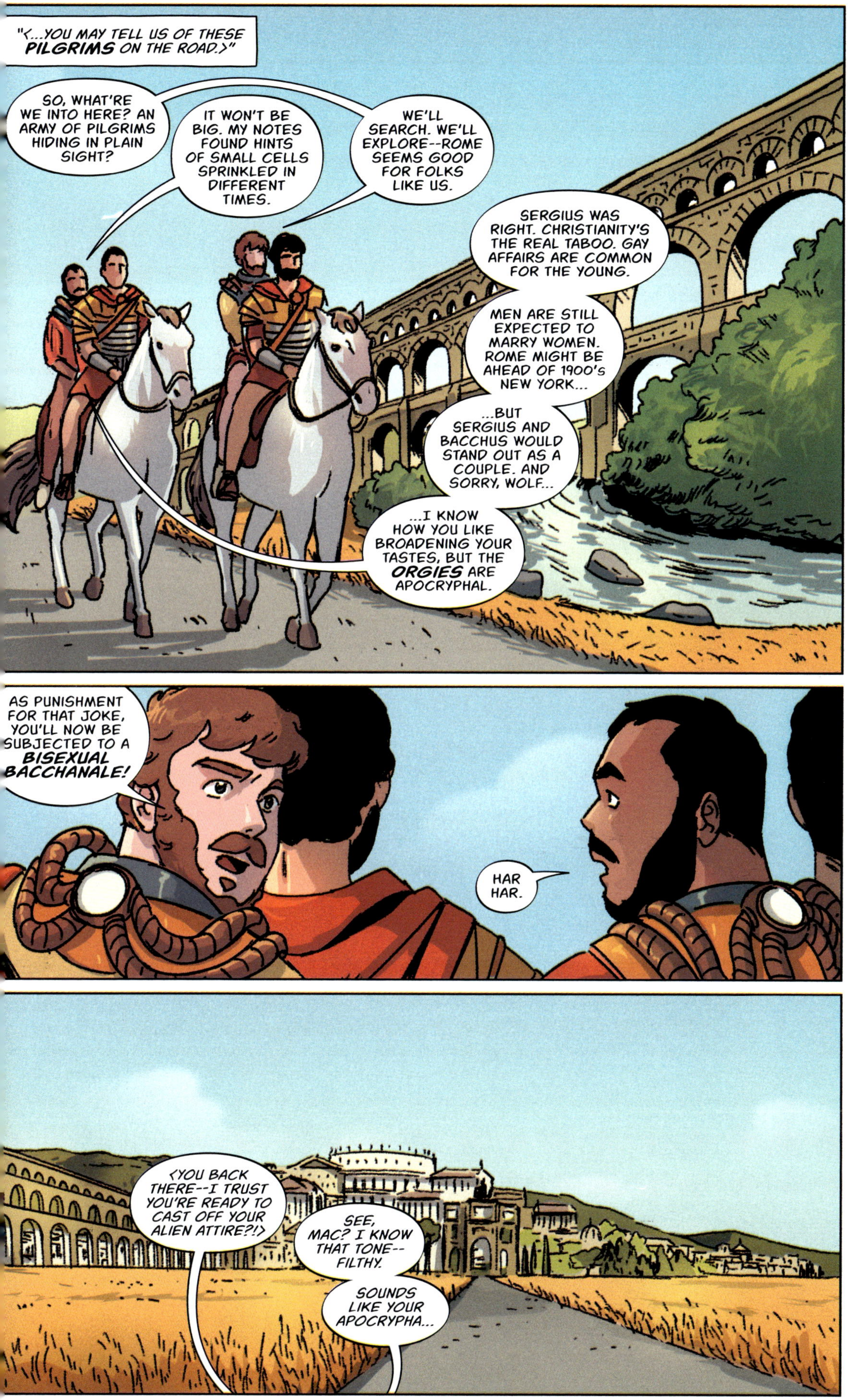
"‹...YOU MAY TELL US OF THESE PILGRIMS ON THE ROAD.›"
SO, WHAT'RE WE INTO HERE? AN ARMY OF PILGRIMS HIDING IN PLAIN SIGHT?
IT WON'T BE BIG. MY NOTES FOUND HINTS OF SMALL CELLS SPRINKLED IN DIFFERENT TIMES.
WE'LL SEARCH. WE'LL EXPLORE--ROME SEEMS GOOD FOR FOLKS LIKE US.
SERGIUS WAS RIGHT. CHRISTIANITY'S THE REAL TABOO. GAY AFFAIRS ARE COMMON FOR THE YOUNG.
MEN ARE STILL EXPECTED TO MARRY WOMEN. ROME MIGHT BE AHEAD OF 1900's NEW YORK...
...BUT SERGIUS AND BACCHUS WOULD STAND OUT AS A COUPLE. AND SORRY, WOLF...
...I KNOW HOW YOU LIKE BROADENING YOUR TASTES, BUT THE ORGIES ARE APOCRYPHAL.
AS PUNISHMENT FOR THAT JOKE, YOU'LL NOW BE SUBJECTED TO A BISEXUAL BACCHANALE!
HAR HAR.
‹YOU BACK THERE--I TRUST YOU'RE READY TO CAST OFF YOUR ALIEN ATTIRE?!›
SEE, MAC? I KNOW THAT TONE--FILTHY.
SOUNDS LIKE YOUR APOCRYPHA...

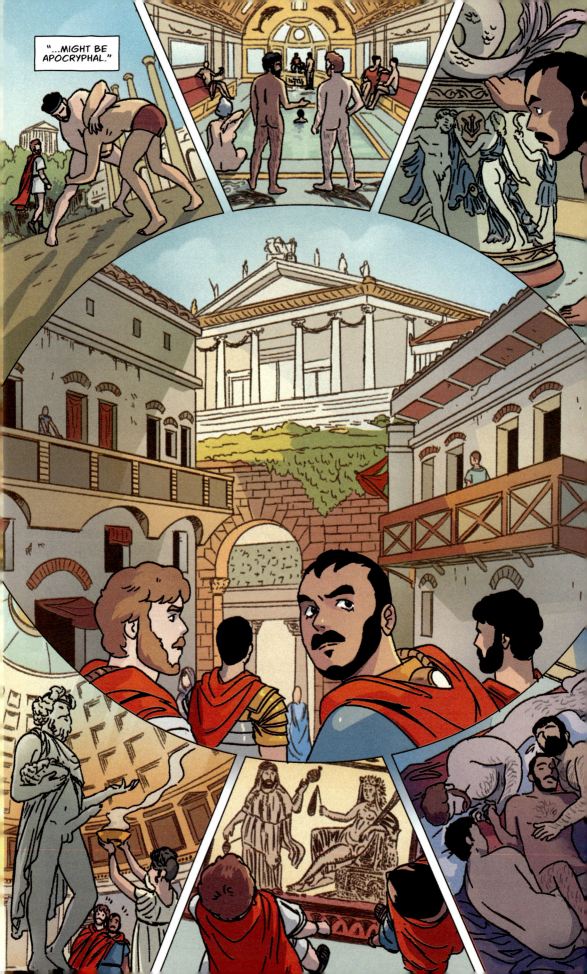

"...MIGHT BE APOCRYPHAL."

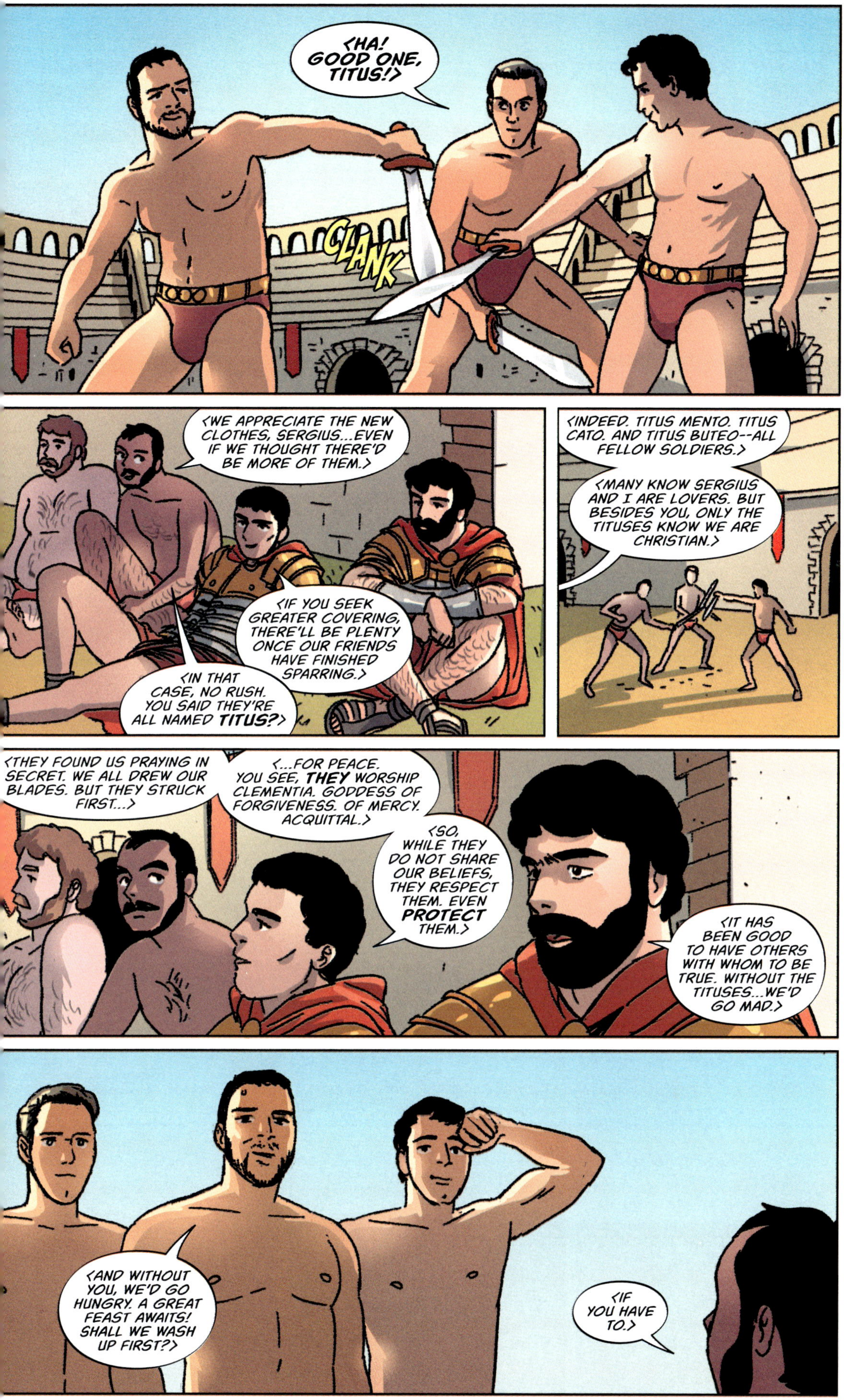

<HA! GOOD ONE, TITUS!>
CLANK
<WE APPRECIATE THE NEW CLOTHES, SERGIUS...EVEN IF WE THOUGHT THERE'D BE MORE OF THEM.>
<IF YOU SEEK GREATER COVERING, THERE'LL BE PLENTY ONCE OUR FRIENDS HAVE FINISHED SPARRING.>
<IN THAT CASE, NO RUSH. YOU SAID THEY'RE ALL NAMED **TITUS?**>
<INDEED. TITUS MENTO. TITUS CATO. AND TITUS BUTEO--ALL FELLOW SOLDIERS.>
<MANY KNOW SERGIUS AND I ARE LOVERS. BUT BESIDES YOU, ONLY THE TITUSES KNOW WE ARE CHRISTIAN.>
<THEY FOUND US PRAYING IN SECRET. WE ALL DREW OUR BLADES. BUT THEY STRUCK FIRST...>
<...FOR PEACE. YOU SEE, **THEY** WORSHIP CLEMENTIA. GODDESS OF FORGIVENESS. OF MERCY. ACQUITTAL.>
<SO, WHILE THEY DO NOT SHARE OUR BELIEFS, THEY RESPECT THEM. EVEN **PROTECT** THEM.>
<IT HAS BEEN GOOD TO HAVE OTHERS WITH WHOM TO BE TRUE. WITHOUT THE TITUSES...WE'D GO MAD.>
<AND WITHOUT YOU, WE'D GO HUNGRY. A GREAT FEAST AWAITS! SHALL WE WASH UP FIRST?>
<IF YOU HAVE TO.>

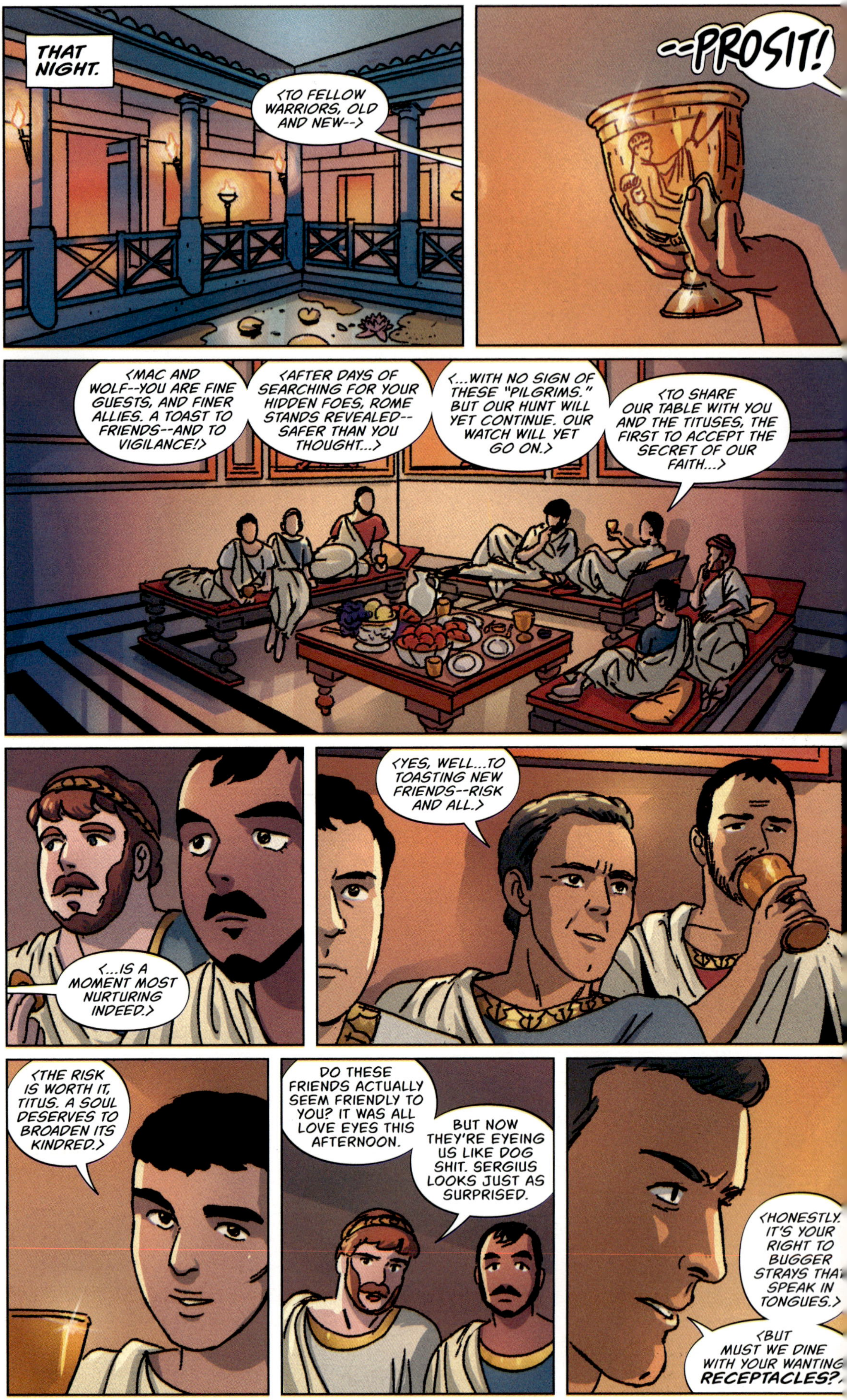
THAT NIGHT.
<TO FELLOW WARRIORS, OLD AND NEW-->
--PROSIT!
<MAC AND WOLF--YOU ARE FINE GUESTS, AND FINER ALLIES. A TOAST TO FRIENDS--AND TO VIGILANCE!>
<AFTER DAYS OF SEARCHING FOR YOUR HIDDEN FOES, ROME STANDS REVEALED--SAFER THAN YOU THOUGHT...>
<...WITH NO SIGN OF THESE "PILGRIMS." BUT OUR HUNT WILL YET CONTINUE. OUR WATCH WILL YET GO ON.>
<TO SHARE OUR TABLE WITH YOU AND THE TITUSES, THE FIRST TO ACCEPT THE SECRET OF OUR FAITH...>
<...IS A MOMENT MOST NURTURING INDEED.>
<YES, WELL...TO TOASTING NEW FRIENDS--RISK AND ALL.>
<THE RISK IS WORTH IT, TITUS. A SOUL DESERVES TO BROADEN ITS KINDRED.>
DO THESE FRIENDS ACTUALLY SEEM FRIENDLY TO YOU? IT WAS ALL LOVE EYES THIS AFTERNOON.
BUT NOW THEY'RE EYEING US LIKE DOG SHIT. SERGIUS LOOKS JUST AS SURPRISED.
<HONESTLY. IT'S YOUR RIGHT TO BUGGER STRAYS THAT SPEAK IN TONGUES.>
<BUT MUST WE DINE WITH YOUR WANTING RECEPTACLES?>

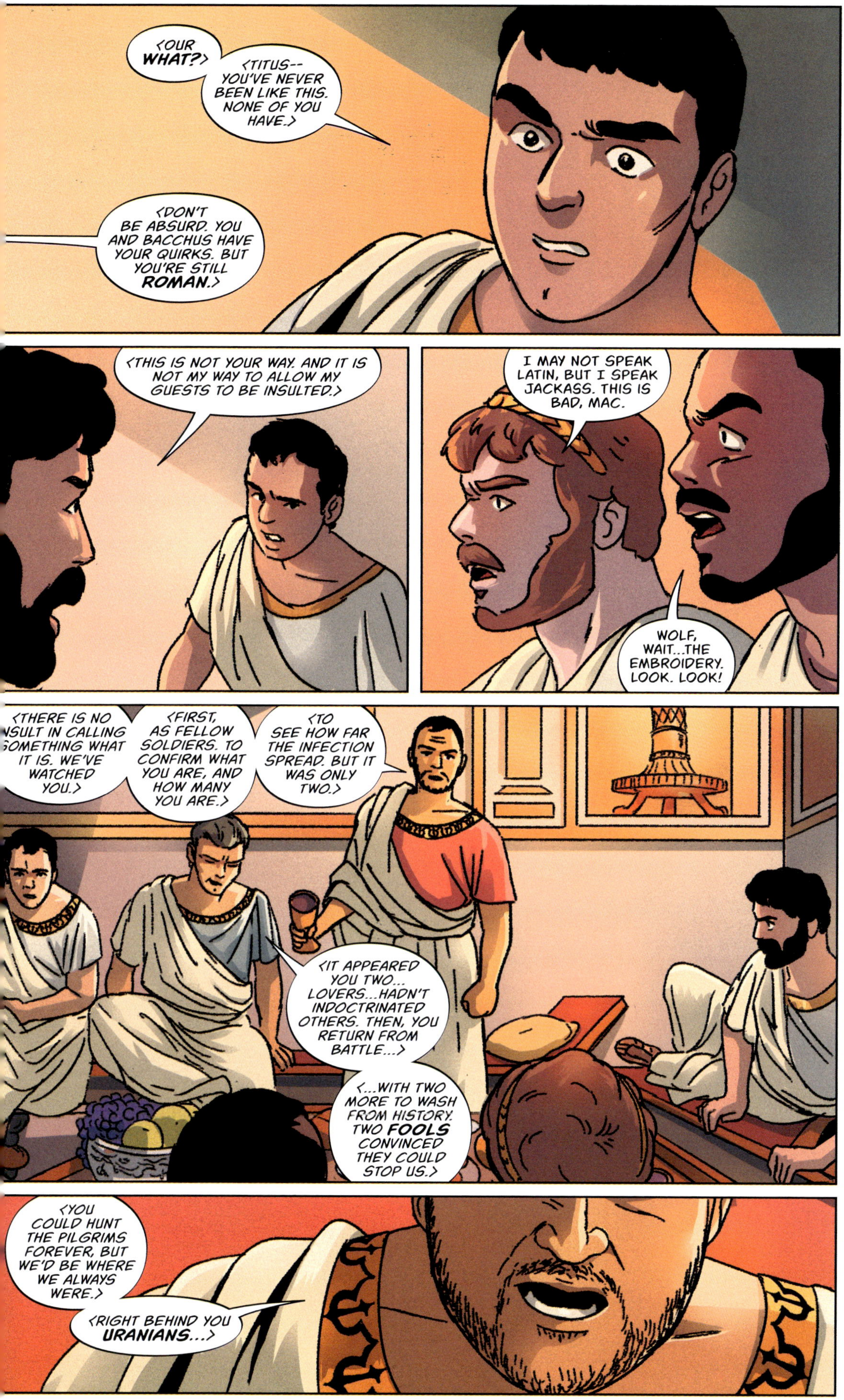

<OUR WHAT?>
<TITUS-- YOU'VE NEVER BEEN LIKE THIS. NONE OF YOU HAVE.>
<DON'T BE ABSURD. YOU AND BACCHUS HAVE YOUR QUIRKS. BUT YOU'RE STILL ROMAN.>
<THIS IS NOT YOUR WAY. AND IT IS NOT MY WAY TO ALLOW MY GUESTS TO BE INSULTED.>
I MAY NOT SPEAK LATIN, BUT I SPEAK JACKASS. THIS IS BAD, MAC.
WOLF, WAIT...THE EMBROIDERY. LOOK. LOOK!
<THERE IS NO INSULT IN CALLING SOMETHING WHAT IT IS. WE'VE WATCHED YOU.>
<FIRST, AS FELLOW SOLDIERS. TO CONFIRM WHAT YOU ARE, AND HOW MANY YOU ARE.>
<TO SEE HOW FAR THE INFECTION SPREAD. BUT IT WAS ONLY TWO.>
<IT APPEARED YOU TWO... LOVERS...HADN'T INDOCTRINATED OTHERS. THEN, YOU RETURN FROM BATTLE...>
<...WITH TWO MORE TO WASH FROM HISTORY. TWO FOOLS CONVINCED THEY COULD STOP US.>
<YOU COULD HUNT THE PILGRIMS FOREVER, BUT WE'D BE WHERE WE ALWAYS WERE.>
<RIGHT BEHIND YOU URANIANS...>

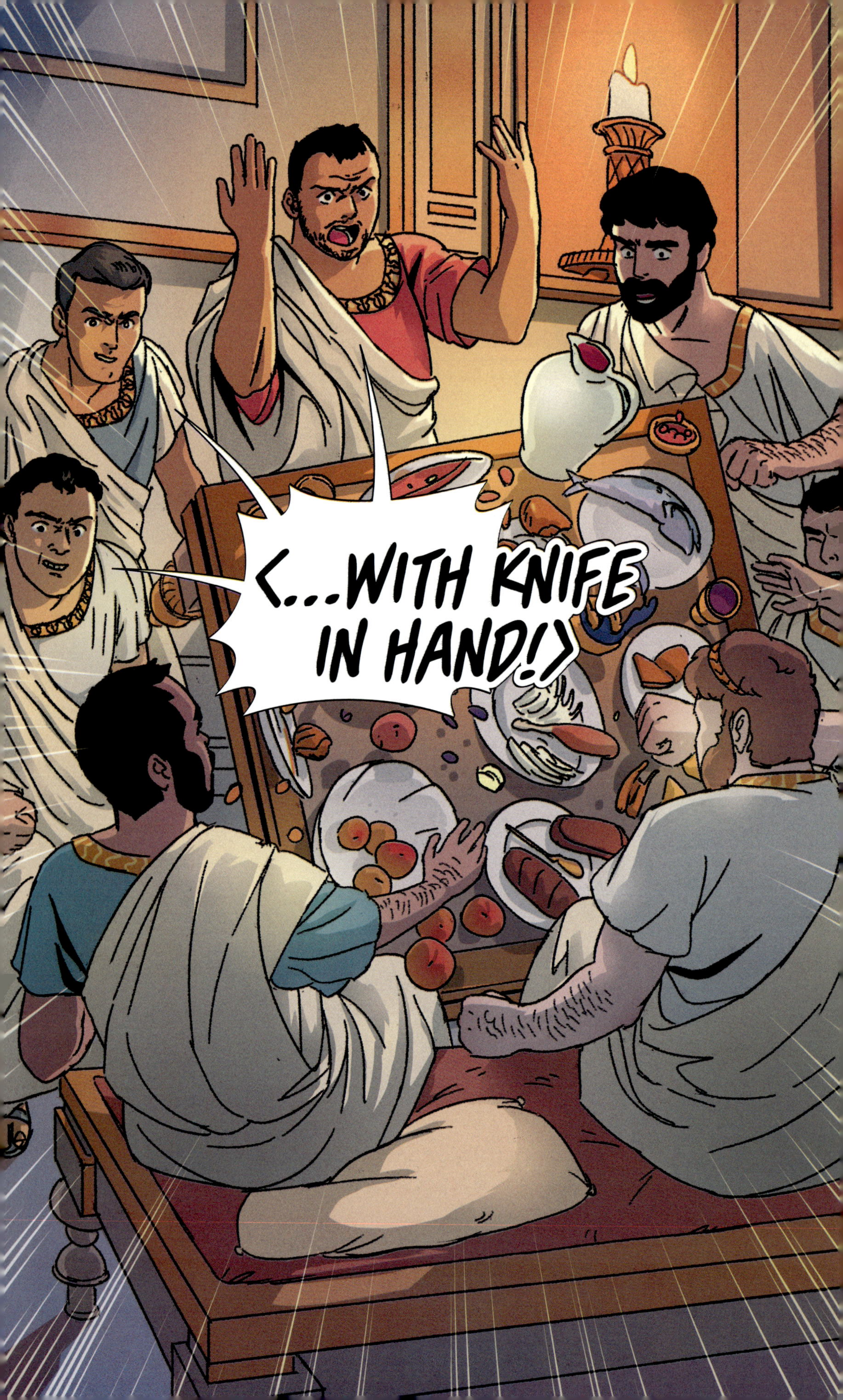
<...WITH KNIFE IN HAND!>

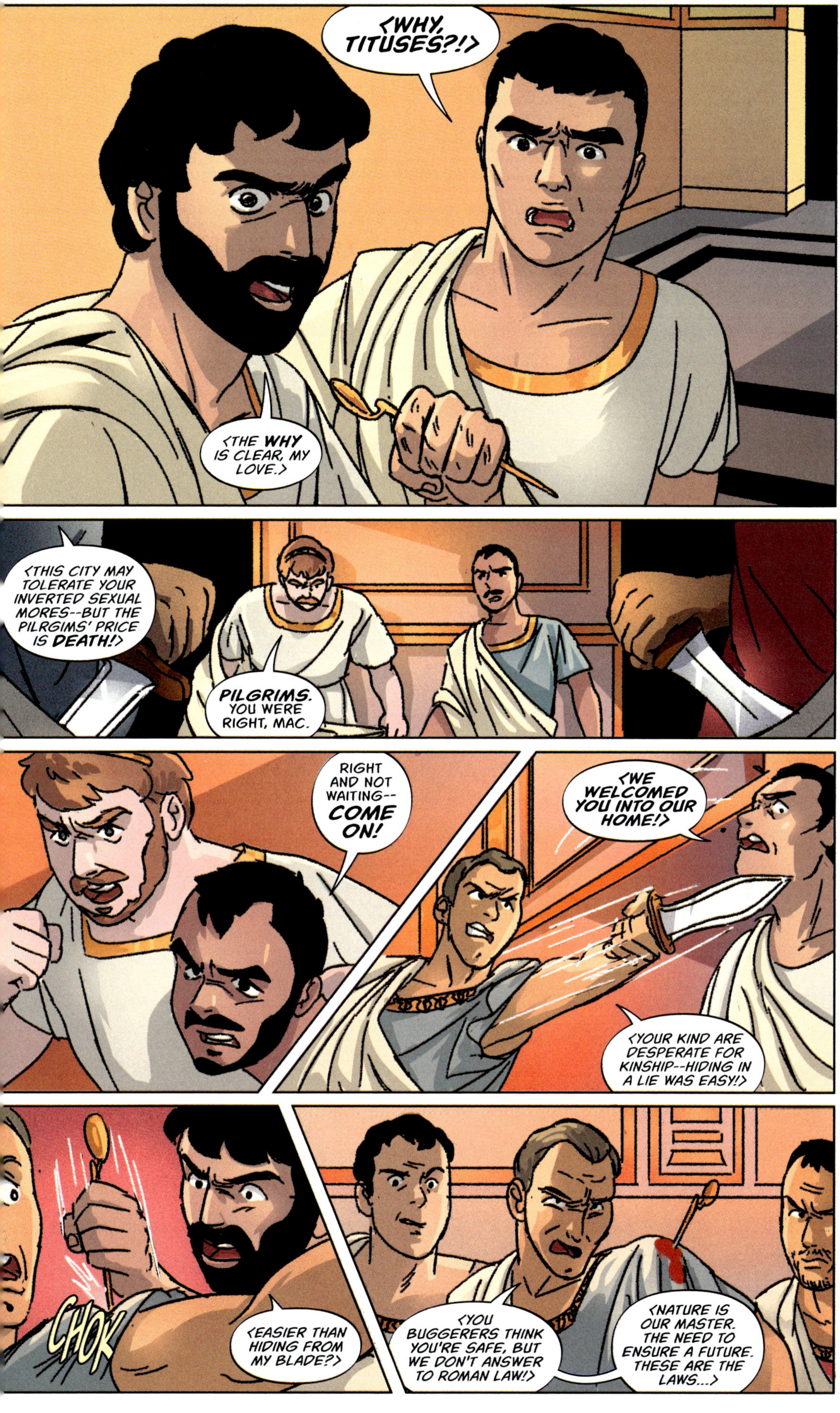
<WHY, TITUSES?!>
<THE WHY IS CLEAR, MY LOVE.>
<THIS CITY MAY TOLERATE YOUR INVERTED SEXUAL MORES--BUT THE PILRGIMS' PRICE IS DEATH!>
PILGRIMS. YOU WERE RIGHT, MAC.
RIGHT AND NOT WAITING--COME ON!
<WE WELCOMED YOU INTO OUR HOME!>
<YOUR KIND ARE DESPERATE FOR KINSHIP--HIDING IN A LIE WAS EASY!>
CHOK
<EASIER THAN HIDING FROM MY BLADE?>
<YOU BUGGERERS THINK YOU'RE SAFE, BUT WE DON'T ANSWER TO ROMAN LAW!>
<NATURE IS OUR MASTER. THE NEED TO ENSURE A FUTURE. THESE ARE THE LAWS...>

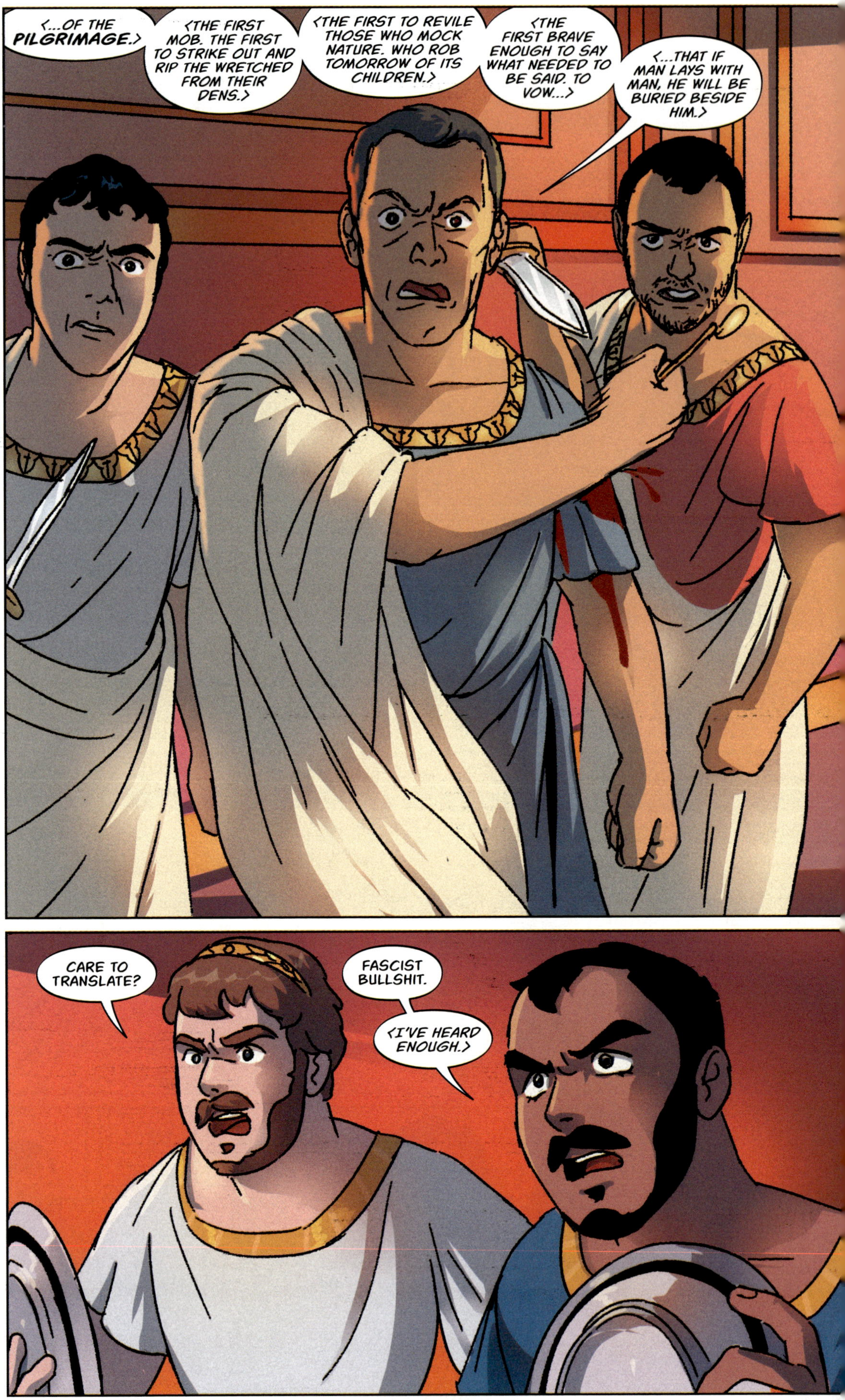
<...OF THE PILGRIMAGE.>
<THE FIRST MOB. THE FIRST TO STRIKE OUT AND RIP THE WRETCHED FROM THEIR DENS.>
<THE FIRST TO REVILE THOSE WHO MOCK NATURE. WHO ROB TOMORROW OF ITS CHILDREN.>
<THE FIRST BRAVE ENOUGH TO SAY WHAT NEEDED TO BE SAID. TO VOW...>
<...THAT IF MAN LAYS WITH MAN, HE WILL BE BURIED BESIDE HIM.>
CARE TO TRANSLATE?
FASCIST BULLSHIT.
<I'VE HEARD ENOUGH.>

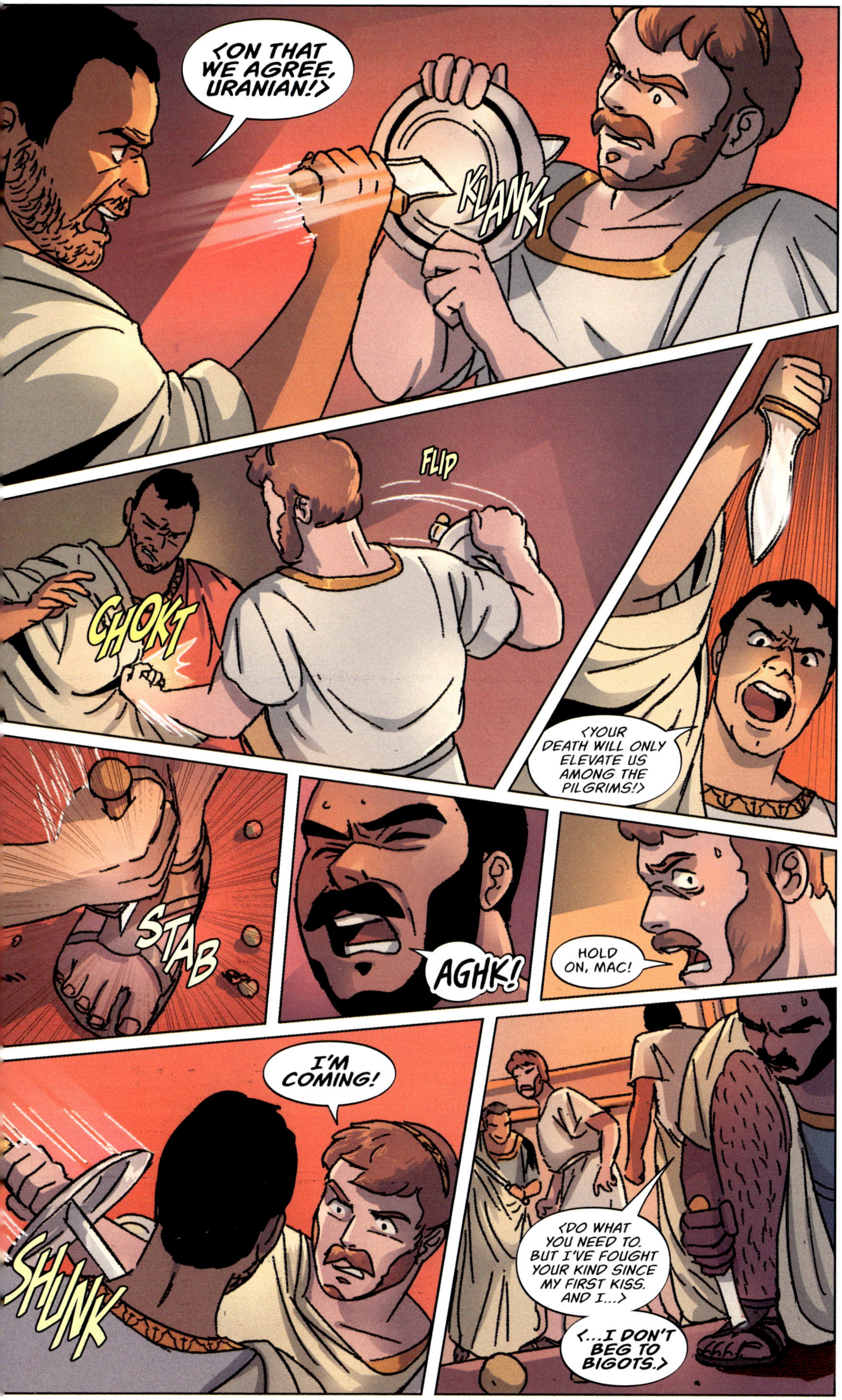
<ON THAT WE AGREE, URANIAN!>
KLANKT
FLIP
CHOKT
<YOUR DEATH WILL ONLY ELEVATE US AMONG THE PILGRIMS!>
STAB
AGHK!
HOLD ON, MAC!
I'M COMING!
SHUNK
<DO WHAT YOU NEED TO. BUT I'VE FOUGHT YOUR KIND SINCE MY FIRST KISS. AND I...>
<...I DON'T BEG TO BIGOTS.>

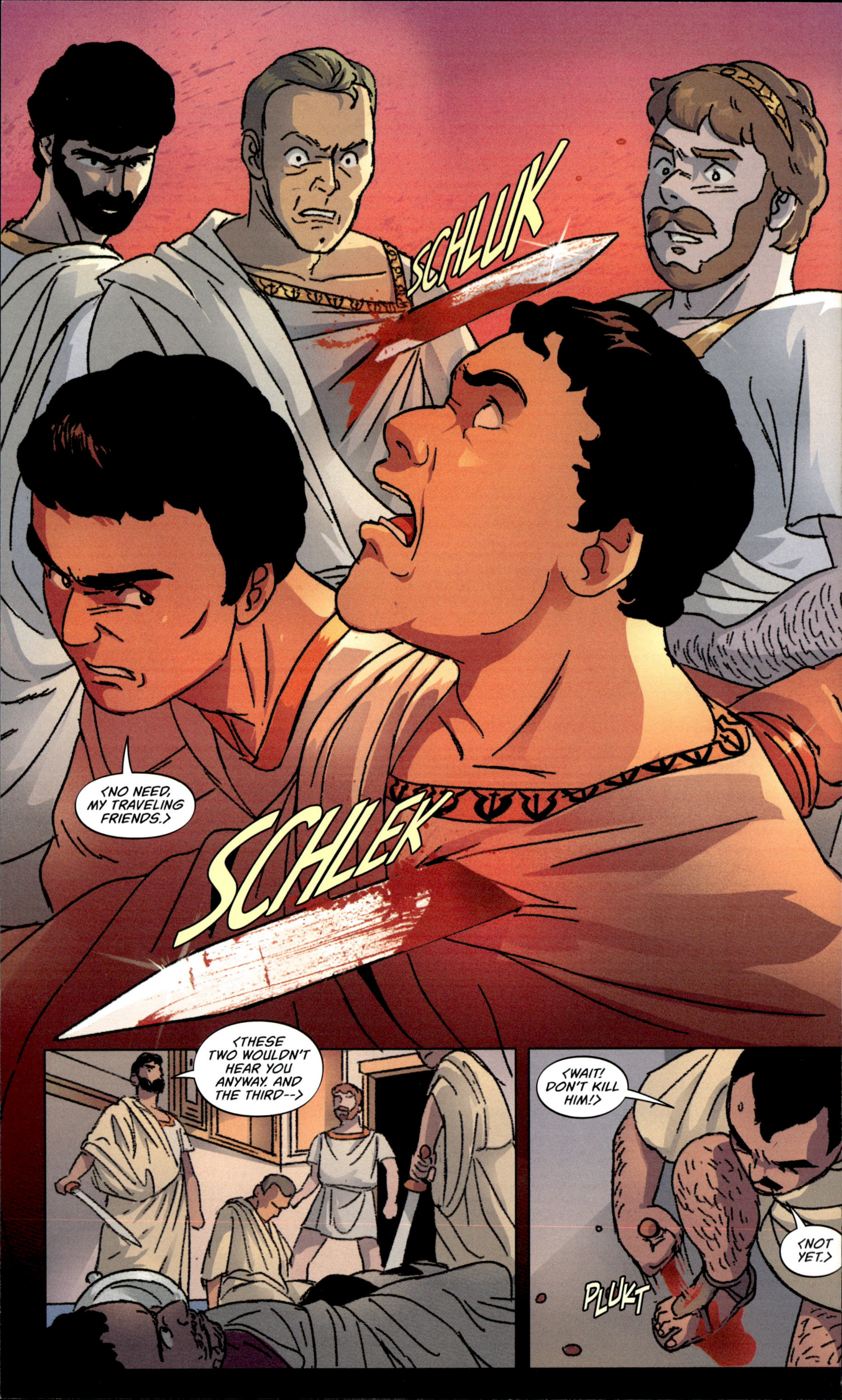
SCHLUK
<NO NEED, MY TRAVELING FRIENDS.>
SCHLEK
<THESE TWO WOULDN'T HEAR YOU ANYWAY. AND THE THIRD-->
<WAIT! DON'T KILL HIM!>
<NOT YET.>
PLUKT

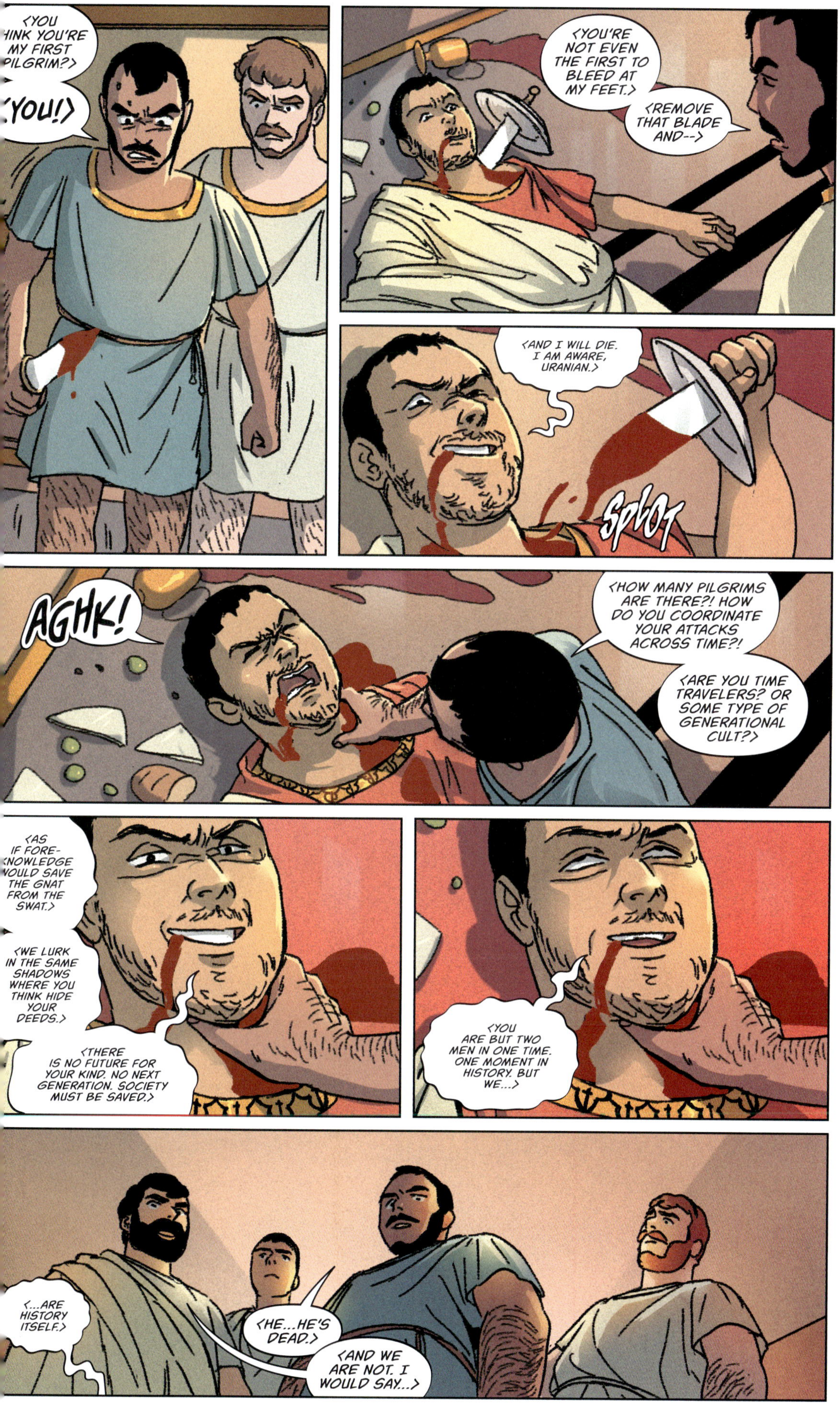

<YOU THINK YOU'RE MY FIRST PILGRIM?>
<YOU!>
<YOU'RE NOT EVEN THE FIRST TO BLEED AT MY FEET.>
<REMOVE THAT BLADE AND-->
<AND I WILL DIE. I AM AWARE, URANIAN.>
SPLOT
AGHK!
<HOW MANY PILGRIMS ARE THERE?! HOW DO YOU COORDINATE YOUR ATTACKS ACROSS TIME?!
<ARE YOU TIME TRAVELERS? OR SOME TYPE OF GENERATIONAL CULT?>
<AS IF FORE-KNOWLEDGE WOULD SAVE THE GNAT FROM THE SWAT.>
<WE LURK IN THE SAME SHADOWS WHERE YOU THINK HIDE YOUR DEEDS.>
<THERE IS NO FUTURE FOR YOUR KIND. NO NEXT GENERATION. SOCIETY MUST BE SAVED.>
<YOU ARE BUT TWO MEN IN ONE TIME. ONE MOMENT IN HISTORY. BUT WE...>
<...ARE HISTORY ITSELF.>
<HE...HE'S DEAD.>
<AND WE ARE NOT. I WOULD SAY...>

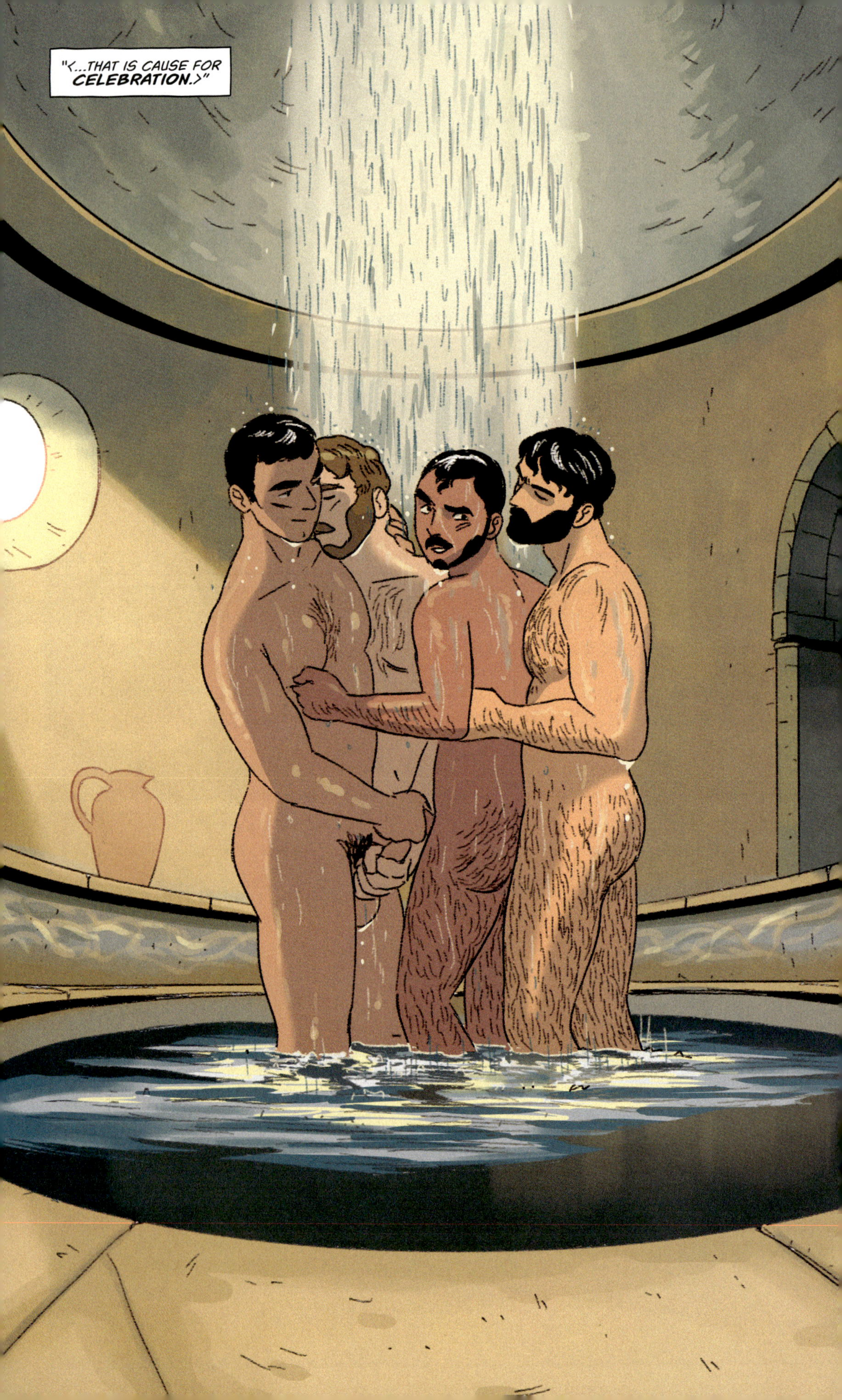
"<...THAT IS CAUSE FOR CELEBRATION.>"

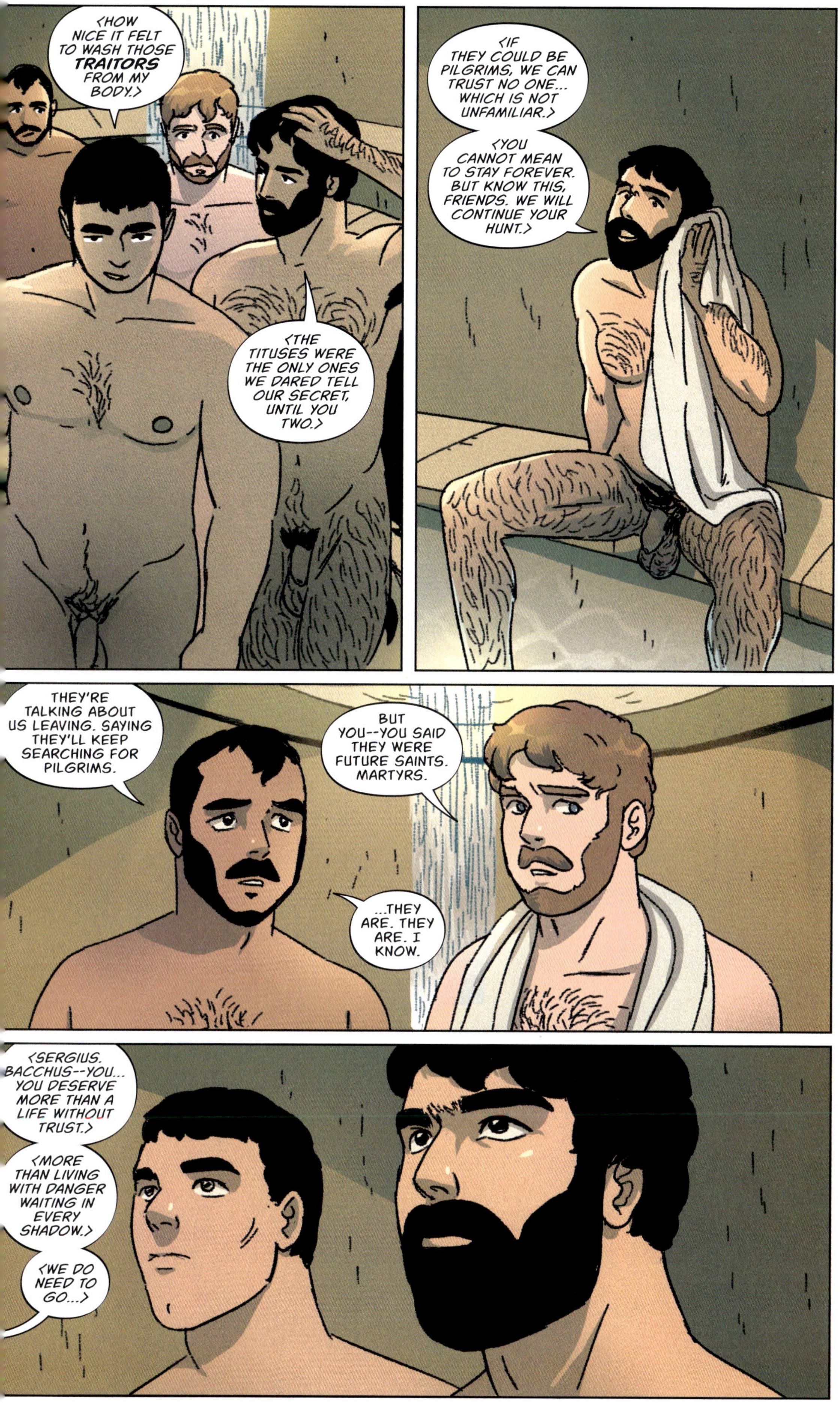

<HOW NICE IT FELT TO WASH THOSE **TRAITORS** FROM MY BODY.>
<THE TITUSES WERE THE ONLY ONES WE DARED TELL OUR SECRET, UNTIL YOU TWO.>
<IF THEY COULD BE PILGRIMS, WE CAN TRUST NO ONE... WHICH IS NOT UNFAMILIAR.>
<YOU CANNOT MEAN TO STAY FOREVER. BUT KNOW THIS, FRIENDS. WE WILL CONTINUE YOUR HUNT.>
THEY'RE TALKING ABOUT US LEAVING. SAYING THEY'LL KEEP SEARCHING FOR PILGRIMS.
BUT YOU--YOU SAID THEY WERE FUTURE SAINTS. MARTYRS.
...THEY ARE. THEY ARE. I KNOW.
<SERGIUS. BACCHUS--YOU... YOU DESERVE MORE THAN A LIFE WITHOUT TRUST.>
<MORE THAN LIVING WITH DANGER WAITING IN EVERY SHADOW.>
<WE DO NEED TO GO...>

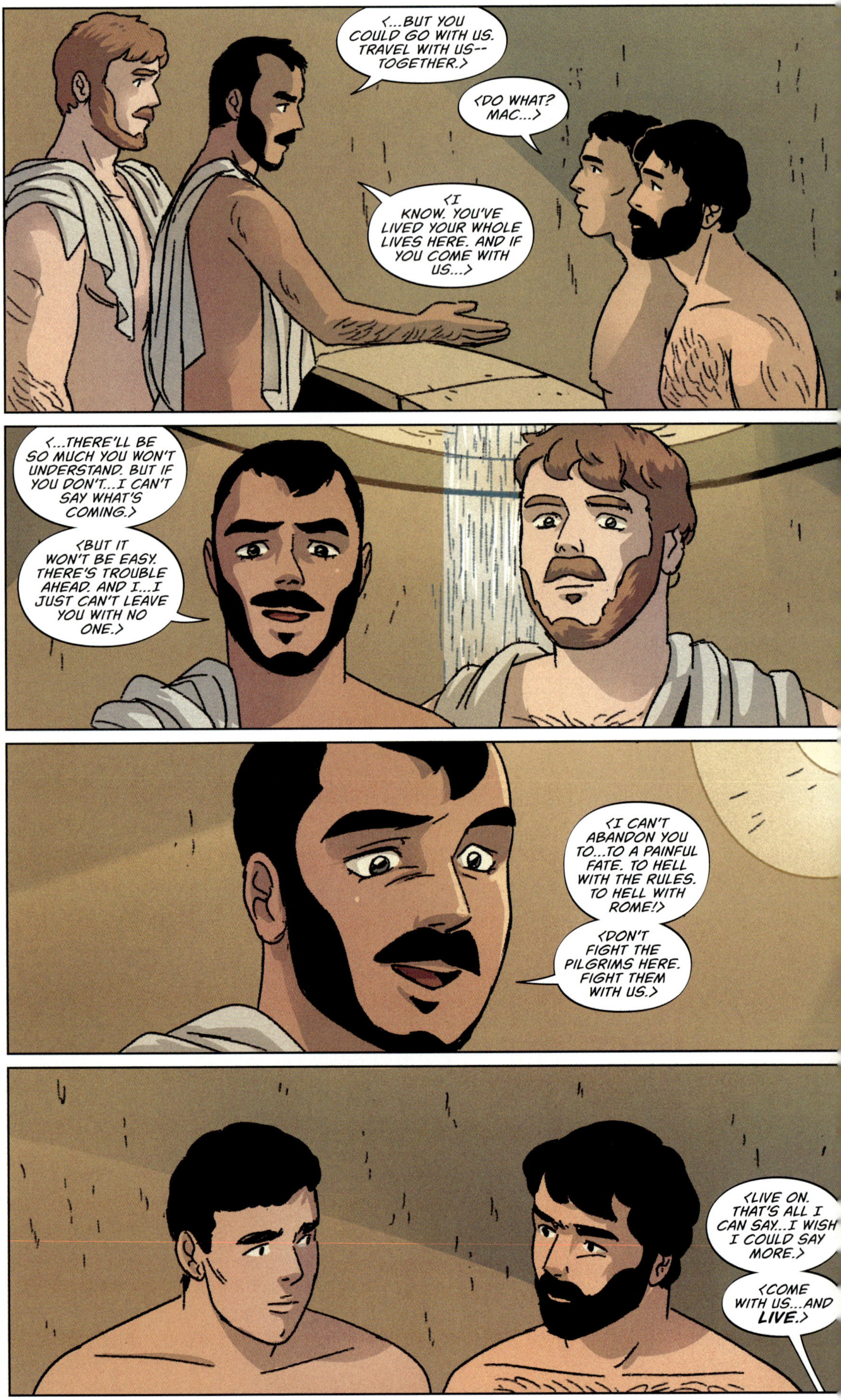

<...BUT YOU COULD GO WITH US. TRAVEL WITH US-- TOGETHER.>
<DO WHAT? MAC...>
<I KNOW. YOU'VE LIVED YOUR WHOLE LIVES HERE. AND IF YOU COME WITH US...>
<...THERE'LL BE SO MUCH YOU WON'T UNDERSTAND. BUT IF YOU DON'T...I CAN'T SAY WHAT'S COMING.>
<BUT IT WON'T BE EASY. THERE'S TROUBLE AHEAD. AND I...I JUST CAN'T LEAVE YOU WITH NO ONE.>
<I CAN'T ABANDON YOU TO...TO A PAINFUL FATE. TO HELL WITH THE RULES. TO HELL WITH ROME!>
<DON'T FIGHT THE PILGRIMS HERE. FIGHT THEM WITH US.>
<LIVE ON. THAT'S ALL I CAN SAY...I WISH I COULD SAY MORE.>
<COME WITH US...AND **LIVE.**>

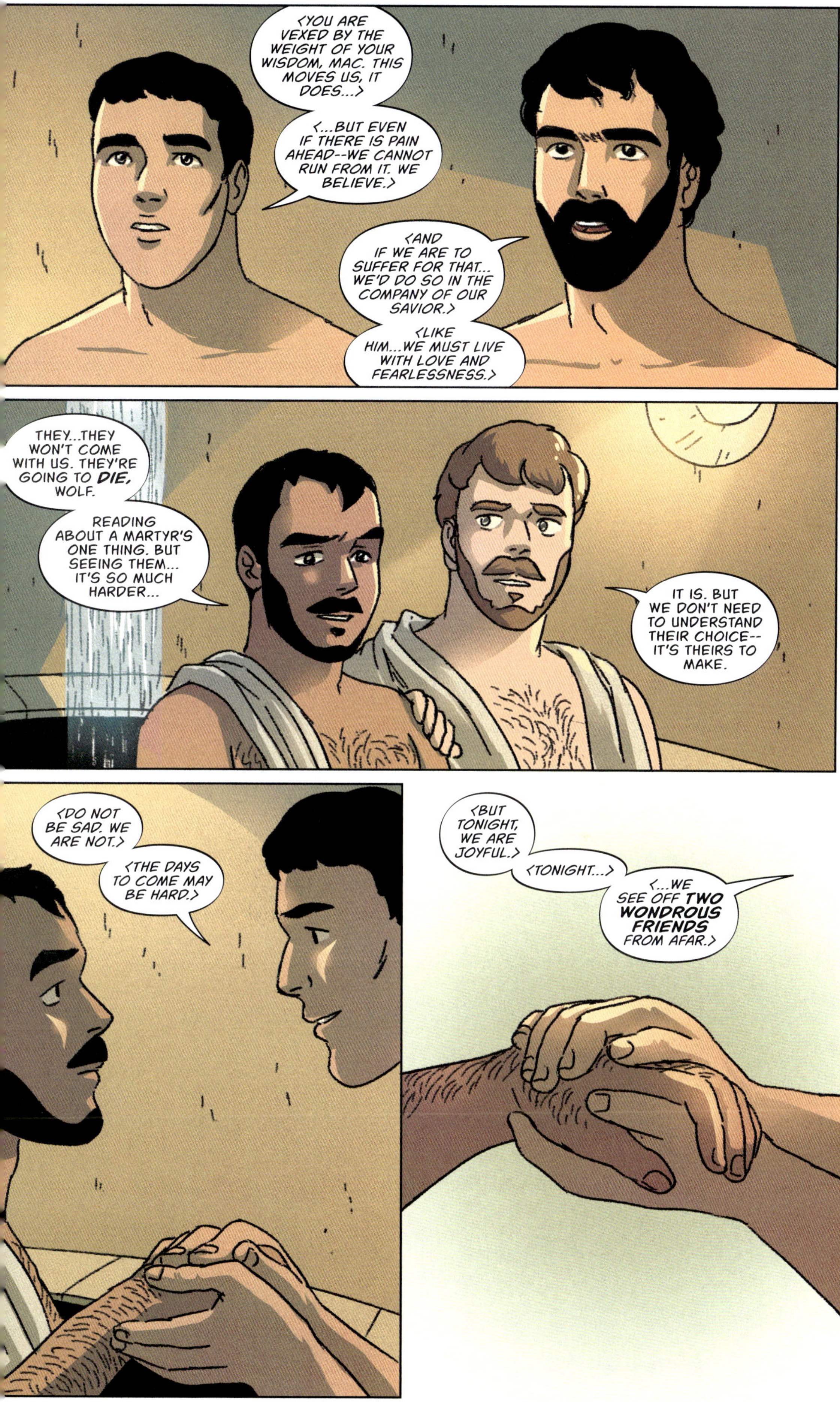
<YOU ARE VEXED BY THE WEIGHT OF YOUR WISDOM, MAC. THIS MOVES US, IT DOES...>
<...BUT EVEN IF THERE IS PAIN AHEAD--WE CANNOT RUN FROM IT. WE BELIEVE.>
<AND IF WE ARE TO SUFFER FOR THAT... WE'D DO SO IN THE COMPANY OF OUR SAVIOR.>
<LIKE HIM...WE MUST LIVE WITH LOVE AND FEARLESSNESS.>
THEY...THEY WON'T COME WITH US. THEY'RE GOING TO DIE, WOLF.
READING ABOUT A MARTYR'S ONE THING. BUT SEEING THEM... IT'S SO MUCH HARDER...
IT IS. BUT WE DON'T NEED TO UNDERSTAND THEIR CHOICE-- IT'S THEIRS TO MAKE.
<DO NOT BE SAD. WE ARE NOT.>
<THE DAYS TO COME MAY BE HARD.>
<BUT TONIGHT, WE ARE JOYFUL.>
<TONIGHT...>
<...WE SEE OFF TWO WONDROUS FRIENDS FROM AFAR.>

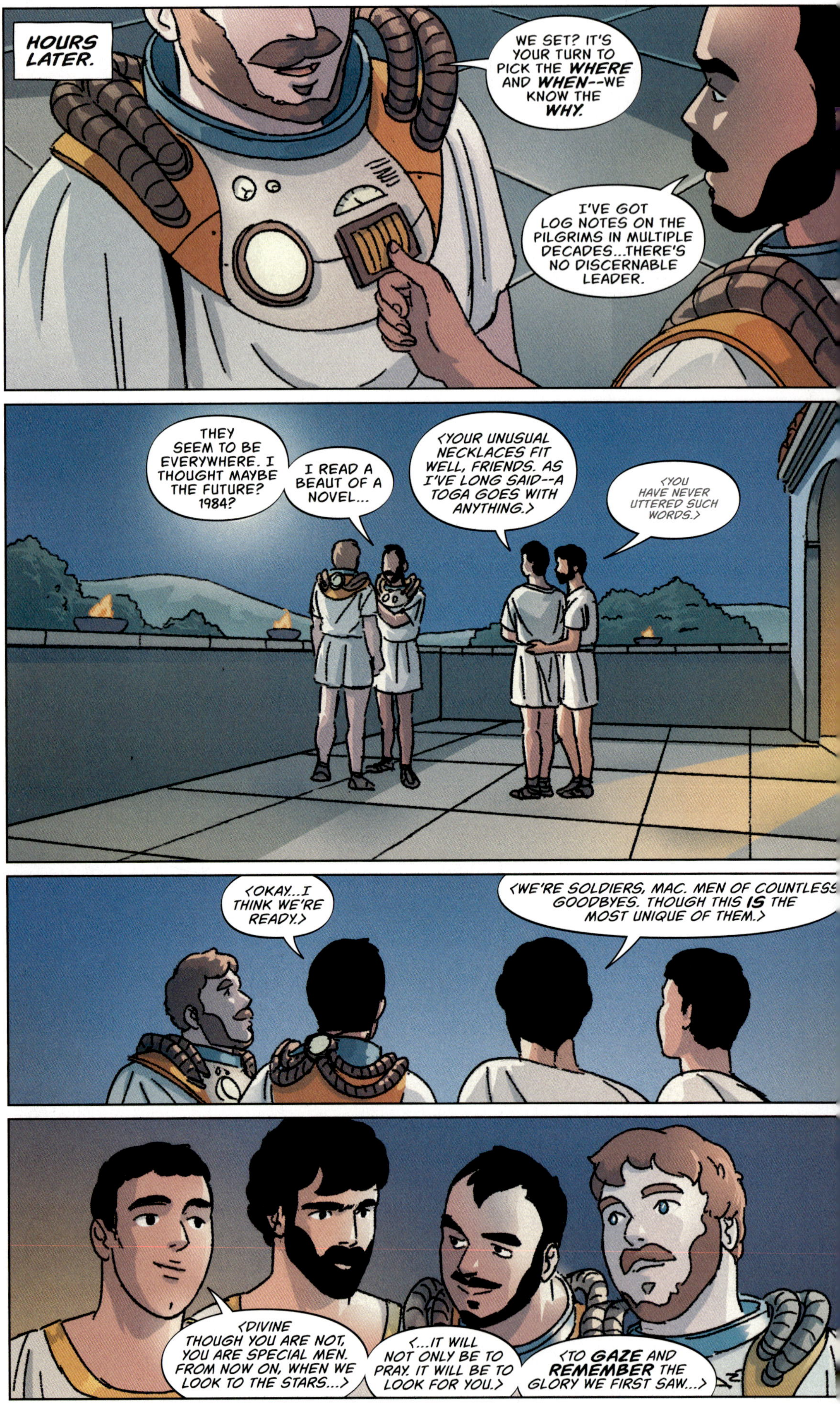
HOURS LATER.
WE SET? IT'S YOUR TURN TO PICK THE WHERE AND WHEN--WE KNOW THE WHY.
I'VE GOT LOG NOTES ON THE PILGRIMS IN MULTIPLE DECADES...THERE'S NO DISCERNABLE LEADER.
THEY SEEM TO BE EVERYWHERE. I THOUGHT MAYBE THE FUTURE? 1984?
I READ A BEAUT OF A NOVEL...
<YOUR UNUSUAL NECKLACES FIT WELL, FRIENDS. AS I'VE LONG SAID--A TOGA GOES WITH ANYTHING.>
<YOU HAVE NEVER UTTERED SUCH WORDS.>
<OKAY...I THINK WE'RE READY.>
<WE'RE SOLDIERS, MAC. MEN OF COUNTLESS GOODBYES. THOUGH THIS IS THE MOST UNIQUE OF THEM.>
<DIVINE THOUGH YOU ARE NOT, YOU ARE SPECIAL MEN. FROM NOW ON, WHEN WE LOOK TO THE STARS...>
<...IT WILL NOT ONLY BE TO PRAY. IT WILL BE TO LOOK FOR YOU.>
<TO GAZE AND REMEMBER THE GLORY WE FIRST SAW...>

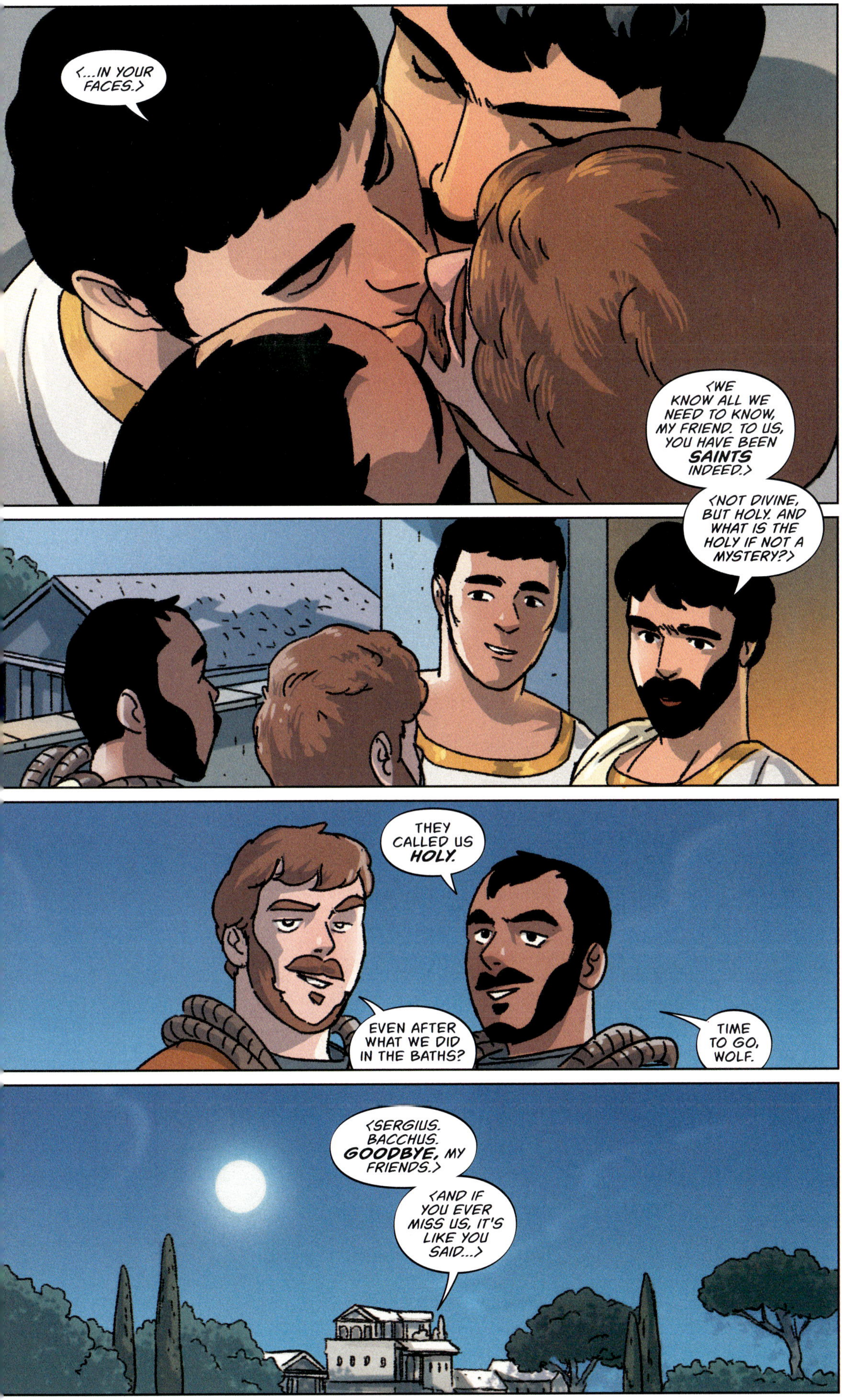
<...IN YOUR FACES.>
<WE KNOW ALL WE NEED TO KNOW, MY FRIEND. TO US, YOU HAVE BEEN **SAINTS** INDEED.>
<NOT DIVINE, BUT HOLY. AND WHAT IS THE HOLY IF NOT A MYSTERY?>
THEY CALLED US **HOLY**.
EVEN AFTER WHAT WE DID IN THE BATHS?
TIME TO GO, WOLF.
<SERGIUS. BACCHUS. **GOODBYE,** MY FRIENDS.>
<AND IF YOU EVER MISS US, IT'S LIKE YOU SAID...>

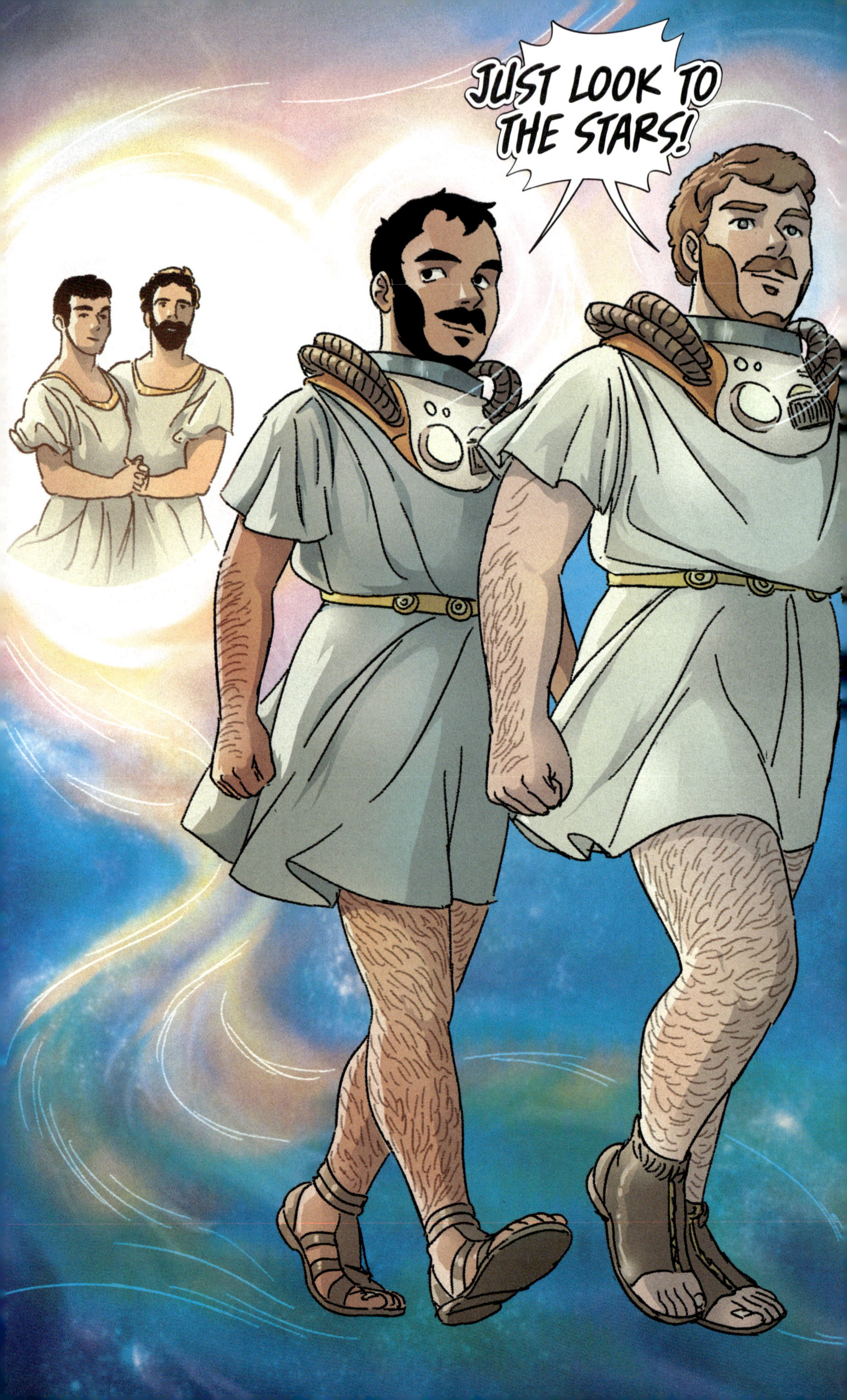
JUST LOOK TO THE STARS!

the covers of

SAINTED LOVE

featuring

GIOPOTA

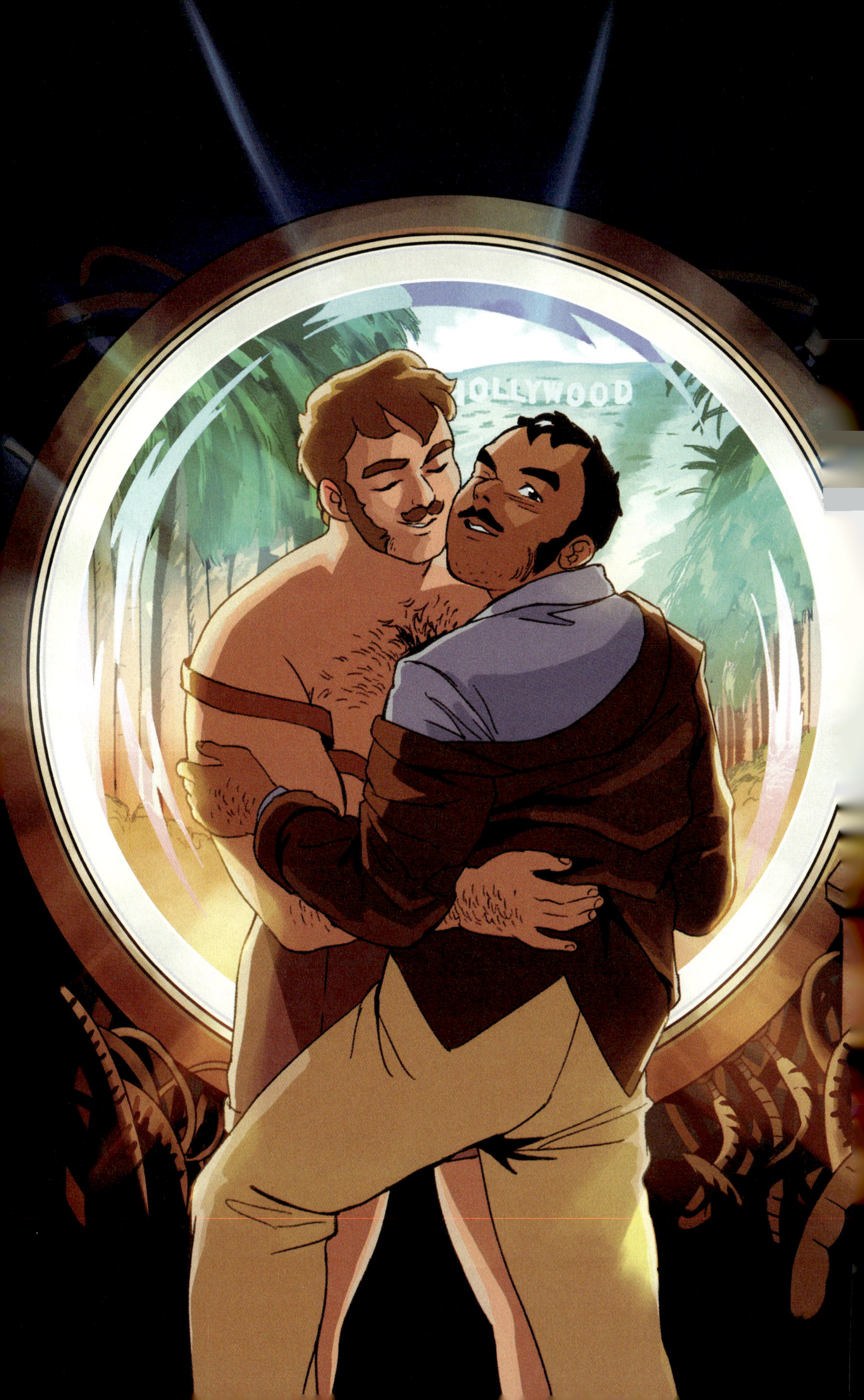
HOLLYWOOD

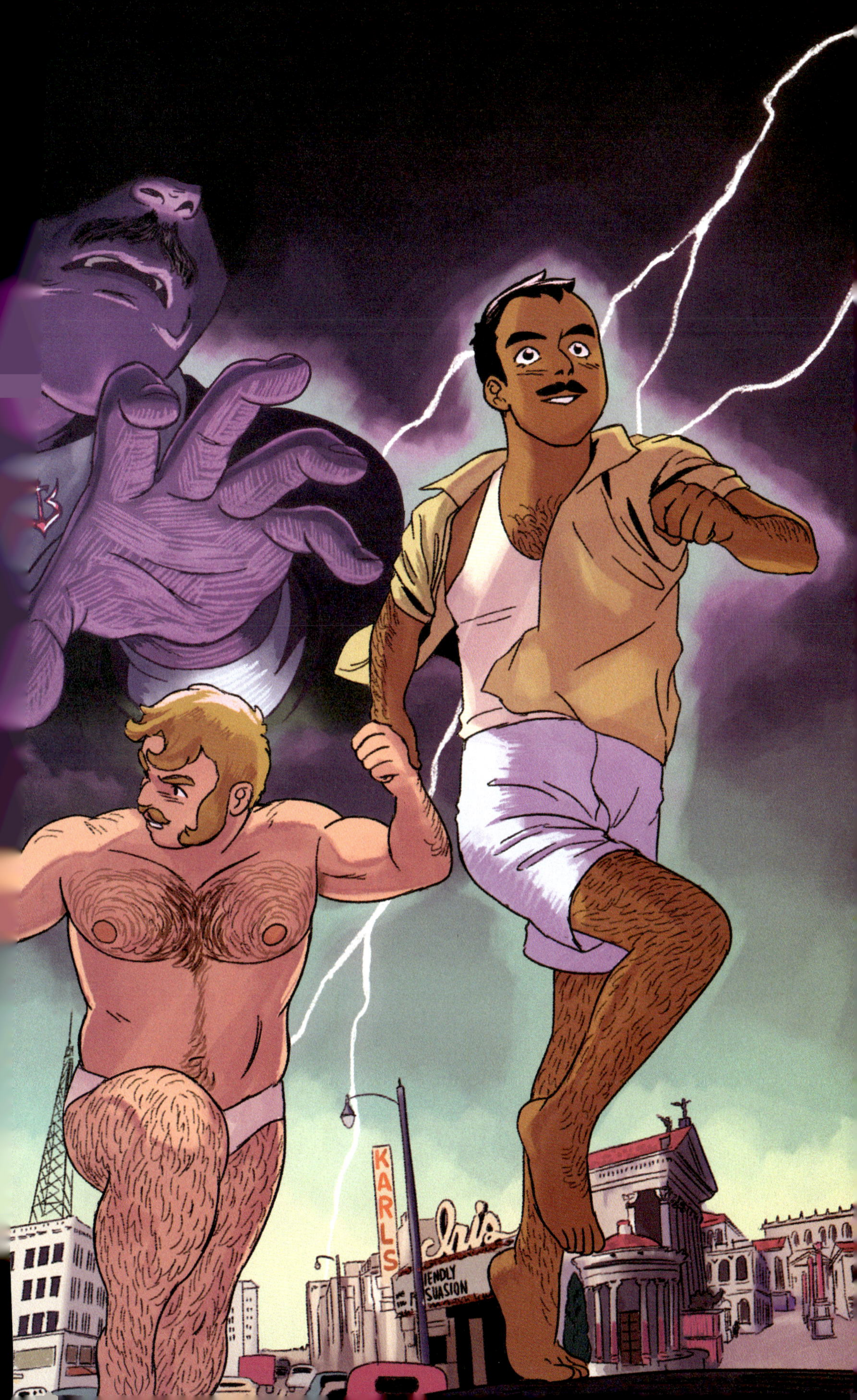
KARLS
Iris
IENDLY
SUASION

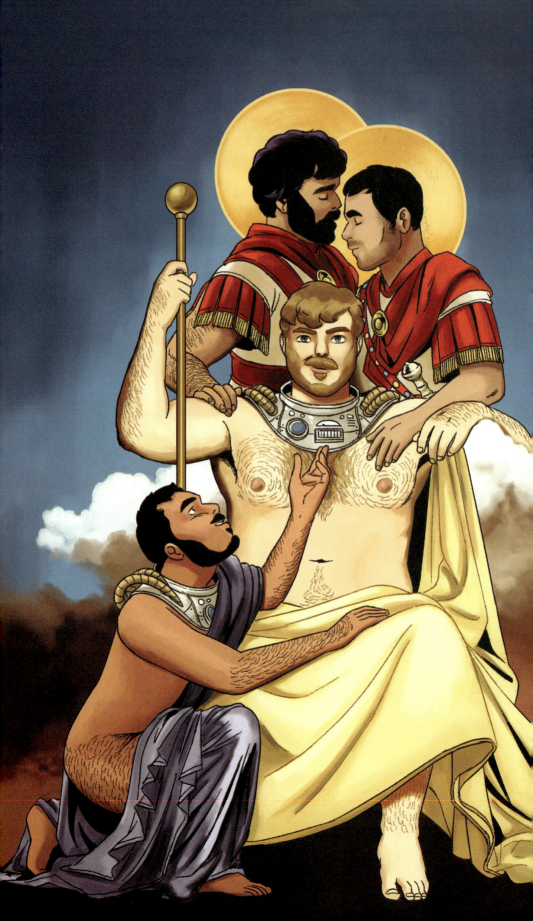

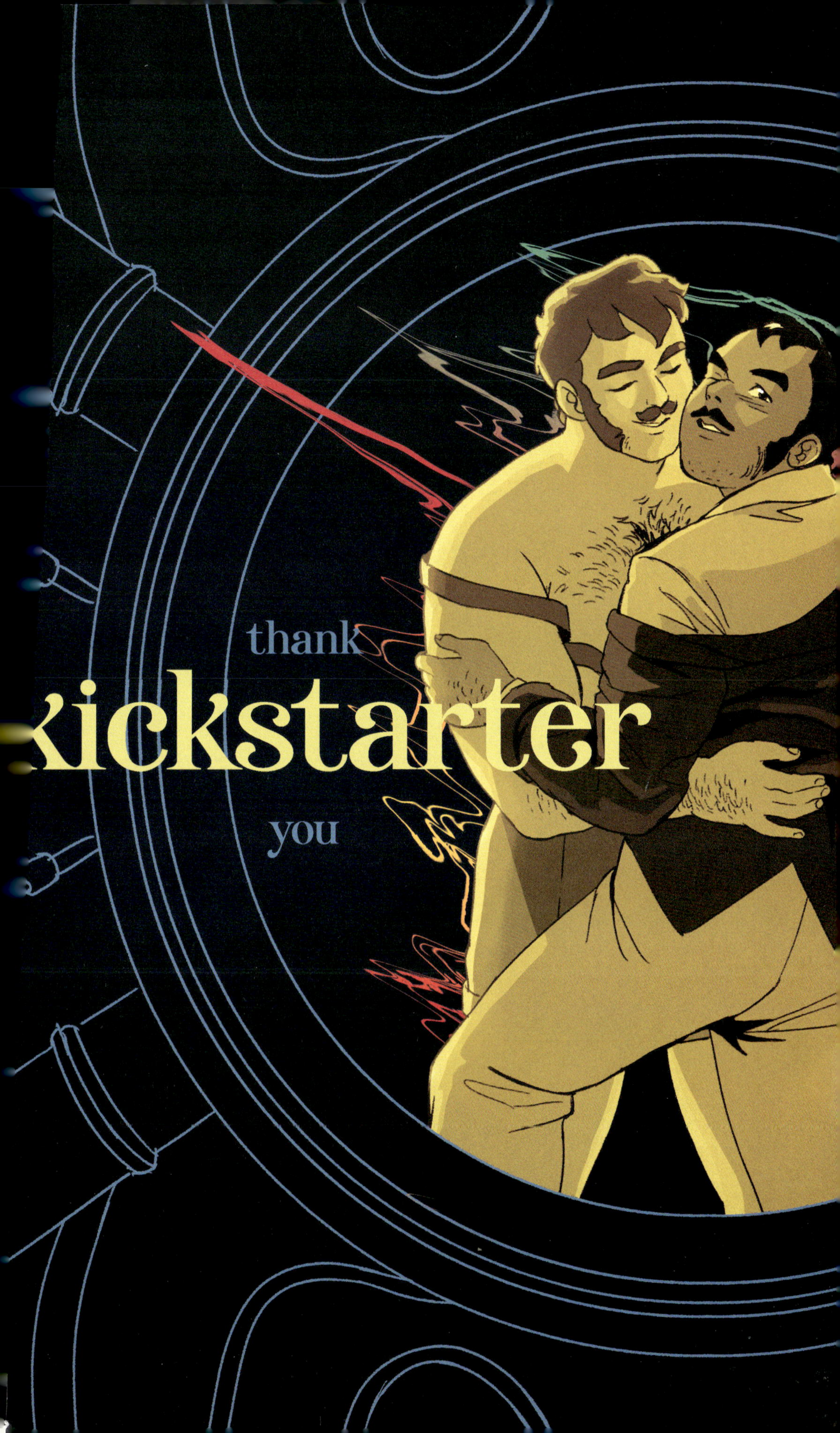
thank
kickstarter
you

JOSH S
ALBERT LIOU
JD RAMEY
JOSIE MEDINA
DORIAN WRIGHT
NOXYLEON
MEGAN MARSDEN
SHANE CLEMENTS
BEN HOWARD
MICHAEL J PURPLE

KAREN KLEBER
DAN GUIDICE
WILLIAM HESSE
MOUSY85
JONATHAN SANDS
JOHN A. RODRIGUEZ
ALBERT CUA
ED BRISSON
MITCH LADD
TIM SAUKE

BRITTA BUESCHER
ROBERT MCDONALD
JEFF ENOS
BRENTT
HENRY DEVILEARS
DAN HAUS
STANFORD M. BROWN
MONTE STARR
PATRICK @ DERBY COMICS
GRADY PARROTT

LANDON WALLISER
HAMISH STEELE
ELENA
ORSOTRASH
ROBERT E. STUTTS
JULIEN BERTRAND
JAN ARRAH
ISOS
NATHAN PIPE
CHAD V CONAWAY

EVAN MEADOW
STEVE MOWRY
DAVY VAN OBBERGEN
EMITOCI
JUAN ROIG
RAY SABLACK
ZACHARY KING
NAESAKITHEBEAR
BEDESCHI MATHIEU
KEVENN T. SMITH

NATURAVIOLENTA
PHIL B.
ALEX SCHLESINGER
MICHAEL DUNN
VALERIA DEL GATTO
CALEB SCHIRMER
KANE ANDERSON
WAYMON HUDSON
FABIEN BATTESTI
SHIPWRECK

ALEX HELM
GUIDO A. SANCHEZ
MIKE CRABTREE
SEAN "WOLF" ETTER
DANIEL TÔ
SCOTT ALLEN
ALEX HANBA
G. RICHARD NEWELL
MATTYFP
MATTHEW GRIFFITH

SEATTLE MIKE
ANDY MANGELS
PELTO
DREW WALLACE
JASON LAVOCHKIN
JOHN COLBERT
SEANAF
MICHAEL SETH
GUS HERRERA
MICHAEL DEMERITT

MAX KATZENJAMMER
CHAN C
KAI TALONPOIKA
JOEL A. S. BUTLER
ZACHARY LINVILLE
THOR HEIDENREICH
PAUL COOKE
MATT ARSENAULT
DAVIDE G.G. CACI
JUDE JONES SCHIRF

HAYYIM OBADYAH
B.D. SUISSE
STACE WALKER
NEAL DEBRECENI
RUBEN CANTU
CHIH-CHENG HSIEH
JC ADAMS
JASON HOGGAN
ELIZA VIERA
ORLANDO LAZA

BRENDA DYNA STAATS
ALEX WALLACE
SPENCER IRWIN
ANILEA ANNULAIRE
JOHNNY ELDER
DEVANTE CHILE
JAKE B
JUSTIN COLUCCI
ANDREW BROADSTON
TJ RUBEL

IAIN CROALL
JACK WILLIS
TOSH FARRELL
PHIL "MOSELEY" GARDNER
BUCK STAR
STEVEN F. WHITE
ERIK J. BROWN
NICOLAS VOVAU
DWAYNE FARVER
JAKE RUNDLE

DREW TABB
NICOLAS SANCHEZ
DANIEL DIEM
TLG
MEGAN SILVERA
SEAN N
B. GONZALEZ
TRAINEWRECK
ROB FORMAN
KETS

GEORGE READER
DENYS HOWARD
RICCI LARICCI
JON MCQUEEN
MATT BACKLUND
JOHN BULLIS JR.
ROBERTONE S
IAN TARAKEY
CODY COULOMBE
AUSTIN SCOTT

SAM HOPPER
RIO KURNIA
MIKAEL
MALPERTUIS
ZIGGI CHAVEZ
SAUL RAMIREZ JR
RAFFAELE & ANDREAS
STUART BUTLER
SAM STEWART
PIE

CRISTIAN ZUNIGA
DWHITNEY B
CHRIS HOUSTON-LOCK
ANDREW C STACKHOUSE
GOENZOGO
ÀLEX FERRÀS
DINON J-F
MIKEY C. SCHELL
ZAKK BRYANT
TARO

YORK THE RED LION
MAREK MONDAY
JENII STEWART
VDH
SYKAEL
ADRIAN MALMGREN
MIKE BROMBERG & KEN REPP
DREW MCCOMBS
TIMOTHY HOWE
WILL S.

MATTHEW GENDASON
BERNARD BENITEZ
SAM SHEPHERD
ANDREA BURGESS
KEVIN CHEVEZ
ISAIAH WADE
JOSH BEVERIDGE
LEE SWAGERT
TY HAMMEL
NEIL ARISTY

PETER BURNS
MIKKI KING
JIM HILL
BENJAMIN PERLEE
CHRIS ROCHA
WALTER & SETH
MATTEO TAMAI
MATTEO HERNANDEZ
JORDAN HAMBLIN
KEVIN TRAN

LUDOVIC L.
JESSICA NICOLE
PUP BADGE
BRYAN J
ALEX BUTLER
BRIAN MONTGOMERY
OLLY WEBSTER
RICHARD C YOUNG
MICHAEL CARPENTER
MARK WINTERS

MATT GARBER
ERIC LAUDENSLAGER
MATTHEW NEISWENDER
DAVID AFONSO
PRASHNIL
J.B. ZIEGLER
A.J. MARTIN
PATRICK WARD
MATTHEW LOWREY
CAL HALL

STEVEN J DAMM
MALTESEGEEK
ALEX V
PIETRO SERDINO
TRAVIS ROY
NATHAN B
BAKER MCDONALD
CALLUM ANGEL
BEN SNOW
LUX DE LUMINE

JEFFREY S WORRELL
PAUL MCNAMARA
STEPHANIE YOUNG
VLAD SEVRIUGIN
PAT HUGHES
MICHAEL E. WIGGAM
JAIME MERCADO
BRYAN HIGA
MORIATY
BEEBADRAWS

MICHAEL MCGAUGHEY
CHANDLER SCHRAMM
LUCAS HARDY
RUSTY THE PUP
KYLE REGO
MEGAN MORRISON
MATTHEW CHIN
BRYBRY
BRADLEY C
EMMANUEL PEREZ

ATOPTHEHILL
R~
SHEILA M. DOUGHERTY
GIANNI RESSI
MIRA
ALLEN CAMPBELL
D FRANKLIN
KENDRA
DAVID
A. KOHLI

MARTIN DUDEK
ALI MOHAJER
TOM B.
JACOB GREGORY DAMMONS
OLIVES ERICKSON
TUCKER LEHMAN
ANDREW HARDIE
FALKENBAX
GEORGE SHARKEY
COTINA S.

MATT S
DENNIS SAMBOLIN-RANDOLPH
D CRARY
SHADIA AMIN
CONNOR C.
PHIL BEECHLER
BRIDGETT FROM VERMONT
BRADEN GREGORY
MAG
JUSTIN ARESOLA

GABRIELE G.
ZEPHYR
MATTEO MANZATI
PATE
JMARIE GREGOIRE
WOODYDRAWZZ
KT
PETER STOCKWELL
GREG STEIRER
ADAM SIMON

ANGELINA XO
COPELAND WOODRUFF
KIMBALL DAVIS
THOMAS KILEY
ANDY BOUGHNER
SPENSER & TRAI
ELLY MULK
MATT DETURCK
PETAR MAMIC
BRUNO PASQUINELLI

JB BEKER
JAMES H. DUKE IV
AJ WHIDDEN

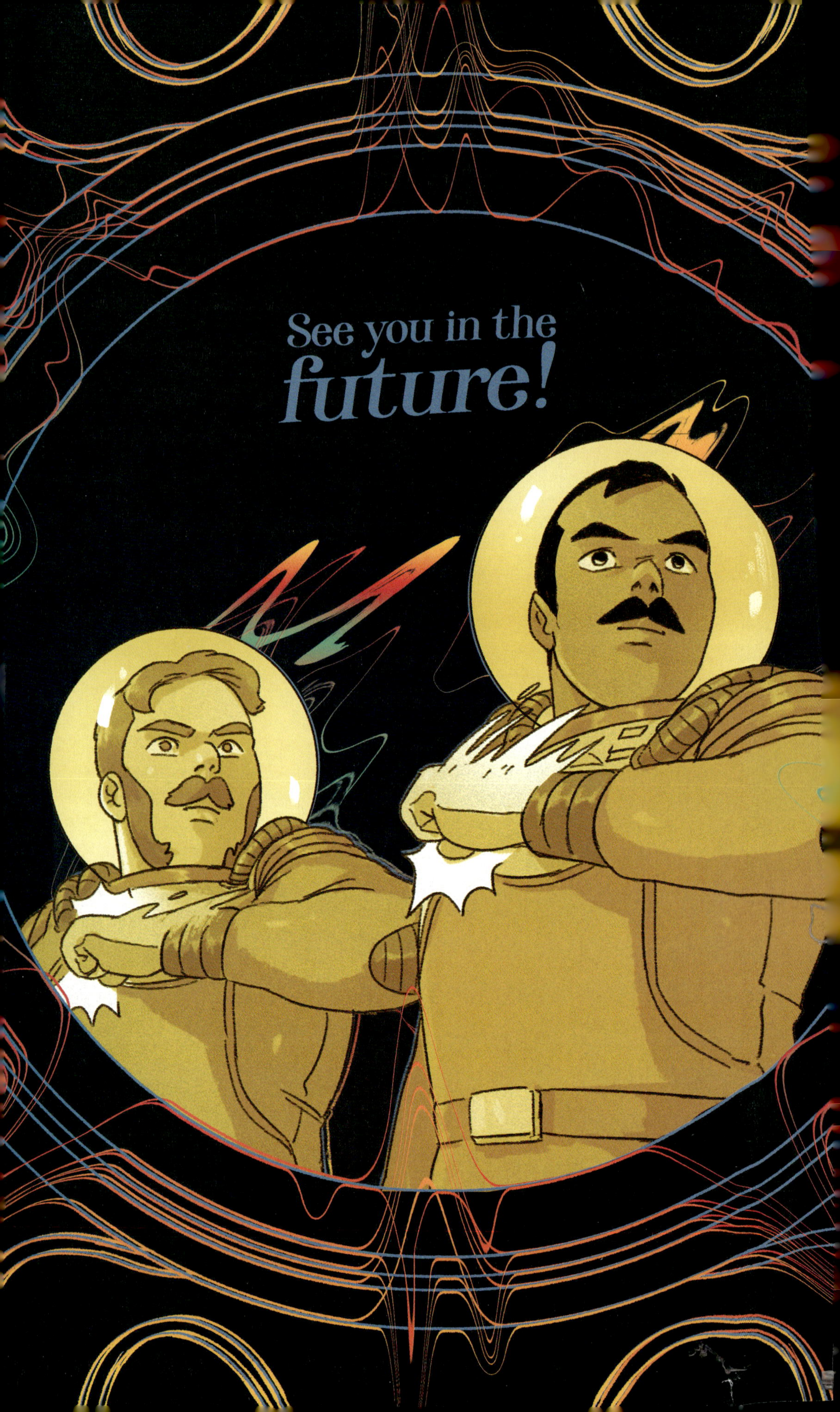
See you in the
future!